BEE COUNTY COLLEGE
DATE DUE

MAR 2 1978		
	BEE COUNTY COLLEGE LIBRARY	
	3800 CHARCO ROAD	
	BEEVILLE, TEXAS 78102	
	(512) 354 - 2740	

27584

KF
228
.T7
T5

Tinnin

Just about everybody
vs. Howard Hughes

27584

KF
228
.T7
T5

Tinnin

Just about everybody vs.
Howard Hughes

Just About Everybody Vs. Howard Hughes

David B. Tinnin

Just About Everybody Vs. Howard Hughes

Doubleday & Company, Inc.   Garden City, New York
1973

ISBN: 0-385-07121-3
Library of Congress Catalog Card Number: 71–157628
Copyright © 1973 by David B. Tinnin

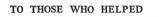

TO THOSE WHO HELPED

Foreword

And so, dear reader, since you opened to this page, I will try to tell you what this book is about, why I wrote it, and how I got my information. Certainly, any author who deals with this subject owes his readers a clear and candid explanation. After all that has transpired, you cannot fail to ask yourself, Is this yet another hoax or still another fanciful biography of Howard Hughes? It is, let me assure you, neither—though in its own way, I am certain that this book tells more about that fascinating and tortured man than ever before has been published.

This book is a story, detailed and documented, of a great human conflict in which Hughes played an essential and leading role. By no means, however, was he the only strong or provocative actor. He was both opposed and supported by a diverse and distinguished group of men whose own creeds and credentials represented a cross section of American society at its highest—and toughest—layer.

The conflict, which centered in a lawsuit, developed into the largest, most expensive, and downright astounding legal battle in the history of American civil litigation. Hence, this book does not rest upon hearsay or rumor. It rests, in the first instance, on the evidence, often painfully extracted by the opposing lawyers from the unwilling other side, that constituted the factual basis of the case. Unlike the great majority of material written about Hughes, this book has one advantage: it is true.

For an outsider, it is almost impossible to imagine the depth and detail of the evidence collected in this case. Naturally, I have not presented the evidence in the cold and sterile way that it is extracted in court or in deposition hearings. I have taken the facts and woven them into what I hope you will find to be an exciting and suspenseful narrative. Yet, by spending countless hours digging through records both in New York and in Las Vegas (where two slightly related suits were started), I was able to reconstruct hitherto secret aspects of Hughes' life and dealings. For example, in one of the Nevada lawsuits, one of his personal nurse-secretaries was called to the stand. His sworn testimony, which ran for hundreds of pages, provided a highly illuminating insight into how Hughes lived in the penthouse atop the Desert Inn and his condition when he undertook one of the most significant acts in his long and controversial career. By the same token, the material seized from Hughes' files in the New York action—the transcripts of his secret messages to aides, the notes of his bankers and lawyers—opened vistas into how the mind of one of the world's two or three richest men actually worked and what his considerations were.

In addition to the collected evidence, I was also helped by the record of the case. Part of the record consisted of the letters between attorneys, their disputes about what material should be surrendered as evidence, their conflicting opinions about the import of court orders. Fortunately, since each side wanted to present its interpretation as forcefully as possible to the court, these episodes are fully documented by affidavits and other sworn testimony. Also, for an understanding of the case, I relied on the arguments by the lawyers in court and their voluminous briefs.

The evidence and court record established both the chronological framework and factual basis for this book. I then sought to research the wider setting of the legal proceedings in an effort to make the book more intelligible and interesting. I am not a lawyer or a financier (I am a journalist), but I learned enough about both to place the events within their proper context and to assess their significance. To fully comprehend these events, it is necessary to understand a bit about how the airline industry operates, to appreciate the importance of the advent of the jets, which totally outclassed all existing aircraft of the day, and to understand the unique position of power and expertise that Hughes held within aviation in those days. At appropriate places, I have provided short —and I promise, not boring—explanations of the workings of high finance and of the law, which are essential in grasping the subtle intricacies on which this case sometimes turned.

To provide that part of backgrounding, I counted mainly on two sources. One was the public record. A huge amount has been written on Hughes, and while most of it is valueless for a documentary book, there is a small amount of reporting that is instructive. By far the most important source within the public domain, however, were the files of the Civil Aeronautics Board, which for more than two decades investigated and kept tabs on Hughes' dealings with Trans World Airlines, the object of the conflict. For days, I poured over the transcripts of questioning of high executives who worked for Hughes by CAB attorneys and examiners. At various points in the book, extracts are quoted from these exchanges. There are other instances, in which the CAB's investigators turned up extremely confidential memos by Hughes' lawyers to their invisible client. Those memos are either quoted or provided the basis for interpretation of otherwise seemingly mysterious and aimless developments.

The reader will also be aware that parts of this book rely on information that goes beyond court record or the findings of a government agency. I sought out a number of people who had played leading or supporting roles in the struggle. I wanted help in understanding the subplots, the personal crosscurrents, the anatomy of some of the incredible turnabouts and surprises with which this book is filled. To a degree that frankly often surprised me, many of these people gave me large amounts of their time, shared their experiences—though recalling them was painful for some—and helped me achieve valuable insights. They also gave me the precious thing that priest, practitioner or journalist can gain—their trust.

In the pages that follow I hope that many of those sources will see much of the information accurately portrayed. The reader should know, however, how I used this material. In all instances I tested it against other accounts, against the legal record. At times the double-checking process involved tracking down a former secretary and trying to get her to recall a certain memo that was dictated by so-and-so on a certain day. It was long and painstaking work, but I now feel that the off-the-record part of the book is as accurate and factual as the part that rests on the testimony of witnesses under oath.

Why did I write the book? Aside from the material motivation for doing what I felt would be an interesting book, I for years had been intrigued by the idea of writing a major work on the inside view of American business. In the mid-1960s I abandoned my first attempt, which was to have been a study of corporations in crises, including Trans World Airlines after it had been taken away from Hughes by the eastern bankers and placed under the direction of a trustee management. I continued, however, to follow the events in the legal battle between TWA and Hughes. By the late 1960s I became convinced that the case provided fascinating material for a book. The drama and complexity of the case came to pose a direct challenge to my own skills as a reporter and writer. Some mountaineers have special mountains that test their prowess, racing drivers their especially challenging courses. I had the Hughes case.

On whose side were my sympathies? On both, and on neither. As the reader will see, the narrative flashes from one set of actors to the other, as one side after the other seizes the initiative. Except for the transitional and explanatory passages, I have tried to keep the author out of the book, to allow the words and actions of the actors to speak for themselves. At the same time, I sought to develop a sympathetic understanding for the aims and agonies of the leading players on both sides in this bit of drama. I do not think that anyone could read the memos of Howard Hughes, written in an alienated penthouse, the windows sealed with black curtains, without feeling a twinge of pity. Nor could—nor should—a writer deal with the brilliant strategies of John Sonnett, the lawyer who conceived the case against Hughes, without experiencing a sense of admiration. Nor could one fail to delight in the irrepressible obdurateness of Chester Davis, Hughes' main legal defender.

My hope is that, on balance, by telling as fully and fairly as I could, both sides of the story, the result is a complete and even-handed account—though I can hardly expect the leading actors in that long and bitter conflict to have achieved the detachment to agree with me.

The idea and concept for this book were completely my own. No person involved in any respect with the case saw the manuscript. In fact, I doubt that anyone even had a very clear idea of exactly what I was doing or how I was handling the material. No person or corporation encouraged me or influenced me in the way I wrote this book or dealt with the various episodes that touch a wide selection of the leading business institutions in the United States. The book speaks for no one and pleads no cases. The interpretation of events, in the final analysis, is mine.

David Bruce Tinnin

Redding, Connecticut–Paris, France
1968–1973

Part One

1. Prisoner in the Penthouse

"Let's not complain about it." Slumped in a chair, a yellow legal pad resting on his lap, he slowly writes those words. Then, as if to impress the injunction more deeply on his mind, he underscores the words with a thick line, not once, not twice, but three times. "Let's not complain about it." It is a message to himself.

Then he writes: "Please watch me carefully and please do not let me go to sleep at all." It is a message for his male nurse-secretaries, who watch over him at all times. He holds the pad up to the plate glass, which separates his climate-controlled and supposedly germ-free quarters from their room. He adds a cautionary afterthought. "But try," he begs, "not to startle me."

He does not want to fall asleep, for he knows that when he does, he often lapses into coma-like states, not waking sometimes for fifty hours at a stretch. When that happens, the nurses have their own phrase for euphemistically describing those long periods of comatose inaction. "The Man isn't working," they say.

But often, even when he is not asleep, The Man still is not, as they would say, "working." Instead he sits, a frail and withdrawn figure, his head held between his hands. His fate is all the more tragic, for he has enjoyed fame, power, and success as few men ever have. By turns, he has been a famous aviator, a daring movie producer, a highly innovative aircraft designer, a powerful investor, a connoisseur of beautiful women. Even now he remains one of the world's two or three richest men. But his present state reflects almost nothing of his wealth or earlier fame. Aging and alone, he scribbles notes to himself: "Let's not complain about it."

This man lives as if he were in prison. His cell, to be sure, is located in a penthouse, a last vestige of the rich and privileged existence he once led. But wherever he may be, whether it is atop a hotel in Las Vegas or London, or some new hideaway, his life conveys the tragic conditions of confinement. He lives in one room, the blinds continually drawn. Only by watching television does he know the time of day or night. When he does eat, he survives on frugal and unimaginative food. Sometimes he almost starves himself to death as if on a fast. He has no luxuries. No distractions. There is no person or thing that comforts him or softens his life. He receives no visitors. He sees and is seen by only the five or six male nurse-secretaries.

He has not been convicted of breaking any law. No court ever passed judgment upon him. Nor did a jury deliberate any charge against him. Yet, as surely as if he had been tried and found guilty, Howard Hughes had become a prisoner. Even as a young man, Hughes displayed a penchant for obsessive privacy and a tendency to retreat into angry isolation when criticized or challenged for his actions. But it was far more than mere idiosyncrasies that brought him to his present state of complete confinement. He was the target of a lawsuit, which led to the biggest civil legal battle in the history of American litigation, and easily the most fascinating. The world probably never again will see a case of the incredible complexity, dramatic turns, and enduring intensity as this one for the simple reason that there never will be another Howard Hughes. By any measure, it was the civil lawsuit of the century. As it worked its way through different courts, it was given different numbers and occasionally slightly different titles. But in essence, it was the very personal conflict that pitted Howard Hughes against leading members of the eastern financial establishment in the struggle for the control of Trans World Airlines.

The battle began very quietly on the morning of June 30, 1961, when a purposeful man in his late forties stepped from his office at 80 Pine Street in New York's Wall Street district and hailed a cab. He was John Sonnett, a lawyer. On that humid morning, he was on a secret and highly sensitive mission. His destination was the Federal Court Building on lower Manhattan's Foley Square. In his black briefcase Sonnett carried two audacious documents. The more important one was called, in the unemotional language of the law, simply a complaint. Yet in this particular instance, it represented nothing less than the legal equivalent of a declaration of war. As such documents go, it was relatively modest in size—only thirty-eight type-written pages. But it touched off a legal conflict of unparalleled proportions.

The case was filled with brilliant stratagems, sudden surprise, and ironic twists. It involved a gigantic manhunt that sometimes took on the aspects of a spy thriller as opposing platoons of private detectives tried to outwit one another in the search for vital documents and elusive witnesses. The case involved an exceptionally distinguished cast of characters, because it matched some of the most outstanding men in the American business community against a person whose habits and business practices were so unorthodox and controversial that he was sometimes called the Huck Finn of American capitalism.

The case involved far more than just a battle of people; it also was a contest of principles. At stake were issues that transcended the narrow torts of law, cutting to the fundamentals of American society. To many people the case seemed to test capitalism's most basic tenet—that of the inviolability of private property. To others the case posed a more subtle question: How should society cope with a man who wields the influence of great wealth but rejects the social responsibility that should accompany the exercise of such power. In a broad sense, the dispute also tested the relative influence and relevance of two distinct and divergent schools of American thought. On the one side was the professional manager, who at the pleasure of his superiors and board of directors serves as a sort of salaried senior civil servant. On the other side was the proprietor, who feels he is entitled to run his company as he pleases for one simple and persuasive reason: he owns it.

The sums in the case were gigantic. All told, the claims and counterclaims amounted to more than one-half billion dollars. In addition, equally huge amounts were involved in developments related to the case. As a side effect of the events that led up to the conflict, a leading American planemaker lost $483 million in three years, the greatest loss ever sustained in so short a time by a United States business enterprise. As a highly ironic result of the suit, the largest sum of money ever to pass at one time into the hands of a private individual passed into those of the man against whom the legal action was directed. It was $523 million.

The amount of evidence and verbal testimony ran to incredible lengths. The documents numbered more than 1,700,000 single pages, filling 694 feet of shelf space. The pretrial testimony—in which some witnesses spent as long as three months on the stand —filled fourteen volumes, each thicker than a Manhattan telephone directory. Subsequent oral testimony filled another dozen or so such volumes.

The abundance of testimony resulted in part from the complexity and breadth of the case. It was also due to the tenacity and ingenuity of the lawyers, who themselves produced a ten-foot-high pile of briefs and counterbriefs. Arguing from diametrically opposed positions, operating on almost unlimited budgets, and aided by squads of assistants, the lawyers fought the case not once but twice through the federal judiciary system from district level all the way up to the United States Supreme Court. At the height of the litigation, more than forty lawyers and investigators were engaged in the case at a cost of about $17,000 a day. The legal fees, court costs, and sundry expenses themselves amounted to a considerable fortune—at least $20 million.

Still, the case's peculiar pathos and drama did not come from its cost or scope. It came from the spectacle of a lone man, though admittedly a rich one, battling against a vast assemblage of powerful and impersonal financial institutions. He was fighting for a very personal cause—to retain sole possession of the country's last individually owned industrial empire. The Fricks, the Rockefellers, and Fords had long since relinquished the absolute ownership of their enterprises. This man alone held out. Eccentric, shy, and pridefully unbending, he waged a determined fight in a most unusual manner. During the entire twelve-year duration of the legal battle, he remained hidden, not once stepping into public view. In the moments of crisis, his actions variously outraged his opponents and perplexed his own lawyers. In the struggle to protect his interests, his greatest handicap was himself.

2. The Ultimate Test

The roots of the conflict between Howard Hughes and the financiers were struck in one of the most dramatic developments in the
history of transportation: the advent of the jet age. It was the early
1950s and the world's airlines were about to undergo a transformation that in its own way was even greater than the one a century earlier when ships switched from sail to steam. For the airlines,
it was a time of promise and anxiety. Promise because the great
speed of the jets would shrink the world by half and make air travel
far more desirable. Anxiety because the new planes would be very
expensive to purchase. Largely because of the competitive nature
of the industry, most of the airlines were financially weak. For
financial help they would have to turn to their bankers or, in the
case of the nationalized foreign lines, to their governments.

The jet age arrived on the sleek wings of a British airliner, the
De Havilland Comet 1. Aircraft are built around engines, and the
British, who pioneered the development of jet propulsion, were
also the first to construct a specially designed airframe whose clean
aerodynamic lines would enhance the superior power of the jet
engine. Introduced by British Overseas Airways Corporation in
1952 on the London–Johannesburg route, the Comet 1 was an instant success with the passengers. Gone were the noise and vibra-
tion of the old propeller-driven planes. The Comet 1 was quiet and
silken smooth. Gone, too, was the straining, groaning, and claw-

ing of the piston engines as they struggled to pull the airplane up into the sky. A true creature of flight, the jet-powered Comet 1 rose effortlessly into the air. Though it suffered a series of tragic crashes due to metal fatigue, a factor that at the time was still not fully appreciated in aircraft construction, the Comet 1 proved the superior appeal of jets over the older piston-engine airplanes. Other British, French, and American planemakers started preparations to produce jetliners. The switch from props to jets was on.

For the world's airlines, however, the switch came too soon and too suddenly. It had, of course, been a foregone conclusion for years that the jet would someday replace the reciprocating gasoline engine as the system of propulsion for civilian airliners. Developed in the 1930s and put into service on military aircraft during the 1940s, the jet engine had indisputably proved its ability to lift a greater load at less cost and to carry it higher and faster than the piston engine. But for the airlines it mattered very much *when* the jets would come into civilian service. Airline executives would have preferred to wait a few more years. In the early 1950s most of the airlines still were engaged either in purchasing or planning to purchase the latest generation of piston planes, the Lockheed Super Constellation and the Douglas DC-7. An early switch to jets would make these piston planes obsolete before the debts on them had been paid off. That would make it more difficult for the airlines to raise funds for the purchase of the new jetliners. As a consequence, airlines in the United States would be more dependent than ever on the banks and insurance companies for the money they needed to acquire the jet equipment.

Despite the obvious disadvantage of an early introduction of the jets, each and every airline president knew that there would be an even greater disadvantage if he did not make the switch in time and got left behind. The first rule for survival in the airline industry is to match your competitors in equipment and if possible to get ahead of them. The reason rests in the peculiar nature of the business. In the United States the airlines are exposed to what many executives would claim is the worst of two worlds. On the one hand, the federal government, which regulates the air-

lines, treats them as if they were public utilities. They are not free
to set fares, determine the rate of return on their investment, or
choose the routes they want to fly. All those basic decisions require the approval of the Civil Aeronautics Board. On the other
hand, the airlines, unlike other utilities, are not granted monopo-
lies, which are the usual reward accorded to companies that operate under similar government restrictions. Quite the contrary,
airlines are exposed to intense competition in which, for example,
at least three and sometimes as many as six fly the same major
routes in the United States.

Internationally, the system is much the same. Like all the
world's major airlines, the American flag carriers belong to IATA
(the International Air Transport Association), which is a cartel
that sets the fares on all international routes. It also establishes the
standards for the meals and entertainment that can be offered
aloft. Because of these controls, an airline cannot offset the fact
that it has older and slower equipment by lowering its fares or offering other enticements such as more lavish meals or better entertainment. Hence, an airline must either fly planes that are as
good or better than its competitors' or face an overwhelming disadvantage. That fact of life was especially valid in the case of the
jets whose speed was almost twice as fast as that of the propeller-
driven aircraft and whose comfort completely outmoded the
smaller prop planes.

In making the selection of the new jets, the airline chiefs and
their financial backers faced difficult and important decisions,
which could decide the fate of the various companies. How many
planes to buy? When to place the order? And above all, which
type of plane to choose? Shortly after the introduction of the
Comet, more than half a dozen various jetliners were being offered by other planemakers, each of whom confidently assured
prospective customers that its plane would operate the most effi-
ciently. But what was the best plane of the future? Was it a turbo-
prop, which used jet engines to turn propellers? Or should one
jump immediately into the pure jets, which were propelled by the
thrust from the whining, tubular engines? And which one would

be most ideally suited for the airline's routes? Those questions were crucial. To be saddled with a plane that was less profitable than those flown by the competition would mean financial weakness and perhaps even ruin.

The problems of the dawning jet age presented a special challenge to Howard Robard Hughes, Jr., who was then the enigmatic owner and undisputed master of Trans World Airlines. More than any other airline, TWA was likely either to benefit grandly or suffer severely from the introduction of the jets. For TWA, the opportunity for benefit rested in its outstanding route structure. As the only American airline with extensive routes both in the States and abroad, it was ideally situated to take full advantage of the jets' ability to haul large numbers of passengers at great speeds over long distances. But jet-age danger for TWA lay in the competition. On its major routes, TWA faced the world's strongest and most aggressive airlines, which were sure to use the new planes as a means to gain an advantage over their competitors.

Howard Hughes was keenly aware of these considerations. To a degree unique among airline chiefs of that time, his background had prepared him to cope with the complexities of the oncoming jet age. Hughes, who was forty-six at the time of Comet 1's debut, had been the deciding factor in TWA affairs ever since 1939, when he first bought into the company. In those days, TWA stood for Transcontinental and Western Air. It had been formed in the early 1930s through the merger of four smaller airlines whose own beginnings dated back to the start of civil aviation in the United States. As an aviator and innovative engineer, Hughes possessed unmatched credentials. In the H-1 racing plane of his own design, Hughes set the world speed record at 352 mph in 1935. Two years later he flew from coast-to-coast in the record time of seven hours and twenty-eight minutes. The next year Hughes demonstrated the feasibility of a global airline as he set another record by flying around the world in ninety-one hours, fourteen minutes, and twenty-one seconds. For three successive years from 1939 onward, he was honored with one or another of the nation's highest aero-

nautical awards, culminating with a specially struck congressional
medal in 1941.

Even as he won fame as an aviator, Hughes became a visionary
exponent of the potential of commercial aviation. He could foresee the time when airliners would streak across oceans and continents at nearly the speed of sound. His ambition was to make
TWA the forerunner in the development of those aircraft. As
TWA's controlling shareholder, Hughes sought to spur the development of new planes, which would bring his dream nearer to
realization. Just before the United States entered World War II,
Hughes and Jack Frye, then TWA's president, conceived the idea
for a new airliner, for which they carefully spelled out the specifications. From those figures Lockheed's great designer, Kelly Johnson, developed the Constellation, which was the United States'
first high-speed piston-driven passenger plane.

During World War II, Hughes, in a tremendous engineering
tour de force, designed and built the world's largest aircraft up to
that time. About the same size as a Boeing 747 or a Lockheed
C-5A, Hughes' plane was a flying boat whose tail towered five
stories high. Powered by eight engines, it was intended to haul
750 troops or seventy tons of equipment high above the oceans,
safe from attack by enemy submarines. Constructed from wood
to save war-scarce aluminum, the "Spruce Goose," as unkind critics called it, was not completed until two years after the end of the
war. Even then, it flew only once—with Hughes at the controls for
a distance of about one mile and at an altitude of about seventy
feet over Long Beach harbor. As Hughes later confessed to close
associates, the big ungainly plane just about scared him to death.
Despite its eight engines, the HK-1, its official designation, was
woefully underpowered. Even so, as a pioneering experiment, the
plane represented a crucial advance in the art of building large
aircraft. For the HK-1, Hughes developed the control system that
enabled one pilot, aided by servomechanisms, to activate the huge
rudder, ailerons, and other control surfaces that govern an aircraft in flight. The flying boat also was a demonstration of the direction of Hughes' thinking. While he envisioned the construction

of passenger aircraft as large as his flying boat, he was the first to concede that such planes would need a greater source of power than the internal combustion engine. Hughes and his hopes were waiting for the refinement of the jet engine.

Thus, as the jet age began, Hughes possessed a great insight into the promise of the new power plants. He also had the aeronautical know-how to evaluate the new planes himself. Unlike the other airline leaders, Hughes was not totally dependent upon an engineering staff for advice and guidance. Furthermore, Hughes had almost complete freedom of action. While other airline chiefs owned only an insignificant fraction of their companies and were thus dependent on the will of boards of directors and shareholders, Hughes knew no such limitations. He had invested more of his own money, at that time some $90 million, in aviation than any other individual in the history of flying, and it gave him the ownership of an overwhelming 78.23 per cent of TWA's outstanding shares. The rest of the stock was scattered among some ten thousand quiescent shareholders.

Hughes held no office in TWA. He was neither its president nor even a director, but he ruled the airline as its absolute master. He appointed the directors. He alone hired—and fired—the president, in the last two instances without ever laying eyes on the men. He never attended a board meeting, but he insisted on dictating the agenda for those meetings and refused to let other issues be raised or discussed. He supervised the advertising, chose the ads, and decided on the budget. Most of all, he delighted in choosing and developing new aircraft for TWA. He even designed the paint jobs. The red dart, which still adorns TWA's jets, was designed by him.

Hughes also had the power and wealth to back up his decisions. As the sole owner of the Hughes Tool Company, also known as Toolco, he each year received tens of millions in earnings, which he was compelled either to invest in one of his enterprises or face a high federal penalty tax for excessive accumulation of profits. Hughes chose to invest in TWA. He used profits from the tool company to finance the purchase of aircraft for the airline. In re-

turn, he took TWA stock as payment. He usually waited until the
price of TWA stock was low so that he received a maximum number of shares for his money.

Whatever Hughes did at TWA was certain to have a great impact on the airline industry and attract the attention of the entire
country as well. In those days, he was the most intriguing and
talked about man in American business. And with good reason,
for he had rolled several sensational careers into what still was a
highly mysterious life. By the early 1950s the slim millionaire from
Houston had established a singular position on the American scene.
He first had become known some twenty-five years earlier as a
precocious movie producer who used the riches of the Hughes
Tool Company to teach himself the art of film-making. His first
attempt, a comedy called *Two Arabian Knights,* won its director,
Lewis Milestone, an Oscar in 1927. Then after two mediocre mov-
ies, Hughes directed his own greatest cinema success. It was *Hell's
Angels,* an epic of World War I aerial combat, which starred
Hughes' discovery Jean Harlow, the platinum blonde who set a
new style in American women.

Hughes' subsequent movies turned increasingly to criticism of
society (he was against injustice and hypocrisy) and sex (he was
for it). His candor in portraying the more intimate details of human relations outraged the censors, who in the 1930s and 1940s
still had great authority. Hughes compounded their outrage by
fighting them in both court and press. His great postwar sensation
was Jane Russell, who starred in his most controversial movie of
all, *The Outlaw,* a hayloft Western about Billy the Kid and a
buxom half-breed girl.

Hughes was compressing several careers into one lifetime. He
also had become one of the nation's most powerful and important
industrialists. As the sole shareholder in Hughes Tool, he presided over the nation's largest and most important supplier of drilling equipment whose products were essential to the operation of
the oil industry both in the United States and throughout most of
the world. He owned Hughes Aircraft Company, which was the
outgrowth of the small shop that produced his racing plane. By

the 1950s Hughes Aircraft had developed into a great science-based company, which made the sophisticated equipment that aimed and fired the guns on United States fighter planes and interceptors. In his role as the decisive influence at TWA, he was responsible for an airline that carried the flag abroad. No other private citizen controlled so many enterprises vital to United States security and international prestige as did Howard Hughes. Though his economic power affected the fate of thousands and hundreds of thousands of his fellow citizens, Hughes never once was called to an accounting in the boardroom or shareholders' meeting.

Despite his great influence, Hughes chose to run his empire in a bizarre and utterly unorthodox manner. It was designed to afford him maximum privacy, protection, and freedom of action. At the heart of his system was his communications center, called variously the "nerve center" or "operations," which was housed in a squat stucco building at 7000 Romaine Street in North Hollywood. A staff of secretaries and guards acted as a relay point. Hughes would dictate messages to the "nerve center" for transmission to aides, bankers, and lawyers. In turn, those who wanted to contact Hughes would call the nerve center, state their business, and according to whatever instructions Hughes had given, the messages would either be relayed to him, held until he called, or ignored completely. At that time, Hughes would also sometimes make calls directly to a few financiers and to some of his aides and attorneys.

Because of his deafness, he preferred to deal by telephone. But he sometimes still consented to personal meetings with a bare handful of financiers. Those meetings usually took place late at night with the rendezvous at some obscure point. The business conference would probably take place in a nondescript Chevrolet parked near the city dump or some equally out-of-the-way place. Nearly always Hughes' tactics were designed to place the person with whom he was negotiating at a disadvantage. He liked to discuss a business deal while flying, and on at least one occasion he managed to unnerve badly the person with whom he was negotiat-

ing by telling him to take the controls while he went to the back
of the plane to relieve himself. He stood smiling in the back of the
cockpit while the anxious executive, a non-flier, wrestled with the
controls of Hughes' souped-up attack bomber.

Anyone dealing with Hughes soon learned that he was acces-
sible only when he wanted to be. He was guarded by a small army
of young men. They were picked for neat appearance, loyalty, and
willingness to obey orders. Many of them were Mormons since
Hughes felt that the religion of Brigham Young rendered its ad-
herents more immune than other mortals to the weaknesses of the
flesh and possible enticements of his enemies.

Hughes honed his technique of conducting business into a fine
art. In those years when his wealth and credit were almost limit-
less, he refused to enter into give-and-take situations and he utterly rejected the imposition of deadlines on him by others. His
attitude was this: Deadlines were devised by other people for
their advantage so why should he even acknowledge them?

Despite his egocentric methods, Howard Hughes evoked a response in others that served his own cause. His remoteness gave
him a fascination and magnetism. Bankers who would not stand
in line to have lunch with any client, no matter how rich he was,
were wildly flattered when Hughes still invited them to dine with
him—or gravely offended when he passed them over in favor of
someone else. Executives and government officials who would
take a call from the President with perfect equanimity were excited beyond measure about a call from Howard Hughes. And
those men of power who had been receiving calls were downcast
when the calls from Hughes came no more.

A few of them, it should be added, were glad when the calls
stopped because Hughes is a long-winded and sometimes whiny
conversationalist, who liked to call in the dead of night when he
was at his best and the other person at his worst. Those who dealt
with him often over longer periods were almost always driven to
absolute fits of frustration. One banker who did business for many
years with him maintains that Hughes operates according to four
principles. One: Never make a decision. Let someone else make it

and then if it turns out to be the wrong one, you can disclaim it, and if it is the right one, you can abide by it. Two: Always postpone any deadline—for a week, a day, or even half an hour. Who knows, the situation may change in your favor if only you have the patience to wait. Three: Divide and conquer—both your foes and friends. Play off everyone against each other so that you have more avenues of action open to you. Four: Every man has his price. The only problem, therefore, is finding out what the price is.

That judgment may be overly harsh, but Hughes evokes harsh responses in those who have finally soured on him. Part of the rancor undoubtedly stems from the fact that Hughes himself cannot accept personal defeat and thus others must take the licking. At the time of the 1947 Senate investigation that questioned the spending of government funds for the flying boat, Hughes swore that if the plane did not fly he would leave the country, never to return. His flight—if only for a few thousand yards—was his vindication. For years the old flying boat sat in a hangar in Long Beach, at the cost of some $90,000 a year, as a memorial to Hughes' refusal to be beaten.

Howard Hughes came by most of his traits rightfully, especially his penchant for secrecy. The family's fortune literally began with a secret and its growth depended upon keeping it. The secret was a drilling bit whose three revolving and interlocking cutting surfaces could drill through rock. Invented by Hughes' father at the turn of the century, the new bit, which completely outmoded the old corkscrew-type ones, opened to exploration vast new oil deposits whose gushers provided the lubrication and power upon which the world rode into the age of the internal combustion engine.

In addition to securing patents for his bit, Howard Hughes, Sr., protected it in other, less conventional, ways too. In the beginning, he carried the bit to the drilling site in a gunny sack and after requiring the bystanders to step back some distance, personally attached the bit to the drilling shaft. Then he left a trusted retainer at the drilling site to prevent anyone from pulling up the bit later and studying its design. Despite his vigilance, Howard's father had to cope with rivals who brought out similar bits. Thanks to the service of skilled lawyers, he was successful in fending off infringements. It was also a lesson that Howard did not forget—the Houston firm that represented his father still represents Howard Hughes.

Howard also inherited his father's attitude toward partners. "Never have partners," his father told him. "They are nothing but trouble." In his early efforts to raise funds, his father had been compelled to take in three partners, who sometimes disagreed with him. As soon as Howard, Jr., inherited Hughes Tool Company in 1924, he persuaded a Texas court to declare him of age though he was only 18 at the time. His first major business transaction was to buy out the partners in Hughes Tool to become the sole owner.

The rigid code that young Howard Hughes had learned made sense in the narrow confines of a toolmaking company, but had less validity in the broader enterprises into which the tool company's profits enabled him to move. Howard's inordinate love of secrecy made him almost totally incapable of delegating authority. Because of his insistence on doing things himself, Hughes always carried a staggering work load. Yet he displayed a strange inability to differentiate between the proper province of a high executive and that of a clerk or mechanic. If anything, Hughes seemed more inclined to turn his searching intensity and brilliance to details and minutiae rather than to questions of policy and over-all direction of this enterprise.

As the jet age began to dawn, Hughes' ability as a manager of great industrial properties was in serious doubt. The doubt arose clearly from two crises in his companies. The first one came at RKO, in which Hughes acquired the working control after World War II, becoming the only individual ever to have sole control of a major Hollywood studio. Fascinated by movie-making, Hughes could not resist flexing his talents as producer, director, writer, and film editor all at the same time. The trouble was, the regular RKO executives and staff resented Hughes' intrusions into their areas of responsibility. The company lost its momentum and sense of direction. Production of movies declined. Ranking executives departed. Hughes closed the studio down for a time, to hunt Communists, he said; most people believed it was to try to halt heavy financial losses. Hughes finally sold RKO to General Tire in 1954.

The other—and far more serious—crisis occurred at Hughes Aircraft, the company Howard had founded in the mid-1930s to build his world-record racing planes. During World War II Hughes built the firm into an important maker of weaponry equipment, most notably a flexible ammunition chute that fed .50-caliber bullets smoothly to the machine guns on bombers. After the war, Hughes, who had an excellent perception of future trends, converted the aircraft company into an electronics laboratory. When the Korean conflict broke out in 1950, Hughes Aircraft was the only company in the nation that possessed knowledge about both electronics and machine guns. Hence, it was called upon to produce the systems that automatically aimed and fired the guns in the United States' jet fighters and interceptors.

The contracts were vital to the United States defense effort, and the company needed to expand its facilities in order to meet the production goals. It also needed stable management. But Hughes stalled and hedged about making any commitments for new facilities. He also refused to grant to the managers the authority that they and their employees felt they needed. The upshot was a revolt by executives and scientists against Hughes. The situation became so bad that the Secretary of the Air Force made a dramatic overnight flight from Washington to Hughes' plant in Culver City, California, to deliver a message to Hughes. "You have made a mess out of a great property," the Secretary told him. Hughes was warned that unless he corrected the situation he would never receive another government contract.

Despite the Air Force's intervention, the company suffered a mass exodus of brilliant scientists and administrators. Hughes Aircraft ultimately recovered from the crisis and went on to make the laser, the Syncom satellite, and dozens of other brilliant developments. Nonetheless, its great original promise was scarred and so, too, was Hughes' reputation.

Hughes' stewardship of TWA had also been marked by upsets —though nothing of the magnitude of those at RKO and Hughes Aircraft. Hughes interfered in the management, tended to harass executives, to second-guess the presidents, and in one unhappy instance fired Jack Frye, who originally had persuaded him to buy into the airline. The main reason: Frye wanted to raise more capital in 1946 by selling stock to the public. Hughes would not tolerate any scheme that would dilute his holdings.

On the positive side, Hughes' wealth, influence, and insight built up TWA from a relatively small airline to one of the nation's four leading air carriers. His wealth enabled TWA to buy its postwar fleets of Constellations. His influence, notably with that of a young senator from California named Richard Milhous Nixon, whose brother Donald received a $205,000 loan from Hughes to pay off debts on a filling station in 1956, helped TWA win important new routes to Europe, the Middle East, and North Africa, enabling it to join Pan American as the second airline to carry the flag abroad. Hughes made Trans Western into Trans World. But even in those early years, his critics detected motives of self-interest. They said that he was spending money for airplanes in order to avoid having to pay penalty taxes on the huge accumulations of his profits from Hughes Tool. Another charge was that he purposefully kept the airline weak and its profits low so that he would be justified in the eyes of the Civil Aeronautics Board and the Internal Revenue Service in supplying unusual amounts of cash to TWA.

Yet, as the airline industry was poised on the verge of the greatest development in its history, no one could condemn Hughes for his stewardship at TWA. The judgment was still in the balance. If he brought TWA successfully into the jet age, it would be a vindication of his control, tangible evidence that he had done for the airline something that no other single person could even have attempted. For Howard Hughes, the beginning of the jet age represented the ultimate test of his stormy and controversial career.

3. The Gathering Crisis

With his customary secretiveness, Hughes embarked in the early 1950s on the search for the ideal jet for TWA. In the past, Hughes had suspected that some of his most advanced concepts, including one for a twin-engine fighter plane that was built by a rival firm during World War II, had been appropriated by his competitors. Thus, as he began his efforts to find the jet that would be suited for both TWA's domestic and international routes, Hughes took extreme precautions for fear his ideas would benefit other airlines before they had helped TWA.

Hughes demanded the utmost discretion from the aircraft manufacturers, who were well aware that to reveal anything about what he was looking for would mean to forfeit the chance of getting his order. Just the same, Hughes also made certain that they knew little about his plans. At that exploratory stage Hughes let the manufacturers do the talking while he stuck mainly to studying the specifications and designs of their proposed jetliners. Basically what he wanted, in addition to the dual-purpose capabilities, was a plane that would be safe, get off the ground fast, and fly at greater speed than any other jetliner that was likely to come into service within the next five or ten years.

Hughes took only one person into his confidence. That was Robert W. Rummel, who was TWA's chief engineer. Howard Hughes had good reason to trust Rummel. Their relationship dated back to 1936 when Rummel, then a fledgling engineer, had performed the stress analysis of the landing gear of the plane in which Hughes set the world speed records. Rummel's assignment had been to test whether the gear of the H-1 racer was strong enough to bear the weight of the high-powered, stubby-winged plane. Later, after Hughes bought into TWA, Rummel happened to join the airline engineering staff, and the two men gradually began to work together on the selection and development of TWA's new aircraft. As a special grip on Rummel's allegiance, Hughes paid him an extra salary in addition to the one he earned from TWA. Taciturn by nature, Rummel obeyed Hughes' instructions to keep their plans and activities secret, even from his superiors in TWA.

As a result, the other ranking TWA executives had no clear idea of what sort of plane Hughes would buy for them or when they would get them. In fact, TWA did not have a hard and fast commitment from Hughes that he would supply the aircraft at all. Even so, most of the TWA people, and especially the pilots, trusted Hughes to get the best jets for them. Hughes prized that trust.

Since the British planemakers were the leaders at the beginning of the jet age, Hughes assembled stacks of technical data about their new planes, notably the Comet 1. After studying the specifications, Hughes, backed by Rummel's advice, concluded that the British jets would soon be surpassed by American ones, which were now taking shape on the drawing boards. He decided to mark time for a while before he placed his orders. Hughes urgently wanted, however, to give TWA the prestige and publicity of introducing jets in the United States. His experience in the movies had made him a master of publicity campaigns, and he obviously hoped that the jets would do for TWA what Jane Russell's breasts did for *The Outlaw,* namely, capture the country's attention. Consequently, Hughes was impatient about waiting for the American jets, which were still five or six years away from service.

Shortly after he dropped the idea of purchasing British jets, Hughes became interested in a small jetliner that Avro of Canada had built. A four-engine aircraft that could carry forty or fifty passengers, it would not have been suitable for TWA's transcontinental and international routes. It could, however, have been used on TWA's shorter domestic routes, which would require a separate type of plane anyhow. After flying the prototype of the Avroliner extensively on the West Coast, Hughes was very impressed and wanted to buy a number of them. But since the Korean War was going on at that time, Avro had to concentrate on the production of F-86 Sabre jet fighters. The Avroliner never became available for sale.

As the months passed, Hughes began to think about building a jetliner himself. He called his plan "Project Greenland." By the mid-1950s, he had two immediate options. He could build the French short-to-medium range Caravelle under license or he could design and construct his own jetliner. Hughes enlisted the public support of LeRoy Collins, then governor of Florida, and leased an extensive tract of land in that state. He told his aides in California to be prepared to move to Florida. Hughes even began to lay the legal ground work for entering the aircraft business. Since there is a federal law that forbids airline operators from engaging in the manufacture of aircraft, Hughes had his lawyers present to the Civil Aeronautics Board an appeal in which he asked for an exemption to that prohibition.

His action stirred intense speculation about his intentions. It seemed to many people, including the governor, that Florida would be the site of the nation's first jetliner plant. But many of Hughes' critics suspected that he was only going through the motions of setting up an aircraft factory in order to extract concessions from the established planemakers. By that time, Hughes was already deep in negotiations with Convair (formerly, Consolidated Vultee Aircraft Corporation), the big San Diego aircraft company. In the converted A-26 attack bomber that he used as his private plane, Hughes would fly down from Los Angeles for conferences with Convair executives and designers. One time, he landed an hour late. "I'm sorry," he apologized to the waiting executives, "but my plane was dirty and I saw a thunderstorm so I decided to make a detour and fly through it to wash off the plane."

Hughes finally made a proposal to Convair to team up with them to build a dual-purpose jet for TWA. It would have to outperform anything on the drawing boards of the two other major American planemakers, Boeing and Douglas. Such a plane was taking shape inside Hughes' head. He needed only the designers and engineers to translate his ideas into blueprints. Hughes had chosen a highly advantageous time to approach Convair. At that moment, the company badly needed ideas and customers. After eight years of producing one of the most successful planes in history, the twin-engine airliners of the 240, 340, and 440 series, Convair was approaching the end of the run. That plane, which ranked second only to the Douglas DC-3 in sales, had established Convair as the postwar world's leading maker of short-range airliners. Yet Convair had not yet developed the airliner to carry the company into the jet age. Though it had important government contracts, including the Atlas missile and B-58 supersonic bomber, Convair was anxious about the future.

Convair was also seriously concerned about its own status and identity. Only a few years earlier Convair, which had been an independent and highly effective corporation, had been taken over by General Dynamics, and the Convair people resented their reduced position as only a division within a large diversified corporation, which had its headquarters in New York City. They wanted to show their General Dynamics bosses that they could take care of themselves. For quite a different reason, General Dynamics was eager for its willful new charge to remain active in the civilian airliner business. As then the nation's largest maker of weaponry, General Dynamics wanted to avoid gaining the unfortunate reputation of an American Krupp. General Dynamics executives felt that Convair's continued success in civilian aviation would improve the corporation's public image and please Washington officials, who frowned on enterprises that survived solely on government contracts.

Thus, Convair accepted Hughes' proposal and the two sides

entered into an informal agreement. Hughes supplied the concepts while Convair designers produced the drawings, and Convair engineers ran feasibility tests of the proposed aircraft. The first one was the Model 18. A four-engine jet with sharply swept wings, it was substantially bigger and faster than other planned jetliners of the time. By building two versions—one with smaller engines for domestic routes and another with larger engines for transoceanic service—Hughes hoped the Model 18 would serve as a dual-purpose airplane. Convair and Hughes wanted to put the Model 18 into production, but Convair had to ask permission from the General Dynamics' board of directors. Despite their eagerness for Convair to make a civilian airliner, the directors were fearful about going ahead on such a big project, which had one customer— Hughes. They vetoed the Model 18.

Convair and Hughes kept on trying. Another one of Hughes' ideas was developed into a design. It was Model 19, which in some respects was a decade ahead of its time. Somewhat reminiscent of the subsequent generation of jumbo jets, Model 19, powered by six engines, would carry two hundred passengers. But Convair rejected Model 19 as too large and ungainly compared to the Douglas and Boeing jets. After that came two more design projects, Models 20 and 21, both of which were modifications and improvements on the earlier four-jet Model 18. But neither of those planes were put into production either.

Meanwhile, Hughes had resumed his contact with Avro of Canada. Avro had designed a six-jet craft that was capable of supersonic speeds and Hughes started to investigate the possibility of a joint venture with Avro to build the plane. But suddenly, Hughes' plans were overtaken by other developments. Earlier, in 1954, the prototype of the Boeing 707 had made its first flight. The big Seattle planemaker had built this one plane as a private venture. Though Hughes had kept in touch with the 707 project, it was not an undertaking that appealed to him. Other airlines were engaged in 707 studies, which meant that any idea he might provide for improving the plane would be certain to benefit his competitors. Furthermore, he had little leverage on Boeing—they were not dependent on him for orders—and it was thus highly questionable whether they would indulge his perfectionist's enthusiasm for suggesting changes.

For a long time Hughes did not have to worry about the Boeing developments because its production lines were tied up by a large Air Force order for tanker versions of the 707, which were used to refuel in flight the B-52s of the Strategic Air Command. But in July 1955 the Air Force gave Boeing permission to build civilian 707s while it continued to produce the KC-135 tankers. The race for the jetliners was on!

Douglas quickly responded to Boeing's challenge by offering to the airlines its own jet, the DC-8. Though Douglas had not yet built a prototype, it really did not have to. The firm's reputation as the world's leading maker of long-range airliners was so good that many airlines were prepared to order the DC-8 even before it flew.

Now the question for the airlines was which plane to order, how many, and when. To the airline that placed the first order would go the preferred delivery position, which would mean the honor of inaugurating jet service in the United States as well as the opportunity to lure passengers away from rival lines that did not yet have jets. While the other airlines were pondering what to do, Juan Trippe, then the president of Pan American World Airways, made a typically clever move. In October 1955 he ordered twenty 707s and twenty-five DC-8s. In that way, Trippe assured TWA's leading international rival that it would be first to fly jets on the blue-ribbon North Atlantic route. A few weeks later American Airlines, TWA's major domestic competitor, ordered thirty 707s. That meant that American would inaugurate jet service across the continent.

Hughes was being left behind, but still he continued to delay. Finally, in February 1956, a full three months after Pan Am's order, Hughes reserved eight 707s for TWA. (A short time later he increased the order to thirty-three 707s, of which fifteen were the shorter-range Transcontinentals and eighteen were the bigger, long-range Intercontinental 331s.) During the months while

Hughes had toyed with one plan and then another, Boeing had gone ahead and produced the very sort of dual-purpose jetliner that he had hoped to develop for TWA. It undoubtedly stung Hughes' sensitive pride that Boeing had managed to beat him to the fulfillment of that concept. Worse yet, other airlines would profit from the idea. In a sudden burst of activity, Hughes sought to overtake his rivals. While other airline executives watched in fascination, Hughes embarked upon what is remembered as the great jet engine caper. Shortly after his initial 707 order, Hughes signed up with Pratt and Whitney, the engine makers, for three hundred jet engines worth $90 million. Engines were in short supply and Hughes undoubtedly was trying to corner the jet engine market. If he succeeded, he could trade his engines to the planemakers in return for earlier delivery positions.

Meanwhile, Hughes seized upon another opportunity that would enable him to overhaul his competitors. The opportunity came from Convair, which, after Hughes had dropped out of their joint project, had designed another jetliner on its own. Known as Model 22, the new design was built around an exceptional engine, General Electric's J-79, the first American-designed jet engine powerful enough to propel a plane at more than twice the speed of sound. It drove Convair's B-58 Hustler, then the world's fastest bomber, and the Lockheed F-104, which had shattered a whole series of speed records. Early in 1956, even before the Air Force took the J-79 off the secret list, Convair had drawn the blueprints of a jetliner that would take advantage of those hot engines.

Exactly two days after the J-79 was declassified, a team of Convair and General Electric engineers paid a visit to Hughes at a beachside villa in Santa Monica. Hughes was entertaining a group of his personal guests, but despite the close proximity of the two groups there was no mixing, except on a single occasion when a beautiful girl fainted onto the lap of one of the engineers.

Still, Hughes found time to study the specifications of the new plane. He was pleased with what he saw. The Model 22 had the one thing that next to safety Hughes wanted most: speed. Propelled by four J-79s, the plane would fly 615 miles per hour, a full

35 mph faster than the early models of the 707 and DC-8. If Howard Hughes could not be first to fly the jets, at least he could fly the fastest. At that time, he was especially sensitive to the speed issue. To his chagrin, the DC-6s of American and United were outrunning TWA's Constellation on the coast-to-coast routes because the Connie lacked the DC-6's ability to fly across the continent without refueling.

"I'll send my men," Hughes told the representatives of Convair and General Electric. He meant that he would send to San Diego a team of TWA engineers under Bob Rummel, who would assist Convair in developing the final design of the new plane.

On February 8, 1956, Rummel, accompanied by a staff of a dozen or so TWA engineers, arrived in San Diego. He set up shop in the small office of a closed-down lumber yard not far from the Convair plant. Then the TWA and Convair engineers began the complex task of reaching an agreement on thousands of details that must be decided before a jetliner reaches the final stage of design.

For publicity's sake, the new plane needed a name. Citizens of San Diego, who were delighted at the prospect of the many jobs the new plane would create, dubbed it "the sweet bird of our economy." Hughes wanted to call it "The Golden Arrow." He hoped that the skin of the plane could be made from oxidized aluminum, which has a golden hue. Unfortunately, tests showed the oxidized panels so differed in shade from one to another that the plane would have looked like a multihued quilt. Jack Zevely, who was Convair's sales vice president, wanted to call the plane "The Sky Lark." But after much discussion, the name became simply a number: the 880. Convair arrived at that sum by doubling the designation of its last twin-engine piston airliner, the 440, since in just about every respect the 880 was twice the plane.

Zevely, wry and likable, who negotiated the contract with Hughes, had a different explanation for the designation. As he told it, 880 stood for the number of negotiating sessions before Hughes finally affixed his signature to the final contract.

Hughes imposed his usual secrecy precautions on their dealings.

To confuse possible spies from competing companies, the two men often met in some seedy hotel in which Hughes had rented a string of rooms so that the conference could take place in a room that was bounded on either side by empty ones. Whenever the layout of the room permitted, Hughes would swing a bathroom door or closet door in front of the locked room door as an additional sound baffle. At other times, Hughes would pick up Zevely at some rendezvous in a nondescript Chevrolet and drive off to park at a deserted spot where Hughes could keep a lookout in all directions.

Hughes was a tireless bargainer. During one all-night session, Zevely complained that he was too tired to carry on. Hughes replied that he had just the thing to pep him up. Though it was 3 A.M., Hughes made some telephone calls. Then, with Hughes at the wheel ("He drives like a demon," recalls Zevely), they careened away in an old Chevy to the RKO lot in Hollywood. Hughes had arranged for a screening of *Jet Pilot,* the film he worked on for years in the late 1940s but had never gotten around to finishing. It had no sound, no start, and no ending, but Hughes had summoned the star to provide a running commentary. Wearing a mink coat over her nightgown, Janet Leigh explained the plot to Zevely, who was so amused by the entire episode that he did, in fact, forget his fatigue.

Hughes had a special reason for being especially insistent in the Convair negotiations. In addition to many engineering changes that he wanted made in the 880, Hughes was pressing for a very unusual financial concession that denied the normal procedures. When ordering aircraft, it is standard procedure for the buyer to make a down payment, usually 10 per cent of the aircraft's cost, which is followed by substantial quarterly progress payments. On delivery, the balance, usually about 20 per cent of the total price, is then paid. In that manner, the buyer assists the manufacturer in bearing the cost of the labor as well as the purchase of parts from outside suppliers, which account for 40–60 per cent of the plane's total cost. In addition, the planemaker is protected against getting stuck with unpaid planes on his hands.

But Howard Hughes, in his all-night marathons, was insisting on a special deal. He offered to make the down payment; then he wanted to pay nothing until the planes were delivered. For Convair, such a setup would mean it would have to provide nearly all the working capital for the construction of the 880s for Hughes.

Such an arrangement would impose a huge strain on Convair's financial resources. Convair would also be taking a gamble whether Hughes would actually have the money ready when the planes were ready for delivery. For Convair, however, an even greater gamble was whether to proceed with the 880 program at all. Aside from Hughes' promise to take thirty 880s, Convair had succeeded in lining up only one other commitment—that of Delta Airlines for ten. Convair unwisely reckoned that it needed to sell only sixty-eight planes to break even (a figure that turned out to be far too small). Even so, Convair's salesmen were not yet near that number. Furthermore, because of a number of design changes, the 880, which originally had been intended to be a relatively small jetliner in the 750–1,000 mile range, had grown in size and range until it came very close to competing directly with the DC-8 and 707. For a variety of reasons, including growing panic at the prospect of the end to Convair's civilian planemaking, the directors of General Dynamics this time consented to the proposal to build a jetliner. On June 7, 1956, when Hughes closed his order for thirty 880s, the contract contained the concession that he needed only to make a down payment of $9 million, the balance payable upon delivery. Unwittingly, Convair had acceded in a matter that later turned out to be extremely painful not only for the Convair Division but for the entire General Dynamics Corporation as well. The stage, in fact, was being set for the largest commercial loss in business history, a debacle that ruined Convair and permanently dented the business careers of a considerable number of top executives, including Frank Pace, then General Dynamics' chairman.

As Hughes completed his first round of jet orders, it became evident to the handful of insiders who were privy to the details of the Convair deal why he had insisted upon such an unusual financial arrangement. In four months, Hughes had ordered sixty-three aircraft worth $315 million. In addition, there was a $90 million order for engines. All told, Hughes' bill amounted to some $415 million. It was by far the largest commitment ever made for an airline—and it was made by a single individual. As things now stood, TWA was to receive a jet fleet that would quickly overtake, outnumber, and outrun those of its competitors. It was a cleverly balanced assortment of aircraft: thirty-three Boeing 707s in two versions and thirty 880s. The mix was ideally suited for TWA's excellent route structure. Now the only question was how Hughes would raise the money.

Even for a man of Hughes' wealth, the orders were extremely burdensome. His aim was to use his own funds to put at least some of the jets into service before he was forced to turn to outside financial help. The reason was that he wanted to retain his absolute control over the airline, and he knew that while the financiers would be glad to give him money, they would take away part, if not all, of his freedom to run TWA as he pleased.

That conviction was only strengthened by the experiences other airlines were having with the banks and insurance companies. In return for five-to-seven year loans for the purchase of the jets, the airlines were being required to submit to a number of restrictive conditions. In some loan covenants, for example, the airlines were forbidden to build new terminals, borrow more money, acquire additional aircraft, or even relocate ticket offices until a certain per cent of their debt had been retired. In some loan agreements there was even a clause that gave the lenders the right to step in and appoint a new management if the old one failed to meet its financial obligations. Hughes regarded such conditions as a grave threat to his position as all-powerful proprietor of TWA. But, he was convinced that once the jets had proven themselves to be profitable investments, the banks and insurance companies would be happy to lend money on less restrictive terms.

His plan was simple. Let the jets prove themselves. "They'll sell like hot cakes!" he would exclaim. Then after the bankers had had a change of heart, TWA could raise the money to reimburse Hughes for the planes he had bought and to finance those that still were to be delivered. In that way, TWA would get its planes,

Hughes would retain uncompromised control over TWA, and he would even be able to make a tax profit by writing off the depreciation charges on the aircraft against Toolco's earnings. If his plan succeeded, he once again would demonstrate that the clever loner could take on the eastern financial establishment and beat it. But as he now embarked on his boldest undertaking ever, there were many financiers who hoped that he finally had overreached himself.

Hughes had based his ability to pull off this financial coup on the continued success of his many enterprises. In the early to mid-1950s, when Hughes formulated the plan, his assumption seemed perfectly justified. But the situation began to change. His first setback was largely self-imposed. In the wake of the employee revolt at Hughes Aircraft and the subsequent threat of the loss of Air Force contracts, Hughes had sought to make a gesture that would show that he regarded his electronics company as a public trust. Accordingly, in late 1954 he set up a non-profit research foundation, the Howard Hughes Medical Institute, to which he transferred the ownership of Hughes Aircraft. It was a gift that was worth $80 million in property alone and at least three times that amount in total assets. It also carried the exclusive right to the aircraft company's earnings, which amounted to from $10 million to $15 million a year. Hughes became the sole trustee of the foundation, but he no longer possessed the power to dip into the aircraft company's resources for his own purposes. In all likelihood, Hughes could have avoided his later financial problems if he had retained free access to the resources of Hughes Aircraft, whose total financial worth certainly doubled, and perhaps even tripled, during the next ten years.

Just as Hughes was placing the big jet orders, problems began to develop in the airline for which he was in the process of pledging his fortune. In January 1956 Ralph Damon, who had been TWA's president for the past seven years, died from a heart attack. Damon had been very well liked at TWA, and despite his inevitable disputes with Hughes, he had run the airline well. After Damon's death, Hughes neglected to appoint a replacement. The airline was administered by a triumvirate of executives who, according to one TWA director, had only one thing in common—mutual antipathy. TWA split into small jealous fiefdoms, and its efficiency went into a spin. After eight years of unbroken profits, including record earnings of $10.3 million in 1954, TWA lost $2.3 million in 1956. Because of the line's weakened condition, A. V. (Vic) Leslie, TWA's senior financial vice president, in 1956 warned Hughes that TWA would not be able to carry the burden for the jet purchases until 1958 at the earliest.

Just as TWA was growing weaker, Hughes temporarily lost the services of his chief lieutenant, Noah Dietrich, who watched over Hughes' financial arrangements. In mid-1956, after quarreling with Hughes over the huge proportions of the jet orders, Dietrich went on a six-month safari to Africa. Dietrich, who had always been skeptical of his employer's sentimental attachment to TWA, no longer was there to try to stop Hughes from bleeding Toolco for TWA's benefit. A short time later, after he and Hughes had parted company for good, Dietrich told a reporter, "I don't know whether Howard knows it or not but he is in the process of liquidating his most profitable enterprises to save the least profitable one."

Though TWA's position was growing steadily more precarious, Hughes allowed nearly all of 1956 to pass before he finally appointed a new president for TWA. Acting largely on the advice of George Spater, then TWA's general counsel and later became president of American Airlines, Hughes tapped for the job a young and energetic Pentagon official: Carter Burgess, then only thirty-nine, who was Assistant Secretary of Defense for manpower. As was his custom, Hughes, who was already becoming a recluse, hired Burgess by telephone. It was a mistake. If he had taken one look at the even stare and determined chin of his prospective president, Hughes would have seen that Burgess was not the man who would tolerate the second guessing that Hughes visited upon his executives.

Still, all went well between the two men at first. Hughes showed his willingness to help TWA by underwriting a small stock offering that raised $70 million to help pay, among other things, for the eleven JetStream Constellations, which Hughes had ordered several years earlier as an interim aircraft to tide over TWA during the transition from the piston-engine equipment to jets. Hughes also guaranteed that Burgess would have the working capital that he needed to bring TWA into good condition.

Burgess, a wartime aide to General Dwight Eisenhower, had an immediate and positive effect on the morale at TWA. Active and dynamic, he flew the line, chatting with everyone from baggage handlers to pilots. His enthusiasm and self-confidence were contagious. "Work harder for Carter" was the slogan among TWA employees in those days. Burgess believed that you gave a man a job and then you let him do it. But it was not a management philosophy that coincided with that of Hughes, who liked to exercise exacting control over his presidents. Soon Hughes began to bombard Burgess with suggestions about how he should run TWA. Hughes, for example, felt TWA needed additional planes to fill the gap before the new jets came into service in 1959–60. He liked two British turboprops, the Vickers Viscount and the Bristol Britannia, both of which he wanted TWA to buy. But Burgess maintained that TWA did not need more interim aircraft. Then the two men tangled on the question of a jet overhaul base in Kansas City. Burgess had given his word to TWA employees that a base of a certain size would be built, but Hughes demanded that the plans should be scaled down. As a result, Burgess felt that his authority had been compromised.

Their next dispute was the crucial one, since it cut to the heart of Hughes' conduct of TWA. By seignorial right, Hughes claimed the privilege of flying TWA's new aircraft. He liked to take out a new plane, make scores of landings, until the tires were worn out. When the JetStreams came into service, Hughes commandeered one. With a TWA crew, he flew to Montreal where he wanted to inspect a Britannia. Instead of returning to New York, as TWA understood he would, Hughes piloted the JetStream to Nassau in the Bahamas where his wife, Jean Peters, joined him at a luxurious beachside hotel. What began as a weekend excursion turned into a week and then into a month. One by one, the

crew drifted back to New York, with stories about how Hughes
had bought them new clothes (they had left with only weekend
bags) and treated them royally. Meanwhile, Hughes stayed on in
the Bahamas. So did the JetStream No. 313.

For old-timers at TWA, Hughes' conduct seemed entirely normal. Many of them remembered occasions when Hughes had appropriated a plane for test flights or had ordered a regular flight
cancelled so that he could use the aircraft to take a party of friends
to Mexico City. But Burgess, a newcomer, was outraged. By the
dint of his own will power, he was trying to wrench TWA into the
black. And where was the owner of the airline? He was flying lazy
circles over the Bahamas in a plane that should have been hauling
paying passengers.

In no uncertain terms, Burgess told Hughes repeatedly that he
wanted the plane back. Meanwhile, Burgess was under great pressure to put No. 313 back into TWA service. The Civil Aeronautics Board was closely watching how Burgess handled the No. 313
problem. From extended telephone conversations with Hughes,
Burgess received the impression that the plane would be returned
to TWA by a certain date, and he told the CAB so. When the deadline fell due, Hughes had not yet returned the plane. Once again
Burgess felt greatly embarrassed. Actually, Hughes kept No. 313
for six months. Finally, as the sole pilot aboard, he flew it non-stop
from the Bahamas to Los Angeles. TWA had been alerted to have
a limousine waiting at the end of a runway at Los Angeles International Airport. As he walked down the airstairs, Hughes snapped
one command. "Change the engines," he said. Apparently, if No.
313 later had engine problems, he did not want to be blamed.

The JetStream dispute heightened the tension between the two
men. Hughes was spending an increasing amount of his time on
the telephone to Burgess with suggestions and admonishments. For
his part, Burgess found it increasingly difficult to run TWA all day
while talking for hours each night with Hughes. Even so, Burgess
did manage to reduce TWA's loss by $900,000 to $2.3 million in
1957.

Finally Burgess got angry. "Why don't you get off my back and let me run the airline?" he told Hughes. As Burgess saw it, Hughes' problem was that he wanted the power, but not the day-to-day responsibility of running a major airline. But Burgess felt that the two elements could not be separated. Fed up, he offered Hughes two alternatives. Either Hughes could appoint an independent board of directors and allow the directors and president to run the company, or Burgess would quit and Hughes could run the airline himself. The choices were sensible, but Hughes chose to ignore them. In December 1957, only slightly more than eleven months after he had become president, Carter Burgess resigned. A group of TWA pilots and executives gave him a farewell present. It was the model of a JetStream with the number "313" emblazoned on its side.

Hughes had failed to make use of Burgess' talents to rebuild TWA, a fact that redounded to Hughes' harm, especially in Washington where Burgess was highly respected. Burgess' exit came at a moment when the federal government and the financial community were becoming alarmed at the worsening condition of the nation's airlines. The recession of 1958–59 had sent airline revenues into a yearlong decline for the first time since the start of American civil aviation in the late 1920s. Earnings were falling sharply at the very time when the airlines needed millions in credit to buy the new jets. After a long investigation, the White House on June 30, 1958, issued a special report on the airline crisis. Written by Paul W. Cherington, a Harvard University transportation expert, the report warned that the nation's airlines faced a severe financial crisis. Cherington noted that all but one of the nation's fourteen major airlines still needed to arrange an additional $763.7 million in long-term financing in order to pay for the jets they had ordered. Of that $763.7 million, TWA accounted for almost half of the unarranged financing.

The White House report was a stark reminder that almost no one except Hughes had much sympathy for his plan to finance TWA's jets himself. To a financier or government official, the plan seemed needlessly egocentric. TWA was a major employer, a carrier responsible each day for the lives of thousands of passengers, and an important representative abroad. No one man's ambition should be allowed to jeopardize the stability and welfare of such an enterprise. Other airlines were arranging for long-term financing. Why shouldn't Hughes? In fact, many of his critics felt that the influence of the banks and insurance companies would be beneficial for TWA and would provide the airline with a corrective buffer against Hughes' interference in the company's management.

As long as his money held out, there was nothing anyone could do to force Hughes to behave in a more orthodox manner. But one month after the publication of the White House report came a jarring disclosure about Hughes' own financial difficulties. In accordance with the regulations of the Security and Exchange Commission, Boeing, which was seeking permission to sell to the public $30.6 million in convertible debentures, was required to make a full disclosure of the state of its business. It had no choice but to reveal that one of its customers had missed a progress payment for 707s. People guessed correctly that the customer was Howard Hughes.

The reason that Hughes missed a payment was that Toolco, the fundament of his fortune, had suddenly ceased to gush forth its accustomed wealth. In mid-1950s the tool company was earning an annual pretax profit of from some $25 million to $30 million. But in spring of 1957 a world oil glut caused a sharp decline in drilling activities. That meant a decrease in the demand for drill bits and other tools that Hughes' company supplied to the oil industry. As a result, Toolco's earnings fell to some $20 million in 1957 and to $15 million the next year. Meanwhile TWA was losing money. Worse still, the resources of Hughes Aircraft were beyond his immediate reach. Furthermore, Hughes already had dipped heavily into his available reserves; Toolco's cash balance, which had stood at a healthy $65 million only two years ago, now was almost totally exhausted. Howard Hughes was by no means broke, but for a man who needed to raise $100 million to $110 million a year for the next three years, he was definitely getting into a financial bind.

As Hughes' position weakened, new questions came into play.

How would the banks and insurance companies treat Hughes? Would they use their power to force him into accepting a loan on their terms, or would they give him the money he needed with few or no strings attached?

The initial skirmish between Hughes and the financiers, which took place during the summer of 1958, gave a hint of a great impending battle. The issue was a $12 million loan to TWA from the Equitable Life Assurance Society and a group of bankers, headed by the Irving Trust Company. TWA had needed the money to meet its payroll in the last months of 1957. When the notes fell due in the summer of 1958, Hughes tried to negotiate for an extension of the loans. But the Equitable, which was TWA's senior lender, told Hughes it would agree to an extension only on one condition: that he promptly set up long-term financial arrangements for the purchase of the jets.

Hughes, who thought it was still too early to turn to the financiers for help, avoided the Equitable's ultimatum by scraping up the money from his own dwindling resources to pay off the notes for TWA.

Hughes escaped the first encounter with the financiers, but he also had tied up more of his millions for the foreseeable future. There was no assurance that he would be able to buy his way out of the next showdown. If he was to be forced against his will to accept help from the insurance companies and banks, he wanted to at least get the very best terms. For that, he needed to get TWA quickly back into shape. Since Burgess' departure, TWA had been without a president. In fact, during the past two and a half years, TWA had enjoyed the services of a chief executive officer for only eleven months.

For help in finding a new president, Hughes turned to his old and most trusted friend, the late Robert Gross, who in 1926 with his brother, Courtlandt, had founded the Lockheed Aircraft Corporation. For years Hughes had relied on Bob Gross for advice and assistance. After mulling over Hughes' problem, Gross suggested a former member of the Lockheed board as a possible candidate. He was Charles S. Thomas, who had recently retired as the

Secretary of the Navy. Wealthy and wanting nothing more than to settle down in his home state of California, Thomas had nonetheless, as a special favor to his old friend President Dwight Eisenhower accepted the position as chairman of the Republican party's finance committee. Thomas was at a fund-raising dinner in Philadelphia when a long-distance call came from Bob Gross. Gross said that Hughes wanted him to become president of TWA and would be calling at twelve that night. Thomas, who had known Hughes years earlier in Los Angeles when the two men had lockers near one another in the Los Angeles Country Club, had friendly memories of him.

At midnight Hughes did indeed call and offer Thomas the job. Though flattered, Thomas explained that a salary meant little to him. Because of his large private income, additional earnings would go mainly for taxes. Though he was aware of Hughes' reluctance to share the stock in his companies with anyone else, Thomas said that unless he received a stock option that would give him a large capital gain, he could see no reason for taking the position.

Hughes replied that he understood Thomas' position, but that it was a difficult time to talk about stock options since he was in the process of trying to increase his TWA holdings from 78.23 per cent to 80 per cent so that he could treat the airline for tax purposes as a subsidiary of Hughes Tool. Hence he could not spare a single share of TWA.

Though the two men were unable to come to terms, Hughes called a number of times during the next four weeks. Finally, Thomas made a counterproposal. He would gamble, as he put it, on a salary for the next two years. After that, if Hughes wanted him to continue as president of TWA, Thomas would expect to be given the right to buy a big block of TWA stock at a low price so he could sell it later and make a large profit. (That would, of course, be taxed then at the standard capital gains rate of 23 per cent instead of the far higher income tax rate that Thomas had to pay on his salary.)

The proposal intrigued Hughes, who was a gambler himself. Hughes hired Thomas, but he reserved for himself two important areas of responsibility—those of arranging the financing for the jets and of advertising. Hughes set Thomas' salary without consulting his new president. Thomas did not even know how much he was earning until he got his first check. When he saw the figures —it worked out to an annual salary of $60,000—Thomas was dismayed. It was only half as much as he had expected. But Thomas did not allow that disappointment to interfere with his sense of purpose at TWA. His experience both in business, where he saved the Foreman & Clark chain of men's clothing stores from bankruptcy in the 1930s, and the government service, in which he served as a wartime aide to Navy Secretary James V. Forrestal, had prepared him to be a first-class troubleshooter. At TWA there was plenty of trouble to shoot at. Because of a lack of leadership, the company was divided into small jealous factions. Morale was low. TWA was not getting the full value either from its people or its planes.

Thomas set up five task forces composed of senior executives to study the airline's operations. At the same time, he wanted to find out what lower-echelon executives felt was wrong. He told each division chief to pick two subordinates who had never had much influence on policy. Summoning these young men to his office one by one, Thomas braced each of them with a challenge: "If you bet I'll not be here too long then this won't make much sense to you. But if you have the nerve to tell me what's wrong with this company, and if you come in here with good suggestions, you're going to have a great future here."

Engaging and sincere, Thomas inspired a sense of trust at TWA. The junior executives responded to his challenge. Within a few months they had brought in recommendations that saved the airline $12 million in operating expenses a year. Thomas' next step was a complete restudy of the utilization of TWA's aircraft. At that time, TWA had no clear-cut idea of where it was making and where it was losing money in its flight operations. Thomas had a task force examine every segment of TWA's routes to determine where flights should be dropped and where they could be added. The result was a complete rescheduling of TWA's flights that put the planes where the passengers were. Thomas also quickly reorganized TWA's archaic management structure. When he took over, he found that thirteen executives representing fourteen major functions in the airline (operations, sales, passenger service, etc.) reported directly to the president. That meant that the president was totally preoccupied with the airlines day-to-day operations and had no time to devote to the vital long-range matters of policy and planning. As a remedy, Thomas created a new post, called "systems general manager," to handle the day-to-day operations of the airline. The systems general manager had two major assistants; one of them ran the flight operations and the other the administration of the company. TWA finally had a modern system of management.

Thanks largely to Thomas, TWA made an amazing recovery. The TWA people liked him immensely. "Two-pants Charlie" they called him in a somewhat ungracious reference to his early days in the men's clothing business. They called themselves the "can-do airline," and they lived up to their name. Though TWA had lost nearly $12 million in the first six months of 1958, the airline turned around dramatically after Thomas' arrival in July and made so much money in the last months of the year that it came within only $700,000 of breaking even for 1958.

As the news of TWA's revitalization spread throughout the airline industry and the financial community, Hughes sensed that it was the right time to start stalking the eastern financial establishment for money. Once again he turned for help to Bob Gross. At Hughes' request Gross flew East to canvass the banking situation. Returning to Los Angeles, he advised Hughes that the banker who might be helpful was George Woods, the chairman of the First Boston Corporation. Acting on Gross' recommendations, Hughes in October 1958 employed the First Boston Corporation at a fee of $25,000 per month to devise a plan for financing TWA's new fleet of jets. In December Woods informed Hughes by telephone that his work had progressed to the point where it would be worthwhile for them to sit down for a face-to-face talk. After Hughes demurred about a personal meeting, Woods reportedly replied: "That is not the way I do business, Mr. Hughes. I am accustomed to dealing with a face, not a voice." So ended Howard Hughes' first attempt to secure financing.

Between Christmas 1958 and New Year's Day, Hughes made another approach to Wall Street. This time he called another old acquaintance, Fred Brandi, who was the senior partner of the investment firm of Dillon, Read & Company. Hughes told him that he wanted Dillon, Read to work up a financial plan and to include as partners in the undertaking two other Wall Street firms, Lehman Brothers and Lazard Frères. Hughes explained that in the past he had worked with these firms on undertakings that had never come to fruition. Now he wanted them finally to participate in a project in which they would earn some money.

It sounded like a reformed Howard Hughes, a transformation that cheered the hearts of Wall Street bankers. There was, however, a reason for his sudden tractability. In January another Boeing progress payment was falling due. He had first missed a progress payment a year before and in the meantime he had managed by a combination of threats of legal action and pleas to have the 1958 quarterly payments extended to January 1959. Now the deadline had almost arrived and he had no cash to meet the accumulated payments of $15 million. Boeing and its bankers were unhappy about the delays because the absence of Hughes' payments was forcing them to use their own funds to pay for the work on his planes. Sensing Boeing's impatience, Hughes felt he could forestall a crisis if he could convince Boeing and its bankers that he would soon have the money to meet his obligations. Accordingly, in January Hughes sent to Seattle a deputation, including a Dillon, Read officer, who testified that a comprehensive plan was being set up to finance Hughes' jets. Boeing, which accepted the explanation, granted Hughes another extension of the progress payments.

The plan that was being worked out was called HALCO, for Hughes Aircraft Leasing Company. Under this plan, Hughes Tool would buy the jets and then lease them on a long-term basis to TWA. Hughes reckoned that the prospect of a large income from the leases would induce the bankers to lend him the money to complete the purchase of the jets. For Hughes, HALCO had the great advantage of enabling him to apply the huge depreciation charges on the aircraft against the profits of the tool company. In that way, Hughes would have been able to write off from $20 million to $30 million a year in depreciation costs against Hughes Tool's earnings.

While the HALCO plan appealed to Hughes, it had an obvious disadvantage for TWA and for TWA's creditors. Under HALCO, the airline would not own its most important pieces of equipment. Charlie Thomas found it unthinkable that a major corporation should not be in possession of its most important money-earning assets. Did United States Steel lease its steel plants or General Motors its automobile factories? Thomas was dead set against HALCO. So were TWA's creditors, for the basic reason that if the airline did not own its own planes, the company's worth would be drastically reduced and the creditors would not be able to secure their loans against TWA's assets. This consideration was especially important to the Equitable, which held notes, guaranteed by mortgages of TWA's piston-engine planes that were not scheduled to be paid off for another ten years.

Faced with such opposition, HALCO died. Howard Hughes had used up one more alternative and several crucial months. By now, circumstances were closing in on him. Three months earlier the first Boeing jet—a Transcontinental model—had been delivered to TWA. With the greatest difficulty, Hughes had managed to pay for it by borrowing money, mainly from the Bank of America and the Irving Trust. In return, he had pledged the 707 as collateral for the notes. Hughes then leased the jet to TWA on a day-to-day basis. The Equitable frowned on the arrangement because it begged the point of finally establishing a stable financing. For more than a year the Equitable had been writing letters to Hughes, urging him to make timely preparations to meet the millions in payments that soon would fall due. But Hughes had never even bothered to reply. Now, as the next 707 was delivered a few weeks later, Hughes again wanted to lease the plane to TWA on a day-to-day basis. But the Equitable said no. Under its old mortgage agreement with TWA, the Equitable could not stop Hughes from supplying the aircraft to TWA, but it did have the power to stop TWA from paying the leasing fees to him. And that is what it did.

Hughes now was in a squeeze. At the rate of three or four a month, his 707s were coming off the production line. To pay for them, Hughes was borrowing heavily from the banks, using up his last source of credit. Yet he could not get back any lease fees from TWA. It was a highly ironic situation. Hughes was, in fact, succeeding in delivering the jets to TWA without surrendering any of his absolute control of the airline. Furthermore, his prediction that the jets would be successful was being richly fulfilled. As the Boeings came into service, TWA recovered and grew ever stronger. Yet in his very moment of victory, the remaining strength of Hughes' financial empire was being bled away.

Hughes was now desperate to reduce his commitments so that in the crunch between his jet orders and his dwindling credit, he would not be ruined. In June 1959 he ordered a substantial cutback in the number of aircraft on order. He cancelled ten of the thirty Convair 880s, reducing his commitment to General Dynamics by some $40 million. At Boeing, he transferred the delivery rights for six of the eighteen 707-331 Intercontinental jets on order, which were scheduled for delivery in late 1959 and the next year, to Pan American World Airways, TWA's major international rival. Pan Am refunded the $6 million downpayment, which Hughes applied to the delivery of Boeing Transcontinentals.

By August 1, 1959, despite Hughes' intense financial problems, he had managed to deliver to TWA all its fifteen Boeing Transcontinentals. As a result, the airline was soaring from success to success. On some days TWA's new jets were making a profit of $200,000. After losing a total of $5.7 million in the previous three years, TWA in 1959 made its second largest profit ever—$9,402,-000. And that, as TWA people liked to say, was only the half of it. Not until the end of 1959 did TWA begin to receive the twelve remaining Boeing 707-331 Intercontinentals, which would enable it to compete on overseas runs against Pan Am, which had been flying 331s across the Atlantic for more than a year.

TWA's strong showing once again provided Hughes with an

opportunity to negotiate from a position of relative strength with the bankers. The airline was so prosperous and well run that Hughes could most probably arrange loans on agreeable terms. Furthermore, he was under increasing pressure to finally do something. Because of the intransigence of the Equitable, he still was unable to receive lease payments from TWA; that money, some $20 million by late 1959, was piling up in TWA's own account. The bankers, to whom Hughes now owed more than $100 million, had begun warning him that his loans were now exceeding the sums he had on deposit. That was a serious matter, for in the first part of 1960 Hughes faced the bulk of the deliveries of the Boeing Intercontinentals and the Convair 880s. That would mean an outlay of some $150 million for the planes alone, not counting spare parts and extra engines that would add another $20 million to his obligations.

Faced with such huge outlays, Hughes in the late part of 1959 finally tried to line up financing. But he did not turn to the traditional sources of credit. Instead, he turned to Convair. Hughes had great leverage over Convair and its parent, General Dynamics. Since he was their only major customer, they had no choice except to be lenient with him. Earlier, in 1958, even though his impending bind was becoming public knowledge, Convair, with the approval of its corporate parent, had allowed Hughes to place an order for thirteen of the new larger and faster Convair 990 jetliners. That commitment had increased his indebtedness to General Dynamics by $85 million to a total of nearly $200 million.

Thus, when Hughes decided to raise money, he went to Convair on the theory that he was so important to them that their lenders, notably the Prudential Insurance Company of America and the Chase Manhattan Bank, would help him in order to rescue Convair. Hughes, who had a keen sense for weakness, also turned for funds to Lockheed, which at the time was in the process of losing $121 million on the turboprop Electra, a plane that had suffered a series of accidents due to a structural weakness in its wings. Hughes made an offer of a two-way deal to both planemakers: he would place a large order for Electras and Convair jets, if the two companies

would persuade their bankers to back a plan that would enable
him to pay for the new planes as well as the ones he had previously
ordered from Convair and Boeing.

The proposal had daring logic to it. There was no doubt that
large orders would have helped both companies—though Convair's
problems were quickly growing beyond the point where a single
customer could do much to save the situation. But Hughes' proposal suffered from the fact that all three parties were, to varying
degrees, financially ill. The bankers did not feel that three sick
partners could make one another healthy. For weeks Hughes tried
to figure out one angle and then another, but neither Lockheed
nor General Dynamics could induce their bankers to give them the
go-ahead. In February 1960 Hughes gave up on the project.

Hughes had used up more valuable time. More importantly, he
had used up what remained of his bankers' patience. By now,
he was totally dependent on loans to pay for TWA's jets. Though
he still had large deposits at the banks to back up his credit, the
bankers were warning him that by very large amounts he had exceeded his loan limits. Hughes, in turn, warned the banks not to
shut off his credit without due notice because he wanted to line
up alternate sources of funds.

Despite their threats, the bankers had nevertheless continued
to provide him with money. Then, on March 5, 1960, in a move
that the Hughes forces claim came without notice and the bankers
say was made only after repeated warnings, the banks cut off his
credit. Hughes' loans stood at some $125 million. Now he could
get no more money. His game was up.

4. Oktoberfest on Wall Street

While the action of the bankers was a grave blow to Hughes, it
was an equally grave one to TWA. For months, Thomas and the
other TWA people anxiously had followed the financial gyrations
of their invisible proprietor. They knew that Hughes was having
problems, but they had thought that their own outstanding performance with the jets would provide him with the opportunity to
set things straight. Unfortunately, Hughes had wasted his chances.
Now the situation suddenly began to get very bad again. Everything that Thomas and the others at TWA had worked so hard for
was endangered. The airline had gotten the Boeing Transcontinentals, but it might get few of the other planes on order. TWA had
spent millions of its own funds in training pilots to fly overseas jets,
on setting up maintenance facilities, and on making the many other
preparations for the introduction of the 880s and Boeing Intercontinentals. But the outlook for receiving all those planes was
bad. Equally bad, TWA's rivals were getting more jets all the time
and taking away TWA's passengers. Already two Intercontinentals
were waiting on the Boeing ramp in Seattle to be paid for. At Convair Hughes had engaged in an incredible series of delaying tactics.
He had even ordered his men to seize three 880s and take them
to an edge of the field. There the planes sat roped off by heavy
hemp and guarded by Hughes' men, who sat under the wings. No
outsider, not even a TWA crew, could get near the planes. In that

way Hughes blocked Convair from presenting the 880s to TWA for acceptance, and thus he did not have to pay for them. TWA could not even count on the fifteen 707 Transcontinentals it already had. They still belonged to Hughes and might be grounded at any moment if the banks foreclosed on their loans to him.

Thomas and his chief aides at TWA were close to despair. If Hughes was thrown into bankruptcy, he would in all likelihood pull TWA down with him. Already that word was being used to apply to the financial affairs of Howard Hughes. As TWA's financial experts looked at the condition of the Hughes Tool Company, they detected signs of insolvency. Hughes was out of cash, out of reserves, out of credit. In the next six months he faced obligations of $125 million. Within the next sixty days, $30 million fell due.

How could TWA save itself from Hughes' impending disaster? Despite its recent profits, the airline was still financially weak, partly because it had strained its own limited resources in spending $53 million in preparations for the introduction of the jets. It most certainly could not hope to raise the $300 million or so to pay for its jet fleet. TWA was also in other troubles. The airline's lawyers were warning Thomas and the other executives and directors that they might be held liable for TWA's precarious position. Though Hughes owned 78.23 per cent of TWA, there were some ten thousand other shareholders who owned the remaining 21.77 per cent; some of them might bring a lawsuit, charging mismanagement and a squandering of corporate assets on preparations for jets that never arrived. In such an event, Hughes would not be involved. He was neither an officer nor a director of TWA. He did his dealings by remote control, but Thomas and the other directors might be held responsible for having failed to protect the interests of all of the shareholders. It was a worrying point, as reflected in notes jotted down by Financial Vice President Vic Leslie. "TWA's current Board," he wrote, "are straw men—and thus will take no action unless forced by the counsel."

But the advice of counsel was very compelling. Though TWA had become accustomed to waiting for and obeying Hughes' commands, the airline directors now had to take action—or face the consequences. The TWA board was meeting in almost continuous sessions. At the session on Friday, March 18, 1960, Thomas declared that it was now up to TWA to help itself. There was still a way out of the dilemma, he said. The solution was to persuade Hughes to go back to an earlier financial plan that had been drawn up the year before and then almost forgotten. It was the Dillon, Read plan, named for the Wall Street house that put it together. Dillon, Read had formulated the financial program after the leasing scheme had collapsed. At Hughes' request, the Dillon, Read plan had gone through numerous revisions, but after the latest reworking in August of 1959, Hughes had ignored it in favor of pursuing his other ideas.

The Dillon, Read plan was a traditional financing setup that would raise $260 million for TWA. Of that sum, $90 million would be provided by the insurance companies and $70 million by a group of six banks headed by the Irving Trust whose senior vice president, Ben-Fleming Sessel, was a TWA director. The remaining $100 million would come from the Hughes Tool Company, which would take TWA subordinated debentures in return for the money it already had spent on the jets. Thomas told the directors that he had assurances from the banks and insurance companies that they were willing to proceed with the plan if Hughes would agree to cooperate.

The directors asked to have the weekend to think. On Monday the board met once more in TWA's headquarters at 380 Madison Avenue. By now the "straw men" had stiffer spines. To a man they agreed with Thomas that TWA had to save itself and unanimously endorsed the Dillon, Read plan. Charlie Thomas wanted to make absolutely certain that Howard Hughes got the message. After the board meeting, Thomas called aside Hughes' lawyer, Raymond Cook, who was also a TWA director.

"Tell Howard if he does not authorize this plan, I'll resign," Thomas said.

Replied Cook, who was also alarmed about TWA's conditions: "I'll do better than that, Charlie. I'll tell him that the whole board will resign." Cook went to a telephone and did just that. Howard

Hughes does not like ultimatums, but he accepted this one with surprising calm. Instead of arguing, he yielded to Thomas' demand and gave his personal approval to the Dillon, Read plan. As a gesture of his support, he pledged to guarantee a $27 million short-term loan, which the banks had promised to extend to TWA to help the airline meet current expenses until the Dillon, Read plan went into effect.

Now that Hughes had given his go-ahead, lawyers for all sides began to draw up the complicated contracts that are involved in long-term financial arrangements. The schedule called for the final closing to take place on July 21, 1960. As the lenders drew up the loan agreement, they naturally discussed what conditions they should insist upon. They were talking about what Hughes dreaded most—convenants and restrictive clauses. He had sought to avoid a long-term loan agreement chiefly because he feared the limitations that the bankers might impose on him. Now there seemed to be no escape. Nor had Hughes exactly endeared himself to the bankers in the past few years. If anything, his behavior had made them more cautious. About the only thing that had changed in the past two years was the interest rate: it had climbed from 4 per cent to 6 and 6½ per cent.

After much deliberation, the lenders decided to include a clause that would prevent Hughes from interfering with TWA's management during the ten-year duration of the loans. In other dealings, the Bank of America sometimes insisted on a proviso in its contracts that gave the bank the right to step in and run the company in the event of an adverse change in management. Similarly, the Equitable occasionally included a stipulation in its loan agreements that provided for the establishment of a voting trust in the event the company defaulted on its debt. Taking a bit from each of those clauses, the lawyers for the lenders wrote a provision into the contract that required Hughes to place his shares of TWA in a voting trust that would be controlled by the lenders if there were any adverse change in the management of TWA that he did not correct within ninety days.

The voting-trust clause represented a definite threat to Hughes, who had a bad record of quarreling with TWA's presidents. The clause, however, was a great vote of confidence in Charlie Thomas. From the start of the negotiations, the lenders had stressed privately to Thomas that they regarded his continued presidency of TWA as the prerequisite to their putting up the millions for the Dillon, Read plan. Their support made Thomas think that he now had some leverage on Hughes, and Thomas needed all the leverage he could get. By now, Hughes, angry at Thomas' independent attempts to save TWA, had turned against him. He harbored some dark thoughts about Thomas, whom he accused of plotting to take TWA away from him. Hughes had quit telephoning Thomas and would not even acknowledge his repeated messages. To his aides, Hughes began to refer to the TWA president as "Mr. Charlie Thomas," an arch formality reflecting his dislike. As an additional expression of his disdain, Hughes in May 1960 engineered a merger proposal between TWA and Northeast Airlines without even informing Thomas in advance. Thomas was furious—and hurt.

When Thomas was hired at TWA in the summer of 1958, his original agreement with Hughes had been a gamble—after two years either Hughes would put him in a large capital gains position or Thomas would leave. The two years were nearly up. Thomas now decided to try and clarify his position with Hughes. He wanted to reach a better understanding about income and his powers and responsibilities as president. Thomas wanted to stay on at TWA and he made a strong case why Hughes should keep him. In messages to Hughes, Thomas stressed the importance of maintaining continuity in TWA's management. Thomas pointed out that if the Dillon, Read financing plan went into effect, TWA would owe $160 million to the banks and insurance companies and $100 million to Hughes himself. Debts of such magnitude obviously required a sound management. Also it was clear to Thomas, as indeed it was to most others in the airline industry, that the airlines faced an exceptionally difficult period of overcompetition as more jets came into service than there were passengers to fill them. It was a period that would call for careful cost-accounting and efficient operations. Furthermore, in the coming year TWA faced union negotiations with the pilots, mechanics, and flight engineers. In order to maintain TWA's continued economic health, it was imperative for the airline to avoid both a strike and an unreasonable wage settlement.

As far as money was concerned, Thomas had given up his hopes of a large capital gains position at TWA because he had come to realize that Hughes would never give him stock in one of his companies. Instead Thomas, then sixty-two, wanted a salary for the rest of his life. He offered to stay on as president and chief executive officer for two more years at $100,000 per year. Then he would stay for one additional year as chairman of the board or senior consultant for $50,000. After that, Thomas wanted a retirement income of $50,000 a year as long as he lived. He also demanded that Hughes should let him run the company free from any interference.

In the midst of these problems, Thomas went back to California on a brief but sentimental trip. It was the fortieth anniversary of his marriage to Julia. As a celebration, he took his wife to the Pebble Beach Lodge on Carmel Bay where they had spent their wedding night in 1920. Their room was bedecked with flowers from friends and their four children. Thomas had hoped to make his wife happy by taking her back to the California they both loved so much, but he was startled to wake up on the morning of his forty-first year as Julia's husband to find her crying. As she looked out over the sunny beauty of Carmel Bay, Julia sobbed, "Oh, Charlie, why do you make me live in New York?"

Why indeed? Charlie Thomas wondered.

While lunching that day with Julia at Cypress Point Country Club, Thomas met an old California friend, who represented the Irvine Ranch interests that were developing a huge tract of land south of Los Angeles into planned model communities. Drawing Thomas to one side, the man whispered, "Now treat this as confidential, but would you consider becoming the president of the Irvine Company?" Thomas said that he would think about it and let him know soon. It was a very interesting offer. It would take

Julia back to California, get Thomas out of his problem at TWA, and give him challenging and worthwhile work.

Thomas returned to New York more determined than ever to sort out his relationship with Hughes, but Hughes was uncooperative. He was incensed that Thomas had made salary and contract demands at a time when the bankers had made it plain that they wanted Thomas to stay at TWA. "You're holding a gun at my head, Charlie," said Hughes. Hughes made a counteroffer: he would meet Thomas' salary request with a contract from Toolco. The proposal went back to an old idea of Hughes'. For months, whenever he did talk to Thomas, Hughes would tell him, "Charlie, I want to get you around here on my side of the desk." By that, Hughes meant that he wanted Thomas to become a vice president of Toolco. Hughes planned to reorganize TWA and his helicopter plants into a new aeronautical division of the tool company and Thomas supposedly would run it.

Hughes did not conceal his outrage at Thomas. He suspected that Thomas was part of a conspiracy to take the airline away from him, and he could not get over the memory of Thomas' action in leading the TWA directors to endorse the Dillon, Read plan.

Hughes' attitude only heightened the dilemma of Charlie Thomas. On the one hand, he felt a great obligation to TWA and to Hughes, for whom he somehow managed to retain friendly feelings. On the other hand, Thomas had severe misgivings. If he accepted Hughes' proposal, he felt he would have less authority than ever as a Toolco vice president since Hughes, as president, would have even more direct power over him. Thomas feared that he was now being used—that Hughes was keeping him around only as window dressing to induce the financiers to go ahead with the closing of the financing plan. Then, Thomas worried, he would be shunted aside. Meanwhile, his legal position was becoming increasingly untenable. Because of Hughes' failure to deliver more jets, TWA was now losing money each day, and Thomas was anxious that he might be held accountable in a lawsuit by the minority shareholders for those losses. He also was increasingly concerned about the deterioration of his own personal relations with Hughes.

In mid-July, a very worried Charlie Thomas went to the Manhattan headquarters of the Equitable Life Assurance Society to discuss his problems and those of TWA with the two insurance executives who were most important in TWA's financial picture. They were James F. Oates, the Equitable's president, and Harry C. Hagerty, Sr., the vice chairman of the Metropolitan Life Insurance Company. The relationship between the two companies was a decisive factor in the financial maneuvers. Since the Equitable already was on the hook for at least $30 million in outstanding loans to TWA, it could not afford to let the airline go under. Furthermore, the Equitable's officers were accustomed to the delays and frustrations that were inherent in dealing with Hughes. But Hughes had no hooks into the Metropolitan, the nation's largest insurance company. Nor was the Metropolitan in the slightest prepared to tolerate his behavior. Hagerty, a devout Roman Catholic layman who was then the dean of American loan officers, felt a deep obligation to help TWA and save the thousands of jobs that otherwise would be lost. But he felt no obligation whatsoever to help Hughes, who, in his opinion, had an unhealthy influence on TWA.

To these two men Charlie Thomas poured out the litany of his complaints about Hughes. He related how Hughes would always stall and delay on decisions, how Hughes could simply not be reached when he needed him most and how Hughes insisted in having the final authority in TWA's affairs. Thomas also told how Hughes was treating him, how Hughes was accusing him of trying to steal his company and charging that Thomas was using duress to get a higher salary. Hagerty had heard enough. Fixing Thomas in his piercing gaze, Hagerty asked him sharply, "Why don't you quit?"

Thomas looked stunned, but his reply came like a reflex. "I think I will!"

Charlie Thomas had to go to Chicago on business. Worried and just about brokenhearted over the situation at TWA, he sat down in his room at the Palmer House. On a piece of hotel note paper, he began to write: "TWA announces the resignation of Mr.

Thomas as President. Having served in that capacity for two years, he was desirous of returning to his family and interests in California." He drew a line under that neat and superficial explanation. Then he began to write what he really felt. First he listed the four main charges that Hughes had made against him. Next he began to fill page after page with a letter to Hughes, pouring out his disillusionment and disappointment. "You have never taken me into your confidence and you have never been available when I wanted you," Thomas wrote. "I know of few people who would have been as patient as I have been or would have tried any harder to help you. It is now a fact that the company is suffering daily losses because of the failure to receive equipment that it was assured it would get. . . . The time has come when I cannot legally or consciensously [*sic*] see those losses occur without taking every possible action to prevent them. Under the circumstances, I am in the regrettable position of either having to resign immediately or take action which I feel certain will be contrary to your desires. I am really sorry to have to do this but I am sure the record will show that *you* forced me into this position." On July 21, the day on which the financing program had originally been scheduled to close, the Hughes Tool Company sent a terse message to the lenders: Charles Thomas had resigned. The news raced and reverberated throughout the financial community. TWA and Hughes had seemed so close to a solution to the financial crisis. Now no one could foresee what might happen next.

Each side blamed the other for Thomas' resignation and the events that followed. Hughes subsequently charged that the lenders had induced Thomas to leave as part of a conspiracy to take TWA away from him. The bankers and insurance company executives maintained that the responsibility for Thomas' resignation rested with Hughes for forcing him into an impossible situation.

Though the causes were disputed, the consequences were clear. On learning of Thomas' resignation, the lenders evoked the management clause in the Dillon, Read plan—though the plan, of course, had not yet gone into effect. They interpreted Thomas' resignation as an unfavorable change in management and refused to proceed with the financing under the old terms. Hughes argued that the lenders should go ahead and give TWA the money. Then, if they had not hired a new president within ninety days, he would surrender his TWA stock to a voting trust run by the lenders.

Hughes' argument made no impression on the financiers. On August 1 the lenders sent their answer to Hughes. It was a jarring one: unless he at once put his TWA shares into a voting trust that would give the lenders control of the airline, they would not consider moving ahead with the financing. To the dismay of Howard Hughes, the lenders had now imposed the very condition that he had feared the most. They wanted to take the control of his airline away from him.

In the same communication, the lenders made it abundantly clear to Hughes that they were prepared to place great leverage on him to force his surrender. Drawing on their power as TWA creditors, the lenders ordered TWA to refuse to accept any aircraft from Hughes even in the remote possibility that he now had enough money to deliver any planes to the airline. In Hughes' opinion, this prohibition was an attempt to cut off him and TWA from lining up any alternate sources of credit and to place them solely at the mercy of the lenders.

That was not all. In an effort to force Hughes into making a prompt decision, the lenders rearranged the due dates for two large loans. They both now would be payable on the same date: September 1, 1960. One loan was for the $27 million, which the banks had advanced to TWA in March on the understanding that the Dillon, Read plan would go into effect. The other was the Equitable's note for $27 million that originally had not been due until 1969. Only one month now stood between Howard Hughes and his impending defeat at the hands of the financiers. Once more he tried to convince the lenders to give him three months in which to select a president satisfactory to all sides. Hughes submitted to the lenders the names of men he was considering for the TWA presidency, notably TWA's senior vice president for finance, Vic Leslie, and James Austin, then the president of Northeast Airlines. But the lenders turned down Hughes' nominations because they felt that neither Leslie nor Austin would make a president who was sufficiently independent of Hughes. Then Hughes challenged the lenders to nominate a president themselves, but they refused to put themselves into the position of picking TWA's next president. Thus, for the third time in four years, TWA remained without a chief executive officer.

What could Hughes do? He could never raise $54 million to pay off those loans. In addition, of course, he faced other enormous obligations in the form of the 707s and 880s that were ready for delivery. But Hughes' very weakness gave him a weapon against the lenders. No major airline has ever fallen into bankruptcy. As a result, airline stocks are regarded by financiers and the public alike as a safe and rewarding investment. But if a major airline were to fail, all that would change. Thus, if the lenders foreclosed on TWA, they would thus be harming one of their own best areas of investment. It was an effective ploy and Hughes obviously hoped to fend off the lenders for a time with such defensive measures while searching for some way to escape from the voting trust. On August 3 Hughes made his first move in that direction by asking Ben Sessel of the Irving Trust to arrange an alternate financing program. Since the Metropolitan had been the one that insisted most strongly on the voting trust, Hughes hoped to escape, or at least weaken, that clause by leaving that insurance company out of the new scheme.

The September 1 deadline passed without either side taking any action. Hughes was greatly encouraged. As he read it, the lenders had only been bluffing and were not ready to take drastic action against him. Furthermore, he had managed to split their ranks by putting Sessel, who led the banking group, to work on a new plan. In mid-September Sessel presented to Hughes' lawyers the first draft of what became known as the "bank plan." It met Hughes' main objective by excluding the Metropolitan from the financing group, thus avoiding the voting trust proviso. The sums involved in the bank plan, however, were smaller. While the Dillon, Read plan would raise $160 million in new money, the bank plan would raise only $135.5 million. Of that amount, $40 million was to come from the General Dynamics Corporation in return for new TWA orders for 23 more 880s and 990s. To Hughes and his lawyers, the bank plan seemed workable except for one apparent flaw. It required TWA to repay $76 million within only five years to the nine participating banks. In view of TWA's weak financial condition, the duration of the bank loan seemed too short to Hughes. When Hughes' lawyer, Raymond Cook, complained about the short repayment period to Ben Sessel, he got a telling reply. "It is time for Howard Hughes to realize that he is in the hands of the banks and will do what we say," said Sessel.

Sessel spoke with confidence, for his bank, the Irving Trust, held Hughes in a powerful financial grip. Hughes had, of course, borrowed heavily to buy the jets; some $50 million of that money had come from the Irving. That loan was now overdue. There was another, even more serious, pressure on Howard Hughes. Years earlier, when he was fighting off suits by minority shareholders in RKO, Hughes had borrowed $14 million from the Irving Trust. He had needed the money in order to buy up the additional stock that enabled him to consolidate his hold on RKO. That loan would become due very shortly—on October 31, 1960. As the security for the $14 million Hughes had pledged his most important possession: his stock in the Hughes Tool Company. At the time Hughes had undoubtedly never imagined that he would ever be hard pressed for money. But now he was hard pressed indeed. As a result, the last bastion of Howard Hughes' financial power was now under attack. If Sessel called that loan earlier or if Hughes was unable to pay it off on October 31 (as now seemed to be the foregone conclusion), Hughes would suddenly find that he no longer was the only shareholder in Hughes Tool. Under the terms of the loan, the Irving Trust had the right to go into the Hughes Tool Company in Houston, open up its secret financial records to the public, and sell off to any buyers $14 million of the company's assets in order to recover its money. To Hughes, such an eventuality would be a catastrophe. He would lose his unique position as the sole proprietor of Hughes Tool. He no longer would enjoy his great freedom of action; other shareholders would be there to question decisions and perhaps even to start lawsuits against him for not running the company as they thought it should be run. He no longer could conduct his business in secret. There would be newsmen prying for stories. Above all, perhaps, it would be a grave personal defeat for Hughes, who did not give up easily. These threats heightened the drama of Hughes' battle. He no longer was fighting only to maintain his control over TWA. He was now fighting to retain his hold over the last great American industrial empire that still remained in the hands of a single individual.

In New York, during the late afternoon of Monday, September 26, 1960, Sessel presented the final version of the bank plan to Raymond Cook. As a pledge of Hughes' cooperation, Sessel insisted that Hughes personally endorse a copy of the memorandum that spelled out the terms of the bank plan. Furthermore, it had to be done by the opening of business the following day. It was an unusually short deadline, but the Hughes' forces managed to meet it. The text of the memorandum was dictated to one of the secretaries in Hughes' communications center in North Hollywood. Then it was taken to Hughes, who was at his home in Bel Air. He signed the memo and it was delivered to a Bank of America office in Los Angeles early Tuesday morning.

Now that Hughes was signed up, the plan was ready to be formally closed. The nine banks were ready to make the loans. The success of the bank plan was now dependent on General Dynamics, which was to extend a $40 million loan, repayable in seven years, to TWA. But the question was, Could General Dynamics swing that loan? In an ironic twist, Hughes was now dependent upon the very company that he had helped to foul up.

At that time, nearly a dozen 880s, for which Hughes had not yet paid, were lined up on the tarmac outside the Convair plant in San Diego where they suffered from exposure to the weather and the ocean air. Some had been pulled off the production line in an unfinished state to make room for the completion of Delta's 880s. The records of what still was to be done on the various aircraft,

especially the complex electrical wiring, were incomplete. Ultimately, Convair had to rip out much of the insides of those planes
and begin again at a huge cost in material and manpower.

Despite their experience with the 880s, Convair and its General
Dynamics parent still wanted to go along with the bank plan since
it would bring more plane orders from Hughes. But General Dynamics no longer was its own master. In 1960 it was headed for a
loss for the year of $80.3 million on the jets, a figure that grew to
a total of $483 million during the next two years. Consequently,
General Dynamics was forced to clear whatever action it wanted
to take with its own creditors, the most important of which was
the Prudential Insurance Company. Wary of dealing with Hughes,
the Prudential refused to allow General Dynamics to participate
in the bank plan. On Thursday, September 29, General Dynamics
told Sessel to count them out. With that, the bank plan collapsed.
Hughes was back where he had been two months ago—hard
pressed financially and at the mercy of the lenders. The quality of
that mercy was quickly becoming more than strained.

Thus the scene was set for what Hughes' foes and allies alike
called the "Oktoberfest." It was a time of almost unbelievable
tension and dramatic confrontations. Until then, the bankers had
not made good on their threats to foreclose on the overdue loans
that were outstanding against Hughes Tool and TWA. But now, as
October began, the bankers seized the balances of TWA and the
tool company that had been on deposit in their banks as security
for the loans. Those balances represented just about all the money
that TWA and Toolco had left. Stripped of funds, TWA and
Toolco now were vulnerable even to a small financial pressure.
If one of TWA's small creditors, say, a food supplier, found that
the airline could not pay its bill, that knowledge, if it got spread
around, would trigger a stampede of the other creditors, who could
force TWA into bankruptcy. The tool company was also on the
very brink of financial ruin. Desperate, the TWA and Toolco officers pleaded with the banks to reinstate their balances. Reluctantly, the bankers agreed to restore the balances until October 5,
provided there were no sizable withdrawals of funds.

Hughes now had a few days in which to find a way out of the predicament. His first idea was to try and bring the bank plan back to life since it offered the chance for escaping from the voting trust. Despite General Dynamics' withdrawal, Hughes still hoped to find some means to make it work. On Wednesday, October 5, the day of the deadline, the tool company sent a letter to Ben Sessel at the Irving Trust "to assure you that the bank plan is susceptible of accomplishment and to commit Mr. Hughes irrevocably to its support." According to the letter, Hughes offered to assume the $40 million commitment that General Dynamics had been unable to meet. To support that commitment, Hughes was having his large real estate holdings appraised and also was trying to borrow money against his oil leases. The banks would carry the same $76 million load as before. As an inducement Hughes offered a major concession to the lenders: he would, in the words of the letter, agree "to recommend to the TWA board of directors the election of a president acceptable to the lenders upon their request." All this time, TWA was still without a president.

On October 6, a crucial meeting took place in Ben Sessel's office at 1 Wall Street. That august address typified the credentials of the participants. George Carver, a Bank of America senior vice president in Los Angeles, had flown in from the coast to represent the world's largest bank. A delegate from the world's largest insurance company was there. So, too, were representatives of nearly a dozen of the nation's most important financial institutions. The financiers possessed some new information about Hughes' intentions. Until then, he had been saying that he would rather be forced into bankruptcy than accept the voting trust arrangement of the Dillon, Read plan. But the day before, in a conversation with one of the bankers, Hughes had changed his tune, saying he would prefer the voting trust to receivership. It was the first indication that Howard Hughes could be forced to accept the voting trust.

As usual, Sessel presided at the meeting. The issue under discussion was whether to accept Hughes' offer to go ahead with the bank plan or again to seize his and TWA's balances. After several hours, Raymond Cook, who had been waiting tensely in an adjoining room, was summoned to join the meeting. When he entered, he noticed that the atmosphere was distinctly chilly. As Sessel started to tell him that the banks had rejected Hughes' proposal, Cook interrupted to ask why. Someone else started to give an explanation, but Sessel broke in. "Let's not beat around the bush," Sessel declared. "We have made up our minds. The banks do not want to do business with Howard Hughes."

Then Sessel angrily proceeded to apply the great financial leverage that he held over Hughes. The bankers, announced Sessel, had irrevocably decided that the Dillon, Read plan must be put into action as the only feasible way of saving TWA from otherwise certain financial ruin.

They demanded that Hughes pledge his support, in writing, to the Dillon, Read plan. Unless Hughes met their conditions, the banks would at once confiscate the balances of the Hughes Tool Company and TWA. Sessel also warned that the Irving Trust would foreclose on the tool company's overdue loans and throw the company into bankruptcy. In addition, he vowed that if Hughes tried once more to resist the Dillon, Read plan, he would declare him in default on his $14 million personal loan from the Irving Trust. That would give the bank the right to go into the tool company and sell off assets in the amount necessary to recover the amount of the loan.

When Sessel finished with his list of threats, it was 3 P.M. He wanted Hughes' reply delivered in writing in a Bank of America office in Los Angeles by five. "Tell him," Sessel ordered Cook, as he started to leave the room to telephone Hughes, "that if he does not agree, I will be on the steps of the Hughes Tool Company in Houston on Monday morning to take over the Hughes Tool Company!"

Cook telephoned Hughes at his Bel Air home. Hughes and Cook felt that Sessel meant what he said, for they knew that he had already engaged the Houston law firm that was the rival of Cook's to handle the personal bankruptcy proceedings against Hughes. For Hughes, surrender meant the loss of control of TWA, but continued resistance could mean the ruin of his entire financial empire.

He chose surrender. He dictated the required reply to a secretary who typed it on Hughes Tool stationery. It was delivered to a Bank of America office in Los Angeles before the five o'clock deadline. The text of the letter was then phoned to 1 Wall Street where the bankers were standing by. To their satisfaction, Hughes agreed to all the major points. He asked for only one concession. Though he agreed to submit to the voting trust, he asked to be given the right to pay off the loans and thus dissolve the voting trust at any time without "premium or penalty."

The bankers had no objection to granting this concession, nor did the representatives from the insurance companies. Through Cook, who was present at the discussion, Hughes got the impression that the concession would be formally included in the terms of the Dillon, Read plan. Psychologically, it was an important point for Hughes since it would lessen the onerous nature of the voting trust if he knew he could get back his company whenever he could pay off the loans.

But everyone had failed to reckon on the obduracy of Harry Hagerty, the chief loan officer at the Metropolitan Life Insurance Company, who had been out of town at the time of the October 6 meeting. When he returned to New York on Tuesday, October 11, Hagerty vetoed the provision that Hughes should be able to pay off the loan without penalty before its full ten-year term was completed. Hagerty insisted that the lenders should be assured of earning the full 6½ per cent return on the loan even if Hughes did pay it off earlier. Consequently, he demanded that Hughes pay a penalty for buying out the voting trust. When Hughes heard about that, he regarded the penalty clause as another piece of damning evidence that he was the victim of a giant conspiracy to rob him of his right to run TWA.

Hagerty's veto meant that this deal, to which Hughes and the bankers had agreed on October 6, was now off. Fearing that Sessel would make good on his threats, Hughes moved to try to put together an alternate plan. On Friday, October 14, Hughes sent a message to Sessel in which he reiterated his agreement to submit to the voting trust as long as he had the right to pay off TWA's indebtedness without penalty. To get Hagerty out of the picture, he offered to have Toolco take over the Metropolitan's position in the loan consortium—though where he would raise the money was certainly another question. But by now the lenders were completely fed up with Hughes' cliff-hanging, last-minute maneuvers. The constant negotiations, angry confrontations, and endless frustrations had taken a toll of the nerves on both sides. People were tired and irritable. High blood pressure was becoming the occupational disease of those who dealt with Hughes. Hughes also was suffering from the tension. Normally polite and well modulated on the telephone, he now yelled and screamed. Some people who telephoned him at the time said that he sometimes broke off his normally interminable conversations by explaining, "The doctor says I have to hang up now."

This time the bankers at once rejected Hughes' new proposal. Either he submitted to their terms—voting trust, penalty, and all—or they would throw him into bankruptcy. That was it. And that was final.

Hughes did not react. Though other mortals, if faced with such a drastic situation, would undoubtedly have felt compelled to spring into action, Hughes waited to see what his opponents would do. He did not have long to wait before his opponents opened a well-orchestrated attack. In letters postmarked Wednesday, October 19, the Equitable and the Metropolitan, in identical terms, informed TWA and Hughes Tool Company that they were willing to proceed with a final closing of the Dillon, Read plan if Hughes would accept both the voting trust and the penalty clause. On the same day, the Irving Trust sent a similar letter to TWA and the tool company, stating that the banks regarded the acceptance of the voting trust and the penalty clause as essential to their own participation in the program. Once again, the lenders gave Hughes a deadline: October 21, a day that TWA and Hughes people still remember as "Black Friday." Once again Sessel repeated the litany of threats. He explained that only because of confusion over the penalty clause did the lenders fail to make good on their threats in September. This time they were in agreement on the terms. Unless

Hughes submitted to their demands by five o'clock on Friday, they would force him into bankruptcy, seize the tool company, and sell off part of its assets to meet his obligations.

The Hughes Tool Company and TWA did not receive those letters until the very day on which the ultimatum was to expire. Cook and Raymond Holliday, the tool company's executive vice president, were in New York. They quickly contacted the lenders. Sessel stormed into the TWA headquarters for a showdown with Cook and Holliday. He wanted Hughes to endorse the letters from the insurance companies and his bank as an acknowledgment of his acceptance of the terms. Cook telephoned Hughes, but Hughes took the position that he should not commit TWA to the 6½ per cent interest rate of the Dillon, Read plan. He argued that the rate had been placed high because he controlled TWA. But now, if he was losing control, why should the airline be saddled with high interest costs? Therefore Hughes said that he would accept the Dillon, Read plan on one condition—that TWA's directors voted to approve it. In order to enable the TWA board to convene in New York for the vote, Cook asked Sessel to extend the deadline for one business day to five o'clock Monday, October 24. But the lenders were suspicious. The TWA had already endorsed the Dillon, Read plan in March. Why should it be asked to vote on the voting trust and penalty clause that concerned only Hughes? Sessel regarded the request as simply another of Hughes' stalling maneuvers. He would tolerate no more of that. In another fiery showdown, he bluntly told Cook that the banks would not extend the deadline for even one second. Sessel telephoned the insurance companies and urged them to join the banks in holding the line against granting any extension of time.

This episode led to a complete breach between Hughes and Ben Sessel. The next day the Hughes Tool Company sent to Sessel a sharply worded letter that abrogated its endorsement of the Dillon, Read plan. It also threatened him with legal action. "The full results of your actions are difficult to predict, but you are hereby notified that Hughes Tool will hold you accountable for any damages suffered by it directly or indirectly," said Toolco's letter.

Even as Hughes was fenced in by the lenders, TWA was sliding into an increasingly hopeless situation. While its competitors were adding more and more new jets to their fleets, TWA had not received any new aircraft for five long months. On October 25, following the showdown between Hughes and Sessel, the banks made good on their threats by seizing the balances of TWA and Toolco. Both companies were left without funds. As one Toolco insider put it, "We did not even have enough money to buy stamps." Howard Hughes was calling his few remaining banker friends to try to figure out a way to rescue himself from the impending disaster. "How many sails will I have to cut adrift?" he would ask. TWA was in equally bad shape. Some of TWA's balances were not large enough to cover its loans so it ended up in debt to the banks. At any moment, one or more of TWA's creditors could have forced the airline into bankruptcy. As a precaution, TWA had in secret already drawn up an application so that it could beat its creditors in filing for Chapter 10 bankruptcy proceedings if and when a showdown came. There was also the threat that either Boeing, General Dynamics, or both might become weary of having finished jetliners sitting undelivered at their plants because Hughes did not have the money to pay for them. They might decide to declare a default under the purchase contracts with Hughes and thus be free to sell TWA's jets to someone else. That could start a rush on Toolco, which in turn would throw TWA into receivership.

In fact, TWA's precarious situation helped protect Hughes from the worst consequences of his dispute with the lenders. "Don't you dare push TWA to the wall," he would tell the bankers in telephone conversations. The bankers knew they could not move against Hughes without gravely injuring TWA and that they did not want to do. Accordingly, Sessel refrained from the ultimate threat of taking over Toolco. During the weekend of October 22–23 Hughes was wrestling with a dramatic idea. After more than two years of total disappearance from the public scene, he was considering coming out of seclusion to do battle with his enemies. "I am going to come out of my coffin," Hughes told some aides. Meanwhile, his lawyers were drawing up petitions for court orders that would prohibit Ben Sessel and the Irving Trust from interfering with Hughes' attempt to seek financial help elsewhere.

Just at that time a new and unexpected development took place that spared Hughes from making the decision to come out and fight. Gregson Bautzer, a sauve Hollywood lawyer, who for years had handled sensitive assignments for Hughes, thought that he had found a way out. Bautzer had turned up a rescuer. He was Colonel Henry Crown, the Chicago industrialist who only the year before had merged his own highly profitable Material Services Corporation (a construction goods supplier) into General Dynamics. Crown had thus become the largest single investor in the General Dynamics just when the Convair jet program began to eat up the General Dynamics profits. He was understandably concerned, and by offering to help Hughes, he hoped to help General Dynamics and himself.

The anatomy of the deal that Crown offered to Hughes ran like this: Hughes would commit TWA to buy Convair aircraft for the foreseeable future, thus helping to bail out General Dynamics. He would also sell a large block of his TWA shares to Colonel Crown at a price well below the market level. In return, Crown would use his influence to raise a loan of $150 million or so for Hughes, who could then pay off his most pressing debts and avoid being forced into bankruptcy or the voting trust. Most of the money would come from the Bank of America, putting the bank in the peculiar position of belonging to Sessel's banking group, which was trying to bring Hughes to heel, while at the same time trying to save Hughes from the grasp of Sessel's group. Under the Crown plan the financing for TWA's jets would be done through the sale to the public of $165 million in TWA debentures.

Hughes was very enthusiastic. He would escape from the hands of the bankers and keep control of TWA! To celebrate his victory, he was planning to move TWA's corporate offices from New York to Los Angeles. Colonel Crown also recommended a candidate for a still vacant TWA presidency—Frederick Glass, who was the vice chairman of the Empire State Building Corporation, one of Crown's many properties.

The sale of TWA debentures was to be handled by the big Wall Street brokerage firm of Merrill Lynch, Pierce, Fenner & Smith. The officer in charge of the sale was William A. Forrester, Jr., who had worked on an abortive deal with Hughes several years earlier to sell the Hughes Aircraft, a pastime that Hughes pursued on several occasions, apparently to determine the market value of his properties. Hughes and Forrester exchanged a number of messages. One of them—a memo that Hughes dictated to his communications center—revealed a great deal about Hughes' attitude toward Charlie Thomas and the Dillon, Read plan. Hughes' message read: "Charlie Thomas negotiated and developed the deal with Dillon, Read financing without my authority or encouragement from me. He forced it down my throat then at a board meeting at which time he created a coalition of my directors and turned them against me and faced me with a mass resignation of all but one of the TWA directors. I have never liked this plan. I have fought it from the very beginning and I am still fighting it and I assure you that if it is employed it will be over my dead body and if you come up with any suggestion of an alternative plan or any way whatsoever by which I can avoid being forced into the Dillon, Read plan I would be most grateful. It is very flattering for you to say that you do not think I have ever been forced to do anything and maybe there was a time when this might have been a fairly accurate statement, but I assure you that it is not true today and has not been true concerning the Dillon, Read program from its inception. I have fought it hammer and tong from the very first day that I heard of it."

During the last days of October and the first ones of November, Hughes and Crown were very hopeful that a deal could be put together. The Bank of America was willing to go along, not only because the deal would help two of its major clients, General Dynamics and Hughes Tool, but also because it would earn 7 per cent interest on a loan of some $150 million. The Equitable, which, of course, held a veto over TWA's equipment program, raised no objection to the Crown plan as long as it was not asked to contribute any new money. Thus, as Merrill Lynch began scouting the market to determine what sort of reception a sale of TWA debentures might receive, the situation seemed mildly favorable. But Forrester's findings were disappointing. By this time, Hughes' financial problems were so widely publicized that the public had become wary of him. The major airlines were experiencing a severe decline in profits that had pulled down the market value of their stocks. Merrill Lynch concluded that the TWA debentures would face an uncertain reception from investors. The firm, which became very cautious about underwriting the sale, would pledge itself simply to a "best efforts only." That meant it would market the securities as effectively as possible, but it refused to guarantee the results or to buy whatever shares were left unsold.

The attitude of Merrill Lynch bothered Hughes. If he tried and failed to raise the needed capital, his failure would make him more vulnerable than ever to the banks and insurance companies. Such a display of weakness, he reckoned, would stiffen the demands of the lenders and deprive him of whatever freedom of action he still had left. Thus, in late October 1960, Hughes dropped the Crown deal.

As November began, pressures built up on Hughes from other quarters. With increasing alarm, the Civil Aeronautics Board had been watching his conduct of affairs at TWA. On Wednesday, November 2, CAB staff investigators reported to the board that the "crisis stage had been reached at TWA." The CAB staffer who was assigned to keep an eye on Hughes and TWA was Jacob (Jack) Rosenthal, an exceptionally bright and aggressive young government lawyer. Speaking in the guarded phrases of a bureaucrat, Rosenthal warned Cook by telephone that if Hughes did not finalize TWA's financing plan in the immediate future, the board would feel compelled to hold public hearings on the question of whether Hughes should be allowed to continue in control of the airline. Even as Rosenthal served his notice on Hughes, the banks once more began to repeat their threats to throw Hughes out into receivership.

Hughes realized that this time he could not play the waiting game. On the Sunday after Thanksgiving 1960, Howard Hughes telephoned Cook and gave him a new assignment: to contact Fred

Brandi, the senior partner at Dillon, Read, and to ask him if he thought that the Dillon, Read plan could be reinstated. Hughes now seemed prepared to surrender to the plan he had fought "hammer and tong." In answer to Cook's query, Brandi replied that he would canvass the participants and let him know. Within a couple of days, Brandi reported that the plan could be revitalized but that the terms would be tougher this time.

And they were. The lenders demanded that Hughes Tool and TWA make the request for the loan in writing. The letters would have to agree in advance to all major conditions, including an interest rate of 6½ per cent, the voting trust, and the penalty clause for premature repayment of the loan. The letters were quickly prepared by Hughes Tool and TWA. Squads of lawyers for both sides up-dated the loan documents, which had been drawn up earlier. Keath Carver and Robert Gordon, Bank of America vice presidents, took over the preliminary agreements to the Beverly Hills Hotel. Hughes came and signed them.

According to the procedural arrangements, the process of closing the Dillon, Read plan would take place by stages. The first stage was the selection of the trustees, who would administer the voting trust. The completion of this phase would demonstrate each side's willingness to cooperate in the financing and set up the machinery for running TWA under a trusteeship. It was the phase that would trigger the rest of the plan into being. According to the arrangements, it was the responsibility of the Hughes Tool Company first to select its single trustee. After that, the lenders would appoint two trustees, who would control TWA by a margin of two to one. After the naming of the members of the voting trust, the second and final stage would be the formal transfer of Hughes' stock to the trustees, the signing of the loan instruments, and the assignment of the mortgages on the jets to the lenders as security for the loans.

December was just beginning. Unwilling to become entrapped in any more of Hughes' delaying tactics, the banks and insurance companies insisted that the entire financial transaction must be completed before the end of the year—or forever scrapped. Time was short. Everything would have to be done quickly and smoothly. A special session of the TWA board of directors was called for Friday, December 2. The directors expected to hear a report from Raymond Cook about the progress toward the completion of the Dillon, Read plan. Instead, Cook had a report of a quite different sort. As of that morning, he said, his law firm no longer represented the Hughes Tool Company in regard to the financing plan. Cook did not elaborate but earlier that morning Hughes had personally fired him by telephone. Cook, who had helped conceive the Dillon, Read plan and had participated in all negotiations, was now out of the picture. His absence would be felt. Genial and approachable, Cook had managed to retain the respect and confidence of most of the lenders and thus served as an effective buffer between them and Hughes. His replacement, Cook told the directors, was Greg Bautzer, the West Coast lawyer, who had played a leading role in the unsuccessful Hughes-Crown negotiations.

When Bautzer arrived in New York a few days later, his course of action was hardly what the lenders had expected. Instead of proceeding with the closing of the Dillon, Read plan, Bautzer concentrated on trying to revive the old Hughes-Crown deal with General Dynamics and Merrill Lynch. Obviously, Hughes had still not given up his hope of escaping the voting trust. But Bautzer dropped his efforts a day or so later after the Civil Aeronautics Board sent word that it would not approve a financing arrangement in which an aircraft manufacturer would gain a financial interest in an airline as indeed General Dynamics would have done if Colonel Crown had acquired a large block of TWA stock.

The firing of Cook combined with Bautzer's attempt to circumvent the Dillon, Read plan plunged the people at TWA to new depths of depression and hopelessness. Hughes was still, so it seemed, willing to risk TWA's ruin rather than surrender his control of the airline. But a lean craggy-faced lawyer from Texas now grimly resolved that he was at all costs going to stop Hughes from destroying TWA. He was Thomas A. Slack, whose own personal relations with Hughes made the situation extremely delicate from a professional standpoint, and from a personal standpoint highly emotional. After serving ten years as Hughes' personal lawyer, Slack had resigned in 1956. He had also been one of Hughes' closest friends, and the two men had spent literally thousands of hours together. But Slack, unbending and moralistic, had grown increasingly disenchanted with Hughes and with living in California, a state whose relaxed manners irritated him. Slack had moved to a 850-acre farm near Roanoke, Virginia, but he remained a director of TWA and, at Hughes' own insistence, had become a member of the TWA executive committee. In addition, perhaps through an oversight by Hughes, Slack retained his title as vice president and director of the Hughes Tool Company.

As TWA's situation became increasingly desperate, Slack's own agony grew worse. He was angry at Hughes for what he was doing to TWA. He was also angry at himself for not having stood up earlier to Hughes. Slack was torn by divided loyalties; he had been Hughes' friend and lawyer, but now he decided that his first allegiance was to TWA. He thus became Hughes' most active opponent.

Returning to New York after a weekend in Roanoke, Slack was now ready to take on Hughes. The lenders were threatening for the umpteenth time to throw TWA and the Hughes Tool Company into bankruptcy. Through Ben Sessel's lawyers, Slack arranged a meeting with the attorneys for the lenders in his suite at the Waldorf-Astoria. Slack had prepared a short lecture for them. "I am not asking you to do one thing or the other," Slack told them. "But you have threatened us so much now we are deafened by it. You have cried, 'Wolf! Wolf!' a hundred times. It would be unfair to allow TWA to blunder along, thinking that nothing was going to happen, and for you suddenly to go ahead and foreclose." As the lawyers nodded in appreciation of Slack's argument, he continued: "If you are really serious this time, then say so. Send us a telegram saying that you really mean it. But if you are not serious, then for heaven's sake, call off the dogs."

The lawyers assured Slack that this time the lenders were serious. This was the deadline to end all deadlines. They immediately sent a telegram to TWA saying that.

Armed with the new warning from the lenders, Slack embarked on the next part of his plan. It was Tuesday, December 6. A special TWA board meeting took place that day, and among the members present were five directors from the Hughes Tool Company. As Slack well knew, their presence in one place constituted a quorum of the Hughes Tool board. To the surprise of his onetime Toolco colleagues, Slack called a special meeting of the Toolco directors for that evening in his hotel suite. Such action was within the rights of a Hughes Tool director, but the other Hughes directors naturally suspected that Slack was up to something. As they met in his apartment at the Waldorf-Astoria, Slack told them that he was resolved to do everything possible to keep TWA from being thrown into bankruptcy. He appealed to them to do the same.

What they must do, he explained, was to appoint the first voting trustee and thus trip the first phase of the Dillon, Read plan into action. That would demonstrate to the lenders that the Toolco was serious about proceeding with the Dillon, Read plan and would avert bankruptcy for TWA. The directors of the Hughes Tool possessed the power to take this action—if only they dared to act on their own.

Slack tried to goad them into action. "Is there anyone here who can get through to Hughes?" asked Slack. None of them could. As was customary in times of crisis, Hughes had left instructions with his communications center that he was not to be disturbed. Tom Slack understood their dilemma.

"You haven't got a prayer," he told them. "If you fail to take action and TWA is thrown into bankruptcy, Hughes will say he never dreamed that his board of directors would allow such a situation to come about and he will put the blame on you. But if you do dare to take this action on your own, without his approval, you all may lose your jobs. If I were in your position, I know how I would feel. But my stand will be memorialized. I will do everything possible to keep TWA from going into bankruptcy. Hughes wants to gamble. He thinks the insurance companies and lenders won't push TWA to the wall. Well, he may just be wrong this time."

Slack's speech had a great impact on the other Toolco directors, for he had dramatically spelled out the dilemma that faced them. They asked for a night to think over Slack's proposal. Early the next morning, they gathered at TWA's headquarters on Madison Avenue. By a unanimous vote, they named one of their group, Maynard Montrose, to become the first voting trustee. Slack dictated the resolution by the Hughes Tool board to a TWA secretary, Mona Lee McCoy, and waited until she typed it up. Then he carried the resolution to the TWA boardroom where the directors, including Ben Sessel, were assembling for yet another special meeting. Slack handed the resolution to Sessel. It was the evidence that the lenders had been waiting for. The Dillon, Read plan was now in motion.

Shortly after the TWA board meeting convened, a telephone call came for Raymond Holliday. When he rejoined the meeting sometime later, Holliday bent over Slack and whispered in his ear, "That was Howard and he has told me to ask you for your resignation from the tool company board immediately." Then Holliday addressed the TWA directors. He told the directors that Hughes had designated him to replace Montrose as the voting trustee for Toolco. It was a fitting reward for Holliday. Eight months earlier when Raymond Cook had warned Hughes that all the TWA directors, including President Charlie Thomas, would quit if Hughes did not go ahead with the Dillon, Read plan, Cook had unwittingly exaggerated somewhat. One of the eighteen directors would not have resigned: Raymond Holliday.

The next day the details of the Dillon, Read plan were released to the press. Teams of lawyers rushed to amend and update the huge batch of agreements and instruments, which had been drawn up in July and now required modification for the December signing.

The final closing itself involved three steps. First, Holliday, acting on Hughes' behalf, would authorize the transfer of Hughes Tool's 78.23 per cent ownership of TWA to a voting trust. That was to take place on December 28, at the Farmers Bank in Wilmington, Delaware, where TWA was incorporated. The second step called for the formal signing of the loan agreements at which time the proceeds from the loans would be turned over to TWA. That was to take place the next day in lower Manhattan. The final step would take place almost simultaneously in Oklahoma City where the examination and records division of the Federal Aviation Agency would register the mortgages on the jet planes in the name of the lenders.

On Tuesday, December 27, the Equitable and the Metropolitan announced that they had selected their voting trustees: Irving S. Olds, the former chairman of United States Steel who was a partner in the Wall Street law firm of White & Case, and Ernest R. Breech, the former chairman of the Ford Motor Company.

Meanwhile, the Civil Aeronautics Board, which had been watching the crisis at TWA, promptly gave its approval to the proposed transfer of the airline's control from Toolco to the voting trust. "No longer will the directors of Toolco be free to enforce their dictates or those of Toolco's controlling shareholder on TWA," wrote the CAB in its order E-16195. The CAB was so relieved that TWA was being saved from bankruptcy that without even conducting the customary hearing and investigation, it gave the trustees a virtual carte blanche to run the airline. Declared the CAB: "The voting trustees will not be restricted in their power to approve further financing for TWA, nor in their ability to sell, lease, transfer, hypothecate or otherwise dispose of, or manage TWA's assets."

At the same time, the CAB leveled stinging criticism at Howard Hughes. It noted that TWA had received its long-term financing later than its competitors and at a time when the rates were higher. It also pointed out that TWA was falling behind its major competitors both in number of new aircraft and share of the market. "It is evident," concluded the CAB order, "that Toolco's control of TWA, as exercised through Hughes, has presented substantial problems requiring the Board's attention." In view of Hughes' unsatisfactory conduct at TWA, the CAB warned that he would not be allowed to regain control of TWA "without a searching inquiry into the public interest factors affecting this control." The Hughes lawyers countered that the CAB order was only "dicta," words that had no basis in fact. Privately, CAB attorneys conceded that the tough language of the order was a guarantee to the financiers that Howard Hughes would not be allowed to easily regain control of TWA. In fact one of the most important CAB attorneys vowed: "As long as I am here, he will never get back in control."

Under those conditions, it was hardly surprising that Hughes and his aides went reluctantly into that last painful phase of surrender.

The morning of December 28 representatives of the lenders and TWA gathered at the offices of the Farmers Bank in Wilmington for the transfer of the Hughes TWA stock to the voting trust, but Raymond Holliday failed to show up. They waited and waited. No Holliday. Finally he telephoned. He was still in his hotel room in New York, he said. He had been told not to go to Wilmington until he was directed to do so by Bautzer, and Bautzer had not yet given the go-ahead. The lenders contacted Bautzer, who reassured them that Hughes indeed wished to go ahead with the final closing. The hang-up, explained Bautzer, was Hughes' concern about some clauses in the voting trust. The next morning Holliday arrived in Wilmington, but he said he was under orders not to sign anything until he was instructed to do so by Bautzer. Once again the lenders called Bautzer. Bautzer promised that he would relay Hughes' instructions to Holliday as soon as he could. But Bautzer added a catch: he was having difficulty, he said, contacting his client. Bautzer kept sending messages to Hughes, saying, "Howard, this is a red alert!" He was stressing the gravity of the situation to Hughes, but Hughes was not responding. The twenty-ninth, a Thursday, passed. Still no word from Howard Hughes. Still no contracts signed.

Friday was the last business day in 1960. If the loan agreement was not signed on that day, the lenders swore it never would be signed. They would cancel their commitments and invest their money elsewhere in their new budgets for 1961. Then came a breakthrough. During the early hours of Friday morning Bautzer reached Hughes. Apparently at least some of his hesitations were overcome. Bautzer gave the order for Holliday to start signing the first batch of documents. In Wilmington on Friday morning, Holliday put his signature to the instrument that transferred Hughes' TWA stock to the control of voting trustees. The bankers and insurance executives in New York were told that Holliday was now hurrying from Delaware to the home offices of the Chemical Bank New York Trust Company at 100 Broadway where the signing of the loan agreement was now scheduled to take place at three o'clock that afternoon.

It seemed as if everything would work out after all. Then something happened to Greg Bautzer. He had been working day and night—by day with the bankers, by night either on the telephone with Hughes or trying to get through to him. He had kept going only by taking massive vitamin B injections. On the verge of collapse, he felt he simply had to get away from the action. The financiers learned about Bautzer's condition when one of them telephoned his suite at the Hampshire House on Central Park South to check on some detail of the loan agreement. Actress Dana Wynter, who was then Bautzer's wife, said that her husband was exhausted and could not talk with anyone.

At about that same moment Holliday arrived at the Chemical's head office on lower Broadway, but he was in no mood to sign the documents. He pleaded that there were far too many papers for one man to sort out and sign in a single afternoon. Furthermore, he said he needed legal counsel. The bankers called Bautzer's suite again, hoping he had recovered enough to advise Holliday by telephone. This time they learned that he had left for Roosevelt Hospital. One of the lawyers checked with his brother who was a doctor at Roosevelt. Bautzer had indeed checked in, a suspected heart attack victim. Meanwhile, Holliday continued to balk at signing the documents. He wanted time, but time was running out. It was nearly four o'clock in New York. The offices of the Federal Aviation Agency in Oklahoma City were to close at 4:30 P.M. Central Standard Time, or 5:30 New York time. The bankers telephoned the FAA with a request that its offices stay open for a few more hours. The FAA agreed to remain open until 6:30–7:30 New York time.

The last hours of the last business day of the year were running out. The hands of the clock on the wall of the conference room at 100 Broadway moved past five, past six, past seven o'clock. Holliday went off to a side room and made some calls, but he seemed no nearer to signing than before. A warning call came from the FAA in Oklahoma City. They were about to close their office. Then at 7:15 Holliday walked back into the main conference room. He was ready to sign. He did not say what had happened, but in reality he had been talking to Bautzer. From his hospital bed Bautzer had received the final go-ahead from Hughes.

The forty or so assembled financiers, representing the most powerful financial institutions in the United States watched in relief as Raymond Holliday seated himself in one of the tangerine leather seats at the conference room table and put his signature to the documents that closed the financing deal. At 7:25 the instructions were telephoned to the FAA in Oklahoma City to register the titles on the TWA aircraft in the names of the lenders. The Dillon, Read plan was in full operation.

Howard Hughes had lost control of his airline.

The next day Greg Bautzer, feeling better, checked out of Roosevelt Hospital and headed back to the West Coast.

5. Preemptive Corporate Warfare

As a result of the establishment of the voting trust, the effective control of TWA passed from the erratic hands of Howard Hughes into the sure and skilled ones of Ernie Breech. In almost every way the two men were exact opposites. Howard Hughes was a rich boy who always had had great wealth at his command. By contrast, Ernie Breech, the son of a little town blacksmith, had worked his way up in the business world. Hughes was the epitome of the proprietor, Breech the United States' foremost example of the professional manager.

Securing the services of Ernie Breech was a great coup for the insurance companies, though as he later reflected, they never even once said thanks. In late December 1960, as the insurance companies were searching for executives of outstanding reputation to preside over the affairs of TWA, Breech was winding up his business affairs at the Ford Motor Company in Detroit and was looking forward to his retirement in Phoenix, Arizona, where he had just built a house. He was in the process of cleaning out his desk when his telephone rang. The caller was Grant Keehn, the Equitable's executive vice president who later became its president. Keehn asked for a meeting as soon as possible in Detroit. A couple of days later, he flew from New York and after only the briefest formalities, got to the point. Would Breech agree to serve as a

voting trustee and as TWA chairman of the board? Breech demurred, but he did agree to serve as a director.

Breech was concluding an exceptionally distinguished business
career. After serving as a ranking executive at General Motors
Corporation and as president of the Bendix Corporation, Breech
had accepted the challenge in 1946 of seeking to save the Ford
Motor Company, which was losing $10 million a month. Breech's
success in turning failing Ford into a thriving company was a feat
that placed him alongside Alfred P. Sloan, the builder of General
Motors, as one of the great industrial managers in American
history.

Over the years, Breech, a man of strongly held and straightforward beliefs, had built up his own philosophy of business. He
looked upon the exercise of corporate power as a public trust,
and he felt that the rewards of a success in a company should be
shared with the workers and executives as well as with the stockholders. Breech thrived on challenges, and TWA was quite a challenge indeed. He was also motivated by a very nostalgic reason.
In the mid-1930s, when most of the airlines were controlled either
by large holding companies or by the automakers, TWA had been
a subsidiary of General Motors. Breech, then a GM executive,
had been in charge of TWA for several years. Then as now, TWA
was in trouble, and Breech had helped restore it to health by arranging new financing and selecting a new president. That president was Jack Frye, who later appealed to Howard Hughes to buy
into the airline. As Breech listened to Keehn's appeal, he felt that
history was indeed repeating itself.

Still, at the first meeting with Keehn, Breech had only agreed to
serve as a TWA director. A few days later, however, Grant Keehn
called again to explain that the financial institutions were, as Breech
remembered his words, "really over a barrel" to name a voting
trustee. "You've just got to help us, Ernie," implored the Equitable man. The insurance companies had nominated Lucius Clay,
the former military governor in the U. S. Zone in Germany, as a
voting trustee, but the Civil Aeronautics Board had vetoed that
nomination on the grounds that he was already engaged in a phase

of transportation as a director of the United States Lines. At Keehn's urging, Breech agreed to serve as one of the two majority voting trustees.

Thus, in early January 1961, after Hughes had lost control of TWA, Breech found himself in the position of being, in effect, the operating chief of a corporation that badly lacked direction and was heading toward enormous losses. Despite its multitude of troubles, TWA had earned so much in the first six months of 1960 that it managed to finish the year with a respectable profit of $7.8 million. But now, starved for jets, TWA was in a decline that was turning into a steep dive. Furthermore, since Charlie Thomas' resignation in July, the airline had been without a president and it was showing the customary symptoms of confusion and loss of morale. Ernie Breech quickly realized that the recently concluded financing plan represented only one part of the job of saving the airline. TWA needed more jets to become competitive. It also needed a stable management.

TWA's future was now entrusted to the three voting trustees. At their first meeting, which took place on January 16, 1961, Breech was encouraged by the reasonable and cooperative attitude of the Hughes representative, Raymond Holliday. Breech's first priority was to reshuffle the board of directors in order to prepare the groundwork for the appointment of a new management. The three trustees immediately agreed that at the next board meeting on January 26, the present members would be asked to resign. Then the trustees would appoint ten new directors. Six of them would be nominated by Olds and Breech and four by Holliday.

In turn, those directors would select a new president for TWA. On the afternoon before the January 26 board of directors meeting, Breech happened to meet Raymond Holliday at the TWA headquarters on Madison Avenue. After exchanging greetings, Breech recalls that Holliday told him, "Montrose and I are going to '21' for dinner tonight. Come along." Breech, who wanted to become acquainted with the Hughes people, gladly accepted.

It was a delightful evening at the elegant eatery on West Fifty-second Street. While enjoying the company of the two Hughes men, Breech also wanted to make certain that he got a message through to their boss. "You can assure Howard that he has no reason to worry about his company," Breech told them over dinner. "We are going to try to run it, as long as I have anything to do with it, for his benefit as well as for the benefit of all the other shareholders." Breech, who at Ford had run a company that was controlled by one large shareholder, stressed that he would serve Hughes' interest with the same fidelity. "And I predict that he is going to be very happy with the outcome, if he will cooperate," continued Breech. "I want his suggestions through you."

Breech felt that Holliday had accepted the message in a positive spirit and would pass it on that way to Hughes. Any other company owner in America would have been overjoyed to have Breech working for him. The Ford family had paid a fortune for his services. Hughes was getting him free.

Hughes showed no sign of his gratitude. The two men knew each other slightly from a banquet in New York in the mid-1930s. Breech, then the chairman of the North American Aviation, a division of General Motors, was the host, and Hughes, America's most famous flyer of those years, was the guest of honor. Breech gave a short speech before presenting an aviation award to Hughes, who was seated next to him. After Breech's speech, Hughes, perspiring and shaking, stood up and mumbled a few words. After he sat down, Hughes whispered to Breech: "I'd give my right arm if I could talk like you do." Breech replied, "I'd give my right arm if I could fly like you can." It was—and remained—the only communication between the two archetypal adversaries.

The morning after the dinner at "21," Breech and Holliday planned to have breakfast together at the Waldorf-Astoria where they both were staying. Holliday was late. When he finally joined Breech, he apologized for his tardiness, explaining that he had been on the telephone with Hughes.

"I've got some good news, and I've got some bad news," Holliday said.

"Give me the good news first," Breech replied.

"He has agreed to release the Convair 880s to TWA," Holliday said. Since he had lost control of the airline, Hughes had been stalling about whether he would release to TWA the 880s he had originally ordered from Convair. Since TWA badly needed the planes, the news was very welcome.

"And the bad news?"

"I have been instructed that our men are not to show up at the board meeting today," replied Holliday. That meant the planned reshuffling of the board could not take place because there would not be enough directors present to constitute a quorum. Breech was shocked.

"What is it all about?" he demanded.

Mr. Hughes had apparently changed his mind, Holliday explained. If the new directors were to be placed on the board, Hughes felt that election should wait until after the annual shareholders' meeting in April.

It was very embarrassing for Breech and the other newcomers who were trying to organize a new management for TWA. The Metropolitan's Hagerty, Keehn, and he had recruited for the TWA Board six outstanding business leaders, including industrialist Barry T. Leithead, the president of Cluett, Peabody & Company, and Clifford F. Hood, the former president of United States Steel. The directors-designate expected to be elected to the TWA board that day. It was a very inauspicious beginning. The new men had agreed to come on the board after having been assured that Hughes no longer could interfere in TWA's affairs. That promise rang hollow now that Breech and Olds could not even manage to convene a board meeting.

A troubled Ernie Breech flew back to Detroit for a Ford board meeting. While he was there, a telephone call came from Jack Rosenthal, the young attorney at the Civil Aeronautics Board in Washington. In no uncertain terms, Rosenthal told Breech that he better hurry up and find a president for TWA. Breech replied that he was trying to find a president, but that it was not easy. It was difficult, he explained, to persuade an outstanding executive to come to TWA as long as the threat existed that Hughes would get back in control when the voting trust expired in ten years or perhaps even sooner. Rosenthal brushed off that explanation. "If you investigate Hughes right," he said, "he'll never get back into control of the airline anyhow." The young lawyer's remark made a distinct impression on Ernie Breech. There was another person who was talking about investigation of Howard Hughes, but for a different reason. Harry Hagerty of the Metropolitan was insisting that new directors and management must protect themselves against possible lawsuits by minority TWA shareholders by undertaking a full-scale investigation of Hughes' stewardship at TWA. In that way they would avoid being held responsible for any liabilities from the old Hughes era.

Investigation or no investigation, Breech knew that the search for a president was going to be difficult. On February 17 something happened that would make it harder still. On that day, as part of the most extensive labor disturbances ever to hit the airline industry up to that time, TWA's flight engineers struck, closing down all flight operations. Nothing loses money quite so fast as an airline that is being grounded. TWA, which had already lost $4 million in January, suffered a loss of $22.6 million in the first twenty days of February. And the loss was growing ever larger. The TWA situation demanded a fast remedy, but Breech could get no cooperation from Hughes. Breech was becoming entrapped in one of those ironic dilemmas that were inherent in the legal battle for TWA. The airline had done poorly before, but never had it done as badly as this. The trustees, whose takeover of the airline implied Hughes' unfitness to run it, were presiding over TWA's looming financial collapse.

With increasing urgency, Breech made one more attempt on February 23 to assemble a quorum of TWA directors, but the Hughes directors again frustrated the effort by staying away. Faced with Hughes' obduracy, Breech and Olds made a bold decision: if Hughes wanted to fight, they would meet him head on. Acting on their own authority, they ordered a shareholders' meeting to be held on February 28 in Kansas City. At that time they would throw out the majority of the Hughes directors and install a board of their own choosing. If Breech and Olds could not run TWA with Hughes, they would run it without him. Howard Hughes was not accustomed to being treated in this manner, but then he had never before run up against such formidable opponents.

While at the Kansas City meeting, which installed the lenders-selected directors, Breech got a lead on a possible presidential candidate from Francis Reed, a distinguished New York lawyer who was the counsel for the two majority trustees. The candidate was a droll New Englander and former Brown University football player named Charles C. Tillinghast, Jr. At that time, he was the vice president for international operations at the Bendix Corporation, one of Breech's old companies. Breech remembered Tillinghast from before World War II at Bendix. Tillinghast had served as general counsel while he was president. Breech encouraged Reed to ring him up and sound him out about the TWA position. Reed telephoned Tillinghast from Kansas City and made an appointment for him to meet Breech the next evening in the Ford Motor Company suite at the Ritz Tower in Manhattan.

Breech was flying back to New York the next morning for the first session of the newly constituted TWA board. It was a critical meeting. TWA simply had to get more jets to match the expanding fleets of its competitors. Fortunately, Hughes had agreed to release eighteen Convair 880s to TWA. But there was a serious mix-up over exactly which specific aircraft should go to TWA, because Hughes already had given to Northeast Airlines three 880s that originally had been consigned to TWA. During the board's discussion, one of the Hughes representatives, who had been kept on as a director, remarked that the status of those aircraft was still "way out in the left field." To that, Tom Slack, who also remained on the board, immediately replied: "Let's get this straight. The whole management of TWA has been out of the ball park for years." After pointing out that the delays in TWA's receiving the 880s had caused obvious harm to the airline, Slack declared that the board should employ independent attorneys to look into the liability of everyone, including himself, for having allowed the company to blunder into such a mess.

Holliday began to object strongly to Slack's remarks, but Breech, who was in the chair, suddenly remembered earlier suggestions from Rosenthal and Hagerty about an investigation. After quieting Holliday, Breech said that he would accept Slack's statement as a motion to engage independent counsel. The motion was seconded and, over the objection of the Hughes directors, the board appointed a committee of three directors to recommend within sixty days the law firm that should conduct the investigation.

Thus, when Breech and Tillinghast met at the Ritz that evening, the major thrust of TWA's new direction had only been decided. Over coffee, Breech explained the airline's situation. He, of course, accented the positive aspects of the TWA situation, and Tillinghast became mildly interested. He was happy at Bendix, except for one major thing. As the vice president in charge of international operations for a corporation that produced auto parts and aircraft instruments on five continents, Tillinghast was required to travel almost continuously. Though he enjoyed being on the go, he did not enjoy being away from his wife. Despite his salary of $76,500 a year, Tillinghast found that there were not enough dollars left after taxes to take her along all the time. It was not a job that he wanted to do all his life.

The TWA position, on the other hand, offered the opportunity that every ambitious executive dreams of—the chance to run his own company. Also, the wife of an airline president flies free, and Lisette could accompany him on his journeys. There was, however, one grave drawback. It was what the newcomers at TWA called "the Hughes problem." After his talk with Breech, Tillinghast read the voting trust and loan agreements and he saw that Hughes could, with the payment of a stiff penalty, buy out the voting trust and resume his control of TWA. If that happened, the new president, who had been installed by the lenders, undoubtedly would be the first to leave. Only fifty, Tillinghast did not want to throw away the possibility of attaining the top job at Bendix or somewhere else by rushing into an unstable situation at TWA.

Breech and Reed had anticipated Tillinghast's objections. Even in his first telephone call to Tillinghast, Bus Reed had assured him that if he was interested in the TWA post, he would get the same sort of contract Ernie Breech had been given at Ford. Perhaps better than any other man, Tillinghast knew what Reed meant. In 1946, when his Ford contract was being drawn, Breech relied for advice on Bob Gossett, who was a member of the New York law firm of Hughes, Hubbard, Blair & Reed. Tillinghast, who was a member of the firm at that time, actually did the writing of Breech's contract. As protection for Breech, who was giving up a secure position at General Motors for a questionable future at Ford, the contract guaranteed him a large financial gain no matter whether Ford failed or he was fired. It was a precedent-shattering contract. Tillinghast was now offered the same terms. Hughes could regain control and fire him, but Tillinghast would still be left with a large income for life. In Tillinghast's mind, the guarantee took some of the sting out of "the Hughes problem."

For a month Tillinghast pondered the pros and cons of the TWA presidency. He would marshal in his mind a battalion of reasons against going to TWA. Those reasons would march off to do battle with the reasons for going to TWA. Then the order of battle would be reversed, but no side ever won an outright victory. Even as this warfare went on in his mind, Tillinghast was being taken around by Reed to meet the officers at the banks and insurance companies that were backing TWA. Tillinghast's unassuming but confident manner made a favorable impression on the lenders. Tillinghast, however, had not made up his own mind about the job when the TWA board met again on March 20. He had been asked to drop by at that time to get acquainted with the directors. As he shook hands with one director after another, again and again he heard the words, "Hope you'll come aboard." Being in the presence of so many people who wanted him to say yes, pushed Tillinghast over the line. He told Breech that he would take the job.

When the board convened that day, it elected him director, president, and chief executive officer of TWA, his duties to begin April 17. His salary was set at $100,000 a year. As protection against "the Hughes problem," Tillinghast's contract provided that he would receive $50,000 a year until he was sixty-five and then $30,-000 a year for the rest of his life if Hughes regained control and fired him. Ironically, the sums were just about the same as those Charlie Thomas had asked for.

Tillinghast was also given another sort of protection: Ernie Breech. As Breech tells it, Tillinghast made his acceptance of the presidency conditional on Ernie's becoming chairman of the board. There is some suspicion that Breech's arm may have been rotating while Tillinghast turned Ernie's wrist. Breech had gotten so deep into the situation that he did not want to leave the job half done.

At the same meeting in which Tillinghast was elected president, the issue of legal action came up again. After having canvassed a number of firms, Ben Sessel, by now a bitter enemy of Howard Hughes, recommended to the board that the Wall Street law firm of Cahill, Gordon, Reindel & Ohl should be retained to investigate whether TWA had a course of legal action against anyone. Over the objections of Raymond Holliday, the Hughes trustee, the board accepted Sessel's recommendation. A team of Cahill, Gordon lawyers, under the direction of John Sonnett, the head of the firm's trial department, began an investigation of Howard Hughes' stewardship at TWA. Sonnett had exceptional credentials for his new assignment: in the late 1940s he served in Washington as the Assistant Attorney General in charge of the antitrust division. It was experience that would serve him well as he delved into the financial details of Howard Hughes' control of TWA.

The investigation was thus already underway as Tillinghast prepared to take over the airline. During the three weeks while he wound up his old job, he invited a number of TWA officers to drop by his Bendix office in Rockefeller Center for a chat. Among the visitors was Robert W. Rummel, who had been Hughes' old confidant on aircraft selection and development. Under the new management, Rummel retained his old job as vice president for the procurement of aircraft. When he came in to see Tillinghast, Rummel handed him a thick volume of papers. "Here is the equipment program," he said.

Tillinghast realized that TWA needed more aircraft. When he

had been introduced to the bankers and insurance executives, he had inquired as diplomatically as possible whether additional funds would be forthcoming for more jets. In the guarded fashion of financiers, assurances were given that under the right circumstances more money would be available. Nevertheless, Tillinghast had no idea that TWA's equipment program was so large and far advanced. Rummel's papers set out a new major round of jet purchases. Furthermore, his report stressed that now was the time to place the order. While TWA had been paralyzed by strife, its rivals had already ordered more advanced models of jets, which were both faster and more economical than the first generation. If TWA did not want to be left hopelessly behind, it had to act quickly. Rummel's program called for the delivery in 1962 of twenty-six Boeing 707s equipped with new, more powerful fan-jet engines. Of them, twenty were to be Transcontinental 131Bs and six Intercontinental 331s. Until then, Rummel wanted to lease four to six 720s, the slightly smaller version of the 707s.

When Tillinghast looked at the price tag for the program, the amount—$187.5 million—struck him as very large. Of that sum, TWA reckoned it could raise $40.5 million from its own resources; the remaining $147 million would have to be borrowed. In April, as Tillinghast moved into the presidential office at 380 Madison Avenue, TWA announced its financial results for the first quarter of 1961. They were bad enough to make Tillinghast want to leave. Because of the seasonal decline in tourist travel, TWA always did poorly in the first quarter. But never in its history had TWA done nearly that badly. In 1961's first three months, TWA suffered an operating loss of more than $13 million. Even after the application of an income tax credit, there still remained a net loss of $9,580,-000. The flight engineers' strike, which grounded the airline in February, had contributed to the loss. Even so, TWA was losing money on its regular operations at a prohibitively fast rate. Already its working capital was declining so fast that the company might be forced to turn for help to Hughes, who had promised, as part of the Dillon, Read agreement, to support TWA's cash position.

As a company, TWA was fraught with nervousness and anxiety. As a rule, the imposition of a voting trust on any company is a traumatic experience, and it was especially so at TWA. Many of the old-timers had chafed under Hughes' whimsical rule; nonetheless, they felt an intense loyalty to him. They were offended by the attitude of some of the newcomers who seemed to think that everything in the past had been tainted by Hughes and therefore was bad. They felt that such an attitude was unfair, both to Hughes and to them. After all, TWA had been a great airline long before the bankers got their hands on it. When he put his mind to it, Hughes, at least, had known how to run TWA. Despite their flashy business pedigrees, the newcomers did not seem to know how to make TWA work. What did they know about running an airline anyhow? Breech was an automaker, Tillinghast a lawyer. As an added element of nervousness, the veterans at TWA knew that Hughes had an efficient intelligence system within the company that would report how the old-time executives behaved toward the new management. It was a period of great soul-searching and worry for the veteran executives. If they did not cooperate with the new management, they would most probably be fired, or at least demoted. Yet, if they did cooperate, Hughes would hear about it. Vic Leslie, whose association with Hughes dated back many years, likened his situation to the ham in a sandwich—trapped in the middle and bound to be bitten. The tension was heightened by the fact that many TWA people had an almost mystical belief in the ability of Howard Hughes to regain control of the airline any time he wanted it. "He'll be back one of these days," TWA people assured one another. "Howard will never let them take TWA away from him."

In the spring of 1961, after three months of relative inaction, Howard Hughes began to buttress those beliefs by his own actions. The lenders had thought they had won the war against Hughes when Holliday signed over the airline to them in December. Now they had to think again. A new battle was beginning in which the roles were reversed. It was now Hughes who was on the attack and the lenders were on the defensive, their position weakened by the airline's poor record under their custody.

Hughes seized on that proper psychological moment to send his lawyers into action, waving telegrams and uttering threats. He was alarmed by TWA's losses, but he was even more concerned about another issue. In the actions of the new management, he detected the seeds of a scheme to prevent him from regaining control of TWA for even a longer period of time than the ten-year duration of the voting trust. He had been upset when he heard that TWA was planning to buy more aircraft without consulting him. He had thought that the voting trustees would check with him on any major decision, since he did, after all, still own 78.23 per cent of TWA. He was especially disturbed that TWA intended to buy Boeing aircraft. As part of his attempts to gain General Dynamics' participation in his financing deals, Hughes had ordered, for about $80 million, eight additional Convair 880s and thirteen Convair 990s. He wanted TWA to take those planes rather than Boeing's. A telephone conversation with Holliday during that period gives an insight into Hughes' thinking. After Holliday had explained to him that General Dynamics doubted that TWA would accept the additional 880s and the 990s, Hughes replied, "However I obtain TWA's acceptance to this is my own problem. Most likely the Hughes Tool Company will control TWA when the matter comes up."

Hughes had an even more compelling reason for wanting TWA to buy the Convairs. The reason was the way the Boeings were to be financed. The $147 million loan was to be made by the same banks and insurance companies that had forced Hughes to place his TWA shares in the voting trust. In the new loan agreement was a covenant that linked the $147 million financing to the original $165 million loan. The covenant provided that if Hughes paid off the first loan, thus dissolving the voting trust, the second loan would immediately become due. Thus, if Howard Hughes sought to regain control of TWA, he would not only face the prospect of having to pay off the first loan of $165 million, plus a 22 per cent penalty for premature repayment, but at the same time he would also have to pay off the second amount. That would mean the staggering total outlay of some $350 million. Howard Hughes knew that if he wanted to get back TWA any time soon, he would have to do so before the second loan was closed.

While all of this was going on, another development began in the struggle between Hughes and the bankers. It provided the arena in which the other conflicts were played out. That arena concerned the financial arrangements that dated back to the closing of the Dillon, Read plan in December 1960. As part of the transaction, TWA paid to Hughes the grand total of $157,489,-411.93. The amount represented the money Hughes had laid out earlier for aircraft and spare parts, in the long, hectic period before the long-term financing finally went into effect. Of the total sum, $100 million was given to Hughes in the form of a 6½ per cent interim TWA note. The rest was paid out in cash.

According to the agreement, TWA would issue on or before May 31, 1961, $100 million in new debentures. Hughes could then exchange his $100 million note for the purchase of those subordinated securities. Attached to the debentures were warrants that would entitle him later to buy nearly three million additional shares of TWA stock at a per-share price of $20 to $22. The arrangement was designed to be mutually beneficial. TWA would retain $100 million in much needed capital, and Hughes could increase his holdings in the airline at what turned out to be a very favorable price.

In preparation for the sale of the debentures to Hughes, which was set for May 25, 1961, TWA began to draw up the stock prospectus that would have to be cleared by the Securities and Exchange Commission. In accordance with federal laws, the prospectus had to describe fully TWA's business situation and commitments. This prospectus became the focal point of Hughes' attack against the new management. As usual, he was operating through a lawyer. This time it was a new one: Chester Davis, who was chief of the trial department in the Manhattan firm of Simpson, Thacher & Bartlett. Forceful and blunt, Davis was quite a different sort of person from the gracious Cook or the polished Bautzer. If Hughes really wanted to fight, he had picked a fittingly formidable advocate.

In telegrams to the SEC in Washington, Davis declared that the TWA prospectus might be "deficient in certain material respects." He implied that TWA had an obligation to take the Convair jets from Hughes and had been less than candid in not acknowedging that commitment. For two reasons, it was a cleverly conceived move. If TWA acknowledged the obligation, it would then be compelled to abandon its plan to acquire the Boeings. But even if TWA disputed Davis' implication, the disagreement might still delay the completion of the prospectus. That, in turn, would postpone the completion of the Boeing financing because it was highly improbable that the lenders would close a deal with TWA while a major dispute with Hughes was going on.

At the same time, Chester Davis asked TWA for a one-week delay in the sale of the debentures. Davis was seconded in that request by Merrill Lynch whose representatives explained that they had been commissioned by Hughes to make a public offering of the debentures. Instead of keeping them, Hughes intended to sell them right away.

What was he up to? Was Hughes trying to collect enough money to pay off the loans and prepayment penalty to recover control of TWA? That certainly was what it looked like. He needed about $204 million. Through the sale of the debentures to the public, Hughes would get nearly halfway there. But he had other resources. Thanks to $57 million in cash that he had received from TWA, Hughes was solvent again, and his bankers, notably the Bank of America, once more were happy to extend him large loans. Also, the appraisal of Hughes' huge holdings in real estate and oil leases had been completed; the amount came to about $100 million. In addition, the oil industry recession had ended and the Hughes Tool Company was again producing handsome profits. If he could act quickly enough, it was no longer beyond Hughes' financial power to regain control of TWA.

The pressure was now on Tillinghast, who had been president of TWA for only a little longer than one month. Time and timing were now extremely important. The closing for the $147 million Boeing financing was scheduled to take place on May 31, six days after the time that had been set for the sale of the debentures to Hughes. For Tillinghast, it was very important to conclude the financing on that date. If it cancelled the Boeing order after May 31, TWA would lose its deposit. The far more important consideration, however, was the attitude of the lenders, who regarded the new financing as the test of whether Tillinghast could successfully fend off Hughes. This was a crucial matter for the financiers, for while they were willing to do business with an independent TWA, they wanted nothing to do with Hughes. The memories of last year's crises were still too fresh in their minds.

Almost immediately, Hughes' sniping at the debenture prospectus frightened the Prudential away from participating in the new loan. With good reason, Tillinghast feared that another defection might cause all of the remaining lenders to desert him. Then he would be left at the mercy of Hughes. TWA would have no choice but to take the Convair jets and to ask Hughes for money to support its dwindling working capital. Tillinghast knew that if Hughes supplied more aircraft and money to TWA, he would be back in control just as effectively as if he had bought out the voting trust.

Tillinghast faced a crucial decision. Should he grant the one-week extension to Hughes and Merrill Lynch for the sale of the debentures? To do so meant that the date for the debentures would fall one day after the scheduled closing of the financing plan—except, of course, that there would probably be no closing on that date at all if Tillinghast did not settle the Hughes affair first. Yet Tillinghast could not appear to reject the plea of TWA's owner without a good reason. He was, after all, acting on behalf of the trustees, who were charged with administering Hughes' property. Despite the acrimony between the two sides, Tillinghast could not take an unreasonable position toward the request that might later provide Hughes with a cause to start a legal attack.

With those considerations in mind, Tillinghast began to investigate the merits of Hughes' request. He invited the representatives from Merrill Lynch to come by his office for a talk. It was already mid-May, and after questioning the stockbrokers about the arrangements for the public sale of the debentures, Tillinghast was not convinced that they actually could complete preparations in only one additional week. Tillinghast feared that a one-week delay might lead to postponements of two or three or even more weeks. In the meantime, TWA's financing would collapse. Some of the financiers, who earlier had dealt with Hughes, warned Tillinghast about Hughes' propensity for procrastination. In his own mind, Tillinghast also was forming the image of Hughes as a man who would do almost anything to impede or delay the new plans of the new management.

Increasingly, Tillinghast became convinced that Hughes' request for a delay was simply a diversionary tactic that would wreck the Boeing financing plan and would leave TWA once more at Hughes' whimsical mercy. Tillinghast made his first hard decision. Though he realized that not granting the delay would certainly worsen the already bad relations between Hughes and the TWA management, Tillinghast ordered that the debentures would be offered for sale as planned on May 25.

Accordingly, on May 25 the debentures were offered to Hughes. Despite all the threats and requests, Hughes bought them without a grumble. In the wake of the unexpectedly peaceful conclusion of the debenture sale, Tillinghast turned his efforts toward the closing of the Boeing financing, which was to take place the next Wednesday, May 31. But then a telephone call came from Chester Davis. Speaking in a confidential manner, Davis told Tillinghast that he was in possession of some very important information, which he could not disclose until after June 2. Since the information would vitally affect TWA's plans, Davis was asking that the Boeing orders be postponed until after that time. If Tillinghast failed to comply with that request, Davis warned that he would be compelled to take legal action to protect the interests of his client, Howard Hughes.

Tillinghast regarded the Davis demand as simply an attempt to delay the financing deal. Ignoring it completely, he went ahead with the plans to conclude the $147 million loan as scheduled. True to the timetable, the financing for the new fleet of Boeings was completed on May 31 and the new aircraft were ordered im-

mediately. Davis, having failed to frighten Tillinghast, now turned
to Boeing. In a long telegram to the Seattle planemakers Davis
warned that the voting trustees did not have the power to commit
TWA to any aircraft orders without the consent of Howard
Hughes. Furthermore, Davis declared that the Hughes Tool Company was considering legal action against the new management
and the financial institutions that stood behind it. He warned that
anyone who cooperated with the new management might also face
a legal action by Hughes.

Despite that threat, Boeing accepted the TWA orders. But Davis had now issued a grave challenge. He no longer was simply
trying to stop TWA from ordering Boeings so that it would take
the Convairs. Now he was attacking the right of the voting trust
to run TWA. In another of his warnings, he asserted that it was
"the position of Toolco that it was compelled to enter into the voting trust under conditions which would warrant a termination of
the voting trust." Those were fighting words. Clearly, Davis
seemed to be sketching out the basis for legal action.

Even as Davis was issuing his warnings, another set of lawyers
were already at work on a legal case against Hughes. In mid-June
John Sonnett, who personally directed the investigation, presented
his preliminary findings to Tillinghast. After his staff had dug
through TWA and CAB records and had interviewed a number of
people, Sonnett reached the tentative conclusion that TWA had a
case for a private antitrust suit against Howard Hughes. Sonnett,
who believed that he could prove that Hughes had committed offenses against the Sherman and Clayton antitrust statutes, explained that an antitrust action was the most advantageous course
of legal action available to the new management. Under antitrust
provisions, Tillinghast could ask not only for Hughes to pay damages to TWA, but he could also demand that Hughes be forced to
divest himself of his stock in the airline and to leave the company
in peace. That, in Sonnett's words, "would settle the Hughes problem once and for all."

For his part, Tillinghast found Sonnett's recommendations "interesting but not compelling." As he saw it, TWA had already been

the center of so much controversy that another battle with Hughes would harm the new management's efforts to create a fresh and more positive image for the airline. Furthermore, for the moment there was no immediate need to think about a lawsuit because Davis had suddenly embarked on a peace campaign. By this time, June 2 had come and gone, leaving Davis free to discuss the private information he said had come to his attention. Tillinghast agreed to listen, and the two men met, along with several senior TWA executives, on a Saturday morning at the airline's headquarters. His information was hardly startling. It consisted of facts and figures about the performance of the Convair 990, which now had started coming off the production line. Though he was not an engineer, Davis had tried manfully to master the complexities of aircraft operating efficiency and economics. His aim was to persuade Tillinghast and his aides that the 990 was a better plane than the Boeing fan-jets that TWA had just ordered. But Tillinghast and the others remained skeptical and the atmosphere in the meeting became highly charged.

That attempt having failed, Davis asked for a larger meeting at which the lenders, the ranking TWA executives, and the board of directors would be present to hear his presentation on the advantages of the 990. Tillinghast, who suspected that Davis was trying to create divisions within TWA's ranks, rejected the proposal. Still Davis did not give up. In a long letter to TWA ("Chester Davis sure writes good letters," remembers one TWA executive), Hughes' attorney offered the airline, as the first stage toward achieving a cease-fire, the choice of one or more proposals. The first one was that Hughes, in return for the disbandment of the voting trust, would invest $100 million in TWA. The new money would have been enough to purchase a sizable number of new aircraft. Proposal No. 2 was an offer by Hughes Tool to buy an additional $11.2 million in TWA subordinated debentures if TWA would acquire the Convair 990s that Hughes Tool had on order from General Dynamics. The third was an offer to sell at cost the 990s and 880s that Hughes was committed to buy from General Dynamics.

The proposals struck Tillinghast as simply another scheme by which Hughes hoped either to regain control of TWA or to get rid of his unwanted Convair jets or both. As a result, Tillinghast turned them down. This time Davis did not come up with another peace plan. Instead, he resumed his adversary role. As the days of that tense June ticked by, Tillinghast became ever more convinced that TWA, whether it wanted or not, was headed for a legal showdown with Hughes. As he lay awake at night tossing and turning in the bedroom of his Bronxville home, Tillinghast wondered where and under what circumstances Howard Hughes would strike. Would it be in the form of a suit by a minority shareholder, who would be a frontman for Hughes? And what would be the site? Would it be in some obscure town in Nevada where the Hughes millions might have an influence? Would it be in Los Angeles? Would the TWA officers be forced to commute coast-to-coast in order to give their testimony? Could they do that and still have time left to run the airline? What would be the terms of the case? Would it be presented in such a way that Hughes would be able to hide behind a battery of lawyers and never have to risk his own appearance in court?

As he spent one sleepless night after another, Charles Tillinghast pondered such questions. But Tillinghast was also aware that his own lawsuit against Hughes was in some ways pretty startling itself. The suit that Sonnett had proposed struck at the very basis of the American right of private ownership. Tillinghast did not want to dispossess a man of his property. Yet, he felt the issue seemed more complex and more fundamental than that. Since TWA was an instrument of public service, he felt justified in taking the position that such a company should, in his words, "be directed with a more than ordinary degree of responsibility by its owners." In his opinion, Hughes had failed on that count.

Meanwhile, Tillinghast was receiving reports from TWA offices in the field that the Hughes forces were definitely pressing ahead with preparations for a suit. Gordon Gilmore, TWA's vice president for public relations, passed on a tip to Tillinghast that Hughes intended to start legal action in Los Angeles.

On Thursday, June 29, as the executive committee of TWA assembled for a special session at 380 Madison, a thin sheaf of papers was handed to each member. The papers were the outline of an antitrust complaint against Howard Hughes. John Sonnett, who had composed the document, briefed the directors on the case. By a unanimous vote, the executive committee empowered Tillinghast to file a suit against Hughes "at such time as he considered appropriate."

Tillinghast, who considered the next day appropriate enough, telephoned the go-ahead order to John Sonnett. Sonnett picked up his black briefcase and hailed a cab for the short drive to the Federal Court Building in lower Manhattan. Thus began the great Hughes law case.

Part Two

Part Two

6. The St. John Syndrome

On that June day in 1961, as John Sonnett climbed the steps of the Federal Court Building on New York's Foley Square, Howard Hughes acquired an important new antagonist. Until that time, Hughes had been confronted at TWA first by Ernie Breech and later by Breech and Charlie Tillinghast together. But now, as the dispute between TWA's new managers and its old owner entered into litigation, Hughes gained a third major opponent. John Sonnett, a masterful legal strategist and tactician, believed in a simple and direct method of operations. It was to seize—and retain—the initiative. His strategy was the jurisprudential equivalent of the football adage that the best defense is a good offense or the exhortation to the infantryman to take the high ground.

Earlier, as Sonnett had reviewed the events of the past few months, he had seen how Howard Hughes, after losing control of TWA to the voting trust, had rallied and put the new TWA management on the defensive. Using Chester Davis as his spokesman, Hughes had unleashed a barrage of threats against the recently installed TWA executives and directors that challenged their right to run the airline. He also was warning that he would hold TWA's new directors personally liable for the huge losses that the airline now was piling up.

As Sonnett planned the counterattack against Hughes, he hoped to devise a legal strategy that would quickly and decisively give

TWA the upper hand. As he walked down the mauve marble corridors of the Federal Court Building, Sonnett carried in his attaché case two documents that were specifically designed to inflict on Howard Hughes the maximum legal discomfort in the shortest possible time. One of them was a thirty-eight-page antitrust complaint. Among other things, it aimed at forcing Howard Hughes to surrender forever his holding in TWA and to pay to the airline $115 million in damages. The other document, comprising only a few typed sheets, was a petition that requested the court to order Hughes to appear as the first witness to give evidence in the pretrial proceedings.

In a single stroke, Sonnett sought to engage two of Howard Hughes' most intense emotions: his prideful love for TWA and his obsession for privacy. If Sonnett's strategy worked according to plan, Hughes would become ensnared in a dilemma in which he would be forced to make extremely painful personal choices. For Howard Hughes, TWA was much more than just a property. It was something that he had created and built. It was the realization of his own dreams of the great potential of commercial aviation, which he had demonstrated in the 1930s on his world-circling record flight. No man in history had ever put into aviation more of his own money (about $200 million) or more of his own sweat. "I would live in a garret before I would ever give up TWA," Hughes used to tell his friends. His sentiment had not changed. Ever since that fateful day in December 1960 when the financiers took the control of TWA away from him, Hughes had pursued but a single goal: to get it back.

But if TWA was Hughes' love, privacy remained his obsession. By 1961 he had not been seen in public for three years. Sonnett's strategy aimed at placing Hughes in a position in which, in order to protect one of his passions, he would have to sacrifice the other. As Sonnett devised the scenario, the lawsuit would be developed in such a way that Hughes would not be able to defend his interests in TWA without appearing in public. No one knew for certain how Hughes would react to Sonnett's challenge. Could he overcome the fears and anxieties that had compelled him to cut himself off from the outside world? After years of isolation, could Hughes bring himself to face the turmoil and strain of an appearance in public? Or, perhaps even more significant, would Hughes' intense sense of pride allow him to submit to a questioning about his stewardship of TWA?

Sonnett had never met Hughes. Nonetheless, as he had demonstrated in the past, Sonnett had an intuitive sense for dealing with strong-willed men. As a young federal prosecutor in the early forties, Sonnett had won a conviction against John L. Lewis after the old labor chieftain had defied a government ban against wartime work stoppages by calling out on strike his United Mine Workers union. Later, as a private attorney, Sonnett had defeated the combined cast of the Ford Motor Company in the famed *Ferguson v. Ford* suit in which the British engineer Harry Ferguson charged that Ford had purloined his design for a tractor. Among the witnesses whom Sonnett had subjected to withering examinations was Ernest Breech, then the operating chief at the Ford Motor Company. It was an experience that led Breech to be in favor of having Sonnett on his side in the TWA case.

As Sonnett prepared the complaint against Hughes, he carefully studied the peculiarities of the elusive industrialist. It was a rich field for research. To Hughes' enduring disadvantage, he had, especially during the past few years, broken with many of the men who had been his closest advisers. They knew him only too well —knew his fears, his foibles, his method of conducting business. And some of them were so bitter and disillusioned that they were willing and even eager to talk to John Sonnett. He interviewed several of Hughes' former financial advisers who had broken with Hughes during the prolonged wrangling over the financing plan for TWA's jets. They told Sonnett how Hughes' hearing, damaged by three plane crashes and years of exposure to roaring airplane engines, had steadily become worse. Even though it had been made especially for him by the Hughes Aircraft electronics experts, he complained that his hearing aid, which he carried in his shirt pocket, gave him terrible headaches. In their last meetings with him in 1959–60 in Las Vegas and Los Angeles hotels, Howard

Hughes, ever wary of eavesdroppers, had stuffed towels around the window frames and doors of the rooms to "soundproof" the room. Then, after removing his hearing aid, he had asked his advisers to speak as loudly as they could. At the top of their voices, they shouted recommendations about complex financial deals, but even then Howard Hughes had barely been able to hear them. His hearing problem, they felt, made Hughes, always standoffish, even more reclusive than ever.

There was another strong reason for Hughes' hermitlike behavior. It was his phobia about becoming contaminated by germs. So much fictional nonsense (such as Hughes' wearing Kleenex boxes on his feet) had been bandied about in public lore on that subject that a serious lawyer might have been tempted to dismiss the rumors altogether. But men who had often visited Hughes reported that he was genuinely obsessed by the fear of disease and shied away even from shaking hands from fear of contracting some new ailment.

Aside from those two rather well-known handicaps, his poor hearing and germ phobia, Howard Hughes suffered from a very private anxiety that was known only to a very small circle of his most trusted aides. Sonnett may, however, have learned about at least one aspect of that anxiety, since one of Hughes' former lieutenants spoke to outsiders about it. That part of Hughes' anxiety concerned his fear of being declared mentally incompetent. Even at that time, according to this former aide, Hughes had suffered from spells of extreme weakness, which might have been brought on by a combination of the effects of the crashes (he had never given himself time to recover completely), incredible amounts of overwork (he literally kept working until he dropped off to sleep from exhaustion), and an unbalanced and insufficient diet (he frequently subsisted for days at a time on only cookies and milk). When Hughes was stricken by a spell, he would lapse into a semi-comatose state in which he was incapable of carrying on conversations or conducting business. He was fully aware that he suffered from such bouts of weakness and feared that he might be stricken by an attack while he was on the stand. He could imagine the judge, seeing one of the United States' most important industrialists and defense contractors in a state of utter helplessness, declare: "That man needs a guardian."

There was a deeper manifestation of Hughes' anxiety that was an even more closely guarded secret. It concerned his fear of being compelled by outsiders to take actions that were against his will. In his prime, Hughes had exalted in his ability to determine his own destiny and to exert his control over people and events. It was tragically ironic that his own deepest fear would be an inversion of his earlier dominance.

Sonnett may have learned, or guessed, about this other dimension of Hughes' anxiety. During those weeks, as he was conducting his interviews, there was a lot of discussion among TWA directors, especially between newcomers and the few holdovers from the old board, about how Hughes might react to the threat that he would be called upon by a lawsuit to testify in public. There was a good deal of speculation about whether Hughes, if his honor was offended, would come roaring in to defend himself just as he had in 1947 when Senator Owen Brewster accused him of wasting government money on the building of his flying boat. But some of the directors who knew Hughes best contended that he no longer was the same man who had taken on Senator Brewster. The few who had once been closely associated with him were aware that something had happened inside Hughes that made it impossible for him to face people. On at least one occasion, Hughes himself had admitted as much. Shortly before he lost control of TWA, a close friend advised Hughes in a face-to-face conversation that it still was not too late to work out a compromise with the financiers. This man urged Hughes to fly to New York for a personal meeting with the bankers and insurance executives. Hughes paused. "I could no more do that than walk into a den of lions," he replied sadly. "It just isn't in me anymore."

Hughes is no saint but the apprehension about the loss of his free will is hauntingly reminiscent of the warning to Peter in Chapter 21:18 of the Gospel of St. John: "When you were young you fastened your belt and walked where you chose; but when you shall become old you will stretch out your hands and a stranger will bind you fast and carry you where you do not wish to go."

When he had been younger, Hughes had been free and independent to a degree achieved by few men. His wealth, combined with great personal determination, had given him the power to have things done—whether it was starlets hired or executives fired at the tool company—the way he wanted them. As Hughes had conceded in that 1960 message to William Forrester of Merrill Lynch, until the advent of the Dillon, Read plan he had never really been forced to do anything against his will. But that time was past. Hughes, of course, had always been fearful about being kidnapped (hence, he carried no money, thinking that would make him a less inviting target). But now he was obsessed by the anxiety that he could be physically seized by outsiders and taken away and forced to do things against his will, such as signing away his fortune.

As Sonnett fashioned the complaint, it touched on Hughes' deep fear, for the legal action contained the threat of cutting through Hughes' defenses and getting at the man. The suit was not only against his corporate shield, the Hughes Tool Company, behind which he conducted his business. It also was directed at Hughes personally. For Hughes, who was named both as a witness and a defendant, the complaint carried the menace that he would be made subject to the orders of the court. He could be led where he did not want to go.

John Sonnett's mission on that June morning in 1961 took him to the chambers of the Honorable Lloyd F. MacMahon, a judge in the federal court of the Southern District of New York. In a private meeting, Sonnett explained to the judge that TWA had decided to start a lawsuit against Howard Hughes. Sonnett said that there was the possibility, however, that an out-of-court settlement might be reached. Publicity about the lawsuit would imperil the negotiations, because Hughes undoubtedly would resist a settlement that appeared to force him to cave in under pressure. Sonnett asked the judge's permission to file the complaint under seal for several days so that its existence would be kept secret.

Judge MacMahon granted Sonnett's request. He ordered the complaint to be kept under seal until July 11, 1961. The judge also granted Sonnett's request in the petition for Hughes' appearance. He set July 5 as the day on which the Hughes side could argue why Hughes should not be called as the first witness. That order also was kept secret. Thus, to all but a bare handful of people, the onset of the litigation against Hughes remained unknown.

Filing the complaint under seal accomplished two objectives. First, since Tillinghast and Breech feared that Hughes was about to start a lawsuit against them, it beat him to the punch. Second, unless Sonnett had badly misread Hughes' character, the very existence of the suit, in which Hughes was to be called as the first witness, was certain to exert great pressure for a quick out-of-court settlement.

Sonnett sought to send the news about the start of the suit to Hughes through Chester Davis. As soon as the papers were filed under seal, John Nicol, a Sonnett aide accompanied by an assistant United States marshal, arrived at 11:45 with copies of the complaint and petition at Davis' office on the thirty-first floor of 120 Broadway. Davis was not there, but his secretary, Cynthia McBride, telphoned him at a luncheon club. It was a Friday. On hearing that two men were out to serve him with papers, Davis told his secretary to say that he was not coming back to his office that day but instead was leaving directly for a weekend in the country. A few days later, however, Davis did accept a copy of the complaint and the show-cause order regarding Hughes' appearance. Davis passed the word on to Hughes about the litigation.

According to federal court procedure, twenty days must pass between the filing of the suit and the start of pretrial discovery. There was time for talks. A few months earlier, shortly after TWA had retained the Cahill, Gordon firm to study the advisability of a suit against Hughes, Greg Bautzer had tried to head off a legal confrontation. He had come to New York and had, in effect, said: "If TWA thinks it has a claim against the Tool Company or Howard Hughes, I'd like to sit down with you and talk about it." At that time, Bautzer had conducted exploratory conversations with

Ernie Breech and Irving Olds, the two voting trustees appointed by the insurance companies. He had also conferred with Francis Reed, who was the counsel for Breech and Olds. Now with added urgency, Bautzer flew to New York from Los Angeles to resume the talks. Floyd Odlum, a business ally of Hughes, came also to New York on his behalf to seek a settlement.

The signs were encouraging. As Tillinghast later recalled, Hughes appeared to be "very, very concerned about the lawsuit, and looked as if he was making serious efforts to try and get it settled." Bank of America vice president Robert Gordon, who had often dealt with Hughes, scribbled in a desk diary an assessment of Hughes' reaction to the onset of TWA's legal action: "HRH scared by Cahill suit—but worse than expected—they [TWA's lawyers] have concluded that if they get him on the stand—would keep him there for two or three months." Actually, two or three months was a conservative estimate; Sonnett soon was saying that if he got Hughes on the stand, he would keep him there for six months or more.

Bautzer's conversations were highly promising. According to Bautzer, Hughes appeared willing to accept the main TWA demand—that the new management should be allowed to run the airline free from his interference. Bautzer also relayed an offer from Hughes, who proposed to help TWA financially by putting more capital into the airline. The outlook for a settlement appeared so bright that the TWA side felt encouraged to grant a few concessions. On July 6, in a four-way telephone conversation between Bautzer, Davis, Reed, and himself, Sonnett acceded to a request by the two Hughes lawyers and agreed to postpone the deadline for the reply to the show-cause order regarding Hughes' appearance and to keep the complaint under seal for an additional period of time. The extra time was to give the two sides an opportunity to work out an out-of-court settlement. Acting on a motion by John Sonnett, Judge E. J. Dimock the next day extended the seal on the complaint until 10 A.M. on August 1. In addition, the Hughes side was given extra time, until August 10, to state its argument why Hughes should not be called as the first witness.

After spending a short while in New York, Bautzer flew back to Los Angeles. He invited Reed to fly out for further negotiations. In poolside conversations and in late night sessions at Bautzer's home, where Bautzer's wife served coffee, the two lawyers discussed terms of a possible settlement. After three days in Los Angeles, Reed, whom Tillinghast referred to as "vice president in charge of negotiations," returned to New York with a memo outlining the general scope of a compromise. At the regular TWA monthly board meeting in New York on July 19, Tillinghast reported to the directors that encouraging progress was being made toward a negotiated settlement. Hughes apparently also was heartened by the negotiations.

Reed and Bautzer were instructed by their respective sides to draw up a formal out-of-court settlement. The two lawyers were now competing against time; the days during which the suit remained under seal were quickly ticking away. But Reed and Bautzer made good progress. By late July an agreement appeared so imminent that the TWA board was summoned to a special meeting on the twenty-seventh to select an eight-man special committee of directors, who would be empowered to accept an out-of-court settlement on TWA's behalf.

On Friday, July 28, Reed submitted the agreement to TWA's special committee. By any standard, it represented what seemed to be a highly satisfactory settlement for both sides. If TWA would withdraw the suit, Hughes promised to invest $150 million in the airline during the next two years through the purchase of additional common stock and subordinated debentures. The new capital would enable TWA to purchase short-range French-built Caravelle jetliners. Hughes pledged to leave the voting trust in force for its full ten-year life (after which, according to the terms of the 1960 agreement, the airline would revert to his control). Hughes attached only one major string to the settlement. He asked that the airline use about $63 million of the $150 million to take off his hands the thirteen Convair 990 jetliners he had on order from General Dynamics. That would still leave enough money to buy fifteen or twenty Caravelles. The purchase of the 990s seemed a small enough price to pay for a guarantee of ten-years' peace at TWA.

The first reaction of the TWA special committee was to accept the proposal. But the next question was this: how do you settle a lawsuit of the complexity of *TWA v. Hughes?* The mechanics of starting a suit are far more simple than those of ending it. Once begun, a lawsuit assumes almost a life of its own. After the charges have been committed to paper and the complaint filed in court, the suit gains momentum, propelled along by the force of the legal procedure. As it begins to thrash away toward a far-off and distant showdown, a big lawsuit like the TWA action sharpens hostilities, enlists platoons of opposing lawyers, expends incredible amounts of money and human effort, spews out towering piles of briefs, reply briefs, and opinions in such volume as to cost a reader his eyesight, and utterly defies everyone to find a way to end it.

The directors of TWA had started a suit in hopes of a quick out-of-court settlement. Now, as the fulfillment of that goal appeared to be within grasp, they suddenly became very cautious. One reason was that the directors knew that they could be held personally responsible for the outcome of the litigation. They had supported the TWA management in filing the complaint against Hughes, which asked, among other things, for $115 million in damages. Now, if they settled the suit out of court for less than that, someone would want to know why. According to Bautzer, Hughes would have been willing to pay $5 million into TWA for stopping the suit, but that amount was, of course, only a fraction of what TWA was suing for. Even if none of TWA's 10,000 minority shareholders would think of taking legal action against the directors for failing to collect the maximum money for TWA, there certainly would be many attorneys, known in the trade as "strike lawyers," to remind them of their opportunity. In the event a court ruled that the directors had made an inequitable settlement, they could be forced to compensate TWA from their own pockets for the difference between what the airline received from Hughes and what Sonnett's complaint originally asked for.

Since the settlement would bring about a truce between the new management and Hughes, the suspicion would be that the directors had let Hughes off easy in order to have a free hand in running TWA for the next nine and a half years. Thus the directors were aware that a settlement would have to be so demonstrably beneficial to TWA that they could use its terms as their defense in court. The situation was highly ironic. The distinguished directors of TWA, whose business credentials read like a Burke's Peerage of American capitalism, could not drop the complaint against Hughes without rendering themselves open to legal action.

Aside from those implications, the directors had to consider another important factor. As the deadline of August 1 approached for the signing of the settlement agreement, they had to ask themselves whether in their heart of hearts they really wanted to drop the suit. No matter how dearly they wanted a truce with Hughes, the directors could not fail but reflect on what an enormous help the suit had been. Until only a few weeks ago, Hughes had been waging a highly effective corporate warfare, which threatened even to seize their own personal fortunes as a penalty for TWA's growing losses. Then John Sonnett filed a couple of pieces of paper in federal court and what happens? Suddenly all was peace and light from the Hughes side.

Hughes used to frighten off his opponents from pressuring him by saying that he would not negotiate with a pistol held at his head. There was one pointing at him now, and he was behaving very reasonably. No one could be certain how he would act when the legal gun was no longer there. To be sure, Hughes was saying that he would allow the voting trust to remain in effect for its entire ten-year term and would refrain from interference in TWA's management. Without even questioning Hughes' sincerity, the directors, especially those who knew him best, doubted whether his temperament would allow him to live up to his promises. If Hughes, for example, felt that the new management was ordering the wrong type of new aircraft, could he resist trying to reverse the decision? Not very likely. Would he sit quietly in the background if TWA wanted to raise new capital by selling common stock that would dilute his 78.23 per cent ownership of the airline? Hardly.

TWA's directors had to reckon that if they dropped the suit, Hughes might start the same pattern of harassment all over again. And if he did, what could they do? From a purely practical standpoint, one thing they could not do would be to start another suit. It simply would not be feasible to negotiate an out-of-court settlement for the present complaint and then later try again to resort to legal action. The potent charges and sweeping remedies that were contained in the present suit would be put aside by the settlement; the next legal action, even if one were to be started, would not be of the same decisive dimensions.

After much deliberation, the TWA directors reached a conclusion. Any peace plan, they decided, would have to stop short of an outright dismissal of the complaint against Hughes. Instead of dropping the charges altogether, the directors concluded that they would offer an in-between plan. It was quickly transmitted to Hughes. According to TWA's new proposal, Hughes should proceed with his offer to invest $150 million in TWA, and TWA in turn would accommodate him by buying the thirteen Convair 990s. The complaint would be relegated to a limbo status, neither to be pressed nor dropped. Hughes would be required to sign a consent decree. That is an ingeniously ambiguous form of legal ceasefire in which the defendant does not admit his guilt, but agrees to refrain from doing the acts with which he is charged. The consent decree has the advantage for the defendant that he can maintain his innocence and escape prosecution or, in civil cases, avoid a possible fine and other penalties. Under the TWA plan, Hughes would be required to agree to refrain from doing those things with which he was charged in TWA's complaint. But TWA did not intend to drop the complaint altogether. Instead, TWA intended to keep the complaint inactive but alive under the supervision of a federal judge. If Hughes abided by the terms of the consent decree, TWA would let the suit rest in peace. But if Hughes tried to interfere in the airline's affairs before the end of the voting trust term, TWA would dust off the complaint and start up the proceedings against him.

Howard Hughes was understandably wary of TWA's offer. His lawyers were split on the advisability of his signing the consent decree. Bautzer was in favor. "Look, Howard," he said, "I can get you out of this for $5 million. Many of the leading people in America have signed consent decrees. What difference does it make?"

But some of Hughes' other lawyers were advising him in exactly the opposite way. They warned him that his signature on a consent decree would brand him as a wrongdoer in the eyes of the American public. They repeated their earlier advice that the TWA suit was without merit and could be beaten in the courts. They warned that his signature on the consent decree could have damaging consequences for him in Washington. They told him that the decree might be interpreted by some governmental agencies as an admission that he was guilty as charged in the complaint. Such an interpretation could, for example, destroy what was left of his reputation at the Civil Aeronautics Board.

These lawyers based their arguments on an important consideration. Since TWA and Hughes Tool were both chartered in Delaware, they were, so to speak, corporate citizens of the same state. Under the American system of the division of jurisdiction between state and federal courts, a dispute between TWA and Hughes would belong to a Delaware court unless the issue under litigation involved a federal law. In *TWA v. Hughes,* the only ground for federal jurisdiction was Hughes' alleged violations of United States antitrust laws. Thus, Hughes began to fret that his consent to allow the suit to remain alive under the supervision of a federal judge would, in effect, be tantamount to conceding the applicability of the antitrust laws to his case.

Hughes was also concerned about the threat that the suit would continue to hold over him. Just as the TWA directors were suspicious of his future behavior, he was wary of theirs. His main concern was that he might be prevented from taking measures that he would feel were essential to protect his interests in TWA. For instance, he worried about what would happen if he tried to block another loan that would, in effect, perpetuate the life of the voting trust. He feared that TWA would run to the judge yelling, "Hughes is being a bad boy again!" He also feared that Breech and Tillinghast, whom he regarded as no friends of his, could seize on any action—no matter how innocent he meant it to be—to cry, "That's enough!" and start up the suit again. Those were extremely unsettling prospects for a man who already had invested $90 million of his own money in TWA and now was prepared to put in $150 million more. In the final analysis, Hughes reckoned that he might be worse off if he accepted TWA's proposal than if he went ahead and fought.

Unaware of Hughes' reservations, TWA meanwhile was pressing ahead with the settlement procedure. One day before the deadline, TWA's board held another special meeting. At 2:30 Monday afternoon, July 31, the directors met to accommodate an earlier Hughes' request by allowing him to switch $38 million of his new investment from the purchase of debentures to common stock. That would increase his holdings to more than 80 per cent of TWA's stock and would enable him under the federal tax laws to write off TWA's looming losses against Toolco's profits. The directors were also briefed by John Sonnett and Francis Reed on the terms of the settlement. At six in the evening, the board adjourned, leaving behind the special committee, which was to work out the final details and sign the agreement with Greg Bautzer. Of the eight men on the special committee, seven were present that evening at the TWA offices on Madison Avenue. They waited, but no word came from Bautzer. Finally, at about 7:30, the special committee, which included Breech, Tillinghast, TWA vice president Floyd Hall, former Atomic Energy Commission chairman John McCone, and industrialist Barry T. Leithead, adjourned to the Union League Club for drinks and dinner. No messages from Bautzer or Hughes interrupted their repast within the dark paneled walls of that citadel of the eastern financial establishment on Manhattan's lower Park Avenue.

At shortly before nine the next morning, the special committee reconvened at TWA's headquarters in hopes that Hughes overnight had given the go-ahead to sign the settlement. Again, no word from Bautzer. While the directors still anxiously were awaiting a phone call from Bautzer, time ran out. At ten o'clock, in compliance with the order of Judge MacMahon, a clerk in the U. S. District Court ripped the seal off the petition and complaint against Hughes, and the secret battle erupted into public view. There had, of course, been rumblings for months on Wall Street that trouble was brewing between Hughes and the new TWA management. Even so, it had remained a well-kept secret that TWA actually had filed a lawsuit against its longtime master. Now the news that a lawsuit already was in progress caused a sensation in the financial and airline communities across the country. Stories about the case and Hughes blossomed in magazines and newspapers both in the United States and abroad. The cast of characters—Hughes, the loner, v. the elite of American business—made the suit, as newsmen say, "hot copy." One British writer even suggested that the attempt to oust Hughes from the ownership of TWA was the modern corporate equivalent of the ancient overthrow of kings.

The suit intrigued outsiders with the rare spectacle of a corporation suing its majority owner on the charge that he had, of all things, monopolized his own company. In essence, the complaint said, "You, Mr. Hughes, used TWA as a captive market to further your own trade in aircraft and by so doing, you violated the antitrust laws." But aside from its audacious challenge to the rights of ownership, the case raised some serious questions. The most basic of them was simply, could a man be held guilty of dominating a property of which he owned 78.23 per cent? Was it not simply in the capitalist order of things that he who puts up most of the money enjoys the right to control his company? Furthermore, to many experienced observers, it seemed unlikely that monopoly charges could be made to stick in the airline field. Unlike most other American industries, the airlines are exempt by the Federal Aviation Act from the full force of the antitrust laws. Beginning with the first Airmail Act of 1928, Congress has consistently provided that the airlines should be given special, supportive treatment. In contrast to most other enterprises, which must be operated in accord with the antitrust laws whose basic concept is to foster and protect competition, Congress repeatedly has declared that the airlines must be run "in the public interest" and were to be subject to competition only to the extent necessary to develop a healthy transport system.

Congress established the Civil Aeronautics Board as the federal agency to promote and oversee the development of the nation's air transport. It gave the CAB quasi-legal powers to exempt the airlines from the full force of the antitrust laws in instances where antimonopolistic precepts would have handicapped the development of the airline industry. The route structure itself represents a monopoly situation, since the airlines, under the guidance and approval of the CAB, have carved up the air lanes among themselves. But the CAB's sanction protects the airlines from antitrust prosecution. By the same token, if two airlines unite in a merger, the resulting lessening of competition might be a violation of the antitrust laws. The CAB's approval of the merger, however, immunizes the airlines from that aspect of the antitrust laws. The CAB also extends a measure of antitrust protection to persons who have received the board's approval to control an airline. When it grants an order of approval to an applicant, the CAB simultaneously confers upon the person immunity from antitrust laws, "in so far as may be necessary to enable such a person to do anything authorized, approved or required by such order."

Hence many people believed that Howard Hughes was fully sheltered from the antitrust charges in TWA's complaint. The CAB had approved his control of TWA not just once, but three times—in 1944, 1948, and 1954. In fact, after the 1948 investigation, the CAB, in a rare departure from bureaucratic reticence, praised the support that Hughes had given to TWA. Furthermore, Hughes' skilled lawyers had been careful to keep his operations within the shelter of the CAB's antitrust umbrella; without exception, they had gotten specific CAB approvals for all dealings between Toolco and TWA so that, at least in their opinion, those acts would enjoy immunity from the antitrust laws. Each and every lease and sale of aircraft by Toolco to TWA had been cleared by the CAB as being "in the public interest."

Since TWA's allegations rested largely on Hughes' dealing in jets, it seemed unlikely to some veteran airline legal experts that

Hughes could be guilty of antitrust violations, which the CAB had already cloaked with immunity. Many people, in fact, believed that for once John Sonnett, the one-time ace government prosecutor, had picked an unpromising area in which to exercise his mastery of antitrust law. A joke made the rounds on Wall Street about Sonnett's alleged overreliance on antitrust. "If John wanted to replevy a dog," it went, "he'd do it by antitrust."

The choice of antitrust, however, greatly increased the possible penalties for Howard Hughes. If TWA had based its complaint on grounds more customary in business disputes, such as a breach of fiduciary responsibility or misuse of corporate assets, Howard Hughes might at most have been required to pay to the airline the amount of damages it could prove against him. In a case of that nature, he might have been required to compensate TWA for the loss of the use of the Lockheed JetStream that for several months he appropriated for his personal use. Similarly, if Hughes' actions were found to be responsible for the delays in the delivery of the Boeing and Convair jets, he could conceivably have been forced to pay to TWA whatever amount of damages was caused by the lateness of those aircraft.

However, since TWA's complaint was based upon antitrust violations, the airline would be able to seek far more drastic remedies. In a civil antitrust suit, after the amount of damages has been assessed, the sum is then tripled as a penalty. More important, while other business suits inflict only monetary fines, an antitrust action would enable TWA to seek what amounts to the ultimate corporate punishment: the divesture of Hughes from his airline.

Many stanch Wall Streeters, though they had absolutely no sympathy whatsoever for Howard Hughes, felt some qualms about the TWA suit. Some of those who were bothered most were the big financial institutions that had lent the money to TWA. The insurance companies and banks had no love for Hughes. Nonetheless, many of the executives did not wish to become associated with a legal action that seemed to strike at the sanctity of private ownership. The financiers had not been consulted about the advisability of commencing the suit against Hughes. When Tillinghast

phoned them one by one with the information that a complaint
had been filed against Hughes, he later said that many of them
were, in a word, "thunderstruck."

Whatever the criticisms against the action, the complaint itself
was masterfully conceived and executed. It named as defendants
Hughes, the Hughes Tool Company, and Raymond Holliday,
Toolco's chief operating officer. The Atlas Corporation and Northeast Airlines were listed as co-conspirators, but not as defendants.
The complaint charged that the defendants had violated Sections 1
and 2 of the Sherman Antitrust Law by having conspired to restrain trade and monopolize interstate and foreign commerce in
the sale to TWA of jet and non-jet aircraft. The complaint also
alleged that the defendants had broken Section 3 of the Clayton
Antitrust Law by forcing TWA to boycott the products of other
aircraft suppliers. The final antitrust charge was that the defendants
violated Section 7 of the Clayton law by acquiring stock in TWA
in order to convert the airline into a captive market. Atlas and
Northeast were accused of conspiring with the defendants to create
a larger captive market for aircraft through proposing an inequitable merger between Northeast and TWA that would have increased
TWA's needs for jets. The final part of the complaint charged that
after the installation of the voting trust the defendants had sought
to interfere in the conduct of TWA's business.

In establishing the antitrust requirements for the case, Sonnett
identified the Hughes Tool Company, which was best known as a
maker of oil-drilling equipment, as having been engaged "since in
or about 1939 in the development, manufacture, and acquisition
of aircraft." The specific offenses charged against Toolco, Hughes,
and Holliday were divided into two categories: those before and
those after December 1960—the date on which Hughes lost control
of TWA. In the first category, Sonnett listed a long catalogue of
acts by which the defendants supposedly had damaged TWA by
dominating its supply of aircraft.

At first, so the complaint stated, the defendants had planned to
build jets themselves and to sell them to TWA and other airlines.
But after that plan fell through, the defendants refused to allow

TWA either to order or finance jets itself. Instead, Toolco said it would do both, but as a result of its delays in arranging financing for the jets, the interest rate rose from 4½ to 4¾ per cent in 1956, when other airlines were placing orders, to 6 to 6½ per cent in 1960 so that TWA was forced to pay the higher cost. The complaint also charged that the defendants reduced the number of jets on order from sixty-three to forty-seven and, in the process, diverted six Boeing jets, which had been ordered for TWA, to Pan American and arranged for General Dynamics to lease to Northeast three Convair 880s, which had been intended for TWA. Due to Hughes' delays, the jets, which TWA finally did get, were delivered too late so that the airline fell badly behind its competitors in putting the new aircraft into service. In short, TWA got too few jets, too late, at too high an interest cost.

In the post-December 1960 category of alleged offenses, the complaint cited a list of instances in which the defendants supposedly violated the right of the new management under the voting trust agreement to run the airline free of interference by or dependence on Hughes or Toolco. The complaint cited the instances of Hughes' attempt to upset the Boeing orders, to annul the $147 million additional financing, and to question the SEC registration certificate. It also mentioned his attempt to compel TWA to purchase the thirteen Convair 990 jets.

As penalties, the TWA complaint asked:

"That defendants divest themselves of all right, title or interest in the stock of the plaintiff,

"That the defendants pay to the plaintiff $105,000,000 threefold damages sustained by plaintiff, together with costs and attorney fees."

An additional $10,000,000 in damages was requested as compensation for Hughes' interference in TWA's business after December, 1960.

Thus, the total figure amounted to $115,000,000.

The very day the seal was torn off the complaint, John Sonnett and Chester Davis squared off for the first time in court. With utmost care and caution, the two lawyers began to stake out their respective positions. At the start of any so-called "big case," many arrangements must be made. Before a "big case" goes to trial, there is a discovery phase, during which both sides take oral testimony of witnesses, called depositions, and collect documentary evidence. At the beginning of the discovery phase, the court must decide which side has the first turn at examining witnesses; subpoenas must be served to the defendants and witnesses so that they are legally bound to testify; and a schedule must be worked out for the depositions and for the collection of documentary evidence.

The issue on August 1 was vitally important to Sonnett's strategy. It was whether Hughes should be called to testify as the first witness in the pretrial depositions. When Sonnett had filed the suit under seal on June 30, he had also obtained a court order that called upon the Hughes' side to show cause, or, in other words, to state its case why the court should not grant TWA's request to summon Hughes as the first witness. Since Hughes was being summoned as Sonnett's witness, he could only be called first if the court decided to depart from the rule that then prevailed in New York's Southern District, that the defendant generally had the first right to call witnesses. That practice is based on the assumption that the defendants should have the opportunity to learn what the case was against them before the plaintiff could proceed to build up the evidence.

Nonetheless, John Sonnett hoped that he could convince the court to make an exception. He wanted the rule altered only in relation to Hughes. After Hughes had completed his testimony, Sonnett was prepared to sit back and allow Davis to complete his list of pretrial depositions before his turn would come again. In reality, it made little difference to Sonnett what happened next in the pretrial discovery. All he wanted was to get Hughes on the stand first. As a sort of psychological warfare, Sonnett even had public notices printed and distributed about the time and place of Hughes' appearance. Howard R. Hughes was to appear at 10:00 A.M. on August 7 at the Beverly Hills Hotel in Los Angeles, one of his old haunts, to be deposed on matters pertaining to the case *TWA v. Hughes.*

In court Sonnett argued that since Hughes was the key figure, who had information that no one else possessed, he should be put on the stand before his testimony might be lost forever. Sonnett conceded that he had no new information about Hughes' health. Nonetheless, he darkly alluded to press reports about Hughes' supposed ailments. In rebuttal, Davis argued that Hughes should be called to testify only after the defense concluded its questioning of witnesses. "TWA," Davis told the court, "is seeking to capitalize on the well-known reluctance of Mr. Hughes to make public appearances." Then he quickly proceeded to erect legal bulwarks around Hughes. Davis knew that Sonnett was trying to force Hughes in two ways to take the stand: by calling him as a witness and by contending that Hughes was the managing agent of the Hughes Tool Company. According to standard legal practices, the managing agent of a corporation named as a defendant in a suit must appear on behalf of the company. Hughes and Holliday had not yet been given subpoenas, but the Hughes Tool Company had been served twice with subpoenas, which had been handed to two of its employees in New York. Davis conceded that the tool company was bound as a defendant in the case, but he disputed Sonnett's contention that Hughes was obliged to appear on behalf of the company. The reason, explained Davis, was that Hughes no longer was the managing agent of the Hughes Tool Company. In December 1960, Davis explained, Mr. Hughes resigned as president and director of the company. "Since that time," he declared, "he has had no connection with Toolco other than by reason of his continued ownership of all its stock." He added: "Even though Mr. Hughes continues to be the sole stockholder of Toolco, he is not, as sole stockholder or otherwise, subject to the control of Toolco."

Judge Thomas F. Murphy, who listened to the argument, said he would rule later about which side would be given the first turn in calling witnesses. Even so, on August 3, Davis gained a tactical advantage by going ahead and issuing his schedule of depositions,

which were to begin on September 6. His first witness was to be
Ben-Fleming Sessel, the senior vice president of the Irving Trust,
who had done more than any banker to force Howard Hughes to
surrender his control of TWA.

Davis' list of witnesses included thirteen others who had played
important roles in the financial crisis of the previous year. They
included Frederic Brandi and Arthur (Ted) Wadsworth of Dillon,
Read, the two men who had been instrumental in formulating the
financing plan that resulted in Hughes' losing control of TWA;
James Oates and Grant Keehn of the Equitable, who had been
adamant about the inclusion of the voting trust clause in TWA's
financing plan; and Harry Hagerty, the vice chairman of the Metropolitan, who had insisted on invoking the voting trust clause before
his company would loan money to TWA. Also on the list were
Tillinghast and Breech. Davis then obtained an order from the
court instructing TWA to show cause either why TWA's previous
notices to depose Hughes and Toolco officers should not be
quashed or, failing that, why TWA's depositions should not be
delayed until Toolco had completed its examination of witnesses.

In reply to that order, Sonnett argued two days later in court
basically the same tactics he had a few days earlier—that Hughes
was the key to the case and therefore his testimony should be
taken as soon as possible. But Judge William B. Herlands, who
had taken over the case from Judge Murphy, was not persuaded
by Sonnett's argument. He ruled: "Defendant has priority in the
taking of depositions under the general rule that, in the absence
of some special and good reason, pretrial examinations should
proceed in the order in which they are demanded."

With that ruling, John Sonnett's hopes vanished for a quick settlement of the case. It now seemed that he would have to wait until Davis, who was unlikely to be in much of a hurry, had finished
with the examination of his fourteen witnesses before he could
finally call Hughes to the stand. Even so, John Sonnett wanted to
be ready for that day when it finally came. Since Davis already had
made it abundantly plain that the Hughes Tool Company was not
prepared to produce its reclusive owner to testify as the managing

agent, Sonnett knew that now he had no choice except to hunt Hughes down and serve him with a subpoena, which would bind him to appear as a witness.

Thus, on August 8 Sonnett started to organize the search for the invisible Mr. Hughes. Sonnett selected one of his young aides to be huntmaster. Fred Furth, now a successful San Francisco lawyer, was then only twenty-seven. Wavy-haired and athletically tall, Furth, who was a steel worker's son from Gary, Indiana, possessed an irrepressible personality. If clothes are, as expensive tailors like to pretend, a measure of the man, Furth wore his individuality for all to see. In the community of Wall Street lawyers who favored gray, conservative suits, Furth sported bright blue double-breasted ones with wide chalk stripes. In his buttonhole he tucked a carnation. As a badge of allegiance to his esteemed chief, Furth affected a homburg—just as Sonnett did. To Furth, Sonnett entrusted an apparent "mission impossible"—to serve a subpoena on Howard Hughes.

On the same day Furth was assigned to conduct the hunt for Hughes, Chester Davis made a motion to the court that aimed at making the hunt and everything else totally unnecessary. Davis moved that the court dismiss the complaint for the reason that it failed to state a case against the Hughes Tool Company. In reply to TWA's complaint of antitrust violations, Davis stated that (a) they didn't happen and (b) even if they did, it wouldn't make any difference because the CAB's approval of Hughes' control of TWA and all transactions between Hughes and TWA had immunized Hughes from the jurisdiction of the antitrust laws. In fact, argued Davis, the case did not belong in federal court at all. If it belonged anywhere, it belonged to the Civil Aeronautics Board. In a long brief, Davis cited the CAB approval of Hughes' control of TWA and the passages in the Federal Aviation Act that exempts those approved to control airlines from the operations of the antitrust laws.

Since all of Hughes' dealings prior to December 1960 had been cleared by the CAB as being "in the public interest" for running TWA, Davis argued that Sonnett's complaint had no merit whatsoever. As for the second category of alleged violations, which concerned supposedly willful interference in TWA's business since December 1960, Davis declared that Toolco had done nothing more than to call "to the attention of TWA and those now in charge of TWA, matters which it believes might adversely affect TWA and Toolco's interest in TWA."

Davis buttressed his argument by submitting to the court an affidavit from Raymond Holliday whose testimony directly refuted the essential antitrust contention in the complaint—that since 1939 the Hughes Tool Company had been engaged in the manufacture, supply, and leasing of aircraft. "Toolco is primarily engaged in the manufacture of equipment for the oil well drilling industry," wrote Holliday. "Toolco has at no time been in the business of selling or leasing any flight equipment to any airline and the only occasion on which it has made equipment available to any airline other than TWA has been when certain equipment ordered by Toolco for use by TWA has proven to be in excess of the needs or capabilities of TWA."

If all of Holliday's statements were true, what were the grounds for proceeding with TWA's case? Sonnett quickly sought to counter Davis' dismissal motion by submitting a brief to the court in which he challenged Davis' defense that the CAB's approval protected Hughes and his tool company entirely from the workings of the antitrust laws. "The complaint of TWA attempts in no way to interfere with the regulatory authority of the CAB," wrote Sonnett, who was now fighting for the survival of his lawsuit. "TWA is complaining not of what was done or approved by the CAB, but, on the contrary, TWA is complaining of the concerted plan and purpose of defendants, which has been and is being effectuated, to injure TWA in clear violation of the provisions of the antitrust laws.

"It is clear that what the CAB did approve," Sonnett went on, "were specific acquisitions of equipment and other transactions submitted to it, which appeared to further the interests of TWA, on the basis of circumstances known to it, and nothing more.

"What the CAB did not approve and what was presented to the

CAB are the matters alleged in the complaint," declared Sonnett. Playing back the language of the Federal Aviation Act at Davis, Sonnett stated that "the CAB has never required, approved or authorized any combination and conspiracy by the defendants to monopolize the supplying of aircraft in a substantial segment of the interstate and foreign commerce of the United States . . . Nor has the CAB required, approved or authorized any combination to restrain commerce by requiring TWA to boycott all suppliers of aircraft except Toolco." In the same vein, Sonnett went on for sixteen additional paragraphs, citing the alleged violations of antitrust law that the CAB had not approved.

Even as Sonnett and Davis expounded their positions, their respective legal staffs were bombarding the U. S. District Court for the Southern District of New York with a barrage of petitions, subpoena requests, and other papers necessary for starting up a case as complex and large as *TWA v. Hughes*. Already no fewer than six district judges had been engaged in the case. At TWA's request, Judge Sylvester J. Ryan, the chief judge in the Southern District, appointed one judge to handle all aspects of the case. The choice fell upon Charles Miller Metzner, then forty-nine, a former Wall Street lawyer who had been appointed to the federal bench two years earlier. Among Metzner's first duties was to rule on Davis' motion to dismiss the complaint. Without commenting one way or the other on the validity of Davis' argument, Judge Metzner suggested that the Hughes side should withhold its dismissal motion until later. He explained that the U. S. Court of Appeals for the Second Circuit, of which the Southern District is a part, looked with disfavor upon dismissals of complaints before the completion of the discovery proceedings. Because of Judge Metzner's remarks, Davis did not press the motion for dismissal.

Thus there was to be no quick and easy end to the Hughes case. Davis had not won the immediate dismissal he hoped for. But he had won something else—time in which to prepare a defense. As Davis and his colleagues formulated that defense, the CAB began to loom as an increasingly important factor in their thinking. Even if the case remained in the federal courts, it would be very helpful to have the CAB support for the Hughes position, especially in regard to his claim of immunity from antitrust prosecution. And if the District Court should happen to decide that primary jurisdiction in the case rested with the regulatory agency, as the Hughes lawyers believed it did, the good will of the CAB would be a decisive factor.

But the trouble was that Hughes' relations with the CAB at that time were very, very bad indeed. As a result of TWA's long financial crisis, the CAB, and especially the CAB's young and sometimes impulsive staff lawyers, had become thoroughly disenchanted with him. The December 29, 1960, CAB order (that approved TWA's financing plan and the voting trust arrangement) had made extremely critical and damaging remarks about Hughes. In fact, the order had served as one of the cornerstones of the lawsuit against Hughes.

Even so, Hughes now urgently needed influence and sympathy in Washington. The eventual outcome of his great legal battle could well hinge on the attitude of the CAB. As August of 1961 drew to an end, Hughes and his advisers were pondering the ways and means by which they could gain some leverage in Washington.

7. The Washington Maneuver

During the summer and early fall of 1961, whenever the President of the United States spent a weekend at his family's compound in Hyannis Port, a little single-engine plane plied the skies above the small Massachusetts resort town. It towed a banner: JFK PLEASE HELP NEA. NEA stood for Northeast Airlines. The pilots and employees of Northeast wanted to call to the attention of the young man from Massachusetts the fact that unless it quickly received aid, New England's only major airline faced economic collapse. Despite his concern about Northeast, there was little at the time that even John F. Kennedy could do. By 1961 all of the nation's major airlines except Northeast had been off federal subsidy for at least eight years, and even Northeast had been operating without government aid since 1959. It would have made no economic sense for Kennedy to have granted federal assistance to Northeast, because if he made an exception in its case, several other major airlines, notably Eastern and TWA, which were both experiencing heavy losses, would have demanded equal treatment.

No matter how insistently the little plane droned above Hyannis Port or how urgently New England politicians pleaded for help for Northeast, Kennedy remained unmoved. Even so, he could not entirely ignore the fact that the demise of Northeast would have severe consequences. If Northeast collapsed, some two thousand employees in the Boston area alone would be thrown out of work. In towns and cities along the airline's routes in New England and the East Coast, hundreds of other employees would lose their jobs. Throughout New England, Northeast's death also would mean a serious inconvenience for the public. Because of the decrepit state of New England's railroads, a number of towns no longer had passenger rail service. Now some of these communities would also lose their air link to the outside.

There was an additional consequence that would reach far beyond the confines of New England. If Northeast went under, it would be the first time in the history of the United States aviation industry that a major airline had gone bankrupt. In the past the federal government had always exercised its stewardship of the airlines to ensure that they did not suffer a financial collapse. In fact, only a few months earlier, the CAB had saved failing Capital Airlines from bankruptcy by arranging for its merger into larger and stronger United Air Lines. Washington's failure to help Northeast would be regarded by the financial community as a signal that the federal government no longer was committed to its old policy of preventing bankruptcy among the major airlines. Thus, at the very moment when airlines were desperately in need of more funds to finance the next round of jet purchases, they would lose their standing as safe investments. If that happened, the airlines would find it not only harder than ever to raise money but, as a reflection of the risky nature of the investment, they also would be forced to pay higher interest rates.

It was obvious that whoever found a way to keep Northeast flying would earn the gratitude of many New Englanders, including the slim young man who vacationed at Hyannis Port and his powerful brothers. It was equally clear that whoever rescued Northeast would also earn the thanks of the Civil Aeronautics Board, which was gravely concerned about what to do for—or with —that struggling airline. Northeast's death would be taken as evidence that the CAB had failed in its duty as the protector of the nation's airline industry. That failure in turn would put a serious dent in the promising career of the Board's young chairman, Alan S. Boyd, then thirty-nine. Boyd, a Democrat from Florida, who enjoyed the backing of Senator George Smathers, generally was regarded to be in line for higher positions within the Kennedy administration, provided, of course, that the CAB suffered no disasters under his direction.

In the dilemma surrounding Northeast, Howard Hughes sensed a chance to outmaneuver his adversaries. How he must have relished the situation! As in battle for TWA, he once again faced the high and mighty captains of Wall Street—this time in the corporate persons of Manufacturers Hanover Trust Company and the Chase Manhattan Bank, which had made big loans to Northeast. Other powerful figures on Wall Street had refused to do business with him and had called him whimsical and unreliable. Well, he would see how these financial institutions behaved toward him now. If Northeast went bankrupt, its financial condition was so bad that its creditors stood to collect only four cents on each dollar of debts. By the same token, the Civil Aeronautics Board, which had written those unkind words about his ownership of TWA only ten months ago, was unlikely to be so self-righteous this time. It simply could not afford to be, unless it wanted to see Northeast fail.

As he fully realized, Hughes was in an almost perfect position to rescue Northeast if he chose to. Thanks to the Dillon, Read plan, Hughes, who had been out of money in 1960, once again was literally rolling in funds and was looking for somewhere to put them. In addition to the ready cash, Hughes had leverage within the Atlas Corporation, which was the parent company that controlled Northeast. He had come into his present position of strength quite against his own will. Hughes' involvement in Atlas, which dated back to 1955, had been entirely involuntary. Like Hughes' mind, which a friend once described as consisting of an endless web of intertwined ganglia, his business deals were often wondrously complex. Though his goals were often straightforward, the mechanics of his transactions tended to be complicated and filled with plots, subplots, and counterplots that represented the different angles that Hughes simultaneously was trying to play.

This was one of the few instances in which Hughes was outwitted. He was trapped into the Northeast situation by Floyd

Odlum, a clever industrialist and financier who was boss of the Atlas Corporation, which in those years ran construction companies and uranium mines. It also owned Convair, which it later sold to General Dynamics. In addition, Atlas controlled Northeast, which was its least attractive property. Poor Northeast behaved about as well as could be expected for an airline that had two railroads as its parents. Founded in the early 1930s as a regional airline by the Boston & Maine Railroad and the Maine Central Railroad, Northeast had established the unenviable record of never once having made an operating profit in any year. In fact, Northeast's only distinction remained that its original New England routes had been charted by Amelia Earhart, the famed American woman flier. In a burst of speculative optimism, Atlas in the 1950s had bought into Northeast in the hope that the airline could win a route down the East Coast and that, as a result, its stock would climb. Whereupon Atlas could sell out at a big profit. At least, that was the plan. Northeast was still only a loser when Odlum maneuvered Hughes into Atlas. It came about in this way: In the mid-1950s, when Hughes was feuding with the minority shareholders at RKO, a group of them sued him for damaging RKO and wasting its corporate assets. Among other things, Hughes was criticized for hiring "student actresses" at $500 a week and then not making use of their talents in RKO films. He was charged with signing stars such as Merle Oberon, Ann Sheridan, and Gina Lollobrigida to contracts and then failing to provide them with roles in movies.

Hughes was outraged. His attitude was, "Well, if you aren't satisfied, I'll buy you out." And that was what he proceeded to do. He offered $5.00 per RKO share, twice the market price. In order to finance his grand gesture, Hughes personally borrowed $11 million from the Irving Trust Company. As security for the note, he pledged his stock in the Hughes Tool Company. (It was this pledge that later gave Sessel of the Irving Trust such great leverage over Hughes in the financial showdown in 1960.)

Unbeknown to Hughes, while he was buying up RKO shares, so, too, was Odlum, who ended up owning a large amount of stock.

To Hughes' dismay, Odlum then refused to sell out. Hughes had succeeded in buying out the troublesome minority shareholders, but he ended up with an unwanted junior partner. And having partners, of course, was anathema to Hughes. By this time, he wanted to get out of movie-making entirely, even though it meant leaving uncompleted his intended new epic *Jet Pilot,* which was to be a modern version of *Hell's Angels.* He still had not shot the beginning and the end, and those combat sequences, which he had filmed, now were out of date because the aircraft in them were obsolete. Hughes decided to dissolve RKO. He sold off RKO's theater chain to the General Tire and Rubber Company. But then he had to figure out some way to pay off Odlum, who still hung on to his RKO stock. They made a deal whereby Hughes merged RKO's corporate shell, which had more than $6 million in cash in the till, into Atlas. In return Hughes received 11 per cent of Atlas' stock. Atlas, in turn, owned 55 per cent of Northeast. In that way, Hughes became a factor in the control of the airline. Since it is against public policy for one person to participate in the control of two airlines, the CAB stepped in. Jack Rosenthal, the CAB lawyer, compelled him to place his Atlas stock in a trust over which Hughes had no control. The stock was automatically to be voted in the support of the management, and Hughes agreed to dispose of his entire Atlas holdings no later than June 28, 1961.

True to Odlum's speculative design, the airline in 1956 did win a route from Boston and New York to Florida. Even so, Atlas was unable to sell out at a big gain, because the stock did not rise. The reason was that the CAB had granted Northeast only a temporary five-year certificate to fly the East Coast, and the airline's future was still uncertain. Even so, Hughes became mildly interested in Northeast because he wanted to use its north–south route to off-set the seasonal traffic imbalance in TWA's routes, which ran mainly east–west. Meanwhile, though Northeast in the late 1950s had quintupled in size, its financial condition became steadily worse. Because it had only a temporary certificate, it could not raise long-term financing to buy a large fleet of modern aircraft. It had to fly old-fashioned DC-6s in competition against the Electras of National and Eastern, the two established airlines along the East Coast. Then, as National and Eastern prepared to put jets into service, Northeast faced certain ruin, because it could not raise the money to buy jets itself and would be hopelessly outclassed.

In desperation for jetliners, Atlas turned to Hughes for help. He arranged for General Dynamics to lease to Northeast four Convair 880s that originally had been ordered for TWA. By this time, however, Northeast's financial condition was so weak that it lacked the funds even to pay rent for the jets, much less train the crews, stock spare parts, and meet the other expenses of starting up jet operations. Atlas was no help, for in an attempt to support Northeast it had already exhausted its resources. Floyd Odlum had no choice but to ask Hughes for another favor—a loan. Odlum had a compelling argument—if Hughes wanted someday to merge TWA and Northeast, he had better see to it that Northeast survived the present crisis. By now it was the late spring of 1960, and Hughes was already heavily burdened by his jet purchases for TWA. Nevertheless, he managed to line up $9.5 million in credit at the Bank of America and Irving Trust by pledging some of his own TWA stock as a collateral. Hughes granted the loan on one condition: that Northeast immediately present a merger proposal to TWA. The terms of the deal were that TWA would absorb Northeast by giving Northeast's shareholders three shares of TWA stock for every one share that they held in Northeast. The exchange ratio represented the one really amazing and logic-defying aspect of Northeast's situation: though Northeast was continually in financial difficulties, its shares sold in the $30 range while TWA's shares were then trading at only around $10. The main reason Northeast's shares floated at such a relatively high level was that Atlas held a big block of stock. If Atlas had made a move to sell, the per-share price would undoubtedly have collapsed overnight.

The merger negotiations were conducted in secret between Northeast and Hughes' personal lawyers. TWA's president, Charlie Thomas, did not even learn about Hughes' merger plans until shortly before Northeast made public its proposal. Thomas was so outraged at being by-passed in the negotiations that he purposely held up TWA's action on the Northeast offer while his own staff took its sweet time in studying the proposal. After Hughes lost control of TWA at the close of 1960, the Breech-Tillinghast management also considered the Northeast offer and decided against it. (However, as a purely tactical maneuver, the new management in June 1961 did take a position before the CAB in the East Coast route renewal hearings that Northeast should be awarded the run on a permanent basis—but only as part of a merger with TWA.)

Meanwhile, National and Eastern were eager to see Northeast disappear from the route. They claimed that while the two lines had previously made a profit on the run, the addition of a third carrier had meant losses for everyone. In order to block Hughes from continuing to support Northeast, National on June 8, 1960, charged in a complaint to the CAB that Hughes had illegally acquired what amounted to effective control of the airline through supplying loans to Northeast.

The Civil Aeronautics Board duly scheduled an investigation of Hughes' activities at Northeast, but it hardly needed to bother. As soon as National questioned the legality of his actions, Hughes at once ceased financial aid to Northeast. Hughes did, however, go through with his promise to help make available 880s to Northeast. By a supreme effort, Northeast began to place the first of the sleek and beautiful 880s into service well before the start of the 1961–62 winter season.

But even the first cost of starting up the jet operations proved to be too great for Northeast. By the time that small plane began to ply the sky above the Kennedy compound in Hyannis Port, Northeast could no longer pay its bills. In fact, by mid-August of 1961 it was running out of cash so quickly that in another month it no longer would be able to meet its payroll. Northeast's balance sheet was a nightmare: the company's liabilities exceeded its assets by more than $10 million. One after another, Northeast tried to interest Delta, Continental, Braniff, American, and Pan American in a merger. None of them wanted such an unattractive bride. No wonder. At that time, the airline owed $4.5 million in accounts due, including large unpaid bills from its food suppliers, fuel companies, and advertising agency.

In late August and early September the airline's creditors began to grow very restless. Northeast's insurance underwriters warned that they would cancel the airline's aircraft and accident liability coverage unless a $530,000 premium was paid by September 15. Under extreme pressure from the Kennedy brothers, the airline's secured creditors, who held mortgages on the airframes and engines, had earlier agreed to forego payments on both principal and interest to avoid forcing Northeast into bankruptcy. But now, despite continuing behind-the-scene pressure from the Kennedys, the secured creditors threatened to foreclose on Northeast's aircraft within thirty days unless the overdue accounts were settled.

Against that backdrop of looming financial disaster, David Stretch, the chairman of Atlas, once again appealed to Hughes for help. In response, Hughes on September 8 agreed to come to Northeast's rescue, but only on the condition that the CAB would give assurances that he would be accorded a proper welcome. Hughes did not want to extend help to Northeast and then be accused of illegally gaining control of the airline. On September 12 representatives of Atlas, Northeast, and Toolco appeared before the Civil Aeronautics Board in a secret executive session in the CAB headquarters at 1825 Connecticut Avenue in Washington. Chester Davis was accompanied by Raymond Cook, whom Hughes had rehired after firing him the year before. The purpose of the meeting was to try to extract a prior commitment from the board about how it would react to a bid by Hughes to take over control of Northeast.

The behavior of Hughes' lawyers made it clear that Hughes realized, as one board member later put it, that "he had the CAB over a barrel." In no uncertain terms, Davis and Cook wanted to make sure that the CAB would give Hughes preferential treatment. They especially wanted the CAB's pledge that Hughes would not be called to testify personally in the investigation that the board was legally bound to conduct before it could approve his application to take control of Northeast. "There would have to be a hearing of some sort," Raymond Cook told the board. "On the other hand, there are hearings and there are hearings. If there can be some informal or special ways that the board can express itself without the necessity for elaborate hearings, then perhaps that is the way to approach it."

Characteristically, Chester Davis was more blunt. "Let me be very frank and bring out one other thing," he said. "I know as a fact from past experience, assuming it were a proceeding where a lot of intervenors would be allowed, those who desired to achieve a particular result have always exclaimed, 'We must examine Mr. Hughes personally!' and try to take advantage of the well-known fact that he is most reluctant to make personal appearances. If we are going to get involved in a hearing where that is likely to develop, I think that the conclusion that we would reach is that we are just wasting our time."

Chester Davis also made it plain that Hughes was not interested in helping Northeast unless the CAB was very interested in helping him. As CAB Chairman Boyd and the other board members listened in almost unbelieving silence, Davis spelled out the Hughes master plan. Each step logically followed the other, and if the CAB let Hughes take the first one, it would be obliged to allow him to take the others too. Step one: assume control of Northeast, saving it from bankruptcy. Step two: buy out the loans on which the voting trust rested and regain control of TWA. Step three: merge TWA and Northeast.

Davis' explanation of the master plan remained secret, and at the outset of the Hughes maneuver in Washington few outsiders could have guessed at the underlying significance of what some people disparagingly referred to as "Hughes' CAB caper." To the uninformed, it seemed odd that Hughes would invest millions in an airline that was on the verge of bankruptcy. But a millionaire's considerations are not those of the ordinary businessman. To Hughes, Northeast represented a risk of fifteen or twenty million dollars. But he was gambling for an airline empire worth hundreds of millions.

Exactly how the Hughes side regarded the Northeast episode is clearly revealed in a memo that Raymond Cook dictated to Hughes' communications center shortly after he had talked about Northeast with William Forrester of Merrill Lynch. Cook wrote to Hughes that, in Forrester's opinion, "You can probably do better to pick up the airline in a Chapter 10 bankruptcy. . . . Forrester would even say that in the Florida Route Case, Northeast would be stronger under Chapter 10 bankruptcy than under Hughes control. Nevertheless, we are quite aware that you do have other important objectives, which we are not free to discuss with Forrester, such as the following:

"(a) Exploiting the CAB proceedings to restore public favor to you and to the Tool Company. To some extent this is already being achieved,

"(b) Avoiding the possible adverse publicity of a Northeast law suit against the Tool Company in the event of a Chapter 10 receivership,

"(c) Protecting the favorable possibility of employing a Northeast package as a frankly inflated piece of contribution with which to effectuate a TWA settlement,

"(d) The matter of finding a home for six 880s,

"(e) Protecting or restoring value to the Tool Company's $9½ million investment in Northeast."

The Civil Aeronautics Board did not know about Cook's memo. The board was fully aware, however, that Hughes was trying to use the gravity of Northeast's plight as leverage for preferential treatment, and it refused to submit to his pressure. On September 13, the day after the executive session in Washington, the CAB announced its decision. If Howard Hughes wanted to gain control of Northeast, he would have to file a regular application and go through the standard procedure of CAB hearings. The announcement meant that there would be no advance indication of the CAB's attitude toward his application, no shortcut in the bureaucratic procedure. So what did Hughes do? He did nothing. He was confident that Northeast was the hostage of his grand plan and that sooner or later the CAB would have to pay the ransom. The weaker Northeast became, the stronger was Hughes' position.

Despite their repeated threats, Northeast's creditors had not yet forced the airline into bankruptcy. But on October 13, 1961, the Shell Oil Company, which supplied fuel and oil for Northeast's planes, served a final ultimatum. Unless Northeast provided a guarantee to pay its long-overdue fuel bill, which amounted to about $500,000, Shell would cease to supply fuel to Northeast's planes. Northeast managed to stall Shell for a few more days, but on October 20 Shell finally said, "No money, no fuel." Once more Stretch appealed to Hughes for aid. Once more Hughes agreed to help, but only on the condition that the CAB would not penalize him for coming to Northeast's rescue. At Hughes' direction, the tool company informed Shell that it would guarantee the payment of Northeast's fuel payments. On October 31 Northeast and the Hughes Tool Company submitted a joint request to the CAB for immediate board action to enable the airline to receive additional funds from Toolco.

By now, it seemed almost a foregone conclusion that the board would be compelled to allow Hughes to slip into control of Northeast along with the fuel bill. But on November 8 the board handed down an unusual order. Instead of granting an emergency go-ahead to Hughes, the board declared that Hughes had "probably" acquired control of Northeast through his previous loan to underwrite the airline's operations. Any further cash advances by Hughes to Northeast, said the board, would only increase his degree of control. The board's decision did not mention the possibility that Hughes would be punished for having illegally taken over Northeast. But it was a clear warning that the board might decide to hold him in violation not only on the Federal Aviation Act but also on its specific order that barred him from regaining control of an airline without prior CAB approval. Again, Hughes quickly retreated.

As a result, on November 10 the tool company informed Shell that it no longer could stand behind Northeast's fuel bill. In response, Shell ordered Northeast to pay for all fuel deliveries in cash; the fuel-truck driver would collect the cash at planeside before he would tank up the aircraft. But Northeast, whose employees

were a scrambling, determined lot, kept flying. Sometimes Northeast got the money together directly from the cash drawers of the
airport ticket offices; on some occasions the money that paid for
a plane's fuel had come in only minutes earlier when the passengers bought their tickets. It was, however, only a matter of days
—and very few days at that—before Northeast would run completely
out of funds. There was also the ever-increasing danger that one
or more of Northeast's impatient creditors would demand payment on long-overdue bills and force the airline into bankruptcy.

Northeast was on the verge of panic. On November 14 the airline sent another urgent petition to the CAB, asking for a ruling
that would allow Hughes to provide emergency financial aid. By
now, Northeast's plight had become so grave that the board no
longer could fend off Hughes with vague warnings. It had to face
the unpleasant reality that without his aid Northeast would collapse. Faced with the Northeast emergency, the CAB scheduled a
one-day hearing for November 28. Other airlines were invited to
submit briefs and to be prepared to testify on that day.

The procedure was extremely unusual. Normally, CAB hearings
on such a serious subject as the control of an airline would run
for weeks and would be preceded by more weeks of advance warning. Hughes had waited long enough to get what he wanted: preferential treatment. The top executives of other airlines were
disturbed that Hughes was getting away with something. They felt
that if the CAB had declared that any other person had taken control—if only "probably"—of an airline in defiance of the aviation
law and specific board orders, that person undoubtedly would have
been subject to swift discipline. The briefs submitted for the one-
day hearings by the opposing airlines reflected this concern. Wrote
Eastern Airlines' lawyers: "Surely the time has come for the Board
to write 'finis' to the machinations of Howard R. Hughes and his
alter ego, the Hughes Tool Company. Having driven one airline,
with potentially the most lucrative routes in the industry so near to
the brink of destruction that its supporting financial institutions
were compelled to blow the whistle, it is only reasonable to assume
that the next Hughes/Tool victim would speedily be pushed over

the precipice of economic ruin." Added the Eastern brief: "Neither Hughes nor any other man in this country should be beyond the law." In less dramatic language, National Airlines expressed much the same sentiment.

As all parties prepared their arguments for the one-day hearing, the question of Hughes' stewardship at TWA inevitably became entangled in the CAB proceedings. The lawsuit had been underway in New York for the past two and a half months. Rather than avoid a discussion of *TWA v. Hughes* in the Northeast proceedings, the Hughes side welcomed the opportunity to answer the charges. A few days after the filing of Eastern and National briefs, the Toolco forces entered an angry reply that defended the Hughes' actions at TWA. In a pair of lengthy companion briefs, two of Hughes' chief aides—Raymond Cook and Raymond Holliday, who were known to friends and foes alike as "the two Raymonds"— launched the counterattack. Cook's brief, which dealt with the circumstances leading up to the suit, asserted that if anyone had been damaged at TWA, it was Howard Hughes. According to Cook, Hughes was the victim of a vast plot in which the banks and insurance companies had conspired to rob him of his control of TWA. In great detail, Cook, who, of course, had conducted most of the negotiations himself, told how the banks and insurance companies maneuvered Hughes into a position in which he could not get the loans to pay for TWA's jet fleet unless he surrendered control of the airline.

Holliday, who dealt with events after the filing of the TWA lawsuit, charged that the lender-appointed TWA management and the financial institutions were colluding to perpetuate their dominance over the airline while at the same time turning TWA from a money-making property into one that was in the process of recording the largest loss in the history of the airline industry.

As the Civil Aeronautics Board prepared to hear what was called in bureaucratese "The Northeast-Toolco Possible Control Case," that agency was of two minds about Hughes. The two minds belonged to the two distinct divisions within the CAB: the board and the staff. The five board members, especially the three Democrats, were more or less friendly disposed toward Hughes. Of course, it greatly served the board's purpose if it could wrestle down any misgivings about Hughes, since he alone could save the CAB from the fearful repercussions of Northeast's collapse. In addition, several of the board members, who were deeply suspicious of Big Business, felt that Hughes had been victimized by the banks and insurance companies in the TWA affair. After reviewing the events leading up to the lawsuit, one of the board members said privately: "I was appalled at the utter ruthlessness of Wall Street."

Davis and Cook had private, off-the-record sessions with the Democrats on the board. Hughes' lawyers sought—obviously with some success—to defend Hughes' actions at TWA. Some of the board members were, in fact, no longer convinced that Hughes had done all that badly at TWA; TWA's poor financial performance under the new management helped change their minds. TWA had, after all, usually made money under Hughes' control. Now it was going broke at such a rate that already it was looming as a major problem for the CAB. Though Hughes had definite tactical motives for wanting control of Northeast, the majority of the board were blandly prepared to regard him, as one of them put it, as "a romantic old aviation pioneer, who sought to retain a connection with the industry."

The staff members of the CAB, however, were far less generous. While the board makes the final decision, the staff has great influence, for it conducts the investigation and represents the public interest in the cases before the CAB. The staff is composed of civil servants, many of them gifted young lawyers, who use the CAB as a steppingstone into private practice in Washington. A number of staff members, especially those in the Bureau of Economic Regulation, which appears at board hearings as the advocate for the public interest, were wary of Hughes. Some of the most influential staff members shared John Sonnett's suspicion that in the past Hughes had manipulated airlines for his own selfish gain.

Hughes' tactics in the Northeast case only strengthened such suspicions. Though the one-day hearing was scheduled only on the narrow issue of whether Hughes should be allowed to grant interim aid to Northeast, Chester Davis continued to insist that the tool company should not be expected to help Northeast unless the board members indicated that they would subsequently support Hughes' master plan. Furthermore, despite the staff's request for a thorough documentation of Hughes' intentions toward Northeast, Davis refused to submit any such papers. In fact, Davis refused pointblank to commit Toolco to any specific course of action. When questioned about what Hughes would do if the CAB allowed him to help Northeast, Davis would only respond with a standard answer: "Toolco will aid Northeast consistent with the dictates of good business judgment." What did that mean? Did it mean that one day good business judgment would dictate that Northeast should be folded and its losses written off against the Hughes Tool Company's earnings? Or did it mean that Northeast was such sound business for Hughes as a leverage on Washington that he would keep it alive as long as he got his way at the CAB?

As scheduled, the one-day public hearing took place on November 28 before Examiner Merritt Ruhlen in the CAB headquarters in Washington. In preparation for that hearing, Eastern Airlines had assigned private investigators, including a female private eye, to try to track down Hughes, whom the airline wanted to have present for questioning. The woman detective thought she caught a glimpse of his long lanky figure as he slipped from a beat-up Chevy into the Hughes "nerve center" on Romaine Street in North Hollywood, but that was as close as she got. Eastern wanted to force Hughes to testify in the case. But the board obviously did not want to provoke Hughes' displeasure for fear he would withdraw his offer to help Northeast. Despite its efforts, Eastern could not persuade one single board member to sign the subpoena demanding his appearance. In his absence, lawyers for Eastern and National objected that the CAB was altering its procedures to suit the private whims of Howard Hughes. They also raised the old objection that three airlines were one too many on the East Coast route. Northeast, they argued, should be reduced to its original role of a regional carrier in New England.

The Hughes attorneys did not need to say much, because the lawyers for Atlas and Northeast did the talking for them. They pleaded that Northeast desperately needed immediate help to keep flying until southbound winter vacation travelers would start filling up the empty seats. The airline's lawyers recited an appalling litany of facts and figures that documented Northeast's dismal financial situation: the company owed $19,960,000 in current liabilities; it was virtually out of cash; and it was heading toward a $6 million or more loss for the year. Atlas' lawyers explained that the parent company could no longer aid Northeast. Toolco was the only source of help. But, as the Northeast lawyers explained, Hughes required assurances from the CAB that it would not penalize or punish him for supplying assistance to Northeast before he gained the board's formal approval to control the line.

What was the board to do? Should it reverse its policy and grant a subsidy to Northeast? What would that entail? Other airlines would seize upon the precedent to ask for federal help. Overnight the CAB would be besieged with requests for perhaps $60 million to $80 million in subsidy requests to bail out TWA and Eastern. There was also the question of Northeast creditors. If the CAB assumed the financial responsibility for Northeast, the creditors would capitalize on the government's support to demand that Washington pay the airline's long-overdue debts. But the CAB also realized what would happen if it gave even the slightest indication that it was not going to keep Northeast alive. In that event, the airline's creditors would start a stampede for the payment of their bills that would throw Northeast into receivership.

With those considerations in mind, the CAB ended its one-day hearing on Northeast, which had been held on a Tuesday. For the rest of the week the CAB deliberated. Over the weekend the members made up their minds. On Monday, December 4, the board in a brief press release stated that it had "tentatively voted" to permit Northeast to receive interim emergency aid from Hughes Tool Company. Four days later the board, which during Boyd's chairmanship was distinguished for its candor if not for its syntactical brilliance, explained its reasoning in a full order. "In a nutshell," it declared, "we find that Northeast is in such a critical financial condition that it is in need of emergency financial assistance; that without such assistance, it is very likely that the carrier will be forced into bankruptcy; and that such a financial collapse will have serious adverse effects on the public interest . . . We are unable to find any sound reason for withholding from Northeast the opportunity for obtaining emergency assistance from Toolco. Whether Toolco will, in fact, advance the needed funds is not clear on the record before us. All we decide is that the advancement of such funds, pending ultimate disposition of a Section 408 [control application] proceeding, is not adverse to the public interest and meets the approval of the Board."

Howard Hughes had triumphed. To be sure, the board's order did not guarantee future approval of his plan to take over Northeast. Nonetheless, it would be virtually impossible for the CAB later to deny him the right to control the airline he had saved from bankruptcy. Besides, for the foreseeable future, Northeast would undoubtedly remain so weak that without his help it would not be able to survive. The CAB reckoned that Northeast, simply to stay in business, would require at least $7.7 million during the next year. Thus, for all practical purposes, the board's "nutshell" opinion meant the CAB would later be compelled to grant Hughes full control of Northeast. And when it did, the CAB's approval would imply that he was a fit person to run an airline. That endorsement would, in effect, cancel out the harsh words that the CAB had directed at him only a year earlier and that formed part of the basis for the lawsuit against him. Less than one year after he was unceremoniously forced out of control of TWA, Howard Hughes had managed to return to the airline business. The crucial first phase of his master plan to regain control of TWA was succeeding brilliantly. Now he needed to find ways of bringing to bear his newly won power in Washington on his legal problems in New York.

8. A Finely Balanced Conflict

*The entire affair is being played out in five acts
and three scenes in front of the CAB.*

—Howard Hughes
December 14, 1961

Actually, Howard Hughes was understating the scope of the "entire affair." It was indeed being acted out in five acts and three scenes in front of the CAB, but it was simultaneously being played out on other stages, too. Since one set of developments often had immediate effects on what was happening on the other stages, the conflict turned into an extremely complex interacting struggle. "In the well-ordered and codified world of modern large-scale business," commented *Fortune,* "Hughes is a distracting legend, and the TWA conflict a Greek spectacular with a chorus of fifty lawyers from ten law firms with a million and a half documents chanting versions of its mysteries while the central character himself remains invisible." Even as Howard Hughes was establishing a position in Washington that ultimately could help him turn the tide of battle, other developments were underway in New York that threatened to place the airline forever beyond his grasp.

On December 4, the very day Hughes won formal CAB approval to aid Northeast, a secret meeting was being held in Ernie Breech's apartment in the Ritz Tower on Manhattan's Park Avenue that could frustrate the comeback plans of Howard Hughes. In addition to Breech, TWA was also represented by Tillinghast. The two other participants were from Eastern Airlines: Captain "Eddie" Rickenbacker, the airline's chairman, who had directed Eastern's destiny since the 1930s, and Malcolm MacIntyre, a former Under Secretary of the Air Force, who was Eastern's president. The roots of the meeting reached far back into the history of American aviation. Nearly three decades earlier, when both airlines had been controlled by General Motors, Rickenbacker, who was then Eastern's general manager, had wanted to merge Eastern and TWA, which at that time had been under Breech's supervision. After Breech in December 1960 once again had been put in charge of TWA, Rickenbacker had rung him up and reminded him of the earlier merger plan. Breech and Rickenbacker had had further conversations, which led to the Ritz Tower meeting. The purpose of the get-together was to discover whether the two airlines could find ways and the will to merge into one single system, which would have become by far the nation's largest airline with some $800 million in annual revenues. For Howard Hughes, a merger of the magnitude of Eastern-TWA represented a threat to his plans. Since Eastern was roughly the same size as TWA, the merger would have diluted his stock ownership so that he could not have hoped to exercise the tight control over the merged airline that he once held over TWA.

Hughes could be expected to oppose any merger that would weaken his control of TWA. He had caused Northeast in mid-1960 to submit a merger proposal to TWA, but that was a merger of a different sort. Since Hughes owned an interest in Atlas, which controlled Northeast, and since Northeast was a relatively small airline, with annual revenues of only about $35 million, its merger into TWA would have enhanced, rather than threatened, Hughes' dominant position. But, in a sense, Hughes could only blame himself for having gotten TWA interested in merger possibilities. When Tillinghast took over as president in early 1961, TWA already had conducted studies about the desirability of a merger with Northeast. In general, TWA executives had favored the proposal. Breech, Tillinghast, and TWA's new directors, however, demanded a re-examination of the proposal. They were put off, above all, by the financial terms of Northeast's offer, which called for swapping three shares of TWA for each Northeast share.

In the first months of his presidency, Tillinghast, who did not want to be limited to only the Northeast proposal, ordered a full-scale review of merger possibilities for TWA. The studies were carried out under the direction of Thomas F. Huntington, a former executive at the management consulting firm of Cresap, McCormick & Paget. Merger kits were prepared that consisted of transparencies of routes of other airlines. By placing the transparencies on a TWA route map, TWA executives could get an idea of which other airlines or combinations of other airlines would best complement TWA's system. For several weeks TWA executives spent a great deal of time working with their merger kits and examining figures from other airlines on aircraft utilization, number of passengers carried, and related statistics.

At this time—it was the late spring of 1961—similar studies were in progress throughout the airline industry. The advent of the jets, which represented a radical technological improvement, had brought the need for correspondingly drastic changes in the organization and management of the nation's airlines. The airlines were still organized to deal with planes that flew only half as fast and carried only a third to a half as many passengers as the new jets. The need for change was heightened by economic problems. At the time of the introduction of the jets, the American economy was in the recession of the last years of the Eisenhower administration. In the early 1960s the economy was beginning to recover, but the growth of airline travel nonetheless lagged far behind the optimistic projections that had been made in the mid-1950s, when most of the airlines ordered their first jets. Meanwhile, the jets themselves had proved to be so much more efficient and trouble-free than anyone had dared hope that the airlines ended up with more planes than they needed. Too many jets were carrying too few passengers. As a result, earnings of the major airlines fell sharply to crisis levels. In speech after speech, CAB Chairman

Alan Boyd warned that overcompetition and overcapacity were undermining the stability of the airline industry. The airlines, he said, had better start thinking about mergers before the government was forced to step in and recommend consolidations. At the time, Boyd and many other people felt that the United States' eleven major airlines should regroup into three or four major nationwide systems so that they could make better use of the swift big jets.

TWA was anxious not to be left out of any such consolidation. On May 9, 1961, Tillinghast held a meeting of the airline's management policy committee, which had been considering merger possibilities. By this time, Northeast, which had received only two of its new 880s from Hughes in time for service during the winter tourist season, was sinking ever more deeply into financial distress. On polling the TWA executives, Tillinghast found that Northeast now rated only third in preference as a merger partner. The overwhelming first choice was Eastern whose great flow of north–south traffic would have offset almost perfectly the seasonal imbalances in TWA's east–west pattern. The second choice was National. In terms of evening out the peaks and valleys of TWA's traffic flow, National and Northeast rated just about the same. But National, which was financially stronger and better equipped, was the more attractive merger partner.

Tillinghast wanted to be very careful about whom TWA proposed to. He feared that the CAB might grant TWA only one turn at merging. Therefore, he wanted to be certain that TWA sought the partner that would provide the greatest benefits. At the May 17 meeting of the TWA board, Tillinghast reported to the directors that a broad study of merger possibilities was underway. By then, since TWA's own financial condition was becoming grave, most of the directors agreed that the airline should, in Tillinghast's words, "put out an anchor to windward."

While the merger studies continued, Tillinghast had experiences as a passenger that deeply affected his own feelings about Northeast. During the summer of 1961, Tillinghast's family vacationed at the Massachusetts resort of Wianno on Cape Cod, and he tried to commute by Northeast on the weekends between New York

City and Hyannis, the airport nearest Wianno. He managed to make it only half of the time. Tillinghast realized that often the weather was to blame. Nonetheless, he became acutely aware of Northeast's reputation for unreliability among its passengers and the run-down state of its equipment, which included ancient DC-3s. Tillinghast, who was trying to enhance TWA's image of efficiency and modernity, had no desire to become associated with Northeast.

Even so, Northeast had an increasingly urgent desire to be associated with TWA. David Stretch, the chairman of Atlas, repeatedly telephoned Tillinghast to ask for a meeting. In between his requests, Stretch also expressed his annoyance that Tillinghast was encouraging TWA's financial vice president, Vic Leslie, to dun Northeast for an overdue bill. Northeast owed TWA $1.3 million for the rental of a Boeing 707 that it had leased during the preceding year. Stretch said that he thought it was unbecoming for TWA to demand payment from a company to which it was practically engaged. But Tillinghast only took Stretch's unwillingness to settle the account as another reason for regarding Northeast as an unpromising merger partner. Still, even though Tillinghast was cool to a Northeast merger, some old TWA hands continued to look upon it with favor. In early summer of 1961 Northeast's application for permanent certification on the East Coast route was scheduled for hearings before the Civil Aeronautics Board. Tillinghast authorized TWA to take a position before the CAB that sounded as if TWA was still interested in Northeast. In a letter July 6 to the CAB, TWA's lawyers wrote that "Northeast's authority south of New York should be renewed as part of a merger operation and TWA is the only logical candidate for such a merger." The letter raised the hopes of poor struggling Northeast and later provided the Hughes forces with an opening to charge that the Northeast merger was dropped not for economic reasons but because of the lawsuit.

On June 12 Tillinghast had lunch with Stretch and James Austin, who was the president of Northeast. In telephone conversations, Stretch had kept insisting that TWA should either accept or reject the merger proposal, which Northeast had continued to extend to TWA. Stretch had also refused to consider an adjustment on the three-to-one swap of the shares. Now, in the luncheon discussion with Tillinghast, Stretch indicated he was prepared to be flexible and would be willing to bargain about a different exchange rate, which would more realistically reflect Northeast's worth. Tillinghast, however, replied that the threshold question was not one of ratios but a broader issue of whether Northeast would make a good partner for TWA. Austin, who was deeply committed to keeping Northeast alive, explained how the airline hoped to reduce operating expenses by eliminating service at small airports and switching to regional airports in New England. He also made heartening forecasts about Northeast's performance for the remainder of the year, but Tillinghast felt that Austin was unduly optimistic.

At TWA's monthly board meeting on June 21, Tillinghast told about the luncheon meeting with Stretch and Austin and said that he did not feel that TWA should seek a merger agreement with Northeast until he was satisfied on two points. Those were whether Northeast could ever be profitable and whether it was prudent to use up what might be TWA's only merger opportunity on Northeast. But Stretch continued to telephone Tillinghast. "When are we going to get together?" Stretch would ask. Tillinghast would apologize for still not having a definite answer about whether TWA would or would not commit itself to a merger with Northeast. On August 1 Tillinghast reversed the routine by telephoning Stretch, but it was not the sort of news Stretch had hoped for. Tillinghast told him that Atlas and Northeast had been named as co-conspirators, but not as defendants, in an antitrust suit against Hughes that had been opened that day. Understandably, Stretch was outraged and told Tillinghast that he did not think it was fair for TWA to have included Atlas and Northeast in the case. But Tillinghast tried to reassure him that the merger could still take place, provided that it was in TWA's best interest.

Accordingly, Stretch pressed for another meeting, and Tillinghast arranged one for 2:00 P.M. on August 15 in his office. In addition to Tillinghast and Stretch, Breech and Austin were also there.

Stretch began by complaining about the suit, but Tillinghast interrupted him to say that the issue was under litigation and should be left to the lawyers. Switching to the merger proposal, Stretch sought to highlight Northeast's advantages to TWA by saying its losses could be used as a deduction against income tax. Tillinghast replied that since TWA unfortunately was piling up its own losses, that was a dubious asset. In that unencouraging strain, the conversation continued for about an hour. The meeting ended with both sides saying, well, we're sorry but . . .

Though economic factors were paramount in TWA's deciding against Northeast's proposal, the lawsuit nonetheless inserted hostilities and issues into the situation that rendered useless any future talks. Northeast, by this time under severe pressure from its creditors, careened toward a crisis, while TWA became increasingly concerned about its own looming economic troubles.

TWA's problem bore down especially hard on Breech, who keenly remembered from his early years at Ford the aching worries of a financial squeeze. Until now, Breech had not been excited by the prospects of a merger as a solution for TWA's problems. But a conversation in September 1961 ignited his highly infectious enthusiasm. Breech was a member of the President's Business Council, which was composed of the nation's sixty or so leading industrialists. He had gone to a council meeting at the Homestead, the gracious resort hotel in Hot Springs, Virginia. During a break in the talks, Breech struck up a conversation with one of the other members. And that member happened to be Juan Trippe, the founder and president of Pan American World Airways. Trippe and Hughes had once been friends and used to fly off together for weekends. But after TWA won its first international routes after World War II, the old friendship developed into an intense rivalry.

In the Homestead conversation, Trippe agreed with Breech that, yes, the airlines were indeed in trouble. Yes, they had to find a way out. Soon the two men, who were two of the nation's finest business strategists, found themselves concurring that it made little sense for the two big U.S. international airlines to engage in wasteful competition against one another when foreign airlines were ganging up on them. For years Juan Trippe had been known for his advocacy of the "chosen instrument" concept, by which he meant that Pan Am should be the sole, or chosen, U.S.-flag carrier abroad. As the two men talked, Breech could see that a merger with Pan Am could solve TWA's problems by forming an airline that could compete more effectively with foreign airlines, which for the first time in history now were carrying more passengers across the Atlantic than TWA and Pan Am combined.

After his talk with Trippe, Breech spoke of the attractiveness of mergers at TWA's September board meeting, which was held in St. Louis. As a result, the directors agreed that Tillinghast should make the pursuit of a merger one of his major objectives. There was another reason for the decision. TWA's traffic was continuing to slump; it had declined 8 per cent so far that year. By contrast, TWA's earlier planning had anticipated that the traffic would grow by precisely the same percentage. Thus TWA's results were lagging 16 per cent behind the projections. In practical terms, that meant that TWA's overhead cost of equipment, terminals, payroll, and the like were so great that they were eating into TWA's working capital. Nine months earlier, TWA's working capital had amounted to a healthy $42 million. But if TWA's present slump continued, the airline would run out of cash entirely within the next six months. Tillinghast told the board that he had written to Raymond Holliday about TWA's problem but that Holliday had responded that the lawsuit ruled out any help from Hughes Tool Company. Tillinghast also reported that on September 7 TWA had entered into an agreement with France's Sud Aviation to buy twenty short-range Caravelles, which would cost about $100 million. The directors realized that if TWA was going to pay for new aircraft, which it needed to replace on short routes the old prop-driven Martin 404s, and if TWA was going to meet all its other financial obligations, the airline was going to have to find a partner who could help pay the bills.

The question was who? As the search began in earnest in late September 1961, TWA focused first on the domestic scene. The primary reason was that, despite foreign inroads in the oversea market, TWA's international operations still were making a handsome profit. But the domestic part of the company was accounting for more than $3 million a month in operating losses. In their earlier studies of merger possibilities, TWA executives had rated Eastern as the most desirable merger. Thus, Breech, who months earlier had received a call from Rickenbacker, took up the merger subject with him. Meanwhile Tillinghast got in touch with Malcolm MacIntyre. After work one day in late September, Tillinghast arranged to pick MacIntyre up in his TWA limousine and the two men were chauffeured to their homes in Westchester County. During the ride, they talked about a merger. Both agreed that one of the main problems was that TWA and Eastern alike were losing money and were short of cash.

Through his web of contacts in Manhattan's airline and financial communities, Juan Trippe learned of the Eastern-TWA talks, which supposedly were being conducted in secret. One day in the early fall, Trippe reached for his telephone and dialed an Oxford number. The private telephone burred on Tillinghast's desk at 380 Madison Avenue. It was a direct line that did not go through the TWA switchboard and the number was changed frequently; those were precautions that Tillinghast took against the Hughes people, who he feared would try to bug his line.

When Tillinghast answered the phone, he heard the soft, genteel voice of Juan Trippe. As Tillinghast recalls it, Trippe said, "Now I don't want to push you or interfere in your affairs, but I understand that you are having talks with Eastern and I wonder if I could be of help in any way." Continuing to speak in his quick, almost hushed manner, Trippe who liberally interspersed his conversations with "don't-you-knows," suggested that perhaps he could alleviate the cash problems that would confront the TWA-Eastern merger by buying TWA's international routes. Tillinghast thanked him for his interest, but said that negotiations had not yet advanced far enough with Eastern for him to think about such things as selling off part of the TWA system. Tillinghast promised, however, to keep Trippe's offer in mind.

TWA and Eastern continued to have talks, including the December 4 meeting in Breech's apartment in the Ritz Tower. But Tillinghast found that MacIntyre, who had never shared Rickenbacker's interest in the TWA-Eastern merger, was growing increasingly distant. MacIntyre told Tillinghast that he had two main objections to a merger. One was he did not want to become involved with the "Hughes problem," which was understandable. The other objection was that he had no interest in branching out into overseas operations. That was less fathomable, since oversea traffic was the fastest growing segment of the United States airline business. But Tillinghast soon divined the cause of MacIntyre's preference. TWA was being two-timed by Eastern. Though Tillinghast says that MacIntyre never mentioned it to him, the Eastern president was, in fact, also engaged in merger negotiations with crusty old C. R. Smith of American Airlines, which was the nation's second largest domestic airline. It had lost its first-place ranking earlier in the year to United, which grew as a result of the takeover of ailing Capital Airlines. Contacts between Eastern and American had been made a few months earlier by representatives of the Rockefeller family and the Equitable, which had helped finance Eastern's and American's jets—as well as those of TWA. By the end of December, MacIntyre was so involved in the negotiations with American that Tillinghast gave up on Eastern as a lost cause. But he continued to watch the Eastern-American talks, as did just about everyone else in the airline industry. The Eastern-American merger would produce by far the country's most competitive airline, whose network of routes would reach into almost every major market. Whether flying north–south or east–west, passengers could travel with the same airline. That is a great advantage in attracting frequent travelers. With the combined Eastern and American fleets at its disposal, the new airline would be able to outschedule its opponents, bracketing the competition's flights with its own departures and arrivals. As a general rule, the airline that has the most frequent flights attracts proportionally more passengers than do the airlines that have less frequent flights. Because of its magnitude, the American-Eastern merger was certain to trigger a whole series of defensive mergers and start the fundamental reshaping of the nation's airline industry that CAB Chairman Boyd and many others felt should take place.

On January 18, 1962, American and Eastern publicly announced their decision to seek the approval of their respective shareholders and the CAB to form a single airline that would carry the name "American." The announcement spurred Tillinghast into a surge of activity. Tillinghast knew that since TWA was the weakest of the major trunk airlines, it would suffer most severely from a combination of American and Eastern. He flew to Minneapolis to sound out Donald Nyrop, the president of Northwest Airlines, about the possibility of a merger, but Nyrop remained silent when Tillinghast asked him about what position he himself would want in a merged airline. Tillinghast also flew to Miami, where he talked with Ted Baker, then the president of National. He spoke by telephone with Delta President C. E. Woolman. During this period, Tillinghast dispatched Emmett O. Cocke, a TWA senior vice president, as emissary to the West Coast. There Cocke talked with Terrell Drinkwater, the president of Western Airlines, and Robert Six, the chairman of Continental Airlines. Tillinghast was hoping that he might be able to put together a three-way merger in which TWA would link up with two of the smaller airlines. But the same reply came from the other airline presidents: they had known Howard Hughes for many years and personally liked him but they would not dream of becoming associated with any venture in which he was involved. Only Bob Six held out some hope. Six, who was often in contact with Greg Bautzer, intimated to Cocke that he had a plan, which had already received Hughes' blessing. Six then flew to New York where he and Tillinghast had two meetings. Their talks, however, never reached the point where Six unfolded his plan. At best Tillinghast could figure it out, Six's proposal centered around a TWA-Continental merger in which Hughes would donate his TWA stock to a foundation and thus collect a huge tax break. In return, the new airline, in which Six expected to be chief executive officer, would settle the TWA suit against Hughes.

In the midst of his unsuccessful attempts to find a merger partner, Tillinghast rang up Juan Trippe and reminded him of his earlier offer of help, and asked if he could get together with him for a talk. The two men began a series of secret meetings, sometimes in midtown coffee shops, sometimes in the Irving Trust's suite in the Waldorf-Astoria. At first Trippe was only interested in buying TWA's oversea routes. He offered, for example, to trade Pan Am's 30 per cent stock interest in National, which was held in a trust plus a sizable hunk of cash for TWA's international routes. The stock in National would give TWA leverage in trying to effect a domestic merger with National. Trippe also offered to cede Pan Am's New York–San Juan route to TWA. But Tillinghast insisted that he was not interested in dissecting TWA; he wanted either a full-scale merger with Pan Am—or nothing. That presented far more complex problems for Trippe, who was trying to get the best deal possible for Pan Am while his old competitor was temporarily weak. Trippe realized that if he could succeed in acquiring only a part of TWA in return for a fair price, he stood less chance of becoming embroiled in the legal dispute with Howard Hughes than if he sought to take over TWA in a merger. Trippe knew that a merger was certain to involve him in the "Hughes problem." That consideration, however, did not stop Juan Trippe for long. Within a short time, he was expounding to Tillinghast a plan by which the two airlines could merge and at the same time solve the "Hughes problem."

Trippe knew that in a straight share-for-share exchange of stock between TWA and Pan Am, Hughes would end up owning something like 30 to 35 per cent of the merged airline. Since the rest of the stock in both airlines was scattered among thousands of shareholders, Hughes would have become the controlling power in the merged airline when he finally regained control of his shares from the voting trust.

Trippe's plan was intended to permanently lock Hughes out of control. It worked like this: In the merger, Pan American World Airways would become a holding company whose main asset would be a majority of the shares in the new TWA-Pan Am airline. The airline, in turn, would be a separate company. Pan Am shareholders would receive stock in the holding company, but none in the airline. TWA stockholders, including Hughes, would be given stock in the new airline but none in the holding company. Thus Trippe, who would become chief executive officer of both the holding company and the airline, would be able to outvote Hughes through his control of the holding company. Under those terms, the merger indeed seemed like good business to Juan Trippe. In a single stroke, he would double the size of his airline, gain for Pan Am the long-sought access to the United States domestic market, and dispense with his most potent competitor.

Though the terms may have seemed harsh, Tillinghast felt that he had no choice. He began to negotiate seriously for a Pan Am-TWA merger. More than ever, TWA needed that "anchor to windward" if it was to avoid being swept under in a storm of financial problems. As 1961 ended, TWA was headed for the largest one-year operating loss until that time in airline history—$38.7 million.

Meanwhile, however, Howard Hughes was going ahead with his own plan to win back control of TWA before anyone could merge it out from under him or take it away from him through the anti-trust suit. Having granted Hughes the right to supply emergency aid to Northeast, the Civil Aeronautics Board set up an accelerated schedule for investigating and deciding about his application to take over the airline. But even before the investigation began, Hughes pressed on with his effort to acquire control of Northeast by taking over Atlas' 55 per cent stock interest in the airline. The arrangements were handled by Raymond Cook. At 10:30 on the evening of December 13, 1961, Cook phoned a message for Hughes to the communications center on Romaine Street. "We believe that it is essential," said Cook, "that we immediately tie up Northeast with an option from Atlas . . . This will not prevent you from making a different and better deal along the line of a firm commitment to buy out Atlas for cash as you are now contemplating."

At ten the next morning, Hughes' reply was telephoned to Cook. "Raymond," admonished Hughes, "I am sure you believe sincerely in the fairness of what you propose, but when you say that we can take an option at one price and then go ahead and negotiate and possibly close a firm deal of a much lower basis without the acquisition of the option having hurt us, I just do not believe that you yourself believe this.

"As you know," Hughes' message continued, "the entire affair is being played out in five scenes and three acts in front of the CAB." Hughes was cautious about any action that later could provoke the CAB's criticism. He explained: "Now if we take an option at the figure you are discussing and then try to negotiate at a lower figure, the CAB will say we led Atlas down the garden path."

Hughes instructed Cook to present to Dave Stretch at Atlas two alternate offers for immediate acceptance. The first offer, as Hughes put it, was: "$3.5 million cash for Atlas stock in Northeast—no strings, no conditions, no option." He instructed Cook how to present the deal to Stretch. Said Hughes: "Naturally this would assure Atlas that we have made a firm commitment to save NE from bankruptcy, and therefore the major asset to be derived out of the deal by Atlas would be the virtual assurance that Northeast will be put back in healthy financial condition and converted into a profitable enterprise for all the Northeast stockholders. I think the absolute all-out, horror-filled tragedy of Atlas permitting Northeast to go bankrupt to the financial destruction of the stockholders is something so serious that it would destroy public confidence in Atlas." Hughes continued: "Heaven knows how much we will have to put into Northeast to save it, but a conservative guess would be $20 million of our money, not bank loans which would be on top of this."

Hughes also outlined the second offer: "Exchange of my stock [in Atlas] plus $1 million cash for Atlas' holding in Northeast"— Hughes had originally paid somewhat more than $6 million for his Atlas holdings. "If anyone wants to argue that my stock in Atlas is not worth $6 million today, there is one pretty good answer to that," Hughes told Cook. "Atlas management had full control of my $6 million plus and if it is not worth $6 million today, the responsibility lies in only one place—Atlas—and it is from this same Atlas that we are contemplating buying Northeast, so I think due adjustment is owing us." Under either plan, Hughes offered to write off Toolco's $10.2 million in loans to Northeast and not to hold Atlas in any way responsible for them. In assessing the value of the loans, Hughes applied his earlier argument. "The same answer applies if anyone wants to argue that our $10.2 million investment in Northeast is not worth that amount today," he said. "We have kept our hands off 100 per cent and Atlas has managed Northeast without any interference from us, so any loss in the $10.2 million is Atlas' responsibility."

Thus briefed, Raymond Cook proceeded to close the deal. But Atlas insisted on a higher price than Hughes had offered. On December 28, 1961, Hughes agreed to pay $6 million for Atlas' 55 per cent ownership of Northeast, and the control of the airline passed to Hughes Tool. Combined with his original 11 per cent, Hughes controlled potentially 66 per cent of Northeast, a very big chunk of a very ailing airline.

As 1962 began, the focus of the struggle returned to the lawsuit. Even as the merger talks and Northeast crisis had been in progress, the lawsuit had been gathering momentum. On September 6, 1961, Sonnett and Davis met in their first pretrial hearing before Judge Metzner. It was the first of nineteen such hearings in addition to numerous informal sessions in the judge's chambers. When Judge Metzner took over the case in mid-August, he had deferred ruling on the motion by Chester Davis to dismiss the case. In the September 6 hearings, Davis warned that the tool company intended to file counterclaims and also made a new motion for summary judgment in the case. By that, Davis meant that he wanted Judge Metzner to make a decision only on the basis of the complaint. It was an unlikely request since the complaint raised many factual questions that required investigation. Nonetheless, the motion, if successful, would have ended the discovery proceedings and thus would have spared Hughes the threat of a personal appearance. But the next day Judge Metzner ruled that Davis' new motion should "be held in abeyance" until a later date.

Next, controversy developed over the surrender of documents in the case. Both Toolco and TWA had drawn up lists of thousands of documents, which each side demanded from the other. As a reflection of its owner's secretive ways, Toolco was extremely reluctant to turn over any documents, let alone the ones demanded by TWA, which related to Toolco's innermost financial and tax secrets. But in two separate orders in December, Judge Metzner ruled that the tool company would be required to turn over the papers requested by TWA for inspection and copying. These included communications between Hughes and Toolco officials and Toolco's balance sheets and profit-and-loss statements for the years 1939 through 1960 and income tax returns for the years 1939 through 1961. "The scope of proof is quite broad in these [antitrust] cases," wrote Judge Metzner, "and under the liberal Federal Rules, wide latitude is permitted in the deposition discovery proceedings."

Meanwhile, TWA was already producing for inspection and copying hundreds of thousands of documents, which Toolco had requested. The timing of the production of the documents was linked to the schedule of witnesses, which finally had been established. Davis was to begin calling his witnesses on January 5, 1962, so he would need TWA's documents first. The first witness was to be Tillinghast. He was to be followed by a procession of other TWA officers, past and present, insurance executives, and bankers. In all, Davis had sent out deposition notices for fourteen witnesses. According to the schedule, Davis would complete his questioning of witnesses on April 3, 1962, and after that, TWA's parade of witnesses would begin. At the top of TWA's list was, of course, Howard Hughes.

Right on schedule, Tillinghast was sworn in as a witness at ten on the morning of January 5. The hearing was held in a conference room in Chester Davis' office at 120 Broadway.

The procedure for depositions is more relaxed than a hearing or trial in a courtroom. The lawyers sit around a table, usually are allowed to smoke, and generally do not stand when they speak. The lawyer who does the questioning is granted considerable leeway in conducting his investigation. Sometimes the court appoints a "special master" to supervise the proceedings, and sometimes the lawyers handle it on their own. But as in a courtroom, the witness is under oath and the answers are recorded by a reporter. The purpose of depositions is to give the defendant an opportunity to explore the charges against him and to enable the plaintiff to establish testimony that supports his complaint. Once the evidence—both oral and documentary—has been collected and sorted out, the two sides then can participate in so-called "Rule 16 proceeding" in which the issues in the case are defined. After the issues have been delineated and the evidence reduced to manageable proportions, the case can move to trial.

From the opening of *TWA v. Hughes,* Chester Davis had contended that the complaint had no merit and that the charges were contrived conclusions that had no supporting facts. Now, as the depositions began, Davis' tactic was to try and prove through Tillinghast's own admissions that (a) the charges had no factual basis, and (b) he had no personal knowledge of the offenses. If Davis was successful, it would bolster his contention that the suit had been filed simply to force Hughes to accept an out-of-court settlement that would have placed TWA forever beyond his reach. That, in turn, would put pressure on the court to reconsider Davis' earlier motion for dismissing the case. It would also help create a public atmosphere that would be more friendly to Howard Hughes, the poor old underdog millionaire.

The atmosphere was tense as Tillinghast settled himself into the witness chair in Davis' office. Seated around a large table were a handful of lawyers, including John Sonnett, who was there to advise Tillinghast. A cigarette glued to his lower lip, Sonnett was poised to needle Davis if the occasion arose.

Davis commenced by asking Tillinghast to describe what he knew about TWA before he took the job as president. "I was in a broad way familiar with TWA's background and its chronic inability to retain a chief executive officer," answered Tillinghast.

Davis pressed him for specifics. In reply Tillinghast declared: "There had been a parade of presidents."

"Describe the parade of presidents, if you please."

Tillinghast: "Well, there originally was Jack Frye . . ."

Davis (interrupting him): "Are you personally familiar with the circumstances under which he left?"

At that instant, Sonnett broke in with a biting comment to Davis: "Just a minute. Which question do you want him to answer? Everytime he starts to answer it, you come up with another one. If you will relax a bit and let him give you an answer, you will save your time."

Davis (tensely): "I don't think it is necessary for you to refer to my relaxing. I am perfectly relaxed, as everyone in this room is aware . . . The witness is obviously not a friendly witness, and I would appreciate a little latitude in my efforts to get at the facts."

Davis resumed the questioning by asking Tillinghast to describe what he had referred to as a "parade of presidents." Tillinghast replied: "Well, I knew that there had been quite a succession of presidents at TWA. I am not sure that at each point in time I could identify the names and tenures of each of them, but I knew that Jack Frye had been followed by Ralph Damon—no, he was followed by La Motte Cohu, I believe, and then there was Ralph Damon and then Carter Burgess and then there was Charlie Thomas, and anyone who was in the aviation industry, or read the public press was aware of the fact that there had been a parade or succession or whatever you want to call it, of presidents of TWA."

"Have you completed your answer now in describing the parade of presidents," asked Davis, who obviously sensed that Tillinghast's knowledge was somewhat less than encyclopedic.

"Yes," replied Tillinghast.

"Do you know when Mr. Frye left as president of TWA?"

"Well, it was in the 1940s—1945, 1946, somewhere along there."

"Do you know the circumstances under which he left?" asked Davis, going for the clincher.

"I do not," replied Tillinghast.

"And you never inquired as to the reasons why he left?"

"I never had occasion to."

Davis went on through the list, making the tacit point that Tillinghast seemed to know very little about his predecessors or their problems. Tillinghast did, however, say that he had had lunch with former President Carter Burgess, who had mentioned that some people at TWA were also on the Hughes Tool payroll and that he was not sure of their loyalty.

"Would you at this point," asked Davis, "describe what you did when you did become president of TWA to determine or ascertain who might be on the payroll of TWA who was not entirely loyal to the interests of TWA?"

"I did nothing," Tillinghast replied.

"Nothing at all?" asked Davis incredulously.

"Nothing at all," confirmed Tillinghast. "I felt, when I took office," he explained, "that it would be a mistake for me to go in and start snooping around and create the impression that I didn't have confidence in the loyalty of the people of the organization, and I would rather make the mistake of overlooking some disloyalty than to create a general feeling of suspicion and concern. For that reason I have done nothing in the way of a witch hunt or a search for those who are unfaithful."

"But you believe there are some that are unfaithful to the interests of TWA?" asked Davis.

"I have no reason today to think they are," said Tillinghast.

"So you think Mr. Burgess was in error when he said to you at this luncheon meeting that there were a number of people or might be a number of people whose loyalty to TWA might be questioned?"

"I think circumstances have changed," replied Tillinghast.

"What circumstances have changed relating to the loyalty of employees to the interests of TWA?" Davis shot back.

"You have no longer the situation that you used to have where Mr. Hughes used to personally contact various people in various echelons of the organization and deal with them directly," replied Tillinghast evenly. "Under those circumstances, in my view, you are much more apt to get a lot more divided loyalties or disloyalties than you are under the present situation."

On that note the first day's deposition ended. By the time questioning resumed on Monday, January 8, Davis had gotten hold of Tillinghast's desk diary, which TWA had surrendered to Toolco as evidence in the case along with the thousands of other documents. Using the diary as a reference for dates, Davis wanted Tillinghast to reconstruct the details of virtually everything—his hiring, his discussions about his employment contract, his conception of the voting trust, his relations with Breech, what Reed said to him on the evening of February 28, and so on and so forth. It was a time-consuming process. At the noon break that day, Davis offered to make arrangements for Sonnett and Tillinghast to have lunch at the conveniently close Bankers' Club. Sonnett declined. "I hope we will be finished by this afternoon and won't have the problem tomorrow," he said

For once, John Sonnett, who normally was the most hardheaded of realists, was engaging in a bit of fantasy. It was true that, according to Davis' schedule, he was to complete the deposition of Tillinghast in two days and then march through the testimony of three TWA vice presidents in one day each. But perhaps even Sonnett could not have foreseen the course the depositions would take. As the afternoon session began, Davis reminded Tillinghast that one part of the complaint was directed against Toolco's alleged interference in TWA's business after December 1960. The alleged interference had been carried out principally by Davis, who peppered TWA, the SEC, Boeing, and the New York Stock Exchange with letters and telegrams that warned, among other things, that Toolco disputed the right of the new management independently to conduct TWA's business. "Which communications did the complaint encompass?" asked Davis.

Replied Tillinghast: "Mr. Davis, let me say I am referring to all the letters you wrote, which were very numerous and lengthy and considerable, from the period beginning about the fifteenth of May and continuing through the period really up to the present."

"Those are the communications which you feel constitute interference in the affairs of TWA?"

"Oh, I didn't say that, Mr. Davis," replied Tillinghast. "I think some of the letters were appropriate, perhaps proper statements of position to management, and others were unwarranted interference in the management of TWA."

Thereupon, Davis asked Tillinghast to sort through the entire batch of letters and telegrams and attach a paper clip to those that he felt constituted unwarranted interference in TWA's affairs. In all, there were about sixty communications. Tillinghast put clips mainly on the communications that referred to Hughes' insistence that TWA should buy the Convair 990s from him and to Toolco's objections to the SEC about the wording of the TWA stock registration. But it was slow progress. Furthermore, Tillinghast was unable to explain the specific offense committed by the communications that he did clip. He conceded that individually they appeared to be innocent. They constituted an offense, he said, only because of the intention with which they were written.

Just then, Sonnett looked around the hearing room and spotted three additional listeners whom he asked to identify themselves. To his chagrin, he learned that they were Richard Hannah, Hughes' longtime public relations man, who had brought along Richard J. Cook of the *Wall Street Journal* and an *Aviation Week* reporter. Sonnett thought that he had an understanding with Davis that the depositions were to be secret. He accused Davis of not informing him that the press would be present and implied that Davis was attempting to try the case in the newspapers.

"Who is trying to try something in the press?" cried Davis. "I charge you with trying to try something in the press, and I did not file a complaint under seal either. I assure you I have no objection to the world knowing what I am doing."

Sonnett asked sarcastically about what attitude Davis would have toward open depositions when TWA's turn came to call witnesses.

"I have told you," said Davis. "The Hughes Tool Company has no objection to permitting any part of these proceedings being public."

"Including all depositions?"

"Including all depositions."

"And that of Mr. Howard R. Hughes?" asked Sonnett.

"I have nothing to do with Mr. Howard R. Hughes personally," declared Davis. "I represent the Hughes Tool Company."

On the morning of January 9, Tillinghast's third day of depositions, the hostility between Davis and Sonnett remained high. With elaborate politeness, Sonnett made a point of introducing to the assembled lawyers an aide who had not attended the previous hearings. Then Sonnett added that his assistant was attending in his capacity as a lawyer and not as "a public relations man or reporter."

Davis retorted: "You mean Cahill, Gordon does not publicize . . ."

Sonnett (interrupting): "We don't do what you have . . ."

Davis (breaking in): "We don't prepare the kind of complaint you have prepared."

Sonnett: "It should be a matter of regret to you."

Davis: "I hope, if I have the occasion to do so, I will avoid the temptation."

During the depositions that day, Davis took Tillinghast through more of the letters and telegrams. On January 10, which was Tillinghast's fourth day of deposition, Davis dealt at length with the reasons for TWA's selection of Boeings instead of the Convair 990s that Hughes wanted TWA to take off his hands. Under Davis' quizzing, Tillinghast conceded that he did not know the exact price at which the 990s would have been made available to TWA. It was obvious that without the exact figure, a comparison of the total operating costs for Boeing and Convair aircraft could hardly have been exact.

Meanwhile, Sonnett was becoming disturbed about the slow progress of the deposition. Instead of finishing with the testimony of four TWA executives in the first week as scheduled, Davis had already spent nearly four days on Tillinghast. At that rate, Sonnett feared that Tillinghast's deposition could go on for weeks. In mid-afternoon Sonnett brusquely interrupted Davis' questioning to ask how much longer Tillinghast's testimony would continue. Davis was less than enlightening. "At the moment," he replied, "I am not able to tell you how long the depositions of Mr. Tillinghast will last." He did explain, however, that he would not be able to continue the questioning the next day because he had to go to

Cleveland where a case of his was coming up in the federal court there.

By now Sonnett was only looking for an excuse to break off the depositions under the current arrangements so that he could persuade the court to appoint a special master to preside over proceedings. Sonnett, who hoped that the presence of a special master would force Davis to speed up the depositions, pounced on Davis' impending absence as the pretext for picking a fight. Judge Metzner's ruling, he declared, had clearly stated that the depositions must continue on a day-to-day basis. If Davis was not prepared to abide by the court's order, Sonnett would consider the depositions ended. It was then 3:15. Sonnett challenged Davis to accompany him to Foley Square to seek a ruling from Judge Metzner about whether he meant what he said when he ordered the discovery proceedings to go forward on a day-to-day basis. "The answer," Davis replied, "is that I am not going to see Judge Metzner this afternoon." With that, Sonnett declared that the depositions were ended. Gathering up his papers, he escorted Tillinghast from Chester Davis' office.

The action had the desired result. On Sonnett's motion, Judge Metzner did appoint a special master to oversee the depositions. The special master's distinguished credentials reflected the importance of the case. He was James Lee Rankin, the Solicitor General of the United States during the last three years of the Eisenhower administration. His compensation was fixed by the court at $60 an hour, the cost to be shared equally by Toolco and TWA. However, Sonnett's hope was quickly dashed that the special master would compel Davis to quicken his pace.

When the deposition of Tillinghast resumed, after a month's break, on February 13 under Rankin's supervision, Sonnett once again asked Davis how much longer the TWA president would be questioned. Davis replied: "If I have to go back to 1939, because it [the complaint] is predicated upon some motive or course of conduct since 1939, we could anticipate a pretty long period of time."

Rankin, who seemed cautious about the substance of TWA's case against Hughes, did not dispute Davis' statement. "You have a right," Rankin told him, "to exhaust what Mr. Tillinghast and those other important officers of TWA know about the controversy, and I am sure counsel recognize that."

Davis had put the recess to good use. For months he had warned his opponents that Toolco would file a countersuit. John Sonnett mockingly referred to the much-heralded counterattack as "Chester's atomic bomb." During the morning session on February 13, he announced that he intended to file Toolco's countersuit and the company's answer, or defense, to TWA's complaint later in the day.

During the lunch break, Davis entered his "atomic bomb" in the Federal District Court. The news quickly swept through Manhattan's financial district that Howard Hughes had launched a countersuit. Reporters cornered Tillinghast in the hearing room at Davis' office just before the start of the afternoon session. What was his reaction? they asked. Tillinghast, whose boyhood as a headmaster's son was still reflected in his manner of speech, replied that in the presence of the special master, he had best maintain "correct deportment."

Though Tillinghast retained his New England aplomb, Chester Davis' "atomic bomb" nonetheless had severe repercussions. Having already regained the initiative at the Civil Aeronautics Board in Washington, Howard Hughes was now in the process of seizing the upper hand in the legal proceedings in New York as well. The "atomic bomb" consisted of two parts, one of which was predictable and the other quite astonishing.

The predictable part was Toolco's defense to TWA's charges of antitrust violations and conspiracy. In a forty-one-paragraph answer, Davis restated his already familiar position—that the alleged offenses did not constitute violations of the antitrust laws, and hence the court lacked jurisdiction in the case; and that the complaint failed to identify a course of action upon which claims could be based; and that even if the alleged violations had taken place, they did not cause damages to TWA. Davis again rebutted the basic point on which Sonnett's antitrust charges hinged—that Toolco was engaged in the development, manufacture, and lease of aircraft for use in interstate and foreign commerce. He also reasserted the argument that since Toolco's control of TWA had been approved by the CAB, Hughes, Toolco, and Holliday were immunized from the workings of the antitrust laws. Finally, in regard to Toolco's alleged interference in TWA's affairs in the period since December 1960, Davis repeated his earlier contention that all acts were taken on advice of counsel in order to protect Toolco's legitimate interests.

But if Davis' defense was familiar, the countersuit—the second part of the "atomic bomb"—was novel and bold. In fact, it left Sonnett in the shade. He had filed a thirty-eight-page complaint, asking for $115 million in damages. Toolco's countersuit was almost twice as long and three times as costly. It comprised sixty-eight typed pages and asked for a grand total of $443 million in penalties and damages. The legal reasoning behind Toolco's countersuit was nothing less than ingenious. To just about everyone's surprise, Davis did not contest Sonnett's charge that TWA had been damaged. He agreed with it. In fact, he even assessed the damages at $10 million more than Sonnett did—$45 million versus $35 million, bringing triple damages to $135 million. The difference was in who was to blame for those damages. While Sonnett put the responsibility on Hughes, Davis placed it on TWA's new management and the financiers.

In the countersuit, Toolco sued both on its own behalf and that of TWA. Named as additional defendants were four financial institutions that either made or arranged the $165 million loan that forced Hughes to put his TWA stock into a lender-controlled voting trust. The institutions were the Equitable, Metropolitan, Irving Trust, and Dillon, Read. Also named as additional defendants were the men who opposed Hughes in the battle for TWA: James F. Oates, the president of the Equitable; Harry C. Hagerty, vice chairman of the Metropolitan; Ben-Fleming Sessel, senior vice president of Irving Trust; Breech; and Tillinghast.

Toolco's countercomplaint contained five major counterclaims and one minor one. Each of the major counterclaims spelled out a long and detailed elaboration of the alleged offenses. The first one concerned the establishment of the voting trust and employment of Tillinghast. Toolco charged that the Irving and the insurance companies had entered a conspiracy to force Toolco to surrender control of TWA and then engaged in self-dealing to perpetuate the life of the voting trust beyond its ten-year life. Tillinghast's employment contract, which in the event he was fired provided for an annual $50,000 income until 65 and $30,000 after that, was attacked as a waste of corporate assets.

The second counterclaim alleged a violation of Section 408 of the Federal Aviation Act of 1958, which makes it unlawful for any person engaged in any phase of the aeronautics to acquire control of an air carrier in any manner whatsoever without prior approval of the CAB. Toolco charged that for years the Equitable and Metropolitan had been engaged in a phase of aeronautics because of their dominant position as lenders of long-term capital to the airlines. With the establishment of the voting trust, so Toolco argued, the insurance companies gained control of TWA without the approval of the CAB. Asserted Toolco: "The creation and continued existence of the Voting Trust was and is contrary to the public policy of the United States."

The third counterclaim charged violations of the Sherman and Clayton antitrust laws. According to Toolco, the defendants entered into a conspiracy to restrain interstate commerce by preventing TWA from obtaining loans from sources other than the defendants. Part of the conspiracy was to force Toolco to surrender control of TWA by denying it access to other banks and by insisting upon the establishment of the voting trust as a condition for loans. As a consequence of the illegal conspiracy, so the third counter-complaint charged,

"(a) TWA's jet equipment program was disrupted and the delivery of jet equipment which had been ordered by Toolco from General Dynamics for the benefit of TWA was delayed;

"(b) TWA has been compelled to obtain financing under unfavorable terms and at higher interest rates than it would have otherwise had to pay;

"(c) TWA's assets have been wasted;

"(d) TWA has lost valuable opportunities;

"(e) the business and affairs of TWA have steadily deteriorated."

As an illustration, Toolco cited the airline's precipitous financial decline: "During the years from 1947 through 1960 TWA realized earnings before taxes of $95,600,000. Upon information and belief, TWA in 1961 lost in excess of $30 million without regard to accelerated depreciation of piston aircraft and before applicable tax credits." Toolco claimed that TWA had been damaged in excess of $45 million, "which amount may become substantially greater as a result of the conspirators' continuing unlawful activities."

So much for TWA's damages. The fourth counterclaim declared that because of the conspiracy, Toolco had been damaged in excess of $77 million. The fifth counterclaim charged that the plotters also had aimed at perpetuating the voting trust beyond the ten-year limit prescribed by corporate law in Delaware. The sixth counterclaim, which was relatively minor, asked that TWA pay Toolco $168,000 in interest on an earlier loan.

Toolco's prayer for relief contained a long list of penalties and remedies. Among other things, Toolco asked that the voting trust should be terminated and that the defendant bank and insurance companies should be enjoined from advancing the due date on any of TWA's loans. Toolco also asked (1) that the pension and annuity clauses of Tillinghast's employment contract should be declared null and void; (2) that the Equitable, Metropolitan, and Irving should be perpetually enjoined from refusing to deal with TWA while it was controlled by Toolco; and (3) that all defendants should be permanently forbidden to interfere with Toolco's right as a shareholder in TWA. Davis had questioned Sonnett's choice of antitrust as the basis for TWA's action against Hughes. Nonetheless, he based his own countersuit on the Sherman and Clayton laws. Thus he, too, was able to triple the damages. In the prayer for relief, Davis asked that the additional defendants should pay damages of $135 million to TWA and $308 million to Toolco. The grand total was $443 million.

In important respects, Davis' countersuit was the mirror image of Sonnett's, though each looking glass reflected a different picture. The damage was done. But who was the doer?

9. Who Shot TWA?

I do not think that the fight between TWA and
Howard Hughes should be converted into a three-ring circus.
—John Sonnett
February 15, 1962

After the filing of Toolco's massive countersuit, Sonnett was understandably concerned that his own case would be submerged in a legal morass. Davis' counterattack immediately changed and complicated the legal battle between Hughes and TWA. The growth in size of staffs now engaged in the litigation posed problems. As a result of the countersuit, four new law firms, adding a total of twenty or more lawyers, joined the proceedings. More important, the goals of the additional defendants, who had been forced into the case by the countersuit, did not at all coincide in many respects with those of John Sonnett.

Sonnett, on behalf of TWA, was suing Howard Hughes himself as well as Toolco the corporation and Raymond Holliday the company officer. The additional defendants being sued in a countersuit by Toolco were not parties to Sonnett's case and therefore did not to the same degree share his overriding aim to engage Hughes personally in the litigation. They wanted to examine Hughes all right, but only to prove that Toolco had no case against them. By contrast, Sonnett wanted to collect out of Hughes' own mouth most of the evidence on which his case rested. The additional defendants sought only to have the charges against them dismissed. But Sonnett was trying to collect $115 million in damages for TWA.

If Sonnett and the lawyers for the additional defendants had differences in aims, they also shared a number of mutual concerns. One of the main ones was a common suspicion about the nature of Davis' "atomic bomb." On closer examination, Sonnett and the other lawyers concluded that Toolco's countersuit actually was not a true countersuit at all. By definition, a countersuit is one in which you sue the people who are suing you. Davis' countersuit did not do that at all. It did not sue TWA, which was suing Hughes, Toolco, and Holliday. Instead, on behalf of TWA as well as of itself, Toolco sued parties who, with the exception of Tillinghast and Breech, were in no way involved in the TWA action against Hughes. Only Davis' sixth counterclaim, the minor one concerning loan interest, actually conformed to the concept of a countersuit. All the rest of the countercharges were new claims against the financial institutions, the financiers, and Breech and Tillinghast personally, not as TWA officers.

The suspicion that Sonnett and the other lawyers felt about the countersuit was only heightened by the parallel maneuvers that Davis undertook. If his long-range goal was to collect $443 million for Toolco and TWA from the additional defendants and to dissolve the voting trust, as the countersuit maintained, his short-range objective certainly seemed to be to tie up Sonnett and the other lawyers in protracted pretrial proceedings that would delay for months, perhaps even years, the appearance of Howard Hughes. Meanwhile, Hughes could capitalize upon his newly won leverage at the CAB to complete his master plan for regaining control of TWA. Then Hughes could most assuredly find some way to have TWA settle the case against him. After that, all that would remain would be the countersuit. Even if that line of attack failed, Davis had developed an effective fall-back position. If he retained the first turn at questioning witnesses both in the suit and countersuit, he could try and build a record that would support Toolco's charges of collusion and conspiracy between TWA's new management and the additional defendants.

Either way, it was absolutely essential for Davis to keep the right to call witnesses first. He had, of course, already won the right to prior discovery in *TWA v. Hughes*. Now, in a swift maneuver, Davis sought to transfer that advantage to the countersuit as well by pointing out that his witnesses in the countersuit were the same ones whom he had already notified to appear for questioning in the TWA action. After that, Davis coolly invited the lawyers for the additional defendants to join the deposition proceedings, which were already underway in his Broadway office. The lawyers for the additional defendants did indeed join the deposition hearings in Davis' office, but they were furious about the procedural strait-jacket into which Chester Davis had firmly laced them. They argued that a new case had now begun in which Toolco was the hunter and they the hunted. Thus, they demanded the first right to examine witnesses from the Hughes side in order to determine the case against their clients before they allowed them to submit to questioning by Davis.

Tillinghast's deposition was momentarily shoved aside as the lawyers for the additional defendants pleaded with the special master to make changes in the schedule of witnesses. They were willing to allow Davis to complete his questioning of Tillinghast and of the three other active TWA officers. But after that, the lawyers for the additional defendants asked to question Hughes about the basis of Toolco's countercomplaint. In rebuttal, Davis stuck to his position that he had the indisputable right to examine without interruption all the witnesses whom he had subpoenaed.

John Sonnett was understandably distressed about the intrusion of the countercomplaint into his case. During an argument before the special master, Sonnett declared: "I do not think that the fight between TWA and Hughes should be converted into a three-ring circus in which Hughes is wrestling around half the time with others in the process of defeating or delaying our course of action." The special master, however, did not feel that he had the power to alter the list of depositions, which had been affirmed only a few days earlier by Judge Metzner. The lawyers for the additional defendants appealed Lee Rankin's ruling, and on February 23 they presented their arguments in a pretrial hearing before Judge Metzner.

The hearing was held on the motion of Bruce Bromley, a distinguished partner in the Manhattan firm of Cravath, Swaine & Moore, which represented four of the nine additional defendants: the Metropolitan and its vice chairman, Harry Hagerty, and the Equitable and its president, James Oates. Since Bromley had served one year in the 1940s on the appellate bench, he was usually addressed by court and colleagues alike as Judge Bromley.

"I must say," Judge Bromley told the court, "that what Mr. Davis has done appears to me to be a very clever device indeed—having gotten an order giving him complete priority in an action and having that order signed, sealed, and delivered, he then serves this massive claim against nine additional parties and insists that the schedule, which Your Honor set, be adhered to without regard to the rights of the additional defendants to exercise their traditional and normal right of discovery as soon as practicable." Judge Bromley continued that unless his side had the opportunity to question witnesses from the Hughes side, it would be forced to "sit back in ignorance" while Davis developed his case. He concluded: "I do not see how anybody can possibly object to all of us, who have had very little connection with this litigation being given an opportunity to discover on what basis in the world we are sought to be held liable for half a billion dollars before we undertake the task of posing proper objections to this vast parade of witnesses."

Two other lawyers for the additional defendants supported Judge Bromley's plea. They were Peter Kaminer of Winthrop, Stimson, Putnam & Roberts, who represented the Irving Trust and Ben Sessel, and Charles L. Stewart of Dunnington, Bartholow & Miller, who represented Dillon, Read & Company. "I think there are a lot of games being played here," Kaminer told the court. "I think that the game is that Mr. Hughes doesn't like to be examined, and that is why we have all of these very devious schemes of serving notices for examination of witnesses, getting an order setting forth a schedule, and then all of a sudden these witnesses become defendants in a half million dollar suit . . ."

Judge Metzner corrected Kaminer's slip of the tongue. "Half a billion," he interjected.

"Your Honor is so right," replied Kaminer.

"I am impressed, Mr. Kaminer. I have got to admit that," conceded Judge Metzner.

"I am scared, Your Honor," said Kaminer. "These figures are a little more than I am used to."

When Sonnett's turn came to speak, he once again sought to protect his case from becoming derailed by the other proceedings. "Why the rush about filing the countersuit?" he asked rhetorically. "Well, it is perfectly simple, I think, what he [Hughes] is up to," he continued. "The effort is to create a diversion in TWA's case, to slow that case down to a walk, to strangle—just as he strangled TWA in the past. And now, by creating a procedural morass, he hopes to bog down this case and bog it down for good. I am sure meanwhile he hopes that he will get some pat on the back from the Civil Aeronautics Board for being willing to put money into Northeast, and maybe get a whitewash in that way."

Sonnett went on: "I know one thing for sure: what he is trying to do is prevent the TWA case from being progressed as it could be speedily and come to trial." Sonnett characterized Davis' countercomplaints as a "mishmash," "strictly phonies." "The only counterclaim," he declared, "that seeks anything from TWA, which might be called a counterclaim truly, is the $170-odd thousand from TWA. I am prepared to submit that matter on paper to Your Honor for a ruling and if he is right, we will pay the judgment within twenty-four hours. But other than that, all he [Davis] is doing is saying that since December of 1960, when the voting trust went into effect, this big conspiracy has been in existence to take control of TWA away from Hughes and give it to the banks and insurance companies. If every word of that were true—if every *single* word of it were true—it would not be a defense to any aspect of TWA's cause of action alleged in this complaint. It is apples and oranges."

In order to speed up the progress of his case, Sonnett asked the court to establish a system of alternating depositions so that he and Davis could take turns calling witnesses. Sonnett requested the court to order Tillinghast's deposition to be ended by the next week and to allow him to summon Howard Hughes as the next witness.

Speaking last, Chester Davis feigned surprise that the other lawyers were so upset over the fact that the Hughes side retained the right to call its witnesses first. Davis defended as fair and equitable the special master's refusal to modify the schedule of depositions. In regard to the timing of the filing of the counter-claim, Davis argued that he actually was doing the witnesses a favor since now they knew the charges against them and could protect their own interests when they were called to testify. Disputing Sonnett's "apples and oranges" view of the two lawsuits, Davis contended that Toolco's answer and countersuit constituted a full and complete defense to TWA's complaint. "Whether we call it counterclaims or affirmative defense is not particularly important," he declared. Then in a somewhat convoluted manner, Davis explained his theory behind the countersuit: "If TWA was deprived of equipment, if the financing of TWA injured TWA, as is claimed in [Sonnett's] complaint, and we can show that that was a result of the course of conduct, or conspiracy by these other people—if only on the issue of damages (as to, Did we cause the injury or did they?), the same set of facts, plus the addition of the prayer for relief, might well also constitute a basis for additional relief.

"There is a conspiracy, certainly concerted action, among these various defendants," Davis continued. "These are not bare naked allegations. The depositions taken to date, the documents obtained to date, establish a course of conduct, which unquestionably requires an inquiry." In a rebuttal to Bromley's contention that the additional defendants needed an opportunity to probe the basis of the accusations against them, Davis argued that the charges in countercomplaints were so detailed and specific that the additional defendants did not need to question Howard Hughes to find out what they had done wrong. "Your Honor," Davis asked, "where do you think they are going to find their misdeeds? In our files? Through our people? Or in their files? Where are the facts to be found as to whether or not there has been an unlawful course of conduct on the part of these additional parties? Through the tool company? Or through their own files and their own witnesses?"

As the hearing ended, Judge Metzner said he would rule at a later time on which side would be given priority of discovery in the countersuit and how that would affect Davis' depositions. Meanwhile, Davis on February 26 resumed the Tillinghast deposition. More lawyers representing the additional defendants crowded into the conference room in Davis' office so that extra chairs had to be placed around the table. While eight to ten lawyers had been in attendance in the earlier sessions, the number now swelled to twenty or more. At the same time, twenty or thirty other lawyers were at work on other aspects of the case. That was costing Howard Hughes a lot of money, because he was paying all of Toolco's costs and, in theory at least, was also bearing 78.23 per cent of TWA's expenses.

The depositions were costing Charles Tillinghast more than money. He had been president of TWA for less than one year, and he should have been spending his time learning how to run the airline. Instead, he was being forced to spend day after day testifying in exacting detail under Chester Davis' forceful questioning. Even while he was engaged in the deposition, Tillinghast tried to keep up with his job at TWA. Early in the morning, he would commute to Grand Central from his home in Bronxville and walk the four blocks to his office at 380 Madison Avenue, arriving usually about 8:00 or 8:30. He would get as much work done as he could by 9:30 when it was time to be driven downtown to Chester Davis' office on lower Broadway. The deposition started promptly at 10:00. At 12:30 or 1:00 the hearings recessed for ninety minutes for lunch. During the break, Sonnett generally took Tillinghast to his club, the India House on Hanover Square. There, amid the mementos of the clipper ships and the sail-borne Far East trade of a century ago, Sonnett and Tillinghast for a few moments were able to relax. Sonnett was a believer in the medicinal qualities of the martini. At lunch he took two himself and prescribed the same number as an elixir for the tensions that afflict witnesses. Tillinghast, who in legal matters followed his distinguished counsel's advice, ordered two; but exercising his innate Yankee caution, he drank only one and a half. The hearings resumed at 2:00 or 2:30 and continued until about 5:00. After that Tillinghast would be driven through Manhattan's rush-hour streets to his office where he would usually put in two or three more hours of work before being chauffeured home.

Tillinghast was a wary, sometimes pugnacious witness. "Chester," he once mused, "does not evoke warm feelings in a person." The relations between the two men had already been soured by the events of the preceding year. In spring 1961, when Davis had tried to induce Tillinghast and the new TWA management to buy Toolco's leftover Convair 990 jetliners, the two men had crossed tempers several times. Furthermore, Davis' line of questioning in the deposition, especially since the filing of the countersuit, was hardly flattering since it pursued the unproven assumption that Tillinghast was a part of a vast illegal conspiracy.

While another witness might have been unnerved by the long stint under Davis' questioning, Tillinghast, who had the advantage of being schooled in the art of litigation, was not. His first job had been as a New York deputy assistant district attorney in Thomas E. Dewey's office in the late 1930s, and he was quite capable of trading verbal punches with Davis. On one occasion, while questioning Tillinghast about his meeting with former TWA president Charles Thomas a few weeks earlier, Davis expressed utter amazement that Tillinghast had not asked Thomas about his knowledge of the background of TWA's jet orders. Without batting an eye, Tillinghast replied: "Because I knew that for each five minutes I talked with Thomas, I'd spend an hour on the stand with you."

On another occasion as Davis was trying to develop his point that TWA did not have valid reasons for rejecting Hughes' offer of the Convair 990 jets, he inquired about what TWA officers thought of his explanation of the comparative qualities of the

Convairs and Boeings. (Davis, you may recall, in the spring of 1961 had given a long lecture to a group of TWA executives about the superiority of the 990 over the Boeing 707, which TWA had chosen to buy.) "I believe the remark was made, if you will pardon me," said Tillinghast, "that it was a rather unenlightening presentation and exhibited more a desire to divert our attention than to add to our knowledge about the technicalities of aircraft."

Despite the putdown, Davis repeatedly pressed Tillinghast for his thoughts and actions concerning the Convair vs. Boeing issue, because it had become a central point in support of the alleged conspiracy charges. Davis' theory was that Tillinghast decided on the Boeings in order to have a reason to borrow an additional $147 million from the same lenders that controlled the voting trust and thus make it more difficult, if not impossible, for Hughes to regain control of the airline. The new financing arrangement, of course, provided that if Hughes did manage to buy out the voting trust by paying off the original $165 million loan and its early repayment penalty, the new loan for $147 million would immediately become due and payable.

During one exchange, Davis asked Tillinghast:

"Is it your view as chief executive officer of TWA that such a condition was most harmful to TWA?"

"No, I don't think it is most harmful to TWA," responded Tillinghast. "I think it's more a theoretical problem than an actual one, Mr. Davis."

"Because of the unlikelihood of the tool company being able to purchase the obligations underlying the voting trust?"

"Because, Mr. Davis, I don't think that any large stockholder of TWA is likely to take any step of this magnitude without having made some provision for their refunding."

"In other words," retorted Davis, "you are relying on the fact that the tool company, after this new financing was accomplished, would realize that if it made an effort to exercise whatever rights it had under the financing of 1960, TWA would be put into a serious financial condition."

"It seems to me obvious, Mr. Davis, that if the tool company is going to end the voting trust, it has got to have a refinancing plan that is sufficient and adequate for TWA. I am quite prepared to take the risk that the tool company would not be so foolish as to seek to end the voting trust without a complete financial solution."

But Davis continued to pursue that line of questioning: "To what extent did you or TWA make an effort to obtain financing other than from these particular leading institutions without such a requirement?" he asked. By requirement, Davis meant the continuation of the voting trust. He was trying to find out if Tillinghast had sought to borrow money from insurance companies and banks other than those that had already loaned the $165 million to TWA.

"I personally made none," replied Tillinghast.

"You probably thought it would be a useless exercise to try and obtain financing of this magnitude . . ."

Tillinghast (breaking in): "Without a voting trust?"

Davis: "Without a voting trust."

"That's correct," affirmed Tillinghast.

On a number of other occasions, Davis grilled Tillinghast about the reasons for starting the suit against Hughes. Davis' purpose was to show that the case itself was part of the conspiracy to take TWA away from Hughes. In reply to Davis' questions, Tillinghast gave a candid account of TWA's legal strategy. He told of a conference with John Cahill, then the senior partner of Cahill, Gordon, and John Sonnett, in which the two lawyers recommended an antitrust action. Testified Tillinghast: "Mr. Sonnett said that he felt as he looked at this situation and saw the dispute that had come up over the Boeing acquisition and the pressures that had been brought to bear to interfere with that, that there wasn't any real solution to this problem, short of a divestment of Hughes' interest in the airline.

"He said," continued Tillinghast, "that when the voting trust was set up, people felt that at last they had the problem solved and had some stability and then it was just a matter of time before another controversy arose." Tillinghast recalled that Sonnett told him: "I think that you will have to face the fact that it is very unlikely you will be free of controversy so long as this relationship exists.

"For that reason," said Tillinghast, "[Sonnett] thought a divestment proceeding was what was really needed in order to solve the problem. He said that it seemed abundantly clear that TWA was too large and too important to its stockholders and the public to be the plaything of an eccentric man, and that he felt that in the last analysis a court would come to the conclusion that a continuation of this relationship was just inconsistent with the public good and with the good of others having a legitimate interest in the company."

Davis was not satisfied. "Isn't it true," he asked, "that one of the purposes of the suit was to scare Mr. Hughes?"

"No, Mr. Davis," said Tillinghast, "the purpose of the lawsuit was to get some claims of TWA settled and to bring an end to the warfare that then seemed to be going on, and our interest was in getting something settled, not in scaring Mr. Hughes."

Next Davis inquired about a report relayed by telephone from Ben Sessel to Bank of America Vice President Robert Gordon to the effect that the Cahill firm had concluded that if they got Hughes on the stand, they would keep him there for two or three months. Tillinghast demurred that he could not recall the exact details. But Davis insisted on refreshing Tillinghast's memory. "Do you recall," he asked, "what was said about the general strategy of starting a lawsuit, deciding upon an antitrust course of action, getting an order to show cause for the deposition of Mr. Hughes, the advantage of forcing talks with the tool company, and the threat of what could take place in the lawsuit—do you remember that kind of discussion?"

Sonnett heatedly objected to Davis' line of questioning. "Mr. Rankin," he told the special master, "that is obviously a misstatement of the entire record, and I object to it. It implies some reflection on the professional standing and ethics of myself and my firm, which I resent. The facts are not as Mr. Davis summarized them. The evidence in this record is quite clear. Insofar as Mr.

Hughes is concerned, he will be on the stand for a good two or three months. Like anyone else, he will submit to the procedures of the courts."

The special master sustained Sonnett's objection regarding the form of the question, but Davis persisted for hours along that line of inquiry. He finally extracted from Tillinghast a pithy statement of TWA's reason for choosing to sue Hughes on antitrust charges. The TWA president explained that Sonnett told him "that the relief obtainable on an antitrust action would, in fact, make TWA whole for any damages that it had suffered and that the best people were defendants in antitrust actions, and that he felt that one of the reasons for bringing an antitrust action was that it didn't have the social approbriums [sic] attached to it that some other types of action did, and he thought Mr. Reed's chances of working out something with Mr. Bautzer would be improved rather than diminished if we avoided anything that would point an unpleasant finger at Mr. Hughes personally."

Sonnett, still angry, had his own answer for Davis. "Let me state it now," he declared. "You have asked for it. I did not recommend a suit charging Hughes with being a thief because I thought it wasn't in the interest of TWA. Just keep pushing me, and we will see what happens."

"You will see it all right," replied Davis.

"Suppose you will just stop making speeches and get on with your deposition," snapped Sonnett. "You are wasting your own time under the court's order."

As March 1962 began, it did not seem as if Davis would ever get finished with Tillinghast. They went round and round, covering in exhausting, often repetitious detail such subjects as TWA's equipment problems, TWA's relations with Toolco, Tillinghast's experiences with some of the old-time executives at TWA, and his efforts to find a merger partner for the airline. Another reason that no end was in sight for Tillinghast's deposition was because an increasing percentage of question time was being taken up by arguments of the lawyers about arrangements for the surrender of the documents and disputes about the order of witnesses. After the lawyers for the additional defendants joined the deposition proceedings, this percentage grew to perhaps 25 to 35 per cent of each day's session. While the arguments raged about him, Tillinghast would open his attaché case and spend the time pouring over TWA reports. His reading was generally depressing: engine trouble delayed a jet's departure by two hours; an opinion by TWA's financial staff that as long as the company was tied up in litigation, it was impossible to raise the $100 million for the Caravelles on order; a report that TWA's working capital was nearly exhausted; a traffic forecast that passenger loads would continue to decline.

If ever an airline needed both peace and a full-time president, it was TWA. In the late afternoon of March 6, after Tillinghast had spent most of the day in the hearing room absorbed in gloomy TWA reports while the lawyers argued about other subjects, Sonnett openly pleaded with Davis to finish up Tillinghast's testimony. "Let him go back to running the airline," said Sonnett.

Unmoved, Chester Davis continued the examination of Tillinghast. Even so, as the lawyers became increasingly preoccupied with more immediate issues, the deposition was momentarily pushed into the background. On March 5 Judge Metzner had handed down a new ruling on the priority of discovery in the suit and countersuit in which each of the parties won a little and lost a little. Davis was given the right to continue with the witnesses whom he had previously scheduled. However, his investigation was to be limited to evidence that bore on TWA's complaint against Hughes; he was barred from entering into the matters dealing with the countersuit. Sonnett, who had asked for permission to start alternate depositions, was denied that right, but he did have the importance of his interests reaffirmed by the court. "The plaintiff, who instituted the litigation," declared Judge Metzner, "must not be lost sight of in the maze that has resulted from the pleadings." The court also stated that when Davis completed his schedule of witnesses, Sonnett would have the next turn. The court invited the additional defendants either to participate with TWA in its discovery proceedings or to schedule separate depositions at the close of TWA's hearings. In any event, the additional defendants were given the right to examine Toolco first in the countersuit before Toolco could conduct its discovery proceedings against the additional defendants.

It was a complex ruling, reflecting the complicated nature of the case. Judge Metzner said that he would depend upon the special master to keep the various issues untangled. In a discussion before the special master, Sonnett summarized the decision in his own colorful manner: "If Hughes stands before you indicted of attempted murder—assault with intent to kill TWA—he can examine now on the question, Did he or did he not shoot the pistol? And he can examine later on the question whether the bankers also fired a pistol that put a bullet in the body." But in between Hughes' turns, Sonnett would get his chance to question Hughes, and the additional defendants also would have an opportunity to investigate the charges against them.

In early March the lawyers were also busy with the problems involved in the search for documentary evidence. All the parties had employed a vacuum-cleaner method in asking for documents; they requested virtually everything that could be even distantly related to the issue of who fired the pistol at TWA. In addition to reams and reams of financial and tax papers from corporate files, the lists demanded the surrender of the notebooks, desk diaries, and personal records kept by individual executives. TWA and the additional defendants were already producing huge batches of documents to Toolco teams. The procedure for the side doing the copying was to bring photo machines and operators into the opponent's offices at its own cost, make the reproductions, return the originals, and then clear out.

As they went about the job of copying documents at TWA, the Irving Trust and other sites, the Hughes people, reflecting the suspicious nature of their enigmatic employer, were very wary about whether some documents might have been "doctored" before they were surrendered for copying. At one of the financial institutions, a Toolco team came across a document that was crucially important to Davis' entire conspiracy theory in the countersuit. It was an account, handwritten in pencil, that ran for some five hundred pages of legal-size desk pad. Written by a high executive, it was a day-by-day description of the entire history of the complex negotiations and events that finally led to the institution of the voting trust. The diary, which covered the period from 1958 to 1961, included a full and detailed account of the events surrounding the resignation of Charlie Thomas, whose abrupt departure from the presidency in mid-1960 opened the way for the establishment of the voting trust. A few days after copying the document, the Hughes people returned with another machine and several additional experts. They asked to see the original document again. They set up the machine into which, page by page, they fed the original.

It turned out that they were looking for erasures. The document had peculiar spaces between the words within sentences—a pattern that suggested tampering. The machine enabled the Hughes people to detect the original words, which had been rubbed out and in part written over with different words. Their eyes must have burned at what they read. The erasures were not, as the Hughes side undoubtedly suspected, an after-the-fact doctoring of the document to change the substance. The changes had been made for a different reason. Each day, as he talked by telephone to bankers and insurance executives about the various financing plans, the author of the document had simply written down exactly what they had said to him—and they said a lot. When they told him, "I am sick and tired of trying to deal with that [so-and-so]," he had faithfully recorded the great outpourings of profanity and abuse that were heaped on Hughes by the exasperated financial executives, who were fed up with his stalling and procrastinating. In the evenings, he would go back through the text of the day's conversations, erase the profane passages, and substitute Hughes' name or the appropriate pronoun.

The production of documents was a mammoth undertaking. To Toolco, TWA turned over more than a million pieces of paper. The Equitable Life surrendered 35,000; the Irving Trust, 30,000; Dillon, Read, 18,000; TWA's house counsel, the Manhattan law firm of Chadbourne, Parke, Whiteside and Wolff, 20,000; the

CAB, 12,000; the First Boston Corporation, 3,000; Merrill Lynch, 2,500; Atlas, 1,000 and Charlie Thomas, 1,000.

Now it would soon be Toolco's turn to surrender documents for copying by the other side. The court had set March 15 as the date on which the Hughes side should open its files to its adversaries. Sonnett and the other lawyers insisted that the date should be kept.

It was bound to be a traumatic experience for the Hughes Tool Company. Ever since its founding by Howard's father and his partner, Walter B. Sharp, shortly after the turn of the century, the company had jealously guarded its business secrets from the outside world. Under Howard Hughes, Jr., secrecy became an absolute obsession at the tool company. To be sure, on several occasions Toolco had been compelled by other lawsuits to disclose limited amounts of information about its earnings, retained capital, and the like. On a few other occasions, as when Hughes had dangled the possible sale of Toolco before Wall Street investment houses, notably Dillon, Read and Lehman Brothers, he had disclosed a great deal of financial information so that the investment bankers could prepare a prospectus for the sale of the stock to the public. But each time Hughes had backed out, leaving the investment bankers with the impression that he was chiefly interested in getting free of charge a professional assessment of Toolco's value. (In the mid-1950s, when Hughes was sometimes talking about selling out, Toolco itself, minus TWA and its other holdings, was worth about $300 to $350 million.) Hughes had also turned over some Toolco financial data to the Irving Trust when it was acting as his personal bank.

As the time drew near for Toolco's surrender of ducuments, Davis began to warn the financiers that they must not use any financial information about Hughes or Toolco that had been given them in the course of earlier events. Above all, the Hughes Tool Company was gripped by anxiety at the prospect of having outsiders pry into its financial secrets. And those outsiders, in the person of TWA and the additional defendants, wanted to know just about everything. They wanted all tax returns dating back to

1939. They wanted all information concerning Toolco's financial performance since 1938, all information concerning loans and interest rates, all records dealing with aircraft leasing and sales by Toolco to TWA and other airlines. They wanted all documents explaining the reasons behind Toolco's various financial deals through the years. In addition, they wanted all records of dealings between Hughes and his aides—the transcripts of all calls, all memos, all notes.

As the March 15 deadline drew near, Sonnett and the lawyers for the additional defendants began during the deposition sessions to question Davis about Toolco's preparations for surrendering the documents for inspection and copying. During one discussion before the special master, Sonnett needled Davis about whether Hughes had any documents that he might fail to produce. "I don't know whether or not Mr. Hughes made any notes that are called for and that he might be carrying around in his vest pocket," conceded Davis, who continued to insist that he represented only Toolco—and not Howard Hughes. "Obviously I will not be in a position of making any actual representations as to what Mr. Hughes personally has until I am able to reach him," he continued, "and I haven't been able to reach him for several months now."

Two days before the deadline for the surrender of documents, Tillinghast was excused from testifying so that the lawyers could spend the entire day discussing with the special master the procedures for the production of Toolco's documents. Davis maintained that Toolco had the right to mask parts of the tax documents that showed the cost of equipment purchased as compared to Toolco's net income. This category included the outlays for planes that Hughes had originally bought and then resold to TWA. Also, Davis said that Toolco would mask passages in documents and in transcripts of messages that he claimed were "privileged," or confidential, by virtue of their being communications between counsel and client. Presumably, this would include messages between Hughes and his lawyers, even though Raymond Cook, for example, had served as a business agent as well as a legal counselor.

According to the court order, Toolco was directed to begin making documents available on March 15 simultaneously at three locations: in Houston at Toolco's corporate headquarters at 7400 Polk Avenue, in Los Angeles at the head office of Hughes Aircraft in Culver City, and at the "nerve center" at 7000 Romaine Street in North Hollywood. Because Hughes' calls and messages went through 7000 Romaine and important records were believed to be kept there, it was considered to be by far the most important of the sites. The opponents of Howard Hughes made their plans accordingly.

At 10 o'clock on Thursday, March 15, a posse of four lawyers, armed with the court order, arrived at the squat, two-story stucco building on Romaine. They were Paul Williams and Marshall Cox of Cahill, Gordon; John Barr of Cravath, Swaine; and William Bradner of Dunnington, Bartholow & Miller. The four men found the premises tightly locked and apparently empty. They rapped on the front door. No reply. They rapped again. Only silence. Then, in a legal act reminiscent of Joshua's blowing the trumpets around the walls of Jerico, Paul Williams, an elegant, impeccably tailored man of great dignity and decorum, tilted back his head and grasped the court order in both hands. In a stentorian voice, he read to the locked door the contents of Judge Metzner's order, which commanded Toolco to hand over documents to its legal opponents. But, alas, for the four lawyers, no miracle occurred. No doors popped open. The lawyers split up to explore the outside of the building, hoping to find a way in. Bradner rattled a door handle until someone admitted him to the Ping-pong room in the basement.

Finally a few Hughes employees began to surface. They opened the front door but said before they could do anything, they had to ask for instructions from Chester Davis, who was in Los Angeles to oversee the production of documents. They reached him by telephone at the Hughes Aircraft corporate offices at Culver City. Davis sent a message to the lawyers to come there, and he would talk with them. A Toolco auto led them the few miles to the aircraft company's headquarters, which adjoin the plant where Hughes helicopters are built. The helicopter production lines are located in the same huge building, supposedly the world's largest wooden structure, which Hughes erected during World War II to house the assembly of his gigantic flying boat. There, in countless all-night sessions, Hughes, sitting in the cockpit of a flying boat mockup and pulling on the flight controls, figured out how power-assisted mechanisms could be used to enable one pilot to manipulate the huge rudder and ailerons on large aircraft —a breakthrough that helped open the way to the construction of subsequent generations of huge aircraft.

When the four New York attorneys arrived at Culver City, they were led into a large conference room where four boxes of documents had been placed on a table. They were eager to start examining the documents, but Davis said no. He was the host and he insisted that they should first have lunch. Acquiescing to his hospitality, the four men were his guests in the company dining room. After lunch, they returned to the conference room in the austere, almost barrackslike Hughes Aircraft headquarters, which is painted in Hughes' favorite corporate color—dull olive green.

Davis gave the lawyers the go-ahead to begin sorting through the four boxes of documents. In the meantime, the lawyers had had copying machines set up. In a nearby room were three lawyers from the Houston firm of Andrews, Kurth, Campbell & Jones, but they remained unseen by Williams and the other New York lawyers. As the New York lawyers finished inspecting and copying a box of the documents, a Hughes employee took that one and brought a new box of papers, which the Houston lawyers had selected from the aircraft company's files.

But Williams, Cox, Barr, and Bradner were by no means content with examining documents at the aircraft company only. The court order had prescribed simultaneous discovery at three sites, and they demanded that Davis should obey the instructions. Davis replied that he would have drinks and perhaps dinner that evening with them and discuss arrangements for the next day. The meeting place was to be the Library Bar in the Beverly Hills Hilton at seven.

That evening Davis rushed into the Library Bar late. Full of apologies, he explained that he unfortunately could not stay because he had to meet other people that evening. After fifteen minutes and one drink, he hurried off without giving any specific reassurances about the arrangements for the next day. The next morning the four lawyers once again showed up at 7000 Romaine Street and demanded to exercise their court-given right to inspect and copy documents there, but the attempt turned into a replay of the previous day's frustrations. The Hughes employees again refused to admit them and once more rang up Davis, who again was over at the aircraft company headquarters. Once again Davis told the lawyers to come over. He said he had more documents there for them to inspect and copy. Williams demanded that the inspection should start at once at 7000 Romaine but Davis said no. He would refuse to start the discovery process at 7000 Romaine, he said, until it was ended at the aircraft company headquarters.

In disgust, Paul Williams placed a long-distance telephone call to Special Master Lee Rankin, who at that moment was supervising the deposition proceedings in Davis' office. The call went through during the afternoon session while Tillinghast was being questioned by Maxwell T. Cox, Davis' chief assistant (not to be confused with Marshall Cox of Cahill, Gordon). The special master suspended the proceedings to take the call. In a lengthy "Paul and Lee" conversation, Rankin learned the details of Davis' refusal to allow the New York lawyers to start work at 7000 Romaine.

Listening in on an extension, the court reporter transcribed the conversation. After the call had ended, he read the entire conversation to the lawyers in the room. When Sonnett heard about the delay at 7000 Romaine, he exploded. "They are dragging their feet!" he cried. Nonetheless, Sonnett could not immediately demand a contempt-of-court citation, because Toolco was producing documents for inspection and copying at Culver City and at the corporate headquarters in Houston where his young aide, Fred

Furth, had whisked in a fifteen-man crew and set up four copying machines, including one huge copier that could reproduce out-sized documents. In Houston the papers were being supplied smoothly and in great number. The only trouble was that they were being handed over in plain folders so that it was impossible with only a quick scan to identify the documents. Toolco clerks had marked the folders with various colored crayons; each color stood for a different executive. But Furth and his team had no way of knowing which color represented which executive. As far as Son-nett's men could tell, no personal papers of Howard Hughes had been turned over either in Houston or Culver City.

Back in the deposition proceedings in Manhattan, Maxwell Cox explained to the special master one reason for the delay at 7000 Romaine. The Hughes people, he said, were fearful that the copy-ing machines used by the other side could "see" through the pas-sages that were marked with black tape unless the tape was applied to both sides of the paper. And the job of taping both sides of the documents was proving to be very time-consuming.

But Sonnett kept the pressure on. He was counting on the docu-ments in 7000 Romaine Street to help him get a legal grip on How-ard Hughes personally. It was then Friday, March 16. "I think they are entitled to a warning," Sonnett told the special master. "Either stop this and allow our people in 7000 Romaine and pro-duce the documents, including the Hughes documents, or Tuesday we will appear before you in respect of contempt and striking their answer." By that Sonnett meant that he would make a motion to the court to find Toolco in default by refusing to obey the court's order. He would ask Judge Metzner to disregard Toolco's defense and to render a verdict in the case in TWA's favor.

Sonnett's threat produced results. On Monday, March 19, the door of 7000 Romaine reluctantly opened to the four lawyers from New York. In they marched, followed by a platoon of clerks and movers, who carried in copying machines. Marshall Cox, a lean, taciturn Ohioan who had been engaged in the case since its start, directed the setting up of the copying machines. Williams and Barr demanded to be shown through the building, which was overflowing with Hughes guards, who suspiciously eyed the intruders. Williams and Barr rattled door handles and demanded to be let into locked rooms. Most of the rooms contained only reels of Hughes' movies. (The films were periodically unreeled, coated with a chemical preservative, and then rewound and put away again in large metal canisters.) The two men were looking for a secret safe, which they believed was located in a broom closet in the office that had until fairly recently been used by Frank (Bill) Gay, Hughes' chief administrative aide and a Toolco officer. They had received a tip that important papers, including some of Hughes' personal documents, were kept in that safe. They never located it, because the tip gave them the wrong information. There was a safe all right and some of Hughes' papers may have been in it. But it was not in a broom closet. It was secreted in a hallway that led to Gay's former office.

Meanwhile, Marshall Cox was rushing to copy the documents that were being handed over to his staff from the files at 7000 Romaine. Many of the papers were heavily overlaid on both sides with black masking tape, an indication that the lawyers were indeed getting close to Howard Hughes' secrets. All the while, Toolco guards intently watched every move by Cox and his clerks to make absolutely certain that the masking tape was not surreptitiously peeled back from the documents. In accordance with Sonnett's instructions to make the copies first and sort out the material later, Cox was trying to work as fast as possible. Nonetheless, even in haste, he could see that some of the papers were call sheets that recorded the times and texts of Hughes' conversations. He also recognized memos from Hughes to his aides. In rapid succession, some of Hughes' most confidential documents were being photographed and handed back to the guards in return for a new batch.

Then suddenly, in the midst of that frenzied activity, an alarm shrilled. Springing into action, the Hughes guards shouldered Cox and the clerks aside. They shut down the copying machines and began to take them apart. The Hughes guards explained that the alarm was hooked up to a detection system whose sensors registered the presence of X-rays in the room. The guards suspected that Cox was using special X-ray devices to penetrate the masking tape to the secrets beneath. But they searched in vain for an X-ray machine anywhere in Cox's copying equipment. Then one of the guards discovered why the alarm had sounded. The battery of the detection device was running down, and the alarm was a reminder that a new battery was needed. Shamefaced, the guards allowed Cox and his clerks to resume their work. Within three more days, the copying operations were completed at 7000 Romaine and the two other main Hughes sites as well. In all, Hughes and Toolco had surrendered 375,000 pieces of paper.

It was now the end of March 1962. The lawyers took their mountains of photocopies back to Manhattan. The job of sorting through the papers was enormous. As secretaries arranged them into chronological order, the lawyers worked week after week late into the night, studying the thousands and thousands of documents. Placed in the correct order and properly understood, the papers revealed a fascinating story. Many of the innermost secrets of Howard Hughes were in the hands of his opponents. Now they set their sights upon another goal: the man himself.

10.   Man Above the Law

How do you catch Howard Hughes? He is protected by a small army of pleasant but purposeful guards. There is no address to which you can mail a letter and be certain that it will reach him. He lives in hidden-away homes and inaccessible hotel penthouses, which are shielded by closed-circuit television monitors and all sorts of other electronic detection devices. They are virtually impregnable for outsiders. There is not even any way for an outsider to prove that Howard Hughes is in residence in any of his various hermitages. Is he there? No one will acknowledge his presence. When he moves from one place to another, his mode and time of travel usually are planned well in advance and invariably kept secret. He may be driven away late at night in an old undistinguished auto; at one time he owned twenty identical Chevrolets to confuse possible pursuers. Or he may fly away in a helicopter or in a sleek unmarked private jet.

His business is conducted behind a veil of skilled lawyers, whose client's privacy is their primary priority. He cannot be reached by telephone. He may call you, but you cannot call him. Only on very rare occasions are his top aides allowed to telephone him directly; customarily, even their messages must be dictated to operators at his "nerve center" at 7000 Romaine, and his replies, if he deigns to reply at all, are transmitted to them in the same manner. No one, except a small staff of five or six tight-lipped nurse-secretaries, the "Mormon Mafia," as they are called, see him face to face. Otherwise, he remains inaccessible even to his most senior executives. In the spring of 1962, Raymond Holliday, Hughes' faithful aide who was Toolco's chief operating officer, conceded that he had not seen Hughes for a long time and that during the past six months he had had only one message from his employer—and that one was relayed by dictation from the "nerve center." Robert Maheu, a former FBI man who at one time was Hughes' chief of operations in Nevada, worked for The Man in important and highly sensitive positions for fifteen years without once seeing him face to face. "Those who say they do, don't, and those who do, don't say," reflected Maheu about people who claim to have seen Hughes. During the long legal battle, Hughes' lawyers often admitted informally to their opposing colleagues that they did not know where he was. "But you talk with him by telephone," insisted an opposing attorney. "Yes," replied a Hughes lawyer. "But I don't ask him where he is calling from."

Howard Hughes does not walk on the street like an ordinary person. Nor does he go to restaurants or theaters. And even if he did, who would recognize him? His most recent photograph dates from the late 1950s. In the intervening years, Hughes has undoubtedly aged severely. There have been all sorts of reports about what he supposedly now looks like. According to one report in 1970, which originated from within the Hughes camp, he weighed only about ninety-four pounds, had a long beard and hair that reached half way down his back. And also, so the rumor went, he had eight-inch-long fingernails. According to a later report by the United States ambassador to Nicaragua, who said he personally talked with him, Hughes looked fit, weighed about 145 pounds, had short black-and-white peppered hair, and wore a neat Vandyke beard.

One thing that is certain, however, is that the invisibility of Howard Hughes posed great problems to his legal opponents. Some of the sporting aspect of medieval British common law is reflected in American civil litigation: you have to catch your opponent before you can haul him into court. The rules of the chase give the quarry a fair break. Unlike American criminal law, which allows the police, when armed with a judge's warrant for arrest, to break and enter a dwelling anywhere in the nation in search of a suspect, civil law imposes strict limitations on how and where a plaintiff can pursue the defendant. Under the federal rules that govern the procedure in civil cases, a plaintiff can serve a defendant with a subpoena only within the area of the court's jurisdiction. In *TWA v. Hughes,* the service had to take place within the state of New York. Until the subpoena is served, the defendant is not a party to the litigation. He is not bound by the jurisdiction of the court; no proceedings may commence against him; and no penalty may be levied on him. Nor is there any rule in civil law that requires a defendant to make himself available to accept a subpoena. It is the plaintiff's duty to deliver the subpoena. It is the defendant's privilege to try and avoid it. The service is usually carried out by a professional process server, though anyone who is over twenty-one and not a lawyer of record in the case can be sworn in to deliver a subpoena. In order for the service to be binding, the process server must make the defendant aware that a subpoena is being delivered. Usually the process server thrusts it into the defendant's hand, shoves it into his pocket, or throws it at his feet.

When a corporation is the defendant, a subpoena served on a company officer binds the corporation as a party to the suit. Toolco was bound to the case shortly after it began in July 1961 when a subpoena was served a company sales executive at the Hughes Tool office in Manhattan's Rockefeller Center. But TWA was also determined to catch the two individual defendants in the suit, Raymond Holliday and Hughes. For months Holliday successfully evaded Sonnett's process servers. But on January 9, 1962, came a clue about his whereabouts. Abe Pomeranz, an office boy at Cahill, Gordon, had been delivering a message to Chester Davis' office. Descending in the elevator at 120 Broadway, he happened to overhear a conversation between two of Davis' secretaries. Unaware of the identity of the eavesdropper, one of the girls said to the other, "He'll be coming to the Towers at 3:30 tomorrow." Since it was common knowledge that the Hughes lieutenants always stayed at the Waldorf Towers where they maintained permanent apartments, Pomeranz reckoned that the "he" meant Holliday. Abe passed on his deduction to Fred Furth. The next afternoon, when Holliday arrived at the Towers, he was met outside the red-carpeted entrance by a process server. "Good afternoon, Mr. Holliday!" boomed the process server, and handed him a subpoena.

But catching Howard Hughes was quite a different matter. Chester Davis always made a point of stressing that he represented only the Hughes Tool Company and did not represent Howard Hughes personally and that the tool company had no control whatsoever over Hughes, who, added Davis, had no managerial duties at the company. In that way, Davis sought to block Sonnett from being able to summon Hughes to appear as Toolco's managing agent.

There was, however, one other way for Sonnett to compel Howard Hughes to appear in the proceedings. That was by calling him as a witness. Though defendants can be served a subpoena only within the jurisdictional bounds of the court in which the case will be tried, witnesses can be served in other jurisdictions. The plaintiff's lawyers can obtain from the United States District Court in the area in which the witness lives a subpoena that binds him to appear at a designated time and place to give testimony.

Thus, even though it was impossible to serve Hughes as a defendant in New York, it was possible to start a hunt to serve him as a witness in California. One way or the other, John Sonnett knew that he had to make Hughes feel that he personally would become involved in the case. Through a Los Angeles law firm, which acted as Cahill, Gordon's representative on the West Coast, Sonnett obtained a witness subpoena from the federal court of the Southern District of California. In accordance with the deposition schedule that had been approved earlier by Judge Metzner, that subpoena called for Hughes to appear at ten o'clock on the morning of April 23, 1962, at the Federal Courthouse in Los Angeles or at a mutually agreeable site to give testimony. Fred Furth, who was in charge of the hunt for Howard Hughes, was given a $25,000 budget and one main helper and adviser, Albert E. Leckey, a likable and rotund retired FBI agent. Their assignment was to deliver to Hughes the subpoena that would oblige him to appear as a witness.

By now it was already February. While Furth had been concerned with other matters, Leckey had been making contacts quietly in Southern California with people who knew—or who said they knew—something about Hughes' whereabouts. After Furth finished his assignment of copying Toolco documents, Leckey and he began the search for the elusive Mr. Hughes. A tip came in that Hughes and his wife were living in the home of a doctor friend in Rancho Santa Fe, a pleasant resort town about ninety miles southeast of Los Angeles. Furth and Leckey drove there, arriving late in the evening, and checked into The Inn, a hostelry favored by Hughes in earlier times. They had told no one of their mission. The next morning as Furth sat on the spacious veranda planning the day's activities, a Negro butler approached him. "You looking for Mr. Hughes?" he said. "Well, he isn't here." After making discreet and unproductive inquiries at The Inn and elsewhere, Furth and Leckey cruised the vicinity until they came upon an estate that had the earmarks of a Hughes hideaway. The house, its windows shuttered, was well back from the road; a high fence surrounded the grounds; a chain stretched uninvitingly across the drive; and two crew-cut young men, suspicious bulges beneath their arm pits, stood near the gate. Furth got out of the auto and asked if he could go in.

"I'm sorry, sir," replied one of the guards. "This is private property." Furth explained that he had urgent business with Howard Hughes. No response. No flicker whatsoever in the guards' eyes at the name. Not even the slightest indication that they had any connection with Howard Hughes. Furth, a persuasive debater, launched into a stirring speech about the urgency of his mission, its importance to Hughes and so forth and so on. The guards only repeated the short litany about the estate's being private property. Through it all, they remained totally unruffled, restrained, and relaxed. They were doing a job—and doing it exceedingly well. Furth finally gave up. Depressed, the two Hughes hunters drove back to Los Angeles.

If they were going to catch Hughes, they first had to get an idea about where he was and whether he moved around. Together with several private investigators whom they had engaged, Furth and Leckey staked out locations that were supposedly frequented by Hughes aides and employees. For weeks Furth's agents kept a watch on the arrivals and departures at 7000 Romaine. They would jot down license numbers of autos that often visited the "nerve center," would attempt to identify the owners, and later would trail the cars, which they hoped might lead them to Hughes.

The Hughes guards regarded the hunters as a welcome distraction. When they observed that cars leaving 7000 Romaine were being tailed, the guards delighted in decoying Furth's investigators into a chase. They would hop into one of the inconspicuous Chevrolets and lead the Hughes' hunters on a wild run on Southern California's sprawling freeways.

Fred Furth, who liked to live well, concentrated much of his sleuthing on the Beverly Hills Hotel, where Hughes sometimes lived. Since Furth correctly assumed that the Hughes people kept up with all his moves anyhow, he figured that he would get far better service if Toolco made his reservations for him. He also reckoned that his search for Hughes would cause less attention if he gave hotel personnel the impression that he was a guest of Toolco. Thus, through Toolco people, whom he had gotten to know during the document collection, Furth had a room booked at the Beverly Hills. From informants Furth knew that Hughes supposedly sometimes lived in Cottage No. 4 on the hotel grounds. Furth, who was indeed accorded VIP treatment by the hotel staff, had himself moved into Cottage No. 3, from which he could observe Cottage No. 4. Unfortunately, he caught not the slightest glimpse of anyone in the neighboring cottage who even vaguely resembled Hughes in height or age.

While in Cottage No. 3, Furth got a tip that Hughes was living on the third floor of the hotel. That evening Furth began nosing around that floor. He noticed a crew-cut pleasant young man, who was casually sauntering back and forth in the hall. "How's Howard?" asked Furth, as the young man approached. No response. "Where is he?" inquired Furth. No response. The young man, however, seemed to know who Furth was and obviously bore him no ill will. It was simply that he would not respond to questions about Hughes. Furth steered the conversation toward other subjects, but the only topic the young man would freely discuss was religion. The young guard talked so earnestly about the Mormon faith that Furth, a non-churchgoing Christian, got the impression that an effort was underway to convert him to the gospel of Brigham Young.

Furth and Leckey got another tip that Hughes had returned to his rented mansion in Bel Air, a very exclusive residential area of Los Angeles. Armed with a subpoena, the two men drove to the estate's entrance. The shades in the house were drawn, a reflection of Hughes' preference for sleeping during the daylight hours and working through the night. A high wire fence surrounded the estate and a chain was stretched across the drive. Two guards moved out to intercept Furth. "I have some papers for Mr. Hughes," Furth said, handing a copy of the subpoena to one of the guards. Wordlessly, the guard handed it back. For a minute or so, Furth and the guard handed the subpoena back and forth until Furth, in frustration, threw it at the guard's feet and stalked off.

Sonnett had instructed Furth to conduct the search for Hughes in a dignified manner and not to break any laws. Nonetheless, word of Furth's hunt for Hughes got around; the Los Angeles *Times* even did a feature story on the search. The story identified Fred Furth by name and described him as a New York lawyer who worked for the firm of Cahill, Gordon. The result was a great increase in the number of the tips about Hughes' whereabouts. Also, reward seekers, who were sometimes wild and irresponsible bounty hunters, began to offer their services. By telephone, telegram, and letter, offers flowed into the Cahill, Gordon firm from people who volunteered to bring in Howard Hughes—for a price. John Sonnett took the position that TWA could not offer rewards for the capture of Hughes, but that anyone who provided information that led to the service of a subpoena on Hughes would be liberally compensated. One reporter, who had contacts in both the Toolco and TWA camps, says he was offered $5,000 by Leckey if he could tell TWA where Hughes could be located.

Meanwhile, Hughes seemed to be moving around the country, and Furth sent investigators after him. He had reportedly been spotted in Phoenix; a subpoena was obtained for him there, but the process servers searched for him in vain. There were also reports that Hughes had visited New York City, but he could not be found there. Another report said that he was a guest of Gar Wood, the boat builder, on an island south of Miami. Again, private investigators failed to find him.

Leckey loved hamburgers. He and Furth would sit for hours in Los Angeles quick-order eateries, munching what the former FBI agent considered to be the height of delicacies. Furth, whose own tastes ran more toward filet mignon, was always struck by the irony of the scene: two men—one cagey but old, the other young but inexperienced—sitting in a third-rate hamburger parlor and pondering their assignment to catch a man of almost unlimited wealth and resources. At the time Hughes had at his disposal a fleet of three Convair 880s, five Lockheed JetStars, a DC-6, and an assortment of helicopters and small planes.

Actually, the closest Furth and Leckey thought they had ever gotten to Hughes was one morning at an estate in Palm Springs where they had driven in response to another tip. This time no guards blocked their way. They went to the front door and rang the bell. The door was opened by a butler, who answered their questions. Yes, Mr. Hughes had been there last night. The butler had understood that Mr. Hughes was to have stayed longer, but when he went to Mr. Hughes' room earlier that morning, it was empty. Furth and Leckey reckoned that Hughes, forewarned of their arrival, had fled during the night.

To the best of their knowledge, Furth and Leckey never even once laid eyes on Hughes. They did, however, form some ideas about how they thought he operated. They reckoned that his guard force was composed of thirty-five to forty men, all of them of the same general cut: well and conservatively dressed, hair cut short, fresh-faced, disciplined, and totally reliable. Furth and Leckey suspected that Hughes spent much of his time in Mexico. Furth thought that Hughes had a secret arrangement with the Mexican aviation authorities that enabled him to fly across the border without prior clearance. Furth also believed that somewhere in Mexico Hughes maintained a "Shangri La," a hideaway with a landing strip and Telex machines for communications with the "nerve center" in Los Angeles. That suspicion was buttressed by the travel patterns of Bob Maheu and some of the ranking Toolco executives, who made sudden visits to Mexico. Although Furth conducted a search in Mexico City and Acapulco, he was unable to find any trace of Howard Hughes. It was now already March 1962. Despite all the tips about his travels and whereabouts, Hughes remained as invisible as ever.

That was exactly the way Bob Maheu had planned it. Among other things, Maheu was handling Hughes' security, and he had devised a strategy of active defense by which he hoped to keep Furth and his operatives occupied by luring them with false tips into one fruitless search after another. Accordingly, Maheu would have various rumors spread about Hughes' supposed travel plans and hideaways. He even trotted out one of Hughes' former doubles and had him put in an appearance at a few restaurants and resorts in Northern California, but Furth failed to take that bait. Maheu deliberately misled Furth into believing that Hughes had a Mexican hideout by taking a trip to Mexico himself and encouraging Toolco executives to make an occasional detour in that direction.

Maheu and his men also attempted to gain a psychological advantage over the TWA investigators by maintaining a mock belligerency and warning them to keep on their toes and stay on the job. That attitude derived, in part, from a monetary consideration. Since Howard Hughes was still the owner of the vast majority of TWA's shares, he was, in fact, paying almost all of the costs of the hunt for himself. Thus, if he was going to be hunted, it had damn well better be a good hunt. On one occasion Bob Maheu even got the opportunity to deliver that message in person to Leckey, whom he knew from their service in the FBI. For several days Leckey had been tailing Maheu's car in the hope that his trail would lead to Hughes. Maheu was disgusted by the transparency of his former associate's sleuthing. One night, after Leckey had given up the chase for the day and had gone home, Maheu turned his car around so that it headed nose first from the garage. The next morning as Leckey cruised by the Maheu residence in preparation for resuming his tailing operation, Maheu, who had been sitting in his auto, waiting for that moment, shot out of his garage. He quickly overtook Leckey's big Buick and forced it to the curb. "Now get this straight," Maheu told Leckey. "You are being paid to find Mr. Hughes, not to tail me. Mr. Hughes is paying seventy-eight per cent of your salary, and I am going to make sure he gets his money's worth." Shamefacedly, Leckey switched his surveillance to another target.

And where was Howard Hughes? During the entire duration of the search, he did not budge even once from the well-protected privacy of the Bel Air mansion. It was undoubtedly an extremely trying period for Hughes' wife. Even under less confined circumstances, he would have been a difficult mate. Despite his marriage, he insisted on living according to his own egocentric habits. He slept only when exhausted, ate only when hungry, worked mainly at night. Ever fearful of disease, he demanded that his food be kept in a separate refrigerator. Occasionally, Jean Peters would seek to enjoy a bit of outside company by inviting actress friends for a visit. But the atmosphere in the Hughes' mansion was often strained and tense, the visitors reported. Sometimes Jean Peters would go out to a concert. But mostly she shared her husband's chilling isolation.

From a tactical standpoint, however, Hughes' seclusion was a success. Maheu's strategy of distraction succeeded in keeping TWA's investigators from besieging the house and thus drawing unwanted attention to Hughes' presence. Even so, Maheu remained concerned that TWA's investigators or perhaps some free-lance bounty hunter might devise a nefarious scheme to penetrate the security at Bel Air. From contacts in the Los Angeles Fire Department, Maheu picked up a tip that someone (Furth denies it was TWA) was trying to enlist the department's cooperation in a ruse to flush out Hughes. The plot: a helicopter would drop smoke bombs on the roof of the mansion. Sirens shrieking, fire trucks would arrive and firemen would break into the house to hustle out occupants. Among the firemen would be a process server who would slap a subpoena on Howard Hughes. There was also a tip that someone else (again not TWA, says Furth) was seeking the support of the police in a plot that would have sent a bevy of investigators into the Hughes home on the pretext of checking into a report that a felony had been committed there. Among the investigators would be the inevitable process server, who would use the opportunity to place the papers into Hughes' hands. Or so the scenario went. In reality, neither of those schemes went beyond the plotting stage.

To the increasing displeasure of John Sonnett, Howard Hughes was not playing the game that Sonnett wanted him to. After all, TWA's strategy for victory was based on the simple premise that Hughes had to feel threatened and involved. It was no good if he could simply hide away, ignore the case, and let his lawyers cope with it. That would never do. Howard Hughes had to feel the force of the law bearing down on his own skin. But how?

The windows of John Sonnett's eighteenth floor corner office at 80 Pine Street commanded a sweeping view of lower New York harbor. As he sat at his desk, Sonnett would often invite to his office his young aides with whom he liked to discuss the strategy of the case. As he and his assistants pondered various possible moves, countermoves, and their conceivable consequences, Sonnett would often swivel his chair around to gaze out the windows. As he absentmindedly watched the harbor's activity, he would turn his head slightly from side to side, closing one eye and then the other. If his conferees were well acquainted with his habits, they knew that John Sonnett was sighting the Statue of Liberty on the vertical window divider first with one eye and then the other. One day in mid-March, as he kept the statue squarely in his sights, Sonnett mused aloud whether perhaps a new approach was called for in the hunt for Hughes. His listener that day was Fred Furth, who had just returned from further unsuccessful searches on the West Coast. "Should we," pondered Sonnett, "serve interrogatories on the tool company and make them tell us where Hughes is?"

"Great idea, John!" exclaimed Furth with his characteristic impulsiveness, "I'll draw up a thousand of them."

"No, Fred," Sonnett insisted gently, "ten will be enough."

To pose an interrogatory, one party in a case makes a motion to the court for permission to put questions to the opposing side. If the judge grants the motion, the interrogatory then carries the weight of a court order and must be answered under oath.

Fred Furth did a quick and thorough job in framing the questions. They were so detailed and comprehensive and inquired about the whereabouts of Hughes from so many different angles that it would have been impossible for the tool company to answer the questions without fully disclosing the location of its eccentric owner. Furth's questions, which ran for about five typed pages, were directed to all Toolco officers as well as to ten specific employees, including Bill Gay, Hughes' chief administrative aide, and Nadine Henley, Gay's secretary.

As the days of March passed by, the Tillinghast deposition was still—would you believe it?—grinding on. In the mornings before the examination began and in the evenings after the questioning had ended, John Sonnett presented one reason after another to Special Master Rankin for serving the interrogatory on Toolco. By now Sonnett, through the huge Furth-led search, had managed to impress on the public, the court, and the special master that Howard Hughes was ducking service of the subpoena. Since Hughes' testimony was obviously essential to the case, Sonnett argued that Toolco should be ordered to disclose Hughes' whereabouts. By now that argument found a receptive listener in Rankin. He had already several times remarked that, in view of the serious charges being made against Howard Hughes, he was very interested in whether Hughes would show up to testify. Special Master Rankin also kept asking Sonnet if the service of the subpoena had been carried out. Sonnett could only reply that he was trying to serve Hughes but that Hughes was a hard man to find. On March 22 the special master granted Sonnett permission to submit a brief in support of his argument for forcing Toolco to reveal the location of Howard Hughes. After a flurry of counterbriefs and objections by Davis, the special master on April 17 ruled that TWA had the right to serve an interrogatory on the tool company about the whereabouts of Howard Hughes.

From a practical standpoint, there was the question of what TWA would do with the answers once they had them. If Toolco's reply, for example, stated that Hughes was in the upstairs northeast corner bedroom in his Bel Air home and would remain there through July 1, it was obvious that Furth would have no greater success breaking through the defenses than he had before. Hughes could sit behind the guards, high fences, and drawn blinds and remain as physically unapproachable as ever. But John Sonnett sensed that the interrogatory would pose for Hughes' aides a great psychological dilemma, which could lead them into tactical mistakes.

Aside from his immense wealth, Hughes' greatest strength remains his remoteness and the mystery that derives from his inaccessibility. He has made the secret of his whereabouts into a cult, and the keeping of that secret has become an article of faith at the tool company. Sonnett reckoned that the interrogatory about Hughes' whereabouts would put Toolco people in a terrible quandary. Just imagine: Which of the executives would dare to reveal the whereabouts of The Man? Which of them was going to send a message: "Sorry, Howard, the special master says that the game of hide-and-seek has got to end, so I have to tell where you are." No, such actions went against everything Sonnett and Furth had divined about the inner workings of the Hughes empire.

The interrogatory also touched Hughes' phobia about being captured and forced to take actions against his will. As long as no one knew his exact whereabouts, he apparently was less actively obsessed by his old worry. But in the mindscape of Howard Hughes, the disclosure of his whereabouts might arouse his deepest dread: *When you are old you will stretch out your arms and a stranger will bind you fast and carry you where you do not wish to go.*

In addition to Hughes' anxiety, there was another important

consideration. As long as the press was uncertain about Hughes' whereabouts, it left him in peace. But once his hideaway was made public, his solitude would end. Not only would the process servers besiege Hughes' refuge, but the entire scene would be recorded live and in living color by television cameras. The entire posse of the press—the wire services, newspapers, magazines, the whole lot —would document, and intensify, the travail of Howard Hughes.

On the same day that Rankin made the decision about the interrogatory, he handed down a second ruling that also struck at the core of Hughes' obsession for secrecy. That ruling touched upon one of the most sensitive aspects of a client's relationship to his lawyer. It is the so-called "privilege," the legal practice that cloaks in secrecy the communications between client and attorney. Even before the mutual exchange of evidence in March, Chester Davis and Raymond Cook had put the opposition on notice that Toolco was claiming the privilege for a certain number of its papers. Despite a court order for their surrender, Toolco withheld some financial documents, including working papers that dealt with the company's 1960 and 1961 income tax computations. Toolco claimed that the papers were privileged under the attorney-client relationship, because the tax returns were prepared by the Houston law firm of Andrews, Kurth, Campbell & Jones, which had handled Toolco's business ever since the company was founded. In addition, Toolco held back a number of other documents and communications, claiming that they, too, were covered by the privilege.

At the time of the surrender of Toolco documents in Houston, Hughes' lawyers informed Fred Furth that they were withholding several boxes of working papers. Now, as experts for Sonnett and the additional defendants examined the first batch of documents, which had been sorted out from the mountains of Toolco's financial data, those missing boxes began to assume a heightened, perhaps even crucial, significance. After a quick reading of the fragmentary tax papers for 1960 and 1961 that Toolco did hand over, some of the tax experts said that a complete study of the entire batch of working papers would be essential to support Sonnett's contention that Hughes had traded in aircraft to secure tax advantages. At the same time, that material might provide the additional defendants with the evidence they needed to rebut Toolco's accusation that they had damaged TWA by delaying the finalization of the jet financing. The tax experts said that a fuller examination of the accounting procedures used in computing Toolco's tax returns for 1960 and 1961 might reveal that Hughes, and not the additional defendants, was the one who had the compelling reason for delaying the closing of the financing until the last day of the year.

Because of the importance of the working papers, Sonnett and the attorneys for the additional defendants challenged Toolco's use of the privilege to withhold those documents. But Toolco maintained that the working papers constituted a confidential communication between client and counsel and hence were protected by the privilege. Like the bond of secrecy between priest and penitent, the relationship between counsel and client enjoys an inviolate confidentiality. Because of the privilege, a client can confide in his counsel without fear that the attorney will tell anyone else. Neither the court nor opposing lawyers can compel the lawyer or client to reveal what advice, guidance or other information has passed between them.

In order to remain in force, however, the privilege must be exercised only in very specific ways. Otherwise, it can be forfeited. One guiding principle is that the client and counsel must not seek to use the privilege to cover anything other than their two-way communications. The material for which the privilege is claimed must not be passed on to third parties, because the privilege is lost as soon as the client or attorney, either accidentally or intentionally, discloses to outsiders any part of those communications.

Another criteria is the content of the counsel-to-client communication. The information contained in the communication must deal with a legal subject on which advice was sought. Otherwise, the communication loses its privilege. Another test: How did the lawyer acquire the information that he imparted to his client? If the lawyer gained the knowledge while acting as a business agent, the communication does not qualify for the protection of the privilege.

In any event, the privilege is highly fragile and irreparable. Once it has been violated in a single instance in a case, it loses its effectiveness for all aspects of the client-counsel communications for the entire case. One strike and you are out.

Hence, John Sonnett and the other attorneys needed only to prove one violation of the privilege in order to strip the protection of secrecy away from the communications between Hughes and his lawyers in the entire case. Their attack centered chiefly on an episode that had taken place the previous November in the Northeast Airlines proceedings at the CAB. At that time, Raymond Cook, in his capacity as a legal counsel for Hughes, had submitted to the CAB a forty-four-page affidavit in which he described in great detail the maneuvers, allegedly undertaken by the banks and insurance companies, that ultimately forced Toolco to surrender control of TWA to the lender-dominated voting trust. From a reading of the document, it was evident that Cook's information was gained not only in his capacity as a lawyer but also in his role as a business agent. In a companion brief, Toolco's other Raymond—Holliday—who was already charged as a defendant in *TWA v. Hughes,* had declared that he adopted Cook's version of the pre-1961 events as his own. Sonnett and the other lawyers attacked Holliday's statement as a disclosure of the advice given him by his counsel since he was publicly affirming that he was relying on Cook's report about the developments leading up to the lawsuit. They also charged that Cook, who had served as Hughes' chief negotiator with the financial institutions, had acted as a business agent and that his communications, therefore, could not enjoy the protection of the privilege.

Nor was that all. When Chester Davis framed Toolco's gigantic countersuit, he drew heavily upon Cook's affidavit, reproducing entire passages almost word for word. Seizing on those sentences, Toolco's opponents charged that the countercomplaints also contained material that disclosed the advice that counsel had given his client. Furthermore, both Holliday and Davis took the position in court that Toolco's post-December 1960 actions—which TWA at-

tacked as willful interference with the airline's business—were taken
on "advice of counsel to protect the legitimate interests of Toolco."
Davis and Cook thought of the advice-of-counsel defense only as a
temporary tactical maneuver. But Toolco's adversaries argued that
Davis' actions had in themselves made public his advice to his
client, since he had been both counseling Toolco and acting on its
behalf in the post-1960 fracas.

In his ruling, Rankin found Toolco guilty as charged by Sonnett
and the other lawyers. "The affidavit of Mr. Cook and other parties
on the record show quite clearly that in many of the activities of
Mr. Cook on behalf of the tool company, he was acting as a business agent and not merely as a legal adviser," declared the special
master. "He appears also to have passed on to third parties information, positions, attitudes and claims of the tool company concerning numerous specific matters. Whenever Mr. Cook's actions
or those of Mr. Davis or Mr. Bautzer would fit into categories
just described, and they were acting as business agents . . . or
were expected to communicate information to third parties or to
receive information from third persons to be communicated to the
tool company, all of such communications and information and
the full scope of it would not be privileged." Rankin ordered
Toolco to submit the working papers and other documents it
claimed were privileged. He would rule whether they fell within
the scope of the case. If they did, they would have to be surrendered
since Toolco had, in his view, forfeited the privilege.

Even as Rankin's decision struck at the tool company's most
guarded secrets, John Sonnett the very next day made another
major move in his campaign to engage Howard Hughes personally
in the case. On April 18 John Sonnett filed a new suit—this time
in the Court of Chancery in Wilmington, Delaware, the state in
which TWA and Toolco are incorporated. The defendants were
the same as in the New York action: Toolco, Hughes, and Holliday. The underlying material was also the same as in the New York
complaint, but the alleged offenses were different. While the New
York suit charged violations of the federal antitrust laws, the Delaware action alleged mismanagement and breach of fiduciary re-

sponsibility. As the penalty, TWA asked for $35 million in damages from Toolco, a sum which under Delaware law could not be tripled.

Sonnett brought the action in Wilmington to take advantage of an unusual aspect of Delaware law. Under a provision of the state's legal code, the plaintiff in a civil action may apply for a court order to sequester the stock of the defendant. Once the sequester order is carried out, the stock remains under the supervision of the court until the end of the litigation; it cannot be sold, voted, or touched by the defendant, who also is barred from drawing dividends. If the defendant is called to appear in the case and fails to do so, a verdict may be entered against him and a part or all of the stock may be sold off to settle the judgment.

Accordingly, on the same day TWA filed the Delaware complaint, it obtained an order from Vice Chancellor Isaac D. Short II that seized the entire stock of the Hughes Tool Company, then estimated to be worth $250 to $350 million. The court appointed a Wilmington lawyer named Jacob Kreshtool to act as the sequester. He in turn served a notice on Toolco's resident agent in Wilmington that the bedrock of Howard Hughes' fortune—his sole ownership of the tool company—was now under the command of the court and liable to at least partial confiscation if Hughes failed to appear.

Sonnett was now launching a series of swift legal attacks. It was a finely coordinated effort to wrest the initiative away from Davis, who had gained the upper hand through the CAB decision in December and the filing of the countersuit in February. Sonnett knew that he had to act quickly, for he was picking up clues that Davis was also preparing another surprise stroke. Operatives of Howard Hughes, directed by Bob Maheu, had been trying to get hold of the TWA stockholder list, which was on file in Delaware. Sonnett suspected that Hughes and Davis were planning some new maneuver in which they would try to enlist the support of the shareholders behind Hughes' legal counterattack on the lender-installed TWA management, which was running the airline ever more deeply into the red.

Even as a new act was beginning in Delaware, Sonnett was trying to blunt Davis' counterattack in New York. On the same day the new TWA suit was filed in Wilmington, Sonnett argued before Judge Metzner that Hughes' countersuit should be quashed. Sonnett repeated his earlier contention that most of the counterclaims were not proper counterclaims at all but actually constituted a separate suit. He also pointed out that the second counterclaim, which alleged violations of the Federal Aviation Act, did not belong in a court at all but fell instead under the jurisdiction of the CAB. But Judge Metzner reserved judgment on Sonnett's motion.

Meanwhile, as a simultaneous Act Three to the Hughes drama, Tillinghast's deposition was still in progress. The transcript of his testimony already filled a stack of volumes four feet high. Now Sonnett began to lay the groundwork for a motion to end Tillinghast's deposition so that he finally could call Howard Hughes to the stand. Sonnett knew that on July 1 a rule change was scheduled to take place in the Southern District of New York in the procedures that govern the conduct of depositions. Under the old system, the party that had been granted priority of discovery, usually the defendant, had the right to complete the examination of all of his witnesses before the other side could call its first witness. After July 1, however, the new procedures would provide for concurrent depositions. Sonnett wanted either to end immediately Tillinghast's deposition and call Hughes to the stand, or to wait until July 1 and start his own questioning of Hughes even while Davis continued his examination of Tillinghast and the other scheduled witnesses.

Sonnett had to work fast, because he was trying to overcome the big advantage that Hughes was building up at the CAB. Public hearings in the Northeast control case had been held on April 2, 1962, in Washington. Those hearings were proceeded by much the same hulabaloo that took place before the one-day hearings in November. (In the meantime, of course, Toolco had bought out Atlas' controlling position in the faltering airline and had provided Northeast with a revolving credit of $1 million so that it could meet operating expenses. But the airline still badly needed more help.) Hughes' opponents, like the proverbial Greek chorus, again took up the chant that he should appear as a witness. Lawyers for Eastern Airlines maintained their high level of polemic brilliance by stating in a brief to the CAB that "Hughes should humble himself and come forward to testify." Paul Seligson, a bright and aggressive counsel for CAB's Bureau of Economic Regulation, declared that the public interest demanded that Hughes appear at hearings.

Hughes obviously had hoped that the Northeast control case would be decided on the narrow issue of whether the airline could or could not survive without his help. But his opponents, notably Eastern and National, clamored for a much broader inspection of his past behavior. The CAB staff also wanted to expand the horizon of the hearings into the causes behind the TWA complaint against Hughes. In fact, Seligson hoped the Cahill, Gordon lawyers would join him to present a united front against Hughes in the CAB hearings. But they demurred. Sonnett wanted to try *TWA v. Hughes* in the federal court in New York, not before the CAB in Washington. Nonetheless, the merits of the TWA suit became one of the official issues in the Northeast control case.

In the weeks before the start of the April hearings, CAB investigators probed the evidence in *TWA v. Hughes*. They studied the available evidence; they interviewed TWA executives; they examined the court record; they consulted with John Sonnett and his aides. Meanwhile in Washington, dozens of preparatory meetings were held between the various parties in the CAB proceedings to thrash out the parameters of the evidence that would be presented in the public hearings. With the exception of Toolco, Northeast, and Atlas, all the other parties in the proceedings were either opposed to Hughes' control bid of Northeast or highly skeptical about him—or both. And there were quite a few other parties: Allegheny, Braniff, Delta, Eastern, National, Pan American, and Riddle Airlines, and, of course, the CAB's Bureau of Economic Regulation. The CAB staff had requested from Toolco a long list of data and evidence about Hughes' tax positions and business intentions that covered five typed pages.

But Toolco was as cocky and uncooperative as it could be. In reply to the CAB's requests for documents, Toolco said that it first wanted some documents from the CAB. It wanted to see the papers on which the CAB had based its December 1960 ruling, which declared that Hughes was responsible for the delays in the delivery of jets to TWA and had damaged the airline. The CAB did not have any documentary evidence on that subject—and Hughes' lawyers knew it. Those harsh words condemning Hughes had come out of the heads of several young lawyers, who had been eager to force him to surrender control of TWA.

Well, if the CAB could not produce those documents, Toolco did not feel compelled to submit the documents that Seligson had demanded. Pleading its familiar argument that the documents were protected by the privilege, Toolco withheld the most vital papers, which concerned Toolco's taxes and Hughes' plans for Northeast. In order to avoid the disclosure of such information, Toolco's attorneys successfully invoked the privilege some hundred times during the prehearing investigations.

Immediately before the public hearings, the CAB's, Seligson fired off a blistering letter to Chester Davis in which he branded the evidence submitted by Toolco as "entirely inadequate" and severely criticized Hughes for not being willing to testify. Unless more evidence was turned over, Seligson threatened, Toolco's application to take over Northeast would be rejected. He wrote: "Mr. Hughes and Toolco are trying to force the Board to view their transactions through a looking glass of their own design. This course can only result in a distorted view of the facts and a decision grounded upon the logic of Alice's friends in Wonderland."

As the hearings began on April 2, little Alice and her friends might have felt quite at home in the CAB headquarters on Connecticut Avenue. Certainly the opponents of Howard Hughes had to run as fast as they could just to stay in place. In an opening exchange T. A. MacDonald, the attorney for National Airlines, asked Chester Davis "if the tool company can tell me where Mr. Hughes can be found."

"No, the tool company does not know where Mr. Hughes may

be found," replied Davis. He added: "Mr. Hughes is a very independent person with a personal and private life, which I think he is entitled to keep and preserve, notwithstanding his very genuine interest in the aviation industry and his desire to be of as much assistance as anyone is willing to permit him to be."

However, as soon as Raymond Holliday took the stand, Seligson, still perturbed at the incompleteness of Toolco's submitted evidence, pressed him on an issue that cut to the core of *TWA v. Hughes.* That issue was whether one of Toolco's motivations for controlling airlines was to reap tax benefits by leasing and selling planes. Seligson asked: "Mr. Holliday, if the board were to approve the tool company's application here but were to attach a condition for the indefinite future there could be no aircraft transactions between the tool company and Northeast, would the tool company accept such a condition?"

"I am not prepared to say at this time, Mr. Seligson," answered Holliday.

"What would you have to do to find out, sir?"

"I would have to think about it for awhile."

"Would you have to check with Mr. Hughes?"

"I don't think I would."

"Would you be in a position to commit the tool company without again—without checking with Mr. Hughes on that?"

"I think I could, yes. I would have to talk to the board of directors of the tool company."

"What would the board of directors have to do?"

"They would undoubtedly follow my advice in the matter."

"Am I to understand that you control the tool company?"

"No, I don't control the tool company, no. It is controlled by a stockholder, Mr. Hughes."

"Do you speak for Mr. Hughes in this respect?"

"No, I do not. But unless Mr. Hughes speaks for himself, I have to speak for him."

"Are you in a position to speak for him when he doesn't speak for himself?"

"Not without thinking about it, no, sir."

"When you have thought about it, are you in a position to speak for him?"

"We would examine whatever the condition was and if we felt that it fitted into the agreement as we made it with Atlas, then at that time, we would act accordingly."

"When you say 'we' do you include Mr. Hughes in that examination?"

"Not necessarily, no."

"Would you refer the matter to Mr. Hughes?"

"Well, that is entirely—it is unlikely, but it is possible."

"Suppose the board said that in order to get approval, you would have to put up $50 million, would you refer that to Mr. Hughes?"

"I don't think we would have to refer to him at all."

"What would you do in that event?"

"I think we would summarily just say no."

Not content with that reply, Seligson pressed Holliday about what assurances Toolco would give for Northeast's future. But Holliday refused to make specific promises or commitments. Seligson pointed out that, by having acquired Atlas' 55 per cent control of Northeast, Toolco could end up owning 80 per cent or more of the airline—a degree of ownership that would enable the tool company to deduct Northeast's losses from its profits in computing federal income tax. But again Holliday refused to disclose Toolco's tax intentions toward Northeast. In fact, Holliday refused to budge from the standard Toolco position. "The Hughes Tool Company," said Holliday, "will support Northeast consistent with sound business judgment." When Seligson continued to insist on an explanation of what the term "sound business judgment" meant, Holliday snapped: "We have been in business for fifty years, and it is a sound, profitable company. So I think that offers a pretty good measure of guarantee."

During the hearings the CAB's Bureau of Economic Regulation complained that Toolco had withheld some crucial papers altogether and had delivered others too late. Furthermore, because the bureau had not received the close degree of cooperation that it had hoped from Cahill, Gordon, it had been unable to evaluate completely the merits of the *TWA v. Hughes* suit. Even more important, the bureau had been unable to dig up its own evidence to support the charges that Hughes had engaged in unlawful activities while he was in control of TWA. The bureau asked for more time for investigation. But the CAB examiner, Merritt Ruhlen, refused. Said he: "If anybody can introduce evidence to show how Northeast can continue to operate for a reasonable period of time without the help that Toolco is going to give, then I might reconsider my ruling."

No one could submit that evidence. Quite the contrary, the testimony was overwhelming that, without Toolco's continued support, Northeast would be forced into bankruptcy. Though the opposing parties disputed Hughes' right to control Northeast, none of them expressed any willingness to take on the burden of running Northeast themselves without a CAB promise of subsidies or other concessions. Some of them openly advocated letting Northeast die.

On April 20, 1962, Examiner Ruhlen handed down his decision. Hughes could hardly have hoped for a cleaner bill of health. It was in the public interest, declared the examiner, to allow Toolco to assume control of Northeast. While Ruhlen conceded that the Bureau of Economic Regulation had wanted to probe more deeply into *TWA v. Hughes,* he also noted that the bureau failed to accept a challenge from Toolco to supply the documents on which the CAB earlier had asserted that Hughes had damaged TWA. Ruhlen added that he was satisfied that sufficient evidence had been submitted to enable him to draw a conclusion about the validity of the charges against Hughes in the TWA suit. What followed was a stunning blow for John Sonnett. "The record," wrote the CAB examiner, "will not support a finding that Toolco engaged in improper or unlawful activities in regard to TWA or Northeast."

Nor was that all. During the hearings Hughes' opponents also had contended that he had been responsible for the delays in the delivery of jets to Northeast, a charge that echoed the essence of the TWA suit. "The record will not support such a charge," declared Examiner Ruhlen. "It is clear that rather than a detriment, Toolco's actions in this respect were of substantial benefit to Northeast."

The examiner found no merit whatsoever in the charges that Hughes manipulated aircraft sales to TWA for his own benefit—another basic issue in Sonnett's lawsuit. "Toolco evidently ordered ten jet aircraft from General Dynamics for TWA in excess of those finally determined by TWA to be necessary," wrote Ruhlen. "But there is nothing to indicate that this was more than a mistake in judgment on Toolco's part, or that Toolco attempted to make a profit on such transactions at the expense of TWA. Nor does the record disclose that in the operation of TWA, Toolco managed its operations in such a way that tax benefits that should have inured to TWA were obtained by Toolco." Ruhlen's report was sent to the board for final action.

On June 19, in a majority opinion written by Chairman Alan Boyd, the Civil Aeronautics Board handed down its decision. "Northeast is on the verge of bankruptcy," wrote Boyd in his usual disarmingly honest way, "and unless it obtains outside help, it will soon be forced to cease operations. If the carrier is to be maintained in being and its services continued, there are no feasible alternatives to approval of the control applied for." Boyd supported Examiner Ruhlen's decision not to spend time on an extensive investigation of Toolco's record at TWA or of the possible effects of Toolco's management of Northeast. "The condition of Northeast and the necessity for immediate help made the issue not whether Toolco would provide an efficient management, but whether Northeast would have any management at all.

"In summary, the evidence convinces us," Boyd wrote, "that the preservation of Northeast as an operating entity, with the resulting benefits to the traveling public, and to its employees, creditors and stockholders, is, on this record, in the public interest."

There was only a single dissenter among the five board members. "The record is so meager that even the most essential information has not been furnished," Chan Gurney, a Republican, wrote in a minority-of-one dissent. "The most that the record shows is a statement that Toolco will use its best business judgment in promoting the affairs," he declared. "If Toolco is unable or unwilling to commit a definite amount of needed funds based upon a definite plan for the rehabilitation of Northeast, Toolco could permit Northeast to cease operations."

Gurney had a point, but it made no difference now. By a four-to-one vote, the CAB had approved Hughes' control of Northeast and handed him a brilliant and significant victory. The board even officially adopted Ruhlen's position that on its record the TWA suit against Hughes had no merit. The board also, in effect, retracted its earlier criticism of Hughes' stewardship of TWA on which the suit, at least in part, had been based. Howard Hughes must have felt vindicated. No longer was he an outcast from the aviation community. Once again he enjoyed the CAB's full blessing to run one of the nation's airlines. Northeast celebrated the CAB decision by running large ads in forty-two East Coast and Canadian newspapers. They said: "WELCOME ABOARD, HOWARD HUGHES!"

11. One Simple Question

Step One of Hughes' master plan for regaining control of TWA
now had succeeded. His Washington opponents had made a serious error in trying to fight the *TWA v. Hughes* lawsuit within the
limited time frame of the CAB hearings in which Hughes held
Northeast hostage. Now Hughes could embark upon the second
phase of his plan to dissolve the voting trust. But first Hughes
and Toolco's attorney Chester Davis had to repulse Sonnett's
latest attacks.

Davis was concerned about the Delaware case, which threatened
to confiscate Hughes' Toolco stock. Davis could find some comfort, however, in the fact that it would take a long time for the
Delaware proceedings to develop to the point where Hughes could
be called to the stand. That case was still in the deposition stage;
Fred Furth was questioning Bob Maheu about why Toolco had
wanted to get hold of the TWA stockholders list. Davis' most
pressing worry in New York was the TWA interrogatory, which
would compel Toolco to disclose the whereabouts of Howard
Hughes. Special Master Rankin already had instructed Toolco
to answer the interrogatory, which was intended to provide TWA
with the essential information that would enable a process server
to deliver a subpoena to Hughes.

But Davis was fighting back. In mid-May he made a motion to
the special master to quash the interrogatory entirely or, failing

that, to make several changes in wording. The special master scheduled a hearing on the Davis' motion for June 4. At the hearing Sonnett, citing TWA's extensive, expensive, and futile search to find Hughes, insisted that the interrogatory should be answered. He called attention to the admissions by Davis and Holliday in the CAB proceedings that they did not even know where Hughes was. If even Hughes' closest aide and Toolco's counsel did not know where Hughes was, how on earth could TWA be expected to find him? The only feasible way, reiterated Sonnett, was for the special master to compel Toolco to disclose his whereabouts. In his ruling that day, the special master agreed basically with Sonnett's position. Yet, in view of Toolco's obvious reluctance to answer the interrogatory, Rankin wanted to give Chester Davis an alternative. Thus the special master ruled that Toolco could take one of two actions: either Hughes could authorize someone, most likely Davis, to accept service of the subpoena on his behalf, or Toolco would be required to answer TWA's interrogatory by July 1.

Rankin emphasized that if Hughes elected to have someone else accept the subpoena on his behalf, he would have to say so in writing. He should execute a sworn declaration that would be binding and irrevocable. The special master wanted to be certain that Hughes could not in the future either renounce his action by saying that he knew nothing about it or escape through some legal ambiguity. Hence Rankin ordered that "the authorization from Hughes must be in a form satisfactory to counsel of TWA and the special master." In setting such a requirement, the special master also had Davis' welfare in mind. He wanted to be absolutely sure that any statement from Hughes would be so precise that he could not leave Davis in a highly embarrassing situation.

Rankin allowed Davis sixteen days—until June 20—in which to comply with one alternative or the other. But instead of obeying the special master's instructions, Davis continued to dispute the right of TWA to put questions to Toolco at all. Finally, after another flurry of briefs and counterbriefs, Davis appealed the special master's ruling about the interrogatory to Judge Metzner. Because of the time consumed by the appeal, Davis managed to slide by the July 1 deadline without either answering the interrogatory or providing a sworn statement from Hughes to accept the subpoena on his behalf.

But meanwhile, even as Davis sought to avoid answering the interrogatory, Sonnett renewed his efforts to summon Howard Hughes to the witness stand. In a motion to Judge Metzner, Sonnett asked the court either to suspend Tillinghast's deposition so that TWA could begin to question Hughes or to allow TWA to take advantage of the new procedures and start a concurrent deposition of Hughes while Tillinghast's testimony was still being taken.

Yes, Tillinghast was still on the stand. In July, Davis was questioning him mainly about the reasons for starting the suit and his dealings with Vic Leslie, the longtime TWA financial vice president whom Tillinghast had recently forced to resign. Even though Tillinghast had been with TWA for only three months before the complaint was filed, Davis by now had kept him on the stand for six months. Nearly all of Davis' thirteen remaining witnesses were far more intimately acquainted with Hughes' history at TWA than Tillinghast. At Davis' present rate of progress, some of his opponents calculated that he would not be finished with his other witnesses for at least another six years! Perhaps even much longer.

On July 12, after reading the inevitable briefs from each side and listening to the arguments, Judge Metzner handed down decisions on both the interrogatory and the timing of Hughes' testimony. He sustained the special master's ruling that unless Hughes elected to authorize someone to accept the subpoena on his behalf, Toolco should answer the interrogatory. Judge Metzner set July 27 as the deadline for Toolco's reply. On the issue of Hughes' appearance, Judge Metzner once again refused to interrupt Davis' discovery proceedings or to allow Sonnett to hold concurrent depositions. Nonetheless, Judge Metzner did order Davis to end Tillinghast's deposition on or before July 25. Hughes' evasive tactics were beginning to make a distinct impression on the court. "I think it is obvious that Mr. Hughes is in a peculiar situation," said Judge Metzner. "He is obviously ducking service in this law-suit."

Even though the Tillinghast deposition continued, the tension in the case now centered almost entirely on the interrogatory. Chester Davis obviously felt the deadline closing in on him. During the deposition session on July 23, which was four days before due date for the reply, Sonnett asked Davis what action Toolco was taking to supply answer to the interrogatory.

"I have taken no action," replied Davis, who fell back on the fact that he had just applied to the court for some additional modifications in the wording of the interrogatory. "I am not in a position to take any action in transmitting these interrogatories to the tool company until I am in a position to say, 'This is what you are supposed to answer.'" However, Davis' application for changes in the wording could at best only gain a few days of extra time, because Judge Metzner had clearly indicated that he would not tolerate any modification that weakened the sole purpose of the interrogatory—to locate Howard Hughes. In fact, that afternoon Judge Metzner denied Davis' motion for any modification of the interrogatory.

The next day, which was Tuesday, July 24, Davis asked the special master for an extension of the July 27 deadline. He argued that not until the previous day had he been certain what Toolco was to answer and that it would take time to assemble the replies. Unimpressed by Davis' plea, Rankin replied that he had neither the desire nor the power to modify the court's order. The July 27 deadline remained in effect. But the next day—two days before the deadline—Davis appealed the special master's decision to Judge Metzner and asked for an extension until September 25. In response, the court, on July 26, gave Davis half of what he wanted: the deadline for answering the interrogatory was extended to August 27, 1962.

Events the next day, on which the original deadline fell due, made Davis' entire exercise in cliff-hanging seem completely unnecessary, dumbfounding, and downright puzzling. Despite the judge's instructions, Tillinghast's deposition had not yet ended.

Davis had managed to slip past the July 25 deadline by arguing that so many of the recent sessions had been taken up by discussion of other matters that he needed additional time for his examination of Tillinghast. But on July 27 Davis took a few minutes out from questioning Tillinghast to announce to the special master and the opposing lawyers that the issue of the interrogatory was now dead. Toolco had chosen the other alternative. He, Chester Davis, had received authorization from Howard Hughes to accept the subpoena on his behalf.

The next session of the Tillinghast deposition took place Monday, July 30. Mercifully, it was also Tillinghast's last. At the close of that day's questioning, Tillinghast was excused from further examination—at least, for the time being. In the months since his deposition began January 5, he had been on the stand under questioning for forty days, for a total of about one hundred and eighty hours. In what amounted to seven and a half days and nights under the ungentle probing of Chester Davis, Tillinghast had given testimony that took up more than six thousand pages.

What had Davis accomplished through this incredibly lengthy exercise? The most obvious achievement was simply the winning of time. While Tillinghast was on the stand, Howard Hughes used those weeks and months to execute the successful maneuver at the CAB that undermined much of TWA's case against him. Because of his victory at the CAB, Hughes now could hope to regain control of TWA. Almost equally important, Chester Davis had constructed a record of evidence that would be vital in supporting his counterattack in the *TWA v. Hughes* case. Davis' theory of defense was, in effect, to say: "Look, Judge, TWA was injured all right, but we didn't do it. It was Tillinghast, Breech, and those Wall Street fellows. And you know what, Judge? They had it all planned out. It was a conspiracy."

During the questioning of Tillinghast, Davis elicited several telling points that buttressed Toolco's arguments. After extended questioning, Davis extracted from Tillinghast the statement that part of the motivation for seeking an anitrust conviction against Hughes was to force him to divest himself of his TWA holdings.

Davis also was able to demonstrate that Tillinghast was unable to give a spell-out of the specific offenses on which TWA's antitrust case against Howard Hughes rested. That helped Davis to support his contention that the TWA suit was "conclusionary" and lacked factual underpinnings. In the deposition, Davis probed and probed for Tillinghast's knowledge of individual offenses. TWA's president replied repeatedly with the familiar litany of generalized accusation. But never was Tillinghast able to state the specifics. He did not once say, for example, that "on the evening of September x, 19xx, Mr. Hughes, together with so-and-so and so-and-so, forced TWA to buy ten Constellations at $500,000 per plane and by doing so damaged TWA in the following manner and with the following financial consequences."

The special master, for one, was struck by the deficiencies in Tillinghast's deposition. "I had thought," he declared at one of the hearings, "that before we completed the testimony of Mr. Tillinghast, I would be informed about the ultimate facts that the plaintiff was relying upon to support the allegations of its complaint, which are largely conclusions of law but do conform to the requirements of the federal rule concerning such complaints. I did not think that with the chief executive officer of the plaintiff being deposed we would reach a point at the conclusion when I would not know the ultimate facts upon which the plaintiff was relying to establish those various allegations in so far as they had a bearing upon a violation of the antitrust laws. But I did find that I was in that position."

On July 31, the day after Tillinghast's deposition ended, the lawyers met before the special master to discuss the authorization that Davis had said he had received from Howard Hughes. In his earlier ruling Lee Rankin had insisted that the authorization must be in a form that would be satisfactory both to him and to Davis' opponents. In keeping with the ruling, Sonnett proposed to Davis that they should agree on the wording of an affidavit, which Hughes would then execute and swear before a notary public. According to Sonnett's proposal, Hughes in the affidavit should name Davis as his attorney in fact and in law and specifically spell out that he, Hughes, had vested in Davis complete and irrevocable authority to receive on his behalf a subpoena that would require him, Hughes, to appear in person at the Federal Courthouse in Los Angeles to give testimony in the case of *TWA v. Hughes* on September 24. That was the date Sonnett now had chosen as the first day of Hughes' deposition. Sonnett wanted to be certain that the affidavit would be precise and irrevocable so that the service of the subpoena on Davis would be just as binding as the handing of the paper to Howard Hughes in person. Sonnett was anxious about several factors. Like Rankin, he was concerned that Hughes might later renounce the authorization and leave Davis in a precarious professional position. But Sonnett was naturally even more concerned that in such an event, TWA would be left without any legal hold on Hughes if the way to him led through Davis. Sonnett was also worried that Davis still maintained that he did not represent Hughes personally but only Toolco.

Chester Davis, however, bridled at Sonnett's suggestion that they should agree to a form of a written authorization. Said Davis: "I simply announced something on the record last Friday which I thought was a matter of some interest to the special master and counsel, and merely because I saw fit to inform counsel is no basis whatsoever for being subjected to cross-examination or to motions or stipulations." In fact, to the astonishment of the other lawyers, Davis made no move to use the authorization. "They [TWA] served interrogatories. We have a decision of Judge Metzner. Let's leave the matter rest exactly where it is," said Davis, who obviously meant he had until August 27 to answer TWA's questions. Davis was in no hurry to deal with the authorization issue.

Sonnett feigned puzzlement over Davis' reluctance to make an agreement, which would avoid future time-wasting arguments. "I don't quite see why Mr. Davis is so distressed," said Sonnett.

"I am not distressed, Mr. Sonnett," replied Davis.

"If we can't do it in a lawyerlike way, I guess we just have to go ahead with the program Judge Metzner has arranged," declared Sonnett, implying that the interrogatory would have to be answered by August 27.

"I am terrified," responded Davis in mock horror.

"I note, Mr. Davis, you are very flip about how terrified you are," Sonnett shot back. "But you and Mr. Hughes have to learn that the processes of the courts of the United States are not to be treated lightly. We shall continue with every possible effort to make Mr. Hughes subject to the process of this court."

Did Sonnett's warning frighten Davis? Who knows? But the fact is the very next day, Davis reversed his position and as if nothing had happened, sent a letter to John Sonnett. "This is to confirm that I am authorized to accept process on behalf of Howard R. Hughes for his appearance as witness," he wrote. "In order to avoid further effort and expense by TWA to locate Mr. Hughes, I will acknowledge service on his behalf if you will deliver appropriate papers to me." At the same time Davis dispatched a letter to Judge Metzner in which he enclosed a copy of the letter to Sonnett. He also enclosed a photocopy of the written authorization. Davis asked that it be kept confidential and not be made part of the court record.

The deposition proceedings were recessed for August and John Sonnett had left the city for a much-needed rest. In his absence, Robert Zeller, an associate at Cahill, Gordon, was assigned to handle developments in the case. He opened Davis' letter. Zeller telephoned Davis' office to find out if the authorization was in a form which would satisfy Sonnett's criteria. Since Davis had also left for vacation, Zeller spoke with Davis' assistant, Maxwell Cox, who would concede only that the authorization was in writing. Otherwise, he was very mysterious. He would not furnish Zeller with a copy or even permit him to look at the original. As a precaution, Zeller wrote to Judge Metzner on August 2 that unless the authority was precise and irrevocable, TWA's position remained that it refused to accept Davis' claim that he could accept service for Hughes and that therefore TWA expected Toolco to answer the interrogatory on August 27.

While activity in the case lagged under the August heat in New York, there was a sudden spurt of Hughes-hunting in Los Angeles. With the deadline for the interrogatory hanging over Toolco, Sonnett had left instructions to keep up the pressure on Hughes. Leckey had gotten a tip that Hughes had an appointment that would bring him to the Beverly Hills Hotel on Friday evening, August 17. In the event that Hughes did actually circulate in Los Angeles that evening, Furth, who relished the role of a field general, organized the greatest search of all. He hired thirty private detectives, whom he assembled in his spacious suite at the Biltmore Hotel. Furth briefed the agents on their assignment. They were simultaneously to close in on the places where Leckey and Furth, from the earlier sleuthing, thought Hughes might be found. Among the targets for the night were the Beverly Hills Hotel, 7000 Romaine, Hughes' Bel Air home, and a Wiltshire Boulevard office that Hughes supposedly sometimes used. The agents were to operate in groups of three and four, each group containing one man who had been sworn in as a process server. As Furth once joked, "There were almost as many Hughes' subpoenas scattered about the city as there were Los Angeles *Times.*"

While Furth stayed behind in his suite to coordinate their activities by telephone, Leckey and the agents departed on their missions. Lacking a radio communications system, Furth had the agents call in at half-hour intervals and report their findings. If one set of agents phoned that they were closing in on Hughes, Furth could then direct the others to help them. All night the dragnet was cast across Los Angeles. The results? Nil. As usual, no one even caught a glimpse of Howard Hughes. During the August 17 search, United States marshals also attempted to serve subpoenas on Hughes, but they were turned away from 7000 Romaine where they were told that service on Hughes could be effected only through Davis' office in New York. On August 20 Zeller wrote Judge Metzner about the unsuccessful results. He said that TWA would not make any further efforts to find Hughes until it had received Toolco's answers to the interrogatory.

Judge Metzner had also been on vacation. When he returned to Manhattan on August 21 he found Davis' letter waiting for him. Judge Metzner took one look at the photocopy of the authorization and decided that he wanted nothing to do with it. The judge wrote to Davis that he was returning "what you say is a written authorization from Mr. Hughes." Judge Metzner explained that for two reasons—Davis' insistence that the authorization not be made part of the record and his failure to supply a copy to Sonnett —he did not consider the authorization to be properly before the court. "In the circumstances," he wrote, "I will expect that you will comply with the order of the Court of July 26, 1962." That was the order calling for a reply to the interrogatory on or before August 27.

In Sonnett's absence, Zeller kept up the pressure on Toolco. On August 20 he sent a notice to Davis' office, reminding Toolco that Hughes was still scheduled to testify on September 24. Mrs. Lola Lea, an associate in Davis' office, responded the next day with a letter in which she conveyed a message from the vacationing Davis. "Upon his return to New York, he will be glad to make arrangements with you for the service of the subpoena on him, which he is authorized to accept on behalf of Mr. Hughes."

The next day—it was now August 22—Zeller replied in a letter to Mrs. Lea that "We do not believe that our client's interests would be adequately protected by relying upon service of the Hughes' subpoena on Mr. Davis in the absence of irrevocable authority from Mr. Hughes along the lines of that proposed in our draft stipulation. So far as we are aware, that irrevocable authority has not been granted. We therefore await with great interest the service on August 27th of Toolco's answers to our Interrogatory about Mr. Hughes' whereabouts."

On August 24 Mrs. Lea sent a letter by messenger to Zeller. "Your letter points out that you do not know whether the authority of Mr. Davis is irrevocable," she wrote. "May I suggest that the problem would be solved if you were to serve Mr. Davis promptly and before any question as to revocability could arise. I assure you again that Mr. Davis will accept service of whatever subpoena you have obtained whenever you care to submit same to this office." Mrs. Lea added that a copy of the authorization was being filed with the court that day. (Unbeknown to Zeller, Judge Metzner for the second time had refused to accept the photocopy and returned it to Davis' office.) To finally put an end to the argument, Mrs. Lea enclosed in the letter to Zeller a photocopy of the mysterious document, which she asked that TWA treat as confidential.

As Zeller examined the paper, he was utterly amazed by what he saw. Immediately he wrote back: "Now that I have seen the document . . . I must say that I am unable to see why anyone could possibly be interested in having it treated as a confidential document." Continued Zeller, who had developed into quite a letter writer: "I am glad to have your assurance that Mr. Davis will accept service of the subpoena upon Mr. Hughes and to have your suggestion that we serve Mr. Davis promptly in order to avoid any question of revocation. In view of the contents of the document transmitted with your letter [i.e. the photocopy of the authorization], I can see that many questions other than revocation might be raised." Zeller ended his letter by warning Mrs. Lea that TWA expected the reply to the interrogatory on August 27.

And the document? It was a single plain white sheet of paper, which bore no letterhead, no date, no address. It carried no reference whatsoever to the lawsuit, to the time and place of the deposition, or to the court. There was no declaration of a client-attorney relationship between Hughes and Davis, who in the past had claimed that he represented only Toolco and not Hughes. There was only a single sentence typed in the middle of the sheet of paper: "I hereby authorize Chester Davis to accept service on my behalf." Underneath the sentence and slightly to the right on the page was a scrawled signature in ink—"Howard R. Hughes." The statement also lacked the seal of a notary. In short, the document failed on every count to meet Sonnett's criteria.

The August 27 deadline for the interrogatory finally arrived. Despite the court order calling for answers to TWA's ten questions about Hughes' whereabouts, Toolco made no reply. Quite the contrary. In a letter delivered by messenger, Mrs. Lea wrote to Zeller that since Mr. Davis had been authorized to accept the subpoena on Hughes' behalf, "We do not understand what proper interest of your client remains in seeking answers to the whereabouts of

Mr. Hughes." Added Mrs. Lea: "As previously indicated, Mr. Davis is available for you at your convenience."

After business hours had ended on August 27, Zeller went to Davis' office to put the question to him face to face. This was now far too serious a matter to be left to letters. Toolco was in the process of defying a court order. It was risking the severe punishments that can be inflicted for a refusal to obey a judge's ruling. It was opening itself to a motion by its opponents for a default judgment. Toolco's behavior was all the more striking since it came at a time when the Hughes forces had just scored a great victory at the CAB and had built up many important points in the countersuit and Tillinghast's deposition. But now Toolco was taking the risk of losing everything rather than answer what amounted to one simple question: Where is Howard Hughes?

On the thirty-first floor of 120 Broadway, overlooking Manhattan's financial district, Robert Zeller confronted Chester Davis, who had just returned from vacation.

"When does Toolco expect to answer the interrogatory?" asked Zeller.

"Toolco has no intention of replying to the interrogatory," retorted Davis.

The conversation ended. For the moment, there was nothing left to say.

12.   The Game of the Name

The signature of Howard Hughes is almost as rare as a recent photograph of him. He does not write letters to outsiders or sign checks as other people do. For more than a decade, he has not even signed his own income tax return. He has guarded his signature as closely as privacy. And yet who could say that he was wrong? Years later, on the one occasion when a handwritten memo of his was made public, Hughes' precautions seemed fully justified. That single sample of his handwriting was seized upon by a minor American novelist named Clifford Irving who used it to fake the letters that supposedly authorized him to write Hughes' autobiography. But in 1962 Hughes' effort to keep his signature out of the public view was still completely successful. Thus the scrawled name of Howard R. Hughes on a plain piece of stationery attracted intense attention at Cahill, Gordon. That attention in turn led to a sudden and dramatic development.

By this time Chester Davis had been maneuvered into a serious predicament. By refusing to reply to TWA's interrogatory, he had defied the court's order. Davis claimed, of course, that he had a good excuse—that he had chosen the other option, which was to accept the subpoena on Hughes' behalf. But TWA's lawyers absolutely refused to accept the vague and imprecise authorization that Hughes had supposedly given to Toolco's attorney.

Acting swiftly, Robert Zeller began to prepare the argument and affidavits that would support a motion for a default judgment against Toolco. On August 28 he requested a pretrial hearing to present that motion to the court. The TWA move posed a devastating threat to Toolco. In the event of a default judgment, the judge could say, "You, Mr. Toolco, by failing to obey the court's order, have forfeited your right to defend yourself. Therefore I find you guilty as charged by TWA. Pay up."

Judge Metzner scheduled the hearing for September 6. On September 4 Sonnett returned from vacation. His assistants had been preoccupied with the legal implications of the vaguely worded authorization. With a fresh eye, John Sonnett examined the authorization and his interest was caught by something else—the signature.

Sonnett immediately called an old acquaintance from his Washington days to hurry to his office at 80 Pine Street. The acquaintance was Charles Appel, one of the world's leading handwriting specialists. Appel, who had gone to work for the FBI in 1924, had organized and run, until his retirement in 1948, the bureau's handwriting laboratory. During those years his expertise had helped solve thousands of the FBI's cases; his testimony about the handwriting on the ransom note helped send Bruno Richard Hauptmann to the electric chair in 1936 for the kidnapping of the Lindbergh baby. Since his retirement from the bureau, Appel had operated his own private laboratory in Washington for investigation of the authenticity of documents.

Presciently, Sonnett had already collected three other signatures by Hughes that were regarded as genuine. Two of the signatures appeared on a recent note and a pledge agreement with the Bank of America, National Trust and Savings Association. In return for an $11 million loan, Hughes, on February 27, 1961, had signed two documents that committed as security 25,000 common shares and 25,000 preferred shares of stock in the Hughes Tool Company. The two signatures came into TWA's hands through the sequester of Hughes' stock in the Delaware lawsuit. The third signature was on Hughes' commercial pilot's license, a copy of which Sonnett had obtained from the Federal Aviation Agency.

However, because Sonnett had agreed to treat Toolco's matters personally involving Hughes as confidential, he did not feel free to allow Charles Appel to see the entire Hughes signature. Instead, Robert Zeller, who was cleared to handle confidential documents and stayed with Appel until late at night on September 4, gave Appel only individual letters and sets of letters from the Hughes signature. Using a photographic magnifier, Appel greatly enlarged the letters from the signature on the authorization. In accord with the standard practice of handwriting experts, he compared the size, shape, and formation of those letters in that signature with enlargements of letters from the three other signatures. The enlargements enabled him to determine the direction of the motion of the pen, the amount of pressure applied by the writer, and minute differences in the formation of the letters that would remain hidden in an unenlarged signature.

Letter by letter, Charles Appel compared the signature on the authorization, which he called Exhibit B, with the three authentic signatures, which he labeled Exhibits A1, A2, and A3. From the first capital H in "Howard" to the final s in "Hughes" Charles Appel found significant discrepancies between the A and B exhibits. In his report to Sonnett, Appel wrote: "A particularly good example of the discrepancy in the writing motion habits is displayed in the small g, which in Exhibit B resembles the figure 8 because the upper circular form is abbreviated by rounded curves in order to save time. In the examples A1, A2, and A3 it will be seen that the writer in making the small g, after lifting the pen in completing the u, the point is replaced on the paper a considerable distance to the right and is then moved in a very large arc to the left and down to form the lower loop and the upper loop of the g is completed by extending the line up into the h. It is clear," Appel concluded, "that the questioned signature of Exhibit B was written by another writer than the person who wrote Exhibit A1, A2, and A3."

John Sonnett received Appel's findings on September 5. It was the day before he was going into court to make a motion that a default judgment should be entered against Toolco for its refusal to answer the interrogatory. But now Sonnett had an even more important issue. If Appel's findings were correct, and Sonnett certainly had no reason to doubt them, there was now a case of forgery and fraud to be dealt with. Sonnett kept the report about the suspected forgery limited to a bare handful of his colleagues and quickly drew up a detailed affidavit for the court. He also collected supporting affidavits from Charles Appel and Bob Zeller.

When the court convened at 11:30 the next morning, Judge Metzner and the other lawyers were totally unaware of the sensational new development in the case. As John Sonnett glanced around the courtroom on Foley Square, he noticed that nearly all of the familiar cast of characters in the legal battle were present. But there was one important absentee: Chester Davis. No matter. Sonnett began with the speech everyone had expected: an attack on Toolco for its failure to respond to TWA's interrogatory. Toolco's refusal, declared Sonnett, "was willful, deliberate, and inexcusable." Warming to the attack, he cried: "This record of willful and deliberate flouting of specific and unambiguous orders of this court alone warrants the dismissal of Hughes Tool Company's pleadings and the entry of default judgment in favor of Trans World Airlines."

After pausing for effect, Sonnett continued, "I might rest at that point, Your Honor, but something has come to my attention. It has led to the necessity to file affidavits, which contain very grievous charges against the Hughes Tool Company." As he spoke, Sonnett handed the affidavits up to Judge Metzner. The other lawyers suddenly sensed that something new and possibly crucial was happening. The courtroom was absolutely still as the lawyers watched Judge Metzner leaf through the papers.

After a long silence, Judge Metzner looked up. "These are serious charges," he declared.

"The serious charge," replied Sonnett, "is that the Hughes Tool Company deliberately submitted to the court, in an attempt to defraud the court and mislead it, a forged document." Appel's affidavit, explained Sonnett, "set forth in detail his reasons for the conclusions that Howard R. Hughes did not make his signature contained on the so-called authorization." Sonnett continued: "I would like to make it clear that I have no information, nor do I personally believe, that Mr. Davis had any knowledge of this. However, I do represent to Your Honor that on the record before you, it is beyond doubt that someone in the Hughes Tool Company willfully, knowingly, purposefully, in order to mislead counsel for TWA and this court, submitted a forged document. I think on that ground alone Your Honor should strike the answer and give us a default judgment."

The turn of events was stunning. What was happening? Was this a trick or an outrage? Sonnett's charge demanded an explanation. Judge Metzner directed his attention to Mrs. Lea, the poised young lawyer who was taking Chester Davis' place that morning. She could hardly have been more composed and self-assured.

"Why was everyone so excited?" her unruffled attitude seemed to say. "The charges are undoubtedly ridiculous and completely without foundation," she calmly told the court. Choosing her words carefully, Mrs. Lea continued, "The written authorization was merely confirmation of authority, which had been received." As the judge and the lawyers listened intently, Mrs. Lea explained that even if there had been some difficulty about the authorization, it could no longer be said to exist. "At this posture of the proceedings," she said, "I don't think we any longer have a problem. The problem has been mooted," she explained, "for the reason that a United States marshal for the Southern District of California has indicated this morning that he served Mr. Hughes by delivering a copy of the subpoena to Mr. Davis who was authorized to accept the subpoena on Mr. Hughes' behalf. The return has been filed and is in the office of the clerk."

For a second time that morning, the courtroom was thunderstruck. Davis in Los Angeles! The long-disputed subpoena delivered! Stunned and angry, the opposing lawyers could only guess how Davis had managed to pull off such a masterful surprise. What actually had happened was that Davis had decided to dispel the uncertainty that surrounded the subpoena by going ahead and accepting it. Thus he had flown to Los Angeles the day before. Another lawyer, who worked for Hughes on the West Coast, had arranged for a United States marshal named Earle L. Baugher to meet Davis at the Federal Courthouse in Los Angeles when the marshal's office opened at eight the next morning, which was eleven New York time. That was thirty minutes before the pretrial hearing was to begin. Davis, who had shown Marshal Baugher the written authorization from Hughes, executed in the marshal's office an affidavit that was attested by a notary named Woodrow N. Irwin. Davis swore: "I have been authorized in writing by Howard Hughes to accept service on his behalf of a subpoena for his appearance as a witness."

There were only ten or fifteen minutes remaining before the court was to convene in New York when Baugher handed Davis the subpoena, which called for Hughes' appearance on September 24. Davis flashed the word to Mrs. Lea. Thus, moments before Sonnett began to present his motion to Judge Metzner for a default judgment against Toolco, Davis sought to eliminate TWA's grounds for that motion. Davis, however, had no idea that Sonnett would raise the forgery and fraud charge that morning. That was sheer coincidence.

"It seems we are having a lot of last-minute developments to-day," said Judge Metzner in a fine example of judicial understate-ment. "First a charge of forgery and then a statement that Mr. Hughes was already served." Turning to Sonnett, he asked, "Do you know of any service by the United States marshal for the Southern District of California?"

"In the light of the unsatisfactory state of the record, we did make an attempt several weeks ago to serve Mr. Hughes in Bev-erly Hills," Sonnett replied. "The effort was unsuccessful. There-after, I am told—I was not here—that Mr. Davis represented that he was going to be here in court today to deal with this matter. Apparently what he saw fit to do was to go out and to try to blunt the point of this motion [to declare a default against Toolco] and to frustrate it by going to the marshal and saying, 'Look here, I am authorized to take it for Mr. Hughes.'

"I regard what Mr. Davis has done, and I think the court should,

as a nullity," Sonnett declared. "I think that in the light of the very
well-founded charge that a fraud was attempted to be worked on
this court that all matters should be held in abeyance until the court
determines whether to call witnesses in here under cross examination to find out how widespread the scheme was. I don't know
what kind of games Mr. Hughes or the tool company thinks they
can play with the court of the United States. I, for one, do not
think they can play that kind of game."

Judge Metzner, however, decided that he would deal separately
with the issues of alleged forgery and the last-minute subpoena
episode. "We have two problems," he said. "Is Mr. Hughes going
to appear on September 24? By doing that, I suppose he would
validate whatever affidavit Mr. Davis gave to the United States
marshal today to justify acceptance of service of the subpoena on
his part. The other problem is the document, which you claim is
a forgery." Judge Metzner said that the subpoena issue should
stand in abeyance until September 24 to see what Hughes did. On
the issue of the alleged forgery, Judge Metzner gave Toolco's counsel one week in which to file a brief to the court in answer to Sonnett's charge.

Following the astounding developments that morning, an afternoon deposition session was held before the special master. In
order to open the way for Hughes' appearance as a witness on
September 24 and thus test the validity of the authorization, Sonnett made a motion that Davis' discovery proceedings should be
suspended. Rankin reserved judgment on Sonnett's motion, which
was the latter's fifth attempt to break into Davis' schedule of witnesses. After that, the discovery hearings proceeded with Raymond
Cook, as Davis' substitute, doing the questioning. His witness was
TWA's former financial vice president, A. V. Leslie, who had
taken the stand two days earlier.

Leslie, thin and intense, had no reason to be a friend of the
Tillinghast management. Only a few months earlier—on May 12,
1962, to be exact—Leslie had been summoned to Tillinghast's office where he was handed the draft of a letter of resignation—his.
To ease the blow, he also was handed a draft of a consultant's con-

tract that would pay him fees on a diminishing scale for the next three years until he reached sixty when he would be eligible to receive TWA retirement benefits. The timing of Leslie's firing was awkward for TWA's new management. During his deposition, Tilinghast had conceded that he had reservations about driving an angry and disillusioned man into the enemy camp. Nevertheless, Tillinghast decided to fire him anyway. He had several serious objections to Leslie. Among other things, Tillinghast felt that TWA's operations people did not always trust Leslie's financial figures and forecasts and that Leslie did not work smoothly with other TWA executives.

The major issue, however, concerned Leslie's candor. When Leslie talked to CAB investigators and to the Cahill, Gordon lawyers, they got the impression—so Tillinghast reported—that Leslie was holding back information in an effort not to offend Hughes, who had once paid Leslie a Toolco salary in addition to his TWA income. Tillinghast also suspected that Leslie passed unauthorized information to Holliday. Certainly, that could have accounted for Toolco's being so well informed about developments within TWA even after the new management took over. Toolco's high level of intelligence about TWA's innermost discussions infuriated the new management. Surveillance experts were called in to check TWA's board room and executive suites for listening devices, but no "bugs" were found. After his dismissal from TWA, Leslie was hired as financial vice president by Douglas Aircraft and was based at the corporate headquarters in Santa Monica. Since he could not be available continuously for examination, a second witness was also called so that the depositions could proceed without interruption. The other witness was Robert Willard Rummel, TWA's vice president for engineering and aircraft procurement, who for years had been Hughes' closest assistant in the development and selection of new aircraft. Like Leslie, Rummel at some times had been on both the Toolco and TWA payrolls.

Meanwhile, other developments were taking place that threatened to undermine the central point in Toolco's defense strategy. By now John Sonnett's aides had combed through a good part of the evidence that TWA had collected from Toolco. They had also studied the record and evidence at the Civil Aeronautics Board concerning the Northeast control case. The evidence struck directly at Chester Davis' contention that Hughes had severed all managerial ties with Toolco and thus could not be required to testify as Toolco's managing agent.

As Sonnett studied the new documents, he saw repeated evidence that Hughes not only was engaged in masterminding Toolco's over-all strategy, but was also giving instructions down to the smallest detail. As a result, on September 14 Sonnett filed a brief with the court in which he cited some of the evidence that contradicted the argument about Hughes' retired status. The brief supported his earlier motion to suspend Davis' discovery proceedings so that Hughes could be called to testify on September 24. Sonnett was joined in the motion by the lawyers for the additional defendants, who were increasingly eager to question Hughes.

The brief drew heavily on documents that had been collected in the Hughes' nerve center at 7000 Romaine, especially the call sheets, which disclosed the high degree of control that Hughes continued to exercise over Toolco transactions. Sonnett ended his brief with a quote from the transcript of the Northeast hearings that perfectly summed up his own summarized point. On page 1085 of the proceedings, Examiner Ruhlen had become exasperated by the efforts of Toolco's lawyers to draw a distinction between the company and its sole owner. "I think we should stop kidding ourselves that Toolco is some other entity besides Howard Hughes," declared Ruhlen.

In a sense, the special master was also beginning to feel that way. On September 15 at 10 A.M. the lawyers met with him in Davis' office at 120 Broadway. Judge Metzner had empowered Lee Rankin to sort out the problems in the case, and that day, he dealt with two of the most difficult ones in a manner that suddenly made the distinctions between Hughes and Toolco far less important than before. The two problems were (1) the issue of the privileged, or rather unprivileged, Toolco tax and financial documents, and (2) the appearance (or lack thereof) of Howard Hughes.

Those documents were collecting troublesome history. As long ago as April 17, Special Master Rankin had ruled that Toolco had lost its right under the attorney-client privilege to withhold the documents demanded by TWA and the additional defendants. On July 24 Judge Metzner had fully confirmed the special master's ruling. Nonetheless, Davis, who continued to assert that the tax and financial documents were privileged, refused to surrender them. TWA and the additional defendants were especially anxious to get hold of boxes of tax working papers that were held by Raymond Cook's law firm. Fred Furth, who had conducted the document collection in Houston, had requested that Toolco should at least supply a list of all documents it was withholding. The special master sustained Furth's request, and he also ordered Toolco to turn the documents over to him by September 20. He would examine them and rule whether they would qualify to be withheld as being outside the scope of the suit.

The other issue before the special master was the motion to suspend Davis' turn at questioning witnesses so that Hughes could be called to testify the next week. Sonnet argued that the question of Hughes' appearance had now become more important than ever, because Judge Metzner had ruled that the validity of the service of the subpoena on Davis would be determined by whether Hughes actually showed up. Rankin was still reluctant to break into Davis' schedule of witnesses. Yet at the same time he wanted to clear up the question of the validity of the service.

As a result, Rankin made a bold and decisive ruling. To the assembled lawyers he said that he felt that it was no longer necessary to wait for Hughes' appearance or non-appearance to decide on the validity of the service of the subpoena. The special master declared that he "was satisfied that there was authority for the service of the subpoena." Thus he chose to overlook Sonnett's charges about the forgery of Hughes' signature. It was a favorable ruling for Davis, who at least for the moment had the burden of the forgery issue lifted from his shoulders. His relief was short lived. In the next breath the special master clamped the legal grip on Howard Hughes that Davis had been seeking to avoid. Rankin explained that since he considered the authority to be sufficient, he also considered the subpoena to be fully binding on Hughes "to appear on September 24th or, in the alternative . . . at any other time that the court lawfully orders Mr. Hughes to appear in the courthouse at Los Angeles." Rankin explained that he had been so impressed by the evidence in Sonnett's affidavit concerning the close links between Hughes and Toolco that he had decided to slice through the buffer that Davis had been trying to erect between Hughes and Toolco.

"I am," declared the special master, "piercing the corporate veil as to the Hughes Tool Company. I feel that there is such a close connection between Mr. Hughes and the Hughes Tool Company—as evidenced by some of the documents that I have seen and the fact that he is the sole owner of the Hughes Tool Company—that the Hughes Tool Company is responsible with regard to this subpoena and its validity." He continued: "I am bringing what I hope is clear notice of very substantial sanctions, not against Mr. Hughes, but against the Hughes Tool Company." If Hughes either failed to appear or refused to produce documents when ordered to do so by the court, Rankin warned that he would hold the tool company responsible. In that event he would entertain a motion to strike Toolco's defense and to enter a default judgment against it. Rankin did not try to involve the person of Hughes with threats of contempt of court, but he warned him that his fortune was at stake. The corporate charade collapsed. Toolco, the corporate Hughes, was now responsible for the behavior of the private Hughes.

Rankin ordered Davis to communicate his ruling promptly to Hughes, but aware of Hughes' stalling tactics, the special master said that he would not wait for an answer. It was Saturday. If Hughes had not contested the decision by the next Friday, Rankin declared he would regard the lack of protest as acquiescence.

But even as the special master served his unmistakable warning to Hughes, he also put TWA on notice that it would be required to document its antitrust charges before he would allow Hughes to be called to the witness stand. Rankin again expressed his amazement that Tillinghast's testimony had failed to disclose the facts TWA was relying on in its case against Hughes. Rankin said that he was also disturbed at the absence of an explanation as to how the alleged antitrust offenses had any causal relationship to TWA's charges. The failure of Tillinghast's testimony to demonstrate the factual basis of the complaint had, according to Rankin, "an important bearing on what is equitable in asking the testimony of principle witness of the defendant in this case and when that should be required." Therefore Rankin denied Sonnett's application to suspend Davis' discovery proceedings and to start Hughes' testimony on September 24. Instead, the special master explained that he had been growing increasingly concerned about the slow progress of the case. "I believe," he said, "we are reaching the point where it will be expedited by Rule 16 and other procedures." (Rule 16 provides for the plaintiff and defendant to agree upon a definition of the issues in the case.) "I invite any and all counsel during the week of September 24th to apply to Judge Metzner for a pretrial conference," the special master stated. Then he recommended a number of measures for clarifying and speeding up the case. For example, Rankin proposed that if the court designated him to conduct the Rule 16 proceedings, it should also empower him to require John Sonnett and his aides to state "each and all ultimate facts and the witness or witnesses who they expect to testify thereto as to each paragraph of the complaint." The special master also wanted the authority to explore in detail with TWA and Toolco which facts in the case they agreed and disagreed on. Rankin concluded by saying that if the lawyers did not ask the court for a Rule 16 proceeding, he would do so himself.

Rankin's September 15 rulings greatly heightened the pressure on both Toolco and TWA. Howard Hughes was now on notice that if he defied the court order, his alter ego Toolco faced severe, perhaps even crippling, financial sanctions. TWA was on notice that it had to state the underlying facts of the antitrust charges: no more sweeping allegations—just a simple "on the night of whenever it was, Howard Hughes did whatever he did that broke the antitrust laws and caused the following damages to TWA—see exhibits A, B, and C."

Meanwhile, the additional defendants, who were becoming the neglected casualties in the crossfire, were in a dilemma. In order to develop their own defense, they needed to question Hughes, but as things now stood, they would not be able to do so until TWA had finally stated its case.

On Monday, September 17, Chester Davis ended his examination of Rummel a half hour earlier than usual because he had a deal to offer the other lawyers on those controversial tax documents, which Toolco still claimed were privileged. Davis said that Toolco would go ahead and turn over to the special master all the disputed documents. Then came the big "if." The "if" was that the special master should hold the documents until TWA had disclosed the factual basis of its complaint. After the court had established its jurisdiction in the case, Toolco would be willing to permit the special master to hand over the documents related to specific factual issues in the case. It was hardly a generous offer, since the special master had ruled all documents should be surrendered anyway by Thursday, September 20. But as Davis talked on, it became evident that Toolco was highly reluctant to obey that order and was trying to set up an escape route to avoid the danger of incurring a contempt-of-court penalty.

"What I am saying in substance is this," declared Davis. "Toolco is resisting a disclosure of those documents at this time." But since no one took Davis up on his iffy offer, the pressure remained on Toolco to surrender those papers.

Thus the next act in the drama of *TWA v. Hughes* was played before Judge Metzner on September 19. Sonnett had appealed to the court for a reversal of the special master's ruling that had denied TWA the right to question Hughes on the coming Monday. Sonnett had talked so much during the past few weeks that he had almost lost his voice. Nonetheless, he led off with a plea that TWA finally be allowed to call Hughes as a witness. "Hughes," he said, "is the one man who knows the whole story. He is the one who knows best the extent to which the motivations, for what we think are plain violations of the law, were tax motivations. I think that when we take his deposition we could then decide at the end of that whether TWA is going to need another two witnesses or maybe no more witnesses before it would be ready to ask Your Honor to fix a trial date."

Judge Metzner asked Sonnett what he thought of the special master's proposal for holding a Rule 16 hearing in which to define the case's issues.

"I think the suggestion is an excellent one at the right time," rasped Sonnett. "I think at this time it would be idiotic."

"Why?" asked Judge Metzner.

Sonnett explained that the two sides were still too far apart to enable them to agree upon the issues of the case. Judge Bromley and the other lawyers for the additional defendants chimed in with support for Sonnett's view. Judge Metzner questioned Sonnett about why he was not yet prepared to state the ultimate facts of the case. Sonnett's argument was that he could not state the facts until he got them out of Hughes. Maybe he would put Hughes down for 99 per cent of the complaint, but maybe not. "I can't emphasize too strongly that he is the one human being . . . who knows the whole story," Sonnett explained. "He is the one who pulled the strings."

Judge Metzner then recognized Chester Davis, who took exactly the opposite position by arguing that Hughes should not be called to testify until he knew what the charges against him were. "I humbly state," said Davis, who seldom stated anything humbly, "that any principle of justice requires the defendant be aware, be informed in some way as to what it is he is being charged with before he is required to testify. The position and efforts of the tool company have been ever since the complaint was filed to dismiss [it] because the facts do not exist to support the jurisdiction of this court." Continued Davis: "What has been developing [in the depositions] is that Mr. Hughes because of a deep personal interest in aviation and because through the tool company he was a 78 per cent shareholder of TWA did take an active part or interest in the specifications of the aircraft being acquired [and] the type of aircraft to be acquired. Whether or not decisions by TWA with respect to the acquisition of aircraft or its financing should be made by a corporate officer or by a 78 per cent stockholder may be a question that can be raised in some forum, which has jurisdiction over those kind of actions, not here . . ."

Judge Metzner broke in. "Mr. Davis, I hate to interrupt you but you have given me that four times now," he said. "I know it by heart. The question is whether Mr. Hughes should be deposed on September 24 or not."

Davis: "My position basically is that until such time as we do find out what the nature of the claim is which is being asserted by the plaintiff and how the exemption under the Federal Aviation Act is not applicable, we are not ready to be deposed."

Judge Metzner asked Davis how much more time would be needed to finish questioning Leslie and Rummel, his two remaining TWA witnesses.

"Let me put it this way, I don't know what the issue is yet," replied Davis.

"You don't know what questions you are going to ask?" asked Judge Metzner in surprise.

"I do not," affirmed Davis.

"You haven't got a general idea of inquiry before you get into your deposition?" insisted Judge Metzner.

Davis: "If I could do it from 1939 to date and cover all the conceivable events, which might have occurred which have a bearing on the alleged violations of the antitrust law, it is going to take a long time." He urged the court to adopt the special master's proposal for a pretrial conference, which would compel TWA to state the factual basis for its complaint against Hughes. After that conference, said Davis, "I will be in a position to answer your question as to how many witnesses I need and if any and how much time. My strong belief is that when plaintiff is forced to do that, there ain't going to be any more lawsuit because there are no facts that he can state and identify."

Judge Metzner reserved judgment on the motion to call Hughes to the witness stand on the twenty-fourth. Then he shifted his attention to the forgery charge. Both Davis and Sonnett already had submitted detailed papers to Judge Metzner that set out their positions. In his affidavit Davis wrote that when he informed Hughes of the forgery charge, Hughes had expressed "amazement" that anyone would suspect that the signature on the authorization was fake. According to Davis, Hughes said: "Of course, my signature does not look exactly the same all the time. What do they think I use to sign my name with? A machine?" Davis wrote that "He [Hughes] specifically said that he had directed the delivery to me of the writing in question and that it was by him."

Nevertheless, in his affidavit Davis declared that in order to clear up any confusion, he requested Mr. Hughes to acknowledge before a notary public the authenticity of the writing. Davis attached to his affidavit as Annex A a sworn statement by a California notary named Anderson. The California notary declared that Howard Hughes "acknowledged to me he confirms such authorization in writing as follows: 'Chester Davis is authorized to accept a subpoena on my behalf.'" Since the notary swore the affidavit, his signature, and not Howard Hughes', appeared on the statement.

In a reply brief to the court, John Sonnett strongly challenged Davis' explanations. "By a series of misstatements of the record, half-truths, and evasions," wrote Sonnett, "the Hughes Tool Company contends in the Davis affidavit that the matter of forgery and fraud on the Court is insignificant since Mr. Hughes has ratified the alleged authorization. The charge of forgery and fraud, supported by the expert opinion of a leading document examiner, has not been met."

Sonnett pointed out a suspicious feature about Hughes' acknowledgment of the original authorization. He called the court's attention to the fact that Hughes' confirmation to the notary did not conform to the statutory form of acknowledgment in California. The California form requires that the person making the acknowledgment should swear an oath that the signature on the document in question is his. Why did Hughes not use the customary procedure? Also, Sonnett pointed out that Hughes, in his state-

ment to the notary, only "acknowledged" the document and said
it was "by him." "By him" could mean that it was composed or
dictated by him. It did not conclusively carry the meaning that it
was signed by him.

Summing up, Sonnett wrote: "The only conclusion that can be
drawn is that a deliberate and willful contempt of Court was committed in the first place by submitting a forged document and that
a further willful, deliberate, and aggravated contempt has now
been committed by a conscious resort to half-truth and evasion in
an effort to conceal the fact that a fraud had been attempted on
the Court." Sonnett ended his reply brief by asking the court to
punish Toolco for such conduct by granting TWA "a default judgment for the relief requested in the complaint together with such
other and further relief as the Court may deem appropriate."

As the arguments began on September 19, Judge Metzner was
familiar with both briefs. Speaking first, Sonnett zeroed in on the
absence of a clear-cut, sworn statement by Hughes that his signature was the one on the authorization: "At no time did Mr. Davis
get a hold of Mr. Hughes while he was in Los Angeles and ever
say, 'Look here, this thing is getting difficult. Sign this form and
acknowledge it in a regular statutory form and swear that you
signed it.'

"He didn't do that.

"What happened was after we found the forgery, he [Hughes]
decided this is serious enough for him to consent to notice it. He
would therefore go through some ceremonial before a notary
public, and we still don't have his signature on anything.

"I submit to Your Honor," concluded Sonnett, "that it was a
calculated program of frustration in regard to orders of this court.
I don't think Mr. Hughes or anyone else ought to be allowed to
do this."

Judge Metzner seemed definitely struck by the fact that Hughes
had not used the standard statutory form of acknowledgment. He
was curious why Hughes had chosen a roundabout path instead
of making a direct and customary legal statement. Said the judge:
"Tell me, Mr. Davis, if Mr. Hughes left his home and went out
before a notary public and took this time to get through this ac-

knowledgment, wouldn't it have taken less time on his part merely to have signed an affidavit to those facts before the notary public and have furnished another sample of his signature for the court to peruse in connection with his signature affixed to the authorization?"

"Let me explain the problem," replied Davis. "When Mr. Hughes called me on Monday at my request, what he was going to do was write a letter in his own handwriting and put half a dozen signatures for all to look at. I told him no. I was afraid if he did that all I would be doing would be raising another issue of fact as to whether the second signature was a forgery or not a forgery."

"What did you gain by a notary public's acknowledgment as opposed to an affidavit sworn to before a notary public?" asked Judge Metzner.

Davis explained that the problem was that the original authorization that bore Hughes' signature had been in New York, not in California. Therefore, Hughes could not take the original document to the notary and say, "This is my signature." For that reason, the acknowledgment could not conform to the California statutory form, because Hughes could not swear an oath that a signature on a piece of paper was his when that piece of paper was not there. Therefore Hughes had to find another way by which he could get a sworn statement that he had, in fact, given a written authorization to Davis. He solved the problem by repeating the text of the original authorization to the notary, who signed the swearing to show that Hughes had indeed acknowledged that authorization. Said Davis: "It seems to me what took place is a confirmation that the authorization that I received was an authorization by Mr. Hughes. That is the only question that was ever before the court."

Then Davis embarked upon a maneuver that apparently was intended to try to minimize the importance of who did the signing of the original authorization. "I am not interested in what means he used to sign or who he uses to sign," he said. "I am only interested in something which is binding on Mr. Hughes."

Judge Metzner was still inquisitive: "But you still have a little problem too, Mr. Davis. You were faced long before this with claims by counsel that they didn't trust Mr. Hughes and therefore wanted it in writing. And I think the special master adopted that viewpoint when he gave you the choice of answering interrogatories or producing a writing. So you knew that you had a person —for whom you were going to represent to the court that you were authorized to accept service—for whom neither your adversary nor the special master had much faith and that is why they were calling for written authorization filed by Mr. Hughes. When you filed with the court a document purporting to be that and a handwriting expert comes along and says that is not his signature, aren't you in a peculiar position?"

"I don't think so unless my client fooled me," replied Davis. "But he didn't."

Judge Metzner, who did not appear to be satisfied with Davis' explanations, tried to make the point even clearer: "But didn't you understand, Mr. Davis, that after the event, after you became advised that neither the special master nor the adversary trusted Mr. Hughes that when you did produce a document which was then attacked as being a forgery, this was again saying, 'You can't trust Mr. Hughes,' and shouldn't you then have gotten an affidavit sworn by Hughes before a notary public so that you would then have had a document in an independent swearing?"

Davis had his own explanation: "May I suggest what we would have then been discussing? Mr. Sonnett would be standing there and making exactly the same argument. [He would say] 'All that proves, Your Honor, is that the same person who forged the first letter forged the second,' and we would have to have a trial at that time and bring in all these notary publics and bring Mr. Hughes. If I were to produce a man walking into the courtroom and say, 'This is Mr. Hughes,' he [Sonnett] would say, 'Prove it.'

"Let me address myself to what seems to me is the only way to solve these questions of forgery and the question of authorization," said Davis. "There is no issue of fact as to how a thing gets signed. Whether or not a writing is, in fact, an authorized writing —a man may put an X even though he is capable of writing—the law is perfectly clear as I understand it.

"I don't think it would be fair to finish without me making this much of an observation," said Davis. "This relates to these efforts to take the deposition of Mr. Hughes next Monday or any time. TWA has served many notices of deposition for the taking of the deposition of Mr. Hughes. They first took a position that he was managing agent of the tool company and that the tool company could be required to produce him. Then they figured out a better way of annoying and harassing Mr. Hughes and the tool company to coerce some kind of settlement without ever disclosing the merits of the suit. They have had a big hullabaloo about wanting to locate Mr. Hughes. Everybody knows there are a lot of people trying to locate Mr. Hughes, and a lot of people who would like to coerce some money out of either Mr. Hughes or the tool company because of the publicity or notoriety that comes when they raise a claim. We know that; we read the newspapers. So then they asked for interrogatories to be answered by the tool company, interrupting our discovering procedures in the technical sense for that purpose, and persuaded the special master that they needed answers to these interrogatories, which would publicly disclose where Mr. Hughes was so they would be able to serve him.

"Now I get authority to accept service on his behalf. That is not enough. They want to protect me. It has to be confirmed in writing. I obtained that writing. Now they are trying to say it is a forgery."

Chester Davis concluded: "My answer, Your Honor, is nothing is a forgery if it is done with the authorization of the person. I am saying to you, sir, the law is perfectly clear: There is no basis or justification to even say forgery unless you believe it is not an authorized act."

Did Howard Hughes sign the original authorization?

Davis never directly answered that question. In reality, the signature had not been written by Hughes. It had been signed by one of his secretaries. But that bit of intelligence never found its way into the court transcript. Davis had made a clever rhetorical display of avoiding the central issue. But he raised doubts in the mind of Judge Metzner about whether games were being played with the court.

13. Flying Toward the Showdown

THE SCENE: *The gondola of Mark Twain's mythical balloon, which was piloted by an excitable professor. As they float across the Midwest, Huck Finn puts a question to his companion Tom Sawyer.*

"*Tom, didn't we start east?*"

"*Yes.*"

"*How fast have we been going?*"

"*Well, you heard what the professor said when he was raging around. Sometimes, he said, we was making fifty miles an hour, sometimes ninety, sometimes a hundred . . .*"

"*Well, then, it's just as I reckoned. The professor lied.*"

"*Why?*"

"*Because if we was going so fast, we ought to be past Illinois, oughtn't we?*"

"*Certainly.*"

"*Well, we ain't.*"

"*What's the reason we ain't?*"

"*I know by the color. We're right over Illinois yet. And you can see for yourself that Indiana ain't in sight.*"

"*I wonder what's the matter with you, Huck. You know by the color?*"

"*Yes, of course I do.*"

"*What's the color got to do with it?*"

"*It's got everything to do with it. Illinois is green, Indiana is* pink. *You show me any pink down there, if you can. No, sir: it's green."*

"Indiana pink? Why that's a lie!"

"It ain't no lie; I've seen it on the map and it's pink."

As he sat in Chester Davis' law office one day in mid-September of 1962, Raymond Cook suddenly remembered the passage from *Tom Sawyer Abroad* about how Huck thought the colors of states conformed to their tints in the maps of school geography books. He and Davis were terribly concerned by the bad publicity that Howard Hughes had been receiving in the press for his hiding away from the subpoena servers. He had neither broken the law nor, so far, defied a court order by failing to make himself available. Yet by pressing such a massive and extensive hunt for Hughes, John Sonnett had managed to create in the public's mind the impression that the elusive millionaire was a fugitive from justice.

Cook and Davis were trying to devise some way to call the attention of the press to the fact that a very important person on the other side was playing the same game as Hughes. That person was none other than Ernie Breech, who had been named as a defendant in Toolco's massive countersuit. For more than seven months, Davis and Cook unsuccessfully had been trying to serve him a subpoena.

At the time, Cook and Davis were unaware of the reasons behind Breech's reluctance to accept a subpoena. The gist of it was, however, that as soon as Toolco's countercomplaints had been filed in February, Breech had been advised by Francis Reed, the counsel for the two majority trustees, to stay out of New York State. Reed told Breech that his personal fortune might be jeopardized if he became involved in the countersuit. Breech, who had made his millions himself and intended to enjoy them, had no desire to disobey his counsel's warning. To accommodate Breech, TWA's regular monthly board meetings, which customarily had taken place in New York City on the third Wednesday of each month, were being held outside the state, in cities such as Los

Angeles and Newark. The board chairman could thus continue to preside over the proceedings without having to set foot in New York State. The September meeting was scheduled to be held in Boston on the nineteenth of the month.

Cook and Davis were aware that Breech arranged his travel pattern to and from the meetings, to spend an absolute minimum amount of time away from home. Using their knowledge of his travel habits, Cook and Davis assumed that Breech, who spent the summers in Michigan, would fly on the morning of the board meeting from Detroit to Boston and return to Detroit that same evening. The Boston–Detroit air route passes squarely above New York State. So it was that as the two Hughes lawyers pondered how to draw public attention to Breech, an idea was born in Cook's mind. If Huck thought Indiana was pink, why couldn't New York be red (embarrassment) for Breech?

Cook and Davis quickly worked out a plan. A pretty young secretary in Davis' office named Judy McPhail was duly sworn in as a process server by a United States marshal. She was armed with the subpoena that would bind Breech to appear in court as a defendant in the countersuit. On the morning of September 19, Judy, accompanied by her boyfriend, was flown in a private plane to Albany where the American Airlines morning flight from Detroit to Boston touched down. Since it was the most convenient flight for Breech, Cook and Davis surmised that he would be aboard. And indeed he was. The major problem was, how could Judy find him? She had only a photo to help her. When Judy and her boyfriend boarded the plane, the passengers from Detroit were already seated. Without parading up and down the aisle and peering at each face, Judy could hardly hope to spot Breech. If she handed the subpoena to the wrong person and Breech was on the flight, he would slip off at Boston and go home by another route. Rather than risk a mistake, Judy and her boyfriend did nothing until they reached Boston. There she telephoned Cook and Davis and told them about her problem. They arranged to have someone in Boston who knew Breech accompany her to the airport that evening and point him out as he arrived for the return non-stop flight to Detroit.

Blissfully unaware of his opponents' designs, Breech conducted the TWA board meeting, lunched with a group of Boston financiers, and spent most of the afternoon chatting with them. That evening, as he settled himself into a first-class seat aboard an American Airline's Electra, Breech paid no attention to the young couple who sat directly behind him.

Shortly before the plane took off, Judy slipped from her seat and persuaded one of the hostesses to let her enter the cockpit. (It was before the era of skyjacking.) Blushing and batting her eyelashes, Judy told the captain that she was a newlywed—and, "Oh, Captain, we were married in Albany!" As a special favor, would the captain be so sweet as to let her know when the plane passed over the city? Flight 470 had been airborne about an hour when the captain announced on the address system, "We are very pleased to have on board a very lovely young lady who has just been married. The wedding took place in Albany and I just wanted to let her know that the lights below . . ."

At that moment, Judy McPhail took a piece of paper from her purse. Leaning forward, she dropped a subpoena onto the lap of the passenger in front of her.

"Mr. Breech," she said, "that is something for you." Breech was outraged. Turning around in his seat, he told Judy that what she had done was a dastardly trick, that it was illegal, and that it would never stand up in court. Judy only smiled and settled back to enjoy the rest of the flight to Detroit.

"Mama," said Breech as he greeted his wife at the airport in Detroit, "now don't worry, but we are a *cause célèbre*."

Cook and Davis, of course, had never seriously thought that a court would hold that twenty thousand feet above a state constituted a legally acceptable location for the service of a subpoena. Nonetheless, they accomplished their true objective. The incident provoked Breech and his lawyer, Marvin Schwartz, into acknowledging that Breech was avoiding a subpoena. By making public denunciations of Toolco's airborne service, Breech and his lawyer inadvertently conceded that Breech was playing the same sort of game that Hughes was playing—a fact that made headlines in magazines and newspapers across the country.

The Hughes side relished the momentary embarrassment of Ernie Breech. But even so, as the summer of 1962 drew to a close, the Hughes' lawyers could hardly escape the anxious feeling that the case was gathering momentum toward a fateful climax. For Howard Hughes, hidden away in his Bel Air home, the legal situation was becoming increasingly grave. He was scheduled to appear as a witness on September 24. Despite his seclusion behind elaborate security precautions, Howard Hughes must have felt that his enemies were closing in on him.

More than ever, the court proceedings were focusing on Hughes. On September 19, while Judy McPhail was engaged in the airborne pursuit of Ernie Breech, Sonnett and Davis had argued various aspects of the case in yet another pretrial hearing. During the early evening of September 21, Judge Metzner sat down in his chambers to write out his rulings, which he would immediately make public. He chose to pass over the subjects of Sonnett's forgery charge and Davis' motion for a Rule 16 hearing. Instead, the judge concentrated on the most basic issue of all—the appearance of Howard Hughes. In formulating his decision, he adopted the ruling of Special Master Rankin, who six days earlier had "pierced the corporate veil of the Hughes Tool Company" by declaring that Toolco would be held responsible for Hughes' obedience to court orders.

Judge Metzner also adopted Rankin's formula that if Hughes failed to protest that ruling before the close of business on September 21, it would mean that he had acquiesced. Noting Hughes' failure to register an objection, the judge wrote that the service of the subpoena on Davis now was held to be legally binding on Hughes, and he warned that Toolco was responsible for the actions of its evasive owner. Judge Metzner directed Chester Davis to inform Hughes of the ruling by telephone and to post to him a copy of the court decision by special delivery airmail before nine o'clock that same evening.

Davis, however, was able also to communicate some good news to Hughes that evening. Even as Judge Metzner tightened the force of the law on Howard Hughes, he gave him an important break. In order to clear the way for Hughes' appearance on September 24, John Sonnett had asked the court to reverse an earlier ruling by the special master, refusing to halt Davis' discovery proceedings. Metzner, too, was reluctant to break into Davis' examination of witnesses. Thus, he denied TWA's appeal and set a new date for the appearance of Howard Hughes—October 29.

Hughes undoubtedly was vastly relieved by the postponement. But Davis had no time for celebrations. It was a now-or-never situation. His goal had boiled down to this: He had to convince the court that John Sonnett should be forced to state the specifics of the charges against Hughes before the court ordered Hughes to appear as a witness.

On September 25 Davis filed another motion with the court for a Rule 16 pretrial conference. In a supporting brief he contended that at least a preliminary definition of the issues was essential in order to provide a proper framework for the deposition proceedings.

Since Judge Metzner took no immediate action on Davis' new motion, Davis took it upon himself to pressure TWA. He drafted a massive set of questions, covering more than fifty typed pages, which probed for the details behind TWA's allegations. In effect, Davis was saying, "Tell me, Mr. TWA, what are the facts to support your charges that Toolco ever engaged in the business of manufacturing aircraft? Please tell me, Mr. TWA, which aircraft did Toolco produce, what were the names of those planes, and to whom were they sold? Please cite the instances in which Toolco excluded other manufacturers from the commercial airliner market."

On October 11 Chester Davis delivered this formidable interrogatory to TWA. But TWA refused to answer those questions. Instead, Sonnett said he would take the matter up with the special master. Davis responded by, in effect, saying: "If you won't answer my questions, I won't produce Mr. Hughes." He applied to the special master for a postponement of Hughes' scheduled deposition beyond October 29.

On October 25 Special Master Rankin sought to resolve that deadlock. He ruled that TWA should quickly answer Davis' massive questionnaire. "I think that the interrogatories are proper," the special master declared. "TWA could be of great assistance to the progress of the case by answering them promptly." That was a big victory for Chester Davis. Then Rankin turned to the question of Hughes' appearance. The lawyers for the additional defendants were becoming as anxious as Sonnett to question Hughes. In their opinion, they were being taken, at a staggering cost in fees and human effort, through a case in which they did not belong. If only they could put a few questions to Howard Hughes and examine those withheld financial documents, they felt certain that they could make—and win—a motion to dismiss Toolco's countercomplaints. In support of the motion to hold Hughes to the October 29 date, Charles L. Stewart, who represented Dillon, Read, submitted a brief to the special master in which he sharply criticized Davis' delaying tactics. "It is becoming abundantly clear that Toolco is endeavoring to turn this case into a test of economic power and endurance rather than an adjudication of the merits," he wrote. Stewart pointed out that Hughes might even be delighted to have the lawsuit continue endlessly because it would consume funds that otherwise would create problems by piling up as accumulated earnings in Toolco.

Nonetheless, Rankin decided to grant one final postponement. In explaining his decision, Rankin noted that Judge Metzner, whose days were spent trying other cases, had not yet ruled on several important matters in *TWA v. Hughes,* most notably Davis' motion for a Rule 16 definition-of-issues proceeding. Rankin also cited the practical problems involved in the October 29 date. In order to question Hughes, Sonnett, and the lawyers for the additional defendants would have to transport voluminous files to Los Angeles. Offices would have to be set up and staffs transferred from New York. In all, some thirty to forty lawyers, clerks, and secretaries would have to make a temporary move to Los Angeles. The approach of Thanksgiving and the holiday season meant that the New York staffs would either be forced to remain separated from their families during the celebrations or would be required to spend unnecessary time and money shuttling from coast to coast.

Even more important, Rankin was bothered about the still unresolved legal issues in the case. He was especially concerned about the question of primary jurisdiction. From the start, Chester Davis had contended that if TWA's complaint belonged anywhere, it belonged in front of the Civil Aeronautics Board. Rankin now believed that Davis might be correct. After carefully researching the issue, Rankin had become convinced that the United States Supreme Court generally held that primary jurisdiction rested with the federal regulatory agencies (such as the CAB or the Federal Communications Commission or the Securities and Exchange Commission) if they possessed an expertise that should be brought to bear on the controversy before any action was taken by the federal courts. Consequently, Rankin ruled that Davis should have an immediate opportunity to ask Judge Metzner for a decision: Did the court hold primary jurisdiction in the case? Another big victory for Chester Davis.

Then Rankin went on to make his next ruling, which gave Chester Davis an even greater triumph. The special master declared that before Hughes could be called upon to testify, TWA should first participate with Toolco in a Rule 16 hearing. In order to provide the time in which those procedures could take place, Rankin set a new date for Hughes' appearance that seemed a long way off —February 11, 1963. Rankin warned, however, that the February date was to be absolutely final.

As a result of Rankin's rulings, Chester Davis had now moved into an extremely strong position. True, he had been told that the next deadline for Hughes' testimony was irrevocable, and he knew that Rankin was not a man to trifle with. But Davis had also gained precisely the decisions he had been working for all along. He now had the support of the former Solicitor General of the United States for his interpretation that primary jurisdiction in the case rested with the CAB. And if the case went to the CAB, the groundwork was already prepared for a Hughes' victory. Equally significant, Rankin's rulings supported Davis' contention that TWA should be required to state the underlying facts of its complaint before Hughes was called to testify.

Sonnett, badly outmaneuvered, immediately appealed the special master's rulings to Judge Metzner. However, during the autumn of 1962 the judge was so engaged in the final stages of a long and complicated criminal trial that he had little time to deal with the procedural problems in *TWA v. Hughes*. Hence, he took no action on Sonnett's motion. Nor did he make a decision on the two important motions by Davis, who had asked for an immediate Rule 16 hearing and a reversal of the special master's order calling for him to surrender those tax papers, which Toolco still claimed were privileged.

While those issues awaited the court's decisions, Davis pressed on with the deposition sessions. He also continued to emphasize that he still could not fathom what TWA's charges were all about. There was a plan behind his plaints. On December 4 he proposed to the special master that even though he was many, many months behind his schedule, he should be allowed to call two additional witnesses. They were Ben-Fleming Sessel of the Irving Trust Company and Arthur Wadsworth of Dillon, Read & Company. Davis argued that if anybody could supply the facts about Hughes' alleged antitrust violations, it would be those two. For years Sessel had been Hughes' personal banker, and Wadsworth had been the executive in charge of arranging the Dillon, Read financing plan for TWA's jet fleet.

But Davis' opponents attacked his proposal as simply a diversionary tactic. They feared that Davis could spin out the questioning of Sessel and Wadsworth for months and thus cause a postponement of Hughes' appearance on February 11.

Davis undoubtedly had a valid point in wanting to take the testimony of Sessel and Wadsworth, but another factor was coming into play. Davis was wearing out the patience of the other lawyers and the special master. After Rankin heard the arguments on December 4, he immediately told Davis: "I don't want to leave any doubt in your mind or anybody else's. I expect to proceed with Mr. Hughes on February eleventh." Undeterred, Davis appealed the special master's ruling to Judge Metzner, asking for a court order that would allow him to question Sessel and Wadsworth prior to Hughes' examination. Again the court took no action.

While all of those issues remained undecided, Chester Davis continued the depositions of two TWA vice presidents, past and present, and called a third for questioning. The third was Emmett O. Cocke, a bluff and heavy-set man, who in 1959 had been named senior vice president for industrial affairs after serving for many years as the airline's sales chief. Thus, during the last months of 1962, Davis took turns testing the validity of Sonnett's complaint against TWA veterans in charge of sales (Cocke), finance (Leslie), and aircraft procurement (Rummel).

A central element in TWA's antitrust case was that Toolco had supplied the aircraft to TWA only on the condition that the airline should accept financing by Toolco on Toolco's terms. Davis asked Leslie: "Was there any agreement or understanding that you know of or have ever heard about, either expressed or implied, that thereafter all financing by TWA was to be done from or through the Hughes Tool Company?"

Leslie: "I know of none."

Davis: "At any time?"

Leslie: "At any time."

TWA's complaint stated that Toolco had only allowed TWA to purchase aircraft from Toolco, thereby excluding other aircraft manufacturers from dealing with the airline. Raymond Cook asked Leslie: "Have you ever been told by anyone that the tool company or Mr. Hughes in effect said to TWA, 'I will provide you with financing on the condition that you, TWA, agree in the future you will acquire all of your aircraft from me, the tool company?'"

Leslie: "I have never heard of such a statement."

Cook: "Do you know of anything which you could have construed as such a condition?"

Leslie: "No."

A major element in TWA's charges was that Hughes bought

into TWA and increased his holdings in order to dominate the company for his own selfish personal motives. Leslie's testimony provided no underpinnings for that allegation. In reply to questions by Davis and Cook, he explained that in 1946, when Hughes made one of his largest initial investments, the motive had been to help TWA. At that time the airline had been strained to the breaking point by the burden of starting up international routes to Europe and Africa. Hughes' aim, declared Leslie, had been not to dominate TWA but to save it from bankruptcy. (In fact, Leslie in 1960 had been highly critical of Hughes' financial activities at TWA. In a handwritten document entitled "An Appreciation," he had analyzed TWA's dreadful financial dilemma and had placed the blame squarely on Hughes. He wrote that because of the late delivery of the jet aircraft, the Equitable and TWA should sue Toolco and Hughes for breach of contract. But Davis and Cook, who naturally were interested in building a record that supported only their side of the argument, did not question Leslie on that point.)

Hughes' lawyers also subjected Robert Rummel to a long examination. It concentrated on one of the central points of TWA's antitrust complaint. That was the charge that Hughes had conspired to dominate TWA to use it as a captive market for his trade in aircraft and to foreclose the market to other suppliers. "Was that a fact?" asked Davis. "No," replied Rummel, exactly the opposite was true. Hughes had consistently encouraged him to canvass virtually every aircraft manufacturer in the free world in search of the best planes for TWA. Hughes had not restricted competition among aircraft manufacturers. Quite the contrary, Rummel declared. Because of Hughes' support and active cooperation, TWA had been able to encourage aircraft manufacturers to compete with one another in developing aircraft. Said Rummel: "It was a wonderful thing to try to do, I think, to put TWA ahead equipmentwise, but we would not have done this to the degree we did, I am sure, had it not been for Mr. Hughes' interest in those things." He cited the fact that TWA had persuaded Martin to resume production of its twin-engine transports in the late 1940s after it had abandoned the market to Convair. Rummel also said that Hughes had created competition between Boeing and Convair by ordering both 707s and 880s. In his words, Hughes was trying "to get an airplane that was better for TWA than the others appeared at that time to be willing to produce."

TWA's complaint rested on the assumption that Hughes had the power to force TWA to accept the planes that he selected. Not so, swore Rummel. In the case of the Martins, Hughes had favored Convairs and had been engaged in negotiations for their purchase. Yet TWA bought Martins, which turned out to be less efficient than the Convairs. According to Rummel, Hughes in the early 1950s favored switching the TWA fleet from Lockheed to Douglas equipment, but TWA's management had rejected the suggestion. Rummel added that the Douglas airliners proved to be, as Hughes had suspected, faster than the comparable Lockheeds —a reality that, much to Hughes' dismay, gave American and United airlines a coast-to-coast speed advantage over TWA. Again in the mid-1950s, when Hughes wanted TWA to buy Vickers Viscounts, TWA refused. In the late 1950s Hughes had wanted TWA to buy the Bristol Britannia, but once more the TWA management rejected his proposal.

Davis did not, however, press Rummel about another crucial point. That was whether he ever received instructions from Hughes that barred him from dealing with certain aircraft manufacturers, thus excluding them from the TWA market. At that point in the deposition proceedings, Lee Rankin, who felt that the record should not be left incomplete, insisted on taking the examination from Davis. In reply to the special master's questions, Rummel said yes, he had been instructed by Hughes or Hughes' representatives not to deal with Convair about the 990 and not to talk with Lockheed about the Electra.

During his turn on the stand, Emmett O. Cocke, the former sales vice president, had a difficult time recalling most of the events of the past. But he was able to remember in detail his objections to the TWA lawsuit against Hughes. Cocke, who was a personal friend of Northeast President James Austin, had been especially disturbed about the section in the complaint that alleged a conspiracy between Toolco, Atlas, and Northeast to bring about an inequitable merger between TWA and Northeast. Cocke testified that during the executive committee meeting on June 29, 1961—at which Tillinghast was authorized to file the complaint—he had objected that he could not understand the charge against Atlas and Northeast. Cocke said that he had told Tillinghast that in his estimation there had been no conspiracy involved in Northeast's offer to merge with TWA. Cocke recounted that Tillinghast had brushed off his objections by saying, "It's a legal problem," or words to that effect.

From questioning Cocke, Davis collected support for his own conspiracy theory behind the TWA complaint. He probed Cocke for his knowledge about discussions among members of the new TWA board and management about whether Hughes might surrender more readily to an out-of-court settlement if he was threatened with having to testify in public. Cocke replied: "There had been discussions that if it was necessary for Mr. Hughes to make the deposition, there would be a probability that it would be easier to reach a settlement, yes."

Davis: "Do you recall anyone saying anything about Mr. Hughes' attitude taking his deposition or what he might do or not do depending on whether or not his deposition was ordered?"

Cocke: "There have been discussions as to the opinion, and I believe Mr. Slack made this statement that if Mr. Hughes would not want to make a deposition, and if he was forced to make a deposition, or when that time came, the possibility of a settlement would be greater."

Day after day, Chester Davis extracted important evidence from TWA's own officers, who directly contradicted the charges in TWA's complaint. But even as Davis continued to build his record, TWA was being propelled further away from Hughes' grasp. At that very time, TWA was in the process of being taken over by Hughes' old archrival, Juan Trippe.

After Tillinghast was released from the burden of the depositions, he had redoubled his efforts with Juan Trippe to negotiate a merger between TWA and Pan American World Airways. In both August and September, there were rumors that an agreement was about to be reached. Actually, at that time the two men were still, in Tillinghast's words, "haggling like Arab rug merchants" over the terms of the deal. By December, however, they had worked out a merger arrangement. At TWA's regular monthly board meeting on December 19, the directors unanimously granted Tillinghast the authority to enter into a merger with Pan Am. As in the lawsuit, once Tillinghast had the go-ahead, he moved extremely fast. He signed the papers with Trippe that afternoon. The TWA directors met again the next day to approve the deal.

The merger terms embodied Trippe's original concept for a solution to "the Hughes' problem." He would turn Pan Am into a holding company, which would control a far larger block of shares in the merged airline than Hughes. Trippe, who would be chairman of both the holding company and the airline, would then be able to outvote Hughes and exercise absolute control.

Could Trippe and Tillinghast, who would become the airline president, merge TWA out from under Howard Hughes? What was to stop them? In its December 1961 order, which approved the establishment of the voting trust for TWA, the CAB specifically stated that the trustees could exercise all powers normally exercised by the owner. That would presumably include the right to undertake mergers. TWA's two lender-appointed trustees, who would be in favor of the merger, could outvote Hughes' single trustee, Raymond Holliday. Pan Am's shareholders, who had a long tradition of obedience to Trippe's leadership, would surely follow his recommendation. After that, the proposal would have to be submitted to the CAB for approval. If it passed that hurdle, the merger would then require the okay of President Kennedy, since it involved the consolidation of oversea routes. The merger's chance for success, however, was greatly enhanced by the sizable influence that Juan Tripe wielded in Washington.

As Rankin had foreseen, the pace of legal action had slackened during the holiday season. With a sudden burst of activity, it resumed on January 9. A pretrial hearing was scheduled for that day to deal with several crucial issues that had piled up during the past months. In preparation for the hearing, Chester Davis stayed up until 4 A.M. on January 9, putting the finishing touches on a brief to Judge Metzner. It was an impressive document. It ran more than a hundred pages, including exhibits, and contained the documentary basis upon which Davis intended to rely in the final month before Hughes' scheduled appearance. Davis was preparing several avenues of action that had but a single goal: to keep Hughes out of the witness chair.

In his big brief, which was also delivered to Sonnett and the other opposing lawyers, Davis restated his old arguments and outlined his reasons for wanting to question Wadsworth and Sessel. Among other things, Davis cited a letter that Sessel had written on April 16, 1958, to a Mr. Engelman, a TWA shareholder, who had asked whether Hughes was doing well by TWA. In his reply Sessel told the shareholder that TWA should be very grateful indeed to have a rich godfather like Howard Hughes. Davis wanted to know why, if Hughes had been a godfather to TWA, the new management had started a suit against him?

As the lawyers assembled on January 9 in the courtroom on Foley Square, the atmosphere was tense in anticipation of a showdown. Davis spoke first. He began by complaining that so far he had only been able to determine that TWA's lawyers knew what the complaint was about but that nobody else did. If he were allowed to question Sessel and Wadsworth, he would either uncover the facts TWA was relying on in its complaint or be able to prove conclusively that the airline had no basis for its charges. Declared Davis: "As Your Honor knows, in fact, I believe, from the very first day I appeared before Your Honor, I indicated that it was my plan and expectation to bring on an appropriate motion to dismiss as soon as we were in a position to do so."

"You have made six references to that before the court, starting September 1," interjected Judge Metzner. He meant September 1, 1961, but actually Davis had been arguing that point since his first appearance in court in mid-August of that year.

Not easily put off, Davis replied: "I am surprised it is as few

times as that, Your Honor. I am sure it is a burden to have me repeat myself so many times. But it is basic to the issue which I think
is confronting us, and basically the position of the tool company is
if it is entitled to any right to discover what the complaint is about,
we have not had it yet, because we still do not know."

Davis did declare, however, that he had discovered TWA's motive for starting the unjustified legal action against Hughes. He
asked the court to reflect upon Cocke's testimony on how TWA's
new managers had pondered whether Hughes would settle out of
court if he faced the threat of having to testify.

But Judge Metzner once more broke in. "Mr. Davis," he said,
"we have gone through this several times. You are arguing a motion for summary judgment."

"No. I say I want to be in a position to do that," responded
Davis.

"But you will never get to that point until you go through the
proper procedures," declared Judge Metzner. He was reminding
Davis that the court would not accept a motion for summary judgment until TWA had exercised its right to examine Howard
Hughes.

But Davis was far from finished. In a quick change of pace, he
made a dramatic gesture. He had an offer for TWA, he said. For
months the airline had been trying to force him to end his examination of witnesses. All right, said Davis. He would gladly suspend
his examination on one condition: TWA would have to supply
answers to Toolco's interrogatory. After that, the airline could
call to the witness stand Hughes or whomever else they wished
and Davis would happily produce him.

Then Davis stepped aside to let Mrs. Lea state Toolco's position on the privileged documents. Despite repeated orders, Toolco
had still not surrendered all the documents demanded by its opponents. In her argument, Mrs. Lea proposed the novel theory
that the privilege could only be forfeited if the client knowingly
disclosed the advice of counsel. It could not be lost inadvertently.
Ergo, since Toolco had not meant to lose the privilege, it had
not done so. Or so, at least, Mrs. Lea argued. But she added that

Toolco had no desire to suppress relevant facts through the use of the privilege. Hence Mrs. Lea proposed a variation of Davis' earlier offer. If TWA would agree to answer the interrogatory, Toolco would release from the privilege any document that TWA said it needed to draw up its replies.

Now Davis and Mrs. Lea sat back in their chairs at the long table in front of Judge Metzner's bench. It was the opposition's turn. One by one, the lawyers for the additional defendants stated their various objections to Davis' offer, objections that centered on the suspicion that Chester Davis was preparing yet another diversion. Then John Sonnett, badly defeated before the special master, rose to speak. He urgently needed to persuade Judge Metzner to reverse Rankin's rulings, primarily the one that called upon TWA to answer Toolco's interrogatory before Hughes would be allowed to appear as a witness. Sonnett knew that he would have to convince the court that TWA did indeed have a legitimate and persuasive case against Hughes and needed only to put him on the stand to establish the factual evidence behind its complaint. As Davis and Sonnett both realized, the crucial tactical issue in the case now was this: Which would come first—TWA's recital of the facts or the appearance of Howard Hughes?

"When I say that I expect 75 per cent of the evidence we will use at the trial to come out of the mouth of Hughes, I am not saying that rashly," Sonnett told the court. The need to question Hughes was all the greater because Davis and Cook had refused to acknowledge valuable evidence of antitrust violations, which had come out during the depositions. As Sonnett said: "We start out, Your Honor, with a handicap by the fact that the Hughes Tool Company counsel completely disregards the discovery which they have had to date. For example, they would brush aside the entire Tillinghast deposition as if it did not even enlighten them as to claims concerning 1961. It does. And I think it contains very significant evidence relating to the efforts of Hughes to ram 990s down the throat of TWA at the time when the independent management wanted other aircraft.

"They would minimize and disregard the Rummel deposition,

and a reading of that record is very enlightening because every time counsel for Hughes Tool came to an area where it was obvious the witness was going to hurt him, he backed away. And at one point it became so obvious, the special master himself took over the questioning on the subject of whether Hughes had instructed Rummel to boycott airplane manufacturers except the one chosen by Hughes."

Sonnett pointed out that Davis had refused to question Leslie about the handwritten document in which Leslie had asserted that "TWA with Equitable should sue Toolco-Hughes for damages due to implied contract default." Declared Sonnett: "I think what this shows is that none are so blind as those who will not see. If the counsel for the tool company would take a look at the documentary evidence they already have, they would be very much enlightened about various of the problems that face them in this case."

Then Sonnett stated his major point—that TWA was severely handicapped in digging up the facts of Hughes' violation because Hughes had masked his actions in deepest secrecy: "It is provable that it was a cardinal policy that Hughes throughout maintained that there must be secrecy regarding everything. There are documents in which he instructs people, 'Don't make notes of this,' 'Keep this a secret.'" Sonnett picked up several papers from the table as he spoke. They were documents that Toolco, the Bank of America, and others had surrendered to TWA. A master of comic relief, Sonnett read a letter from Raymond Holliday's secretary in Houston to Leslie's secretary in New York. Holliday's secretary complained, "It isn't easy to find out the simplest information. We do carry secrecy to extremes in some cases, in my very humble opinion." She was, Sonnett explained, only trying to find out in which state TWA was incorporated. "I assume," she wrote, "you will not have to get a security clearance and be fingerprinted and all that stuff to furnish this meager bit of information to a fellow employee."

Changing to a serious mood, Sonnett waved other documents that showed that all participants in meetings with Hughes were sworn to secrecy. For the first time in court, Sonnett began to disclose the factual basis of the suit against Hughes. Said he: "What the Hughes deposition is going to establish—and it will be established in the first week of deposition beyond any doubt—is that the motivation for what Hughes did was a financial one. It consisted of tax avoidance. That is what was done and why it was done and how it was done and what led him into the antitrust violations, which he and the others clearly committed."

In support of his statement, Sonnett cited the notes taken by Keath Carver, a Bank of America vice president in Los Angeles, who had had a ninety-minute telephone conversation with Hughes on December 4, 1960. To the hushed courtroom, Sonnett read the jottings that Carver had made from Hughes' comments: "'102 tax situation—it is real bad and three weeks before year end. ML is better—have chairman of the board and only need to get one man (Nixon?) so he would have to set out at once to refinance.'

"Now, there is the proof of why!" cried Sonnett. "It was the 102 tax situation." (The 102 number refers to the paragraph of the old income tax code, which forbade excessive accumulation of profits.) "I think the first week of the examination of Hughes based on things like this plus his income tax returns, which Your Honor had directed that we have, and plus some other documents are going to supply the background and explain why they did get into antitrust violations.

"Now I know of no other way to get that information the way Hughes ran his empire, characterized by secrecy, by being surreptitious, by leaving no trails, by instructing people to keep things secret and by giving them only part of the information, by sitting in the center of the web and pulling all the strings." Sonnett summed up: "I repeat to Your Honor, I believe that 75 per cent of the evidence we will introduce at the trial will come out of the mouth of Hughes during the deposition."

To those familiar with the background of the case, the Carver note was very illuminating. The jottings provided a clue to the reason for Hughes' opposition to the Dillon, Read plan that financed TWA's jet fleet. For Hughes' own tax purposes, the Merrill Lynch financing plan, which involved Colonel Crown, was far superior to the Dillon, Read plan because it would have required a refinancing of TWA's debt. That would have enabled Hughes to have invested Toolco's excess earnings in the new financing and Toolco would have become one of the lenders to TWA. By contrast, the Dillon, Read plan only burdened him with excess cash because it paid back the money he had advanced to buy 707s for TWA. Also it freed TWA from financial dependence on him, thus denying him an outlet for his Toolco profits.

The Nixon mentioned in the memo was indeed Richard M. His brother Don Nixon, who later became a Toolco employee, had received an unsecured loan for $205,000 from Hughes in 1956. When Hughes telephoned Carver on December 4, 1960, he still hoped that financial help from Colonel Crown would enable him to retain control of TWA, and he wished to secure the service of Dick Nixon as a director of the airline. Nixon, of course, had just been defeated in the presidential elections by John F. Kennedy.

The tax avoidance that Sonnett was talking about was of course no crime. If it were, the nation's jails would be filled with millionaires. But it could conceivably be a motive for an illegal course of conduct. That was Sonnett's point. From his study of the available tax documents and related memos, he had discovered that Howard Hughes had often been plagued by the problem of what to do with Toolco's large profits. Hughes' special worry was the federal income tax provision that prohibited companies to pile up large amounts of earnings. Under the tax law, companies had, in effect, three alternatives for coping with large profits: (1) they could pay them out as dividends to their shareholders; or (2) reinvest them in their business; or (3) prove to the tax examiners that the funds soon would be needed to meet business outlays. But if a company piled up excessive earnings without sufficient justification, the federal government could levy a penalty tax of 37½ per cent on accumulated profit over $10,000. Since the penalty tax was added to the standard corporate income tax, then 52 per cent, the result was that Washington could take an 89.5-cent bite from every $1.00 of Toolco's excess retained earnings.

Sonnett and the other lawyers thought they were beginning to

understand Hughes' tax plight. In those days, on annual sales of
$250–$300 million, Toolco regularly brought in net earnings of
$20–$25 million. It was far too much to reinvest each year in
Toolco. The company, which already had some of the world's most
advanced geological laboratories, simply did not require such large
expenditures. There was no compelling reason to cut prices on
Toolco products or to raise the wages of the company's employees;
either move would have thrown Toolco out of step with its competitors. And there was only one shareholder to whom to pay dividends—Hughes himself.

But Hughes did not want the money, because it would only have
gone for personal income taxes. He preferred his established financial arrangement with Toolco. He was paid a $50,000 annual
salary plus expenses. Once each year Hughes crammed his bills in
an old shirt box and had them delivered to Toolco's home office in
Houston. Clerks added them up. Then at their next board meeting, Toolco's directors solemnly voted Hughes a dividend to cover
the total amount. In addition, Toolco, presumably as deductible
business expenses, provided Hughes with his homes, hotel suites,
guards, planes, helicopters, cars, and communications system. It
also, of course, paid for his lawyers. That still left Hughes with his
basic problem: What should he do with $20 or $25 million dollars
a year?

As they studied Toolco's tax returns, Sonnett and the lawyers
for the additional defendants detected what they believed was
Hughes' scheme. It was to put Toolco's excess profits into aircraft
for TWA and then to have Toolco take advantage of the depreciation allowances on the planes and other tax-avoiding measures
before eventually selling the planes to TWA. One of the documents that tipped them off was the Hughes Tool financial statement for 1954, which carried an intriguing item. It was a $17
million downpayment to Lockheed for new Constellations, which
Toolco had ordered for TWA. Since the tool company's earnings
amounted to $20 million for 1954, the payment to Lockheed
greatly reduced Toolco's income tax and probably saved the company from paying a penalty assessment on an otherwise unjustified

retention of earnings. As they sorted and collated other documents for that year, the lawyers came upon a memo by Rummel that was dated December 15, 1954. Rummel wrote that he had protested a decision by Hughes to go ahead with the purchase of the 1694-type Constellations, because the plane was then only in the drawing-board stage. During the final negotiating session with Lockheed representatives at the Beverly Hills Hotel, Rummel had continued to object that it was too soon to sign a contract. At last Raymond Cook, who was in charge of the purchase for Toolco, had summoned him to the telephone. On the line was Howard Hughes, who ordered Rummel to stop bickering and to get that contract signed.

According to John Sonnett, such was the underlying motivation that led Hughes to break the antitrust laws. If only he could get at further evidence, Sonnett contended, he would be able to spell out the detailed offenses. The lawyers for the additional defendants, who also had participated in the study of the documents, were pursuing another angle. From what they had seen, they were convinced that they could prove that Hughes had compelling financial motives for postponing the closing of TWA's financing plan in the 1958–60 period. If they could indeed prove that Hughes was the one responsible for the delay, the lawyers could absolve their clients of the charges in Toolco's $443 million countersuit.

This time no one had to wait very long for the court's decision. The next day Judge Metzner handed down his rulings. One by one, those decisions completely reversed the fortunes in the huge legal battle, demolishing Davis' positions.

No, said the court, Davis would not be allowed to interpose the depositions of Ben-Fleming Sessel and Ted Wadsworth ahead of Hughes' appearance. "The deposition of Howard R. Hughes should now go forward," ruled Judge Metzner. "This deposition was originally scheduled for September 24, 1962, and then adjourned to October 29, 1962. It has now been adjourned to February 11, 1963, and this date will be adhered to in the absence of extraordinary circumstances. It is only fair that the plaintiff be allowed to proceed without waiting for the defendant to complete its deposition proceedings. This is especially true when the plaintiff claims that 75 per cent of the proof necessary to sustain its claim is obtainable from Hughes personally."

In regard to Davis' motion to hold a pretrial hearing for a definition of the issues in the case, Judge Metzner agreed that such a conference should take place. But it should be held *after,* not *before,* Hughes' testimony.

On the issue of TWA's refusal to reply to Toolco's interrogatories, the judge agreed that TWA should respond to them. But not now. Judge Metzner ruled that TWA should reply "within fifty-five days of the completion of the deposition of Howard R. Hughes." Judge Metzner also wrote that he would be willing to entertain Davis' motion for dismissal of the complaint or for summary judgment—but only after Hughes' deposition had ended.

In addition, Judge Metzner ruled on the question of the tax and financial documents that Toolco still maintained were privileged. (The documents included the 1960–61 tax working papers in the three boxes from Houston. Toolco had allowed the contents of the three boxes to be inspected by the special master, who had said that the papers would indeed have qualified for immunity under the privilege if the privilege itself had not been forfeited. Then Toolco had taken back the papers into its own custody.) The court declared that all Toolco documents that previously had been examined by the special master should be turned over to TWA and the additional defendants. He set the deadline for their surrender at noon on January 14. Furthermore, Judge Metzner ordered Toolco at that same time to present to Lee Rankin all documents that had been demanded by the other parties and not yet examined by the special master. Just to make certain that Howard Hughes got the message, Judge Metzner directed Chester Davis to inform Hughes by mail and by telephone about the court's orders. In the seclusion of his Bel Air mansion, Howard Hughes must have felt more keenly than ever that his enemies were closing in on him.

They were indeed. The first attack was directed against his secret documents. At precisely 11:56 on the morning of January 14, a delegation of lawyers from Cahill, Gordon and the firms representing the additional defendants arrived at the New York offices of Chester Davis. They were accompanied by a shorthand reporter.

Chester Davis was absent. In his place, Raymond Cook received the delegation. No time was wasted on formalities.

"Mr. Cook, is the tool company prepared to comply with the order of Judge Metzner of January 10?" asked John Hupper of Cravath, Swaine, who represented the Equitable and Metropolitan.

"Mr. Reporter, please show on the record that Mr. Davis is not present at this time, when the request is being made," said Cook. "I have been shown by his secretary, however, a copy of a letter dated January 14th, from him to Judge Metzner, in which Mr. Davis has made the statement 'The documents have been placed in a sealed envelope and are now in my possession subject to further direction by the Court.'"

Cook continued: "I have also been handed by Mr. Davis' secretary a sealed manila folder which I suppose is an envelope, and it carries this legend on the face. 'January 14, 1963. These are the privileged documents which are produceable pursuant to the Special Master's order of September 15, 1962, and the order of the Court dated January 10, 1963, not to be opened except on further instructions from Mr. Davis.'

"Construing the two together I do not consider, gentlemen, that I am privileged to turn over these documents to you at this time."

Hupper: "Mr. Cook, can you tell us whether or not Judge Metzner has stayed the effectiveness of his order of January tenth?"

Cook: "I have stated all I know about it, Mr. Hupper."

Hupper: "We understand from all information available to us that there is no such stay outstanding, and that being the case, I again call upon you to produce those documents."

Cook: "I have stated all I know on the record."

Hupper: "I must put you on notice that your failure to produce those documents at this time is in our view, it now being twelve noon exact, a violation of Judge Metzner's order and we will so treat it." With that warning, the opposing lawyers trooped away.

By refusing to surrender the documents called for in Judge Metzner's order, Toolco had now directly defied a command of the court. That carried very grave risks. But just as he flew to Los Angeles in the nick of time to blunt Sonnett's earlier attempt to have a default declared against Toolco, Davis this time sought to accomplish the same effect by dispatching a letter to the court. Davis requested a stay in the production of the documents until he could submit a motion to dismiss the case. Until Judge Metzner made a decision on that motion, Davis wrote that "he respectfully refused" to comply with the court order.

But this time Davis' approach was hardly promising. Only four days earlier, Judge Metzner had ruled that he would not entertain such a dismissal motion until after the conclusion of Hughes' testimony. In addition, Davis asked Judge Metzner in his letter or a modification in the procedure that would govern the Hughes' deposition. Until then, it had been assumed that Hughes, like any other witness, would submit to oral questioning. Now Davis asked the court to permit the questions to be transmitted in writing to Hughes, who would respond in the same fashion. That, too, was an unlikely request. Sonnett and the other lawyers were all demanding to question Hughes in person. Tillinghast had spent six months in the witness chair. Why should Howard Hughes be treated any differently?

During the noon hours of January 14 Chester Davis appeared headed for an immediate and disastrous defeat. The transcript of Cook's refusal to obey the court order was rushed by messenger to Judge Metzner's chambers. In anticipation of victory, the legal opponents of Howard Hughes began at once to draft briefs to the court. In those briefs, they moved that the Hughes Tool Company, having deliberately defied the commands of the court, should be declared to be in default and should be subjected to the ultimate penalty for corporate wrongdoing: a payment of $115 million in damages and the forced divestiture of Hughes' holdings in TWA.

14. The Night Court Proceedings

At the very moment Howard Hughes appeared headed for a shattering defeat, a development took place on another front that offered his lawyer a sudden opportunity to reverse the tide of battle. Only three hours after Raymond Cook had refused to obey the court order in Manhattan, the Supreme Court of the United States in Washington handed down a decision that had a direct, conceivably decisive, bearing on the legal conflict between Hughes and the eastern financial establishment.

"The law," former Chief Justice Fred Vinson once remarked, "is what the Supreme Court thinks it is." Vinson's statement was especially true for the complex concepts of civil law involved in TWA's suit and Toolco's countersuit. In such a complicated case, there is no easy assessment of guilt or innocence. There are only questions of precedent and interpretation. The Supreme Court ruling—which both sides had been waiting for—was crucial because TWA's complaint and Toolco's countersuit both raised the issue of primary jurisdiction. Did it rest with the judiciary (as John Sonnett contended) or with the Civil Aeronautics Board (as Chester Davis argued)? Chester Davis had, of course, already gained support for his view from Lee Rankin, the former Solicitor General of the United States. Davis was hoping for support from an even more prestigious quarter.

On the afternoon of January 14 the Supreme Court made public its ruling on a case that dealt with the division of authority between the courts and the CAB. The decision was open to more than one interpretation. Nonetheless, Chester Davis was able to seize on important passages in the decision that powerfully buttressed his argument. The Supreme Court's ruling came in an antitrust case with a very long-winded title—*U.S. v. Pan American World Airways, W. R. Grace & Company and Pan American-Grace Airways*. For short, the case was called *Panagra* after the airline that was co-owned by Pan Am and Grace and was the alleged victim. The complaint, which was filed by the United States Attorney General in 1955, asserted that Pan Am and Grace had monopolized trade and restricted air commerce. Among other things, Pan Am and Grace allegedly had conspired to divide up routes, giving Panagra the continent's west coast while Pan Am had the rest of South America to itself.

The suit had been brought at the request of the Civil Aeronautics Board, which at the time was seeking to improve air service to South America. In order to create a strong second U.S.-flag carrier on those routes, the CAB wanted to free Panagra from its parents and to merge it with Braniff, which would be given permission to fly to South America. For a variety of reasons, including Juan Trippe's great influence in Washington, the CAB felt powerless to act. Thus it asked the Attorney General for help. Consequently, a federal prosecutor filed an antitrust suit in the Southern District of New York against Pan Am and Grace that demanded the two parents be forced to divest themselves of their holdings in Panagra. In 1961 Southern District Judge Thomas Murphy handed down a verdict that cleared Grace (which was represented by Cahill, Gordon) of any role in the antitrust violations. But Judge Murphy ruled that Pan Am was guilty of using its stock in Panagra to restrain trade. For different reasons, Pan Am and the Attorney General both appealed the decision directly to the Supreme Court.

By a five-to-two decision, the Supreme Court declared that the case did not in the first instance belong in a federal court but before the CAB. It directed the District Court to dismiss the complaint for lack of primary jurisdiction. In the majority opinion, written by Justice William O. Douglas, the Court emphasized the distinctive nature of the CAB's regulatory powers. In line with Chester Davis' own argument, the majority opinion stressed that Congress had given the CAB the authority to grant the airlines and their owners immunity from the antitrust laws when the public interest so demanded. Declared Justice Douglas: "If the courts were to intrude independently with their construction of the antitrust laws, two regimes might collide."

The Court held that the CAB's powers should be exercised prior to any action by the federal judiciary. Otherwise, the judiciary might find an antitrust violation in a situation that the CAB could turn around and bless with antitrust immunity. "It would be strange indeed if a division of territories or an allocation of routes which met the requirements of 'public interest' as defined in paragraph 2 [of the Federal Aviation Act] were to be antitrust violations," stated Justice Douglas. He noted that the CAB was ordered by Congress to encourage as well as to regulate the nation's air commerce. Citing the language of Paragraph 411 of the 1958 Federal Aviation Act, Justice Douglas reasoned that the CAB orders, which grant control of an airline to individuals, also give the parties exercising that control "immunity from antitrust violations 'in so far as may be necessary to enable such persons to do anything authorized, approved or required by such orders.'" Thus the Supreme Court decided that even though the CAB had not ruled on the arrangements between Pan Am and Grace, the fact that it could, if it chose to, approve the arrangement and thereby cloak the participants with antitrust immunity, indicated that the case belonged to the regulatory agency. Only after the CAB acted could the case then be referred to a federal court.

To be sure, the ruling was not all inclusive; the Supreme Court declared that the CAB did not have jurisdiction over all aspects of antitrust violations involving the airlines. "We hesitate here," wrote Justice Douglas, "to hold that the new regulatory scheme adopted in 1938 was designed completely to replace the antitrust laws—absent an unequivocally expressed Congressional purpose to do so. Moreover, on the civil side, violations of antitrust laws other than those enumerated in the Act might be imagined. We therefore refuse to hold that there are no antitrust violations left to the Department of Justice to enforce."

Despite those reservations, the ruling seemed certain to stand as a landmark enhancement of the CAB's powers. Certainly, the vigorous dissent by Justice John Marshall Harlan, in which he was joined by Chief Justice Earl Warren, demonstrated as much. "As a result of today's decision," wrote Justice Harlan, "certain questions are placed in the exclusive competence of the Board and will not be the subject of original court actions to enforce the antitrust laws. In effect, a *pro tanto* [partial] repeal of the antitrust laws is contemplated since the law to be applied in the Board proceedings is based not upon the antitrust laws, but upon the 'public interest' and competition to the extent necessary standards of the Board's overall mandate." Concluded Justice Harlan: "By its action today, the Court subjects the airline industry to a crazy quilt of antitrust controls that Congress can hardly have contemplated."

Crazy quilt or not, the Supreme Court's ruling gave Chester Davis enormous encouragement. In the *Panagra* decision, the nation's highest Court was saying that the CAB's special authority took precedence over the federal judiciary in cases involving alleged antitrust violations in the airline industry. What more could Davis have hoped for? Thus, even as his opponents were writing their briefs calling for a default judgment against Hughes, Davis went to work drafting his own brief in which he hoped to persuade Judge Metzner either to quash TWA's complaint entirely or, failing that, to acknowledge the *Panagra* precedent and surrender the case to the CAB.

Before Davis could finish his brief, however, he had a date to keep with Judge Metzner. On January 16 he met with the judge in his chambers to discuss the letter Davis had written two days earlier. It had stated that Toolco refused to surrender the tax and financial documents, which it still claimed were privileged. Sonnett, who was also present at the conference, later reported that Davis asked Judge Metzner for six weeks in which to prepare his brief in which he would move for the dismissal of the TWA lawsuit.

Judge Metzner, however, refused to consider any motion that would cause a major delay in Hughes' scheduled appearance on February 11. He had earlier expressed his opposition to Davis' motion for dismissal before the completion of the examination of Howard Hughes. Nonetheless, the judge said that the Toolco attorney would be given an immediate opportunity to make a motion for dismissal. According to Sonnett, Judge Metzner told Davis: "I cannot prevent you from bringing it on. I have indicated my views. If you wish to bring it on, I will pick a date and set it down. I will look at your papers, which you will have filed before February 1. TWA can have a week to file whatever it wants to file. After looking at your papers, if I find there is any question in my mind requires further consideration, I will postpone the deposition of Mr. Hughes for one week while I decide your motion."

Despite Judge Metzner's obvious reservations, Davis could still hope that the Supreme Court's decision would help him win his motion for a dismissal of the case. But at that very moment Hughes' opponents were redoubling their efforts to tighten their grip on his business secrets. By now, developments in the case no longer were gauged by weeks or even by days; the pace was quickening so that half days became the measure of events. The next morning—it was January 17—Sonnett and the lawyers for the additional defendants sought to persuade the special master to grant them permission to examine the additional Toolco tax documents. The lawyers were following up a motion they had made on January 9. It called upon Toolco to produce new documents in twenty-three various categories, including those that dealt with Toolco's explanations to the tax examiners for its retention of excessive earnings. The information in the documents, the lawyers claimed, would definitively disclose whether Hughes had manipulated TWA for his own tax purposes.

At the time of the initial motion, John Hupper of Cravath, Swaine had submitted to the special master a brief explaining the need for the examination of the additional tax documents, which included all Toolco papers dealing with the company's tax considerations, financial statements, and the working papers that would help explain how Toolco drew up the income tax reports. Now, in the argument before the special master, John Barr, also of Cravath, Swaine, expounded on his colleague's brief. Because of the effort required to sort through the 1,700,000 pieces of paper, which constituted the documentary evidence in the case, Barr explained that the lawyers had only recently managed to study the Hughes financial papers in their proper order. "As so often happens when you get documents put in a chronological order," he said, "they begin to tell a very interesting story." The story, he stated, was that Hughes delayed the financing of the jet fleet as part of a scheme to reap tax savings and capital gains benefits amounting to $25 million or more.

Sonnett then took over and buttressed Barr's statement by pulling out several documents that had been surrendered by the Bank of America. They were handwritten notes by vice presidents who had handled Hughes' banking matters. In one of the notes, dated December 6, 1960, Bank of America's Keath Carver, after a telephone conversation with Noah Dietrich, Hughes' onetime lieutenant, had jotted his impressions. According to the note, Dietrich, who by then had already broken with Hughes, said that Hughes had been the basic cause of TWA's difficulties because his main consideration in running the airline was to overcome his 102 problem. That explained why it was necessary for Hughes to have, as Dietrich was quoted as saying, "a stooge board of directors and policy controlled by him."

The most thorough summation of Hughes' tax dealings came that day from William S. Chandler, of Winthrop, Stimson, Putnam & Roberts, the firm which represented Ben Sessel and the Irving Trust. He had initiated the investigation into the tax angle. Chandler declared that the patterns of Hughes' dealings with TWA had evolved to conform to the modifications in the income tax laws. In 1951, explained Chandler, Paragraph 102 was amended so that money earned through investments was excluded from the category of excess profits, which were subject to penalty taxes. That opened a new possibility for Hughes. If Toolco's excess earnings could be invested for longer than six months in TWA, they would qualify for the relatively low capital gains tax, which took only 25 cents per $1.00 when the investment was converted into cash. By contrast, the standard rate on corporate profits was then 52 cents per $1.00.

This was the reason, asserted Chandler, that when the jet age was just around the corner, Hughes had said, in effect, to TWA: "I'll order the jets and take care of the financing—just leave everything up to me." Chandler recalled how at first Hughes had wanted a leasing plan, whereby Toolco would rent the jets to TWA. For Hughes, such a plan would have had great financial advantages. By retaining ownership of the jets, Toolco would have been able to deduct the depreciation of the jets against the company's pretax earnings, thus drastically reducing the amount of taxable profit. As costly pieces of machinery that someday wear out, the jets are large items of depreciation. The price of a Boeing 707 in the late 1950s was about $6.5 million and its residual value was reckoned to be about $1.5 million. The owner of the jet was entitled to "write off" from his taxable income over an eight-to-ten year period the $5 million that the plane would lose in value. Hence, if Hughes had been able to lease to TWA the entire fleet of sixty-three planes he originally intended to order, he would have been entitled to deduct from Toolco's gross earnings some $500,000 per year for each plane. That would have been a total depreciation deduction of about $31.5 million. That was just about the top amount that Toolco was earning annually before taxes in the early and mid-1950s. Under Hughes' plan, Toolco would have ended up paying little or no corporate income tax.

As an added bonus, the leasing arrangement would have enabled Hughes to invest Toolco's profits in the jets and to treat the income from the leases as a capital gain. Instead of facing a possible 87½ per cent penalty tax on Toolco's retained profits each year, he would have paid only the much lower capital gains tax.

"For two years Mr. Hughes refused to allow any sensible financial plan to come to pass," declared Chandler. "He kept insisting that, if possible, there should be some leasing arrangement. Now what appears from studying these documents is that all the time everybody was wrangling about what kind of financing plan we were going to have, Hughes was, in fact, operating the very kind of leasing plan he had asked Dillon, Read to prepare but everybody refused to let him put it into effect."

During those years, Hughes had, of course, been buying Boeing jets and supplying them to TWA on a rental of $2,500 a day for the domestic-service 131s and $2,900 for the international-range 331s. By the time the Dillon, Read financing plan finally went into effect on December 30, 1961, Hughes had managed to operate his leasing plan for almost two years. At the closing of the Dillon, Read plan, Hughes collected some $25 million in accumulated rentals from TWA. On that deal alone, Chandler claimed that Hughes converted $22 million into capital gains. But since the accumulated rentals only covered the last ten months of 1960, Hughes piled up similar benefits from the TWA rentals, which had been paid to him during the previous year. Chandler stressed that there was no way to determine exactly how much Hughes gained from the delay in closing the financing plan without a study of the tax documents, including the 1959 income tax working papers. Even so, Special Master Rankin refused to make an immediate ruling on the surrender of what became known as the additional tax documents.

Later that same day, January 17, the lawyers reassembled—this time for yet another pretrial hearing in the Federal Courthouse on Foley Square. Since Judge Metzner was trying a criminal case during regular court hours, he attended to *TWA v. Hughes* matters mainly in the evenings. Sonnet called the late-hour hearings "the night court proceedings against Howard Hughes." The issue that evening was Toolco's refusal to surrender the tax documents. However, Chester Davis, who was deep in writing his brief for the dismissal of the case, was eager to test his *Panagra* theories on the court. "It is our position, Your Honor," began Davis, "that particularly since the decision of the Supreme Court in the *Panagra* case that came down, this plaintiff by filing this complaint has improperly invoked the jurisdiction of the court.

"I further submit," declared Davis, falling back on the recommendations of the special master, "that a defendant is entitled to have not only the question of the court's jurisdiction passed on by the court but also to an adequate definition of the issues before the defendant may be required to testify." He said that he would base his motion for dismissal on two major developments. They were the *Panagra* ruling and the failure of TWA witnesses in the depositions to identify any course of action by Hughes that even vaguely resembled antitrust violations.

At the same time, Davis sought to head off the attempts by his opponents to force Toolco to surrender the additional tax data. He said that as long as a motion for dismissal was before the court, he believed that the tool company should not be required to disclose any more information. Furthermore, he protested that a surrender of the new documents would cause Toolco irreparable harm. In regard to the other withheld documents, including those famous three boxes from Houston, Davis insisted that, despite court orders to the contrary, Toolco's privilege on them remained in force. He said that if Judge Metzner overruled him on the question of the privileged documents, he hoped that he would have the opportunity to test that decision in the Court of Appeals.

When his turn came, John Sonnett said that he and the other lawyers were weary of waiting for the surrender of the tax documents. "By a process of trip, stumble, and delay, Mr. Davis has kept them out of my hands for many months, despite the pressure of the court," he declared. "The fact is that the court has directed that we are entitled to the material. I therefore see no mystery about our having it now."

Nor did the court. Two days later, on January 19, Judge Metzner ordered that the "privileged" documents should be surrendered by noon on January 22. In the same order, however, he agreed to hear Davis' motion for dismissal and instructed him to submit his brief by February 1. If Davis' motion was so convincing that it necessitated a delay in the discovery proceedings, the judge said that he would grant a short postponement of Hughes' appearance. But Judge Metzner denied Davis' motion to allow Hughes to remain in seclusion and to participate in the deposition only by answering written questions with written replies. "Contemplated answers to specific interrogatories may not be forthcoming, which would render meaningless subsequent questions," he wrote.

As a result of the January 19 ruling, Davis had only three days in which either to surrender the documents or, for a second time, to disobey the court order. Davis, however, still refused to hand over the papers. He decided to test Judge Metzner's order in the Court of Appeals. The higher court agreed to hear him, and at Judge Metzner's behest, Sonnett and the other lawyers postponed the deadline for the surrender of the documents by twenty-four hours until noon on January 23.

On Tuesday, January 22, Davis tried to convince the Court of Appeals to reverse Judge Metzner's orders of January 10 and 19, which called for the surrender of the "privileged" documents. While Davis' argument to the higher court primarily rested upon his old contention that Toolco's privilege remained in force, he also managed to weave in other familiar themes, notably that TWA had failed to state a case against Hughes and that the federal judiciary lacked primary jurisdiction in the case.

Unfortunately for Davis, he was not alone in the appellate courtroom. Sonnett and Judge Bromley were there, too. They argued that since the case was still in the discovery stage, Davis had no issue that was reviewable by a higher court. After hearing the arguments, the Court of Appeals said it would rule shortly.

But on January 22, even as Davis was arguing in the Court of Appeals, the special master made a decision, which struck even more deeply than ever at Toolco's secrets. On the motion for the surrender of the new material—"the additional tax documents"— the special master declared that Toolco should make those papers available immediately to TWA and the additional defendants.

By noon the next day, January 23, the Court of Appeals had not yet handed down its decision. Therefore, at Judge Metzner's suggestion, Davis was given an extension of the deadline until 5 P.M. for the surrender of the documents. At 4 P.M. on January 23 the Court of Appeals announced its ruling. It was a severe setback for Davis. The higher court, which adopted the view of Sonnett and Judge Bromley, refused to review Judge Metzner's decision.

Beaten on that front, Davis rushed back from the Court of Appeals, which is also located on Foley Square, to his offices at 120 Broadway, where the documents were to be surrendered at 5 P.M.

It was quite a scene. As Davis entered his suite of offices, Rankin and the opposing lawyers were waiting for him. Before he figuratively could take off his hat, the special master began to read to him the court orders that called for the surrender of the documents. Davis managed to excuse himself and to retreat into his private office. He had only a few moments before the deadline expired. What would he do? Would he turn over the documents? Or would he again defy the court's orders?

What did he do? Davis exercised one of his special talents—he wrote a letter. Emerging from his private office, he read aloud to the special master and the lawyers the text of the message, which he already had dispatched by messenger to Judge Metzner. It said: "In view of the irreparable injury to my clients, which would result from prematurely turning over to opposing counsel such documents (as the tax returns and supporting papers), as counsel for Hughes Tool Company I must respectfully decline to comply with your said orders, at least prior to a determination of the motions to dismiss now pending before Your Honor."

After Davis finished reading the letter, John Barr of Cravath, Swaine spoke up. "I want to put you on notice that I do consider this to be in contempt!" he cried. "I assume that it is deliberately done." Just to make certain, Barr added: "May I ask just for the record whether there is any dispute as to whether or not you were as of five o'clock this evening required under existing orders of the court to produce the documents for our inspecting and copying?"

Replied Davis: "There is no question in my mind that the stipulation within which the tool company could comply with the order of Judge Metzner dated January 19, 1963, expired at five o'clock."

"This is deliberate, flagrant contempt of the court's order," declared Bob Zeller, who was taking John Sonnett's place. "We certainly have to reserve our rights to act accordingly."

Davis remained unruffled. "I appreciate that," he said. "So the record may be clear, you should understand that I, as counsel for the Hughes Tool Company, am satisfied that this court lacks jurisdiction over the subject matter of the action. I feel that it is my duty as counsel to refuse to permit any further action on the part of the parties which would cause any injury to my clients until after the court determines the motions which are pending before it and which establish that there is jurisdiction on the premises."

After Davis finished, Special Master Rankin warned him that he, too, considered Davis' refusal to be in contempt of court. Rankin pointed out that Davis was in a procedural dilemma. Even if he managed to have the suit against Hughes dismissed, the $443 million countersuit would still stand. Therefore the defendants in the countersuit would continue to have the right to examine the documents and to call upon Hughes for his testimony. Rankin also sought to impress upon Davis the gravity of his action by emphasizing that all of Davis' appeals and motions had been turned down by the courts and that no judicial process now stayed the effectiveness of Judge Metzner's orders for the surrender of the documents.

"That may be," responded Davis, "unless those orders are errors as a matter of law."

"I do not mean to argue with you, Mr. Davis," answered the special master, "and I am sure you do not mean to. I am only trying to make sure that you are not overlooking any of these things, which I think have a serious bearing on the whole question."

"I have tried not to overlook anything," replied Chester Davis.

But in the rush of events both men had overlooked one thing: the additional tax documents, which the special master had ruled the day before were to be surrendered immediately. Bob Zeller asked the special master to request Davis to hand them over. Davis replied that he was no more prepared to surrender those papers than he was to give up the documents on which he claimed the privilege. On that note of defiance, the confrontation ended.

Davis' opponents quickly sought to capitalize on his refusal for the second time to obey the court's commands. A transcript of the exchange in the Davis' office was rushed by messenger to Judge Metzner. The opposing lawyers wanted the judge to read that Davis once more had refused to comply with his orders.

The next day (January 24) the lawyers for the additional defendants embarked upon a series of maneuvers that concerned Toolco's huge countersuit. They submitted motions to the court in which they asked for the dismissal of the case. Then the next day they filed their answers to Toolco's charges. The banks, insurance companies, and executives rejected Toolco's charge that they had damaged TWA. Predictably, they placed full blame on Hughes for the delays in setting up the financing plan for TWA jet fleet and the resulting losses to the airline. The timing of the filing of the replies met the procedural requirement that defendants must state their defense before they may begin to examine the plaintiff's witnesses. They were preparing for the examination of Howard Hughes.

So, too, was John Sonnett. But Sonnett's tactics did not coincide with those of the additional defendants. As soon as they made their motions to have the case against them dismissed, Sonnett withdrew TWA's own motion for dismissal, which had been made in March 1962. In the event the additional defendants were successful in their motions, Sonnett wanted to be sure that the countersuit was kept alive. In a skillful exercise of legal jujitsu, Sonnett was using the weight of the Toolco countersuit to help his own cause. The continued existence of the countersuit was important to Sonnett for the reasons Rankin had explained to Davis—it provided TWA with another justification for demanding Hughes' testimony and the surrender of the documents.

The next installment in the night court proceedings was played out on the evening of the following business day, Monday, January 28. It was now only two weeks before the scheduled appearance of Howard Hughes, and the proceedings were assuming a heightened atmosphere of suspense. No one could be completely certain about what lay ahead, but almost everyone was convinced that it would be something sensational.

Would, at the last minute, the besieged millionaire come storming out of hiding and, spewing indignation, defend his honor as he had done in the far-off days of the Brewster hearings? Or was he, as some of his former advisers suspected, no longer the same man who faced down the ambitious Republican senator from Maine? Would Hughes' enemies get to look at the secret papers? Or was there a chance that after all Chester Davis would succeed in convincing the court that his theories were correct and thus spare Howard Hughes from the barbs and arrows of a multitude of outraged lawyers?

On the evening of January 28 the one thing that was clear was that Chester Davis was badly tired and harassed. From the start, he had lacked the large staff of associates and clerks that his rivals in the big established Wall Street law firms could call upon. Chester Davis was doing enough work for several lawyers. He was engaged in writing his briefs for the dismissal motion, which was due to be handed in by noon on February 1; he was coping with the demands for the examination of the "privileged" documents and now the additional tax papers; he was fighting a rear-guard action to postpone Hughes' deposition. And if all that were not enough, Chester Davis was also opposing the TWA-Pan Am merger. He was continually receiving telephone calls from the Justice Department, which was investigating the antitrust aspects of the proposed consolidation. On the evening of January 28, as Davis stood in front of the bench, he tried to gain the court's understanding for the distractions that made demands on his time.

Judge Metzner was unmoved. "This is your choice, not mine," he said, breaking into Davis' explanation. The judge, wanting to get on with the case, asked Davis to state his argument concerning the additional Toolco tax documents, which the special master the week before had ruled should be produced. Davis replied that the ruling placed an unreasonable and excessive burden on Toolco. It would take four to six weeks, he said, to search all the files in Houston and Los Angeles and would cost at least $150,000. Anyway, he went on, the great majority of the papers had most likely been turned over already to TWA during last March's production of documents. "I am informed by those who are familiar with those files," declared Davis, "that probably all the documents called for have already been produced and made available to plaintiff and these additional defendants.

"To be sure," he hedged, "that does not include the 1961 tax returns or the 1962 tax returns called for, which is not yet prepared, and that is not available." Davis said that the year-end work of closing Toolco's books was in progress and the people who would be needed to search for the documents were occupied with that job. Davis concluded that the real issue before the court was not whether Toolco would produce documents or whether Hughes would appear. It was whether the complaint should be dismissed.

Judge Metzner reminded Davis of the dilemma that the special master had pointed out to him five days earlier. Said the judge: "Even if you were successful in a motion to dismiss the complaint, you still have the counterclaims totaling $385 [*sic*] million for which Mr. Hughes' deposition is also scheduled."

When John Sonnett's turn came, he handed up to the bench an affidavit in which he argued that it would not be an unreasonable burden to Toolco to produce the additional tax documents. The reason, explained Sonnett, was that the Houston firm had handled Toolco's tax matters for some fifty years and Raymond Cook, by his own admission, had personally handled them for more than ten years. Hence the Houston lawyers should be able, in Sonnett's words, "to collect 90 per cent of the material called for within forty-eight hours."

Then Sonnett, who made extremely skillful use of the Hughes documents already unearthed, launched into a dramatic summation. He was seeking to rebut Davis' argument that TWA had failed to state the factual basis of its case against Hughes. Declared John Sonnett: "I hold in my hand documentary proof from the Bank of America files of statements made by Mr. Hughes himself in 1960 and statements made by Mr. Noah Dietrich in 1960 specifically pointing out that the 102 tax problem had always been and was at the heart of the Hughes problem. I propose to establish on the record to date, and certainly so out of Hughes' mouth when he is deposed, that because of the tax problems of Hughes Tool Company and Mr. Hughes personally, they engaged in the course of conduct alleged in our complaint and that that course of conduct undeniably violated the antitrust laws and was not and could not be exempted or dealt with by the CAB."

At once Davis sprang to his feet and asked the court for an opportunity to answer Sonnett's charges. He said that Sonnett's use of the documents and his whole line of reasoning were totally irrelevant. "I respectfully submit, we are not concerned as to why someone violated antitrust laws," said Davis. "We are concerned with whether they were violated." He declared that it was immaterial whatever the additional tax documents might show, because tax avoidance was not an antitrust violation. "I respectfully submit," continued Davis, "whether or not the tool company did or did not make a profit in transactions, which were reviewed and approved by the CAB, and whether or not the reasons why the tool company acquired 78 per cent control of TWA was because it could employ its cash and thereby avoid an improper accumulation of cash, and whether or not that was done by buying more securities of TWA or by providing funds for the acquisition of aircraft, I just don't understand how that can be said to be serious documents that they would have to have for the purpose of establishing that the tool company or Mr. Hughes engaged in a violation of antitrust laws or how they [the additional tax documents] could conceivably afford a defense to any of the counterclaims."

When Davis finished his convoluted declaration, Judge Metzner fixed him in a steady gaze. Davis was taking great risks, which could lead to severe sanctions. Judge Metzner wanted to know why. During the past two weeks Davis had refused to obey two successive court orders for the surrender of the "privileged" tax documents. He also had failed to comply with the special master's instruction for the surrender of the new batch of so-called "additional" tax documents. (There was, however, a good deal of confusion about which documents had been surrendered and which ones were still withheld. The documents, which by far attracted the most interest, were those in the three boxes from Houston.) Judge Metzner told Davis that he understood that the three boxes had not been made available for inspection and copying by the other side. Davis tried to fend off the judge's question by launching into another convoluted statement. "I don't think the circumstances here indicate that the Hughes Tool Company is not entitled to whatever efforts it is entitled to make in order to protect its rights," he said. "I don't think there can be any question that if, in fact, as we claim we are going to be able to satisfy Your Honor shortly, this complaint lacks merit and is a matter not properly before this court but should be properly before the CAB, I respectfully submit that there is a grave injustice being done by requiring the tool company to do any more than it has already done."

Judge Metzner, however, was decidedly unconvinced by Davis' contention that Toolco should not be required to submit to further discovery proceedings until the motion to dismiss the TWA suit was decided. "You have the boxes of this stuff that you have gone through. Turn it over," he commanded.

"This is what happens when we get the facts piecemeal," countered Davis. He was protesting that there was a mix-up involving the special master's ruling of January 22 that called for the surrender of the additional tax documents and the earlier court orders that dealt with the so-called "privileged" documents. But Judge Metzner pressed Davis about the material in the three boxes. "You have it—haven't you?—and it has been gone through," he said, referring to the fact that the special master had examined the documents in the three boxes and Davis had then taken them back into his possession.

"They have been made available, Your Honor," replied Davis.

Judge Metzner, who was only too fully aware of the long controversy concerning these mysterious boxes, contradicted him. "These three boxes, I understand, have not been made available," he insisted.

"Your Honor, all I know is that Mr. Cook assumed responsibility with respect to that production," replied Davis. "The special master required that something be done, and it was done." Davis explained he had been too busy to attend to the matter himself. He stated: "I am not in a position to analyze what is in those boxes, if there are any such boxes——"

"Mr. Cook is though, isn't he?" interjected Judge Metzner.

Davis began, "Mr. Cook has been engaged as I have——"

"Let us get one thing straight," Judge Metzner broke in. "Has the material in the three boxes been turned over to parties in this litigation?"

"Have they been?" asked Davis.

"Yes," answered Judge Metzner.

"I haven't got the slightest idea," replied Davis.

"Why don't you ask Mr. Cook tonight?" insisted the judge. "If they haven't, turn them over."

"I will do that," promised Davis.

At that moment Judge Bromley, who could tolerate Davis' hedging no longer, cried out, "Of course not! They have been refused!"

"He has had them for a long time," said Judge Metzner.

Now on the defense, Davis fell back to his oldest line. "Your Honor," he said, "I cannot say any more sincerely than I have already said that it seems to me—and I believe I have authority to support it, if I had time to present it—that there is a serious motion to dismiss this complaint."

"You argued that before the Court of Appeals," declared Judge Metzner, who did not seem pleased with Davis' performance in the higher court.

"No, Your Honor," declared Davis, who took the case to the Court of Appeals on one narrow issue. "The only thing I have argued before the Court of Appeals was whether or not the order of this court with respect to the privileged documents was appealable and therefore reviewable."

"I read what you said," responded Judge Metzner, who had received a transcript of the appellate proceedings from John Sonnett. "You went beyond that narrow point."

Davis tried to explain that he had not appealed the case in advance to a higher court. But again Judge Metzner interrupted him. He wanted to know whether Davis would have brought on the motion to dismiss the case if it were not for the pressure of Hughes' appearance on February 11.

Davis responded that the court's January 10 rulings had decided him. "The minute Your Honor indicated to me that Your Honor had decided not to give me a Rule 16 proceeding and no answers to interrogatories, at that point, as far as I was concerned, there was going to be no further opportunity to elicit from the plaintiff what the basis is for this complaint," he said. "At that point, I had no more reason whatsoever but to test the theory which I adhered to from the time this complaint was filed—that this complaint and the subject matter of this complaint was improperly in this court." Davis stressed that none of the TWA witnesses whom he examined "know of any course of conduct violating antitrust laws. They say this complaint is because of what counsel recommended because of their investigation. They asserted the work product and attorney privilege, and here I am." By that, Davis meant that he had been unable to determine what evidence TWA's lawyers told their clients about.

Then Davis, who sought to demonstrate his belief in the emptiness of the case against Howard Hughes, made a startling proposal. "I am so confident of my facts," he continued, "that I am prepared at this date to let this plaintiff, any time he wants, present whatever facts he wants. I will admit every fact he asserts and ask for a decision on the law. I will admit every answer he gives me on interrogatories.

"They can use those facts either for the purpose of construing the complaint or anything else they please, and I ask for a determination of the case on the law and if I am wrong on that, Your Honor, I will make a commitment. Then we proceed to the assessment of damages." Davis seemed to be saying that he was so convinced that TWA could not find any proof of antitrust violations that he would accept without argument any fact that TWA could prove in support of its claims against Toolco and Hughes and he would pay any damages that the court might assess on the basis of the factual evidence submitted by TWA.

Rising to reply, John Sonnett sought to deflate Davis' grand gesture. Assuming an air of bewilderment, Sonnett began. "What Mr. Davis just said—or else I am having trouble with my hearing —is like someone once said, 'Listening to him is like trying to nail a custard pie to the wall.' But if he said that he now admits the allegations of the complaint, TWA now moves for judgment on his admission and for relief sought in the complaint."

"I don't think he said that," replied Judge Metzner.

"I am not sure," conceded Sonnett. "I never know exactly what he is saying except that he wants to use the federal rules [of court procedure] for himself and the tool company, but doesn't want any one else to use them."

Judge Metzner did not respond to Sonnett's observation. Instead, he began to wind up the hearing. He said that he had one question for Davis. It was only a short, almost routine query, but the very asking of it was the first indication that the court was contemplating very serious penalties against Toolco.

"You wrote me a letter January twenty-third," Judge Metzner said. (It was the one Davis sent immediately after his motion to reverse Judge Metzner's orders had been turned down by the Court of Appeals.) "I will refer," continued the judge, "just to the last three lines in the second sentence in that letter, which read: 'I must respectfully decline to comply with your said orders, at least prior to a determination to this motion to dismiss now pending before Your Honor.'

"The question I wanted to ask about those three lines is: Did you make the decision on your own or did you discuss it with your client?"

"I discussed it with my client," replied Davis.

"All right," said Judge Metzner. "That is all."

15. The Price of Privacy

Even as the threat of a default judgment hung over Chester Davis, the arrangements were going forward to take the testimony of Howard Hughes. On several earlier occasions Judge Metzner, Special Master Rankin, and John Sonnett each had suggested to Davis that Howard Hughes might wish to select a site other than a courtroom for his appearance. Rankin and Sonnett proposed that Hughes might feel more at ease if the hearings were held in a hotel suite, one of his familiar habitats, where he could withdraw into another room if the burden of testifying became too great for him. In fact, Judge Metzner earlier had instructed Davis to reply by noon on January 22 whether Hughes desired a different location for his deposition. But Davis, taking the position that his motion to dismiss the complaint would be successful, made no response.

Consequently, preparations were made for the examination of Howard Hughes to be held in the Federal Court Building in Los Angeles. Special Master Rankin wrote to the chief judge for the Southern District of California, who made available a hearing room. Special marshals were engaged at a non-inflationary rate of $12 a day to keep order. Two benches were reserved for members of the press. To hold back the crowds, plans were made to set up police lines outside the Federal Court Building and to cordon off a pathway in the corridors within the building itself.

Fred Furth, who was handling the preparations, took another important precaution. Because of Hughes' hearing problem, Furth installed special amplifying equipment, consisting of loudspeakers placed throughout the room and microphones for the speakers. For Hughes there was a special set of large foam-rubber-padded earphones, which were equipped with a separate volume regulator he could adjust to the desired level of amplification. In his last appearance in a public hearing fifteen years earlier, Hughes had put off the CAB examiner by complaining that he could not hear the questions. "Speak up, young man! Speak up!" Hughes had commanded. This time Hughes' opponents were determined that he would have no problem whatsoever in hearing the questions even if, as one of them put it, "we have to blast his eardrums out."

In preparation for the testimony of Howard Hughes, Sonnett and the other lawyers had begun to ship to Los Angeles filing cases full of documents. During the questioning, some of these papers would be handed to Hughes to help refresh his memory. The lawyers rented office space in Los Angeles and reserved hotel rooms.

In addition to the physical preparations for the hearings, Sonnett and his aides were also planning their strategy. Sonnett's underlying assumption was that Hughes would not appear. Even so, he had to be prepared for the other possibility. No one could be 100 per cent certain that Hughes would not show up. Hughes himself may not have known what he would do. From a purely emotional standpoint, Sonnett hoped that Hughes would appear. From a professional standpoint, he had to be ready if Hughes did show up, to "convict him out of his own mouth," as he had put it.

John Sonnett had to anticipate what Hughes might do. What if Hughes came to the hearing, made a ringing statement of his innocence, and then withdrew, pleading that his doctor had ordered him to make only one appearance? Or what if Hughes agreed to only, say, one week of examination? How should Sonnett orchestrate his questions to meet such eventualities? Which documents should he select from the millions of pieces of paper to quiz Hughes about? And which questions should he ask first?

While Sonnett plotted his courtroom approach, the last days before Hughes' scheduled appearance were racing past. On February 1 Judge Metzner made public his rulings on the issues that had been debated in the pretrial hearing four days earlier. Again they were serious defeats for Chester Davis. Judge Metzner approved TWA's request to withdraw its motion to dismiss the countersuit; hence, even if the counterclaims were dismissed against the additional defendants, the countersuit would provide TWA with an additional justification for calling Hughes to testify. By far the most important ruling that day concerned the surrender of the additional tax documents and the three boxes of working papers. The court rejected Davis' argument that Toolco should not be forced to submit to any further discovery proceedings until a decision had been made on his motion to dismiss the case. Hence, Judge Metzner directed Toolco to hand over immediately to TWA and the additional defendants the contents of three boxes of tax documents. He also confirmed Special Master Rankin's earlier ruling that the additional tax documents should be surrendered as well. Toolco was to begin at once to make those documents available on a day-to-day basis, the entire batch to be surrendered by the time of Hughes' appearance on February 11.

But on February 1, a Friday, Davis made no move whatsoever to comply with the new court order. He did, however, submit to the court that morning the brief that contained his argument for the dismissal of the case. Copies were delivered to John Sonnett and the lawyers for the additional defendants. In response, John Sonnett quickly composed a long brief of his own in opposition to Davis' motion and submitted it to Judge Metzner the next day.

In his brief, Davis relied mainly upon his old argument, which he reinforced with citations from the Supreme Court's *Panagra* decision. He contended that TWA's complaint (a) totally lacked merit and (b), in any event, belonged in front of the CAB and not the federal court. Davis restated his earlier contention that

Sections 408 and 414 of the Federal Aviation Act granted full and complete antitrust immunity to Toolco and Hughes for all their actions at TWA. Not surprisingly, the main point in Sonnett's brief was also familiar—that the CAB's power to grant immunity was limited in scope and did not encompass the antitrust violations alleged in TWA's complaint.

Judge Metzner, who was still tied up in the long criminal case, spent the weekend studying the briefs by Davis and Sonnett. Then he spent Monday night and Tuesday night poring over the reply briefs that each side had submitted on Monday to refute the other's arguments. On Wednesday, February 6, Judge Metzner had an unexpected free afternoon in the criminal trial, and he immediately called a pretrial hearing.

"I would like to say preliminarily," stated Davis, who spoke first, "that I put my energies on the paper that we prepared for submission to the court and I am a little hoarse and hard of hearing today." Therefore, said Davis, he would rely on the briefs he had submitted. Sonnett allowed that he, too, would rest on his briefs.

Judge Metzner quickly got to the point. "I called for this meeting," he said, "on the chance that maybe Mr. Davis could persuade me that the conclusion I had reached on reading the briefs and studying them and checking the law was wrong. Mr. Davis wants me to rely on his papers. Consequently, I will deny the motion to dismiss the complaint. This is the order of the court and a formal opinion will follow in the next day or two."

In less than a minute, his motion to dismiss the case, the maneuver on which Davis was basing his last great hopes, was demolished. But even if Davis was gravely disappointed, he still was thinking fast. "Your Honor," he asked immediately, "may I respectfully request then that in your opinion you certify the matter so that I may obtain a discretionary review by the Court of Appeals?" He meant that Judge Metzner should indicate in his ruling that there was a question of law that merited the attention of a higher court.

"The application is denied," replied Judge Metzner tersely.

Davis persisted: "May I respectfully request Your Honor to stay all further discovery proceedings by the plaintiff until I have had an opportunity to seek a discretionary review by the Court of Appeals?"

"Are you referring to the production of documents under my pretrial order of January nineteenth or the tax papers covered by the orders of February first or the deposition of Mr. Hughes, now scheduled for February eleventh?" inquired Judge Metzner, whose quick recital of the pending processes was an indication of the weight of events that now were bearing down on Davis.

"I was referring to all further pretrial proceedings, Your Honor," said the Toolco attorney. "It seems to me, Your Honor," Davis continued, "that there is at least a very substantial question raised by the decision of the Supreme Court in *Panagra* as to whether or not this court should entertain jurisdiction of the questions raised by this complaint."

"I will tell you what I will do," replied Judge Metzner, relenting somewhat. "I will grant your application to the extent of staying all further discovery or deposition proceedings until five o'clock Friday. That will give you two days to make whatever application you wish to make to the Court of Appeals for a stay."

"All right, Your Honor," agreed Davis. He had now won a breathing space until February 8. But that was the last business day before Howard Hughes was scheduled to be called as a witness. With so little time remaining, Davis was worried that because he would not have an opinion from Judge Metzner for another day or so, he would not know on what grounds he should base his argument in front of the Court of Appeals. "I was wondering what I would have to present to the Court of Appeals as the basis of the court's ruling on the one hand and my position on the other," he asked.

"It is complicated," conceded Judge Metzner, who said that he would make every effort to write up the final opinion. It would probably run about fifteen pages, he stated, and he promised to try to get it to Davis by noon on Friday. But in short, said Judge Metzner, "the answer is I do not agree with you."

"I know I can say that to the Court of Appeals," responded Davis, "but in order——"

Judge Metzner cut in. "I think that if you were to go to the Court of Appeals and, if it's necessary, say to them, 'Judge Metzner disagreed with this position that I took on my briefs,' it would suffice, because all I had before me were the briefs."

But Davis persisted. "I was thinking," he said, "that the Court of Appeals might like to know what legal issue——"

"I think I flatly can say that I disagree with your interpretation of 408 and 414 as applicable to the specific orders involved here upon which you rely, the orders of 1944 and 1950," replied Judge Metzner, referring to two times when the CAB, after lengthy investigations, had approved Hughes' control of TWA. "The scope of the order goes to the fact of acquisition, as I see it. It does not give you a license to engage in subsequent acts which may amount to restraint of trade or attempts to monopolize, and I do not think the words in 414 are necessary to carry out what was authorized or approved by the Board [as] encompassing such activity. That, in brief, is what the fifteen pages are going to say."

Davis asked, "Do I also understand that it is the conclusion of the court that——"

Again Judge Metzner broke in. "Let's have it this way," he said. "You will have an opinion signed by ten o'clock Friday morning."

"Thank you, Your Honor," said Davis. "I would prefer a stay for a couple more days."

"I can go on," stated Judge Metzner, "but you may say what I said from the bench is not what I put in the opinion. I will go over the draft and polish it up."

"I was really hoping for a little more time beyond Friday," pleaded Davis.

"I am afraid not," replied Judge Metzner.

The day's proceedings, however, were far from ended. Davis had prepared a huge surprise for his opponents. He did not mention it himself, but the next speaker did. John Hupper, of Cravath, Swaine, informed the court that earlier that day Chester Davis had dropped another of his "atomic bombs." At noon, through his associates in Washington, Davis had filed a complaint at the Civil Aeronautics Board against the same parties who were the additional defendants in Toolco's countersuit. In addition, he named two new parties as members of the conspiracy to take TWA away from Hughes. They were Pan American Airways and Juan Terry Trippe. During the afternoon Davis had copies of the complaint delivered to the court and the law firms representing the additional defendants. The court and most of the lawyers had not yet seen the copies by the time the pretrial hearing began that day. But everyone immediately understood from Hupper's few words that Davis had embarked upon an audacious new maneuver, which, if successful, would free his side from the great quandary in which it had become trapped.

That quandary was, of course, that Hughes was caught by two lawsuits—TWA's and his own. Even if Davis succeeded on Friday in convincing the Court of Appeals to reverse Judge Metzner's decision and thus quash TWA's complaint, Toolco's mammoth countersuit would remain alive, its continued existence providing TWA and the additional defendants with the legal reason for demanding the appearance of Howard Hughes on Monday.

If Davis was going to keep Hughes off the stand, he had to find some way to suspend or delay the countersuit. Therefore Davis started a new campaign at the CAB where his tactics in the Northeast case had succeeded so brilliantly only a short time ago. His strategy worked like this: As soon as he had filed the complaint at the CAB, he also filed a motion to the District Court in New York, asking that the countersuit be held in abeyance until the CAB had made a final decision about the charges he had just made in Washington. If that ploy worked, it meant that the discovery proceedings, including the scheduled testimony of Howard Hughes, would be postponed indefinitely while the CAB investigated and decided upon Davis' complaint. And Davis had certainly given the CAB plenty to investigate. In his complaint, he charged that the additional defendants had broken the nation's aviation law by illegally gaining control of TWA. Davis also elaborated on his original conspiracy theory by asserting that Pan Am's Trippe and two

other Pan Am directors, all three of whom served on the board of
the Metropolitan, had caused the insurance company to insist on
the voting trust clause that compelled Hughes to surrender control
of the airline. He further charged that Trippe had used his position as a director of the Metropolitan to persuade the Metropolitan
and TWA's other creditors to support his proposal for a TWA-Pan
Am merger.

Even more important, the complaint raised a key legal question
that now became crucial to Davis' strategy for avoiding an immediate showdown in New York. The complaint alleged that the
Equitable and Metropolitan, the two lenders that controlled the
voting trust, had for many years been engaged in a phase of aeronautics through supplying the bulk of the long-term financing to
the nation's airlines. If Davis' point was correct, his charge would
cause some very interesting consequences, because in late December 1960, when the CAB initially approved the change in the
control of TWA from Hughes to the voting trust, the board had
assumed that the insurance companies had not previously been
engaged in a phase of aeronautics. Accordingly, the CAB had not
investigated the possible conflicts of interest involved in the voting trust arrangement. However, if the insurance companies now
were deemed by the board to have been involved in a phase of
aeronautics because of their loan activities, the CAB would be
compelled to conduct an investigation. The Federal Aviation Act
prohibits persons and institutions already active in aviation to acquire control of an airline without a specific waiver from the board.
If the board decided, after an investigation, that the insurance
companies' control of TWA was in the public interest, it could
then grant them protection from antitrust prosecution in so far as
was necessary to enable them to run the airline. By the same token,
persons engaged in one phase of aviation are not permitted to serve
on the boards of other companies involved in aeronautics unless
the board especially approves of the relationship, which it had not
done in the case of Trippe and his two colleagues. Thus that arrangement also needed to be examined by the CAB, which could
either bless or condemn it.

After Hupper had brought up the subject of the CAB complaint in the Federal Court that afternoon, Davis explained his position to Judge Metzner. According to his reading of *Panagra,* the CAB first must decide whether or not it found the insurance companies' control of TWA to be in the public interest. Davis said that if the CAB decided to clothe TWA's two major lenders with the anti-trust immunity, Toolco's countersuit, which rested chiefly on allegations of antitrust violations against the financial institutions, would be meaningless. Until there was a resolution of that question, there was no sense in his pursuing further discovery in Toolco's countersuit. Davis said that he was designating 4 P.M. on Friday, February 8, as the time for his opponents to reply to his motion to suspend proceedings in the countersuit.

"Well, I don't know what I can do for you about your motion," said Judge Metzner. "I am in the ninth week of this criminal trial so I am tied up from ten until five every day, except for this afternoon when we had a lucky break. If you want your decision to be out on your motion-to-dismiss to show the Court of Appeals what I said, it is physically impossible to take this up."

"I appreciate that," replied Davis, who explained that on either the next day or Friday, the last business day before Hughes' scheduled appearance, "I will advise the parties with respect to this Los Angeles date." Before he could continue, Judge Metzner interjected a suggestion.

"May I take your motion and hold it in abeyance and hear argument on it?" Judge Metzner asked.

"Anytime convenient to Your Honor," replied Davis, who was very pleased. Suddenly it looked as if he would win a new delay after all. The fact that the court was going to hear his new motion could provide him with grounds for arguing that Toolco did not have to produce Hughes on Monday.

But Judge Metzner immediately noticed the visible displeasure of the other lawyers. "Mr. Hupper is not satisfied," he remarked.

Hupper, who represented the two insurance companies, certainly was not. "Isn't it perfectly plain what Mr. Davis is trying to do?" he demanded. "He is going to have a decision some time

Friday from the Court of Appeals on whether or not there is any merit to his attempting to get appellate review. At that point he will have something else which he can wave in front of you or some other court, which he will use as a basis for arguing that the deposition of Hughes should not go forward on Monday. There are still unresolved questions——"

Judge Metzner interrupted. "You will agree, Mr. Hupper," he asked, "if the Court of Appeals stays my determination that we are not going to run out to Los Angeles on Monday?"

Replied Hupper: "I would not agree to that as a matter of law for this reason: The charges made against us in this CAB proceeding are entirely different than the charges made by the TWA people against Toolco—completely! We have an additional question here which is a matter of discretion. We have for almost a year now been engaged in this case, brought on by Toolco against our will, the tool company asserting claims of over $330 million against us and alleging that this court had jurisdiction over those counterclaims, and we have——"

Again, Judge Metzner broke in. "Mr. Davis said *Panagra* did not come down until——"

"That is not applicable at all!" exclaimed Hupper. "That involved Section 411." Hupper meant that *Panagra* involved issues that applied only to persons engaged in the aviation industry.

"I read it four times," snapped Judge Metzner. "Don't tell me that!"

"It has not the slightest thing to do with this," countered Hupper. "We are not air carriers and we are not engaged in air transportation. It has nothing to do with this case. There is not a possible basis for it. What Mr. Davis is doing here is using this motion after a year of dragging us down the garden path and spending hundreds of thousands as a last ditch attempt to stave off the deposition of Mr. Hughes. We have a right to examine Mr. Hughes independently of whatever his position in the complaint is. As a matter of discretion, we feel you ought to permit us to go forward on that examination if only for the fact that it would enable us perhaps to adduce facts which would be helpful to you in determining whether or not you have jurisdiction over the subject matter."

Judge Metzner turned to Toolco's attorney. "Mr. Davis," he asked, "do you intend to pursue your counterclaims?"

"Not until we have a determination from the CAB," answered Davis.

"In other words," summarized Judge Metzner, "you want to stay any proceedings regarding the counterclaims in this court until the CAB has spoken first?"

"That is our understanding of what the Supreme Court has held," stated Davis. "Of course, if I am told in some final manner that I am wrong in that regard, I want to be able to resume. That is our understanding of the *Panagra* case. It is a basis for our motion to dismiss. It will be the basis on which we will try to obtain a review at this time, and therefore I don't understand why a defendant is so anxious to be prosecuted if I am willing to stay my claims against the additional defendants." Davis said that he was puzzled why his opponents always accused him of "following some procedure for some improper motive." He tried to turn the tables by asking what was the motive of the additional defendants in wanting to examine Mr. Hughes if he, Davis, was willing to suspend the claims against them until the CAB had made a ruling. "Perhaps Mr. Hupper can explain it more clearly," Davis said.

Instead of Hupper, Judge Metzner recognized Charles Stewart, who represented Dillon, Read. "Mr. Davis," replied Stewart, "as far as Additional Defendant Dillon, Read is concerned, for the first time in this case, after having been in it for a year, we have the opportunity presumably to prove that the counterclaims brought against us are absolutely baseless." Then, addressing the court, Stewart continued: "It is particularly compelling because this so-called complaint, which Mr. Davis has brought before the CAB, is absolutely meaningless as far as we are concerned. Dillon, Read is not an air carrier. It is not engaged in a phase of aeronautics, nor does he claim that we are so engaged. Nothing that the CAB says or does not say can affect us in any way." Stewart asked Judge Metzner to deny Davis' motion from the bench.

"There are other problems in the CAB proceedings, are there not, Mr. Davis?" asked Judge Metzner, turning again to the Toolco attorney. "You allege that Pan American World Airways and Mr.

Juan Trippe were also co-conspirators during the whole time with the additional defendants named in your counterclaim."

"There is no question, Your Honor," responded Davis. "Subsequent to the filing of our counterclaims, I discovered additional facts, which I am bringing to the attention of the CAB. The question basically is whether or not the CAB for all I know—although I don't believe so—may approve this interlocking relationship between Metropolitan and Pan American. That is when we get into the question of where I am disagreeing with your conclusions. It is clear to me, as the Supreme Court said, we are in a peculiar situation if on the one hand the court were to entertain whether or not a course of conduct was or was not in violation of the antitrust laws and then the CAB should turn around and approve it and specifically grant exemption, even though they had never done it before."

The judge then recognized Hupper, who asked for an immediate hearing on Davis' motion to suspend the countersuit. "I am sorry," Judge Metzner told him. "I am not in a physical condition to comply with your request. I am going upstairs now to get this opinion out. I am on trial all day tomorrow. I may have to work on the opinion tomorrow night. I hope not."

"May I express my hope, Your Honor," said Hupper, "that the argument is not set down on the motion so as to interfere with our examination of Mr. Hughes starting Monday. The reason I say this is that we believe very firmly that we have an independent right to examine him quite apart from what happens to Mr. Sonnett. We intend to vindicate——"

Judge Metzner cut in: "What do you think of Mr. Davis' argument that I don't have jurisdiction on the counterclaims as opposed to the complaint?"

Replied Hupper: "I am not sure I understand what his position is, but I do——"

"This is very simple," interjected Judge Metzner. "He is going to take you down to Washington."

Replied Hupper: "I think the very simple reference to these counterclaims will show how completely different they are from the claims made in the complaint [to the CAB]. The first counter-claim——"

"I know," Judge Metzner agreed.

"The only reference that has anything to do with the CAB is the second counterclaim," contended Hupper. "All the others are completely different. I want to join very wholeheartedly in what Mr. Stewart said about the time and expense that we have had to go through to get our first witness on the stand after we had to sit through all the other depositions for a year. We want to proceed with this case and prove that there is absolutely no merit in these claims against us."

Judge Metzner responded: "Well, all I have before me is a motion returnable on Friday for a stay of the discovery proceedings. I am telling you I can't hear you on Friday. It would be impossible. I will try sometime tomorrow to read the complaint with greater particularity than I remember it and try to match them up."

"Do you suppose we could set it for the eighteenth, which is the return date for our motion to dismiss the counterclaim?" asked Hupper.

"It is all right with me," agreed Judge Metzner.

"That's all right with us," affirmed Hupper. "There is a minor thing," he added. "You did stay, as far as the TWA people were concerned, all further production until five o'clock tomorrow?"

"I will put in the additional defendants, too," Judge Metzner quickly said. He apparently anticipated that Hupper might argue that the additional defendants should be allowed to press on with the discovery proceedings, despite the fact that TWA was stopped from demanding further documents from Toolco until Davis had had a chance to present his argument to the Court of Appeals.

Hupper protested: "The situation is different, Judge——"

"Let us not argue with the stay," declared Judge Metzner. "It extends to all the additional defendants."

Judge Metzner was about to adjourn the hearing when John Sonnett asked for thirty seconds in which to make a report. He said that on the day before he had written a letter to Davis in which he demanded that Toolco surrender its 1961–62 tax returns and

financial statements by five o'clock on the present day. While the
court hearing was in progress that afternoon, Nazeeh S. Habashy,
one of Sonnett's aides, had paid a quick visit to Davis' office and at
precisely 4:45 had demanded the documents. A lawyer in Davis'
office named William Grainger had refused to surrender the papers.
The refusal took place before Judge Metzner stayed all discovery
proceedings until five o'clock on February 8.

Habashy had immediately executed a short affidavit in which he
recorded Toolco's refusal to comply with the court order, and the
sworn statement was rushed to Sonnett in the courtroom. With
that paper in his hand, Sonnett said: "I would like to file with the
court an affidavit by one of my associates and serve a copy on Mr.
Davis because this relates to the additional contempt committed
and fully ripened prior to five o'clock today arising out of their
failure to comply in any respect with your order to make a day-to-
day production of tax documents." Sonnett then handed the affidavit to Judge Metzner. It was a second ground for a default
judgment against Toolco.

After the hearing ended, Davis had to think about what to do
next. He had been granted the stay of two days so that he could
apply to the Court of Appeals for a review of Judge Metzner's
denial to dismiss the case. But Davis had to consider the consequences of a defeat at the appellate level. For one thing, he faced
a purely mechanical problem. Though Judge Metzner did hand
down a one-paragraph denial of Davis' motion immediately after
the close of the pretrial hearing on February 6, the complete opinion was unlikely to be ready until ten o'clock on Friday morning,
February 8. At the very latest, Davis would have to go into the
Court of Appeals by three in the afternoon. That was very little
time in which to study Judge Metzner's decision and work up an
argument. Undoubtedly, Davis was also troubled that the proceedings were still only in the discovery phase. Only two weeks earlier
the Court of Appeals had demonstrated its reluctance to consider
a case in which there had not yet been a final decision when it re-
buffed his plea for a stay in the production of the so-called "privileged" documents. If he was again beaten at the appellate level,

there would be no time left in which to try and head off the surrender of the documents and the examination of Howard Hughes. Davis would then be caught in much the same bind as the one on that fateful day in January when he lost the decision in the Court of Appeals at 4 P.M. and one hour later faced the deadline for the surrender of the "privileged" documents. That episode resulted in Davis' first default. He had no desire to be trapped in a replay of that situation.

During the morning of February 7 Davis had a crucial conference with Raymond Holliday, Toolco's chief operating officer. In consultation with him, Davis arrived at a key decision. It was not to seek a review in the Court of Appeals. Even though Judge Metzner actually managed to get his written opinion out on Thursday, February 7, Davis held to his decision.

Chester Davis and Raymond Holliday now were face-to-face with the crisis that had been building up for the past nineteen months. By now they had either exhausted or discarded the legal remedies for avoiding or further delaying the appearance of Howard Hughes. They now had to answer the fundamental question: What price was Hughes willing to pay for his privacy? Would he rather jeopardize his fortune than step into public view? Was his seclusion worth $115 million to him? Was it worth sacrificing his $443 million countersuit and the opportunity to vindicate himself by showing that his opponents, and not he, were to blame for TWA's damages?

In those tension-filled hours, as Davis and Holliday struggled with those questions, Hughes also was debating the central issue: to appear or not to appear. He was receiving conflicting advice. Some of his lawyers were telling him that he did not need to show up because TWA's case had no merit whatsoever. But Greg Bautzer was giving him different advice. "Howard, think of the sanctions," he said. "They are terribly severe. Don't defy a court order."

Did Howard Hughes make a decision? Probably not. Most likely he followed his customary pattern. He went into deepest seclusion and cut communications with his subordinates. On their own, they were left to make the decision. It was an exceptionally grave one. In the past few weeks Toolco twice had defied court orders. If Toolco refused to turn over the documents on Friday and to produce Hughes on Monday, it would commit two additional instances of defiance. Where would that leave Toolco? It would leave it in great danger of contempt-of-court citation, which could mean a heavy fine, perhaps several thousand dollars a day, until it complied with the court's commands. Worse still, Toolco was becoming increasingly vulnerable to a default judgment that could give TWA all that it was asking for—millions in damages and divestiture. At best, the effect of such a judgment on Hughes' finances would be severe; at worst, it could be absolutely disastrous. The burden of raising so much money at one time, combined with the forced sale of his TWA stock, could unravel his fortune and perhaps even force him to sell the bedrock of his empire, the Hughes Tool Company.

Despite the tremendous sums at stake, it was probably not too difficult for Davis and Holliday to divine how Hughes regarded the case. When Hughes first bought into TWA in 1939, he had been shocked to learn that there was such a thing as government supervision of the aviation industry and a CAB, which scrutinized the stewardship of airline owners. But since there was such an agency, Hughes had relied on his lawyers to guide him in abiding by its directives. During all the intervening years they had assured him that his actions at TWA conformed to government regulations. In each of its formal investigations of his control of TWA, Hughes could see in black and white that the Civil Aeronautics Board had approved his control of TWA as being in the public interest and, in one instance, had even commended his generosity toward the airline.

Which of his lawyers or advisers was going to tell Howard Hughes now that he had been misled all those years? Who would say, "Howard, we hate to tell you, but we goofed. Sorry about that, but you'd best appear in court on Monday and explain what you've been doing wrong all these years. By the way, if you don't, you lose $115 million and may be forced to sell off your TWA stock at fire-sale prices and take a loss of maybe another $50 million or so."

At about noontime on February 7 Davis telephoned Special Master Rankin. He had a sensational message. The Hughes Tool Company had made what he described as "a business decision." That decision was to not proceed with any further depositions. The business decision, explained Davis, was based on the fact that Toolco was paying 78 per cent of TWA's expenses in the case as well as its own costs. Therefore, he said, Toolco reckoned that the amount of damages that TWA could hope to collect in the case would be less than the cost of continuing the discovery proceedings.

On the morning of February 8 Davis drew up "a notice of position," which he delivered to the court and the various parties in the case. A brief document of only 150 words, it ended with a terse paragraph: "Toolco hereby elects, subject only to whatever judicial relief it may hereafter obtain, to rest on the merits of its positions as heretofore taken so that it may avoid the burdens and expenses involved in further pretrial and trial proceedings prior to the time that an Appellate Court has the opportunity to rule upon the decisions and orders heretofore made herein."

The sudden development in the case did not exactly catch the legal opponents of Howard Hughes by surprise. Most of them had expected some dramatic last-minute maneuver. Even so, they were puzzled by all the herebys, hereafters, heretofores, and hereins in Davis' notice of position. What was Davis up to?

Sonnett requested an immediate hearing before Judge Metzner. At 5 P.M. that afternoon the attorneys gathered in the District Court. As the hearing began, Sonnett, who often feigned an inability to comprehend what Davis was driving at, expressed his bewilderment about Toolco's notice of position. Sonnett declared: "I don't know whether this consists of a representation to the court that Mr. Davis has been authorized by his client to apply for leave to withdraw his answer and to consent to the entry of a default judgment for the relief requested in the complaint . . . Or I don't know whether, on the other hand, it means that they are just proposing to take no further action on behalf of the tool company in the case and that they will not be present accordingly for Mr. Hughes' deposition on Monday. Since he has been noticed and is under subpoena to appear as a witness, I think if they do not appear on Monday, I would regret not having the pleasure of their company, but the attendance of the Hughes Tool Company is not at all necessary, of course. They can waive their right to cross examination of Mr. Hughes if they so elect."

John Sonnett could afford to be droll. Despite earlier setbacks, his legal strategy had paid off. He had trapped Hughes, just as he had intended to, between two unhappy alternatives: to default the case or to appear in public. Sonnett's remark about going ahead with the deposition of Hughes even if the tool company no longer wished to participate in the proceedings was intended to remind Chester Davis that TWA had the right to demand to examine Hughes on Monday unless Toolco was willing to stop the discovery proceedings by announcing that it was defaulting the case.

Davis immediately grasped the implication of Sonnett's statement. Earlier in the case, Davis had often insisted that he did not represent Hughes because Hughes was not a defendant. But now, as Sonnett expressed his determination to bring Hughes to the witness stand, Davis suddenly began to quote the special master's rulings that had made Toolco responsible for producing Hughes at the deposition. "The Hughes Tool Company is aware of those rulings of the special master," declared Davis, "and the tool company did not seek a review of those rulings and accepted in effect the responsibility placed upon it."

Davis explained that his notice of position was intended to avoid an "unseemly contempt" by electing to stand on the proceedings to date. His aim, he stressed, was to get an order or determination from the lower court that would enable him to obtain a review of the questions of law in the Court of Appeals. "I have tried to prepare a piece of paper which would not preclude or prejudice the rights of the tool company to such an appellate review," he said. "The tool company does want to rest on the merits of its position, and it does so fully aware of the sanctions, which the court in its discretion may impose upon the tool company."

Davis stated that Toolco had concluded, since it also paid most of TWA's legal costs, that the combined expense of shifting the discovery proceedings to California would amount to more than $5 million. "I resisted the figure they came up with," he said, "and I am trying to get a further idea on how they arrived at that figure, but I have been assured upon checking and double-checking that this is the minimum that would be involved and before attempting to address itself as to the probable amount that TWA would be spending." Davis continued: "Under those conditions, the tool company felt that, as a business decision, it would be preferable to stand on the validity or the merits to date and then to obtain some form of reviewable order, depending, of course, on the type of determination that the court may make by reason of the position being taken by the Hughes Tool Company."

Judge Metzner asked Davis if the notice of position meant that Hughes would not show up for the deposition on Monday.

"That is correct, Your Honor," replied Davis.

"And therefore the plaintiff may take whatever proceedings it is advised to take by way of sanctions under Rule 37?" asked Judge Metzner. Rule 37 is the provision in the federal court procedures that applies to default judgments.

"That is correct, Your Honor," answered Davis.

Judge Metzner then asked about what would happen to the counterclaims. Davis gave a re-run of his argument from two days earlier—to wit, based on his reading of *Panagra,* the Civil Aeronautics Board first had to decide whether the acquisition of TWA control by Hughes' opponents had been in the public interest before the counterclaims could be pressed. "In any event," Davis went on, "it is the position of the tool company that the counterclaims may not be effectively pursued at this time in this form, and the relief we are requesting in that regard—and which I was hoping to prepare myself to argue on February eighteenth—was to obtain from the court an appropriate order, which I believe is by leaving the matter docketed but staying all further proceedings therein until after the preliminary questions have been decided."

"I cannot follow you on your argument, Mr. Davis," replied

Judge Metzner, "because in the first place I think it is clear that by virtue of my decision, the CAB does not have exclusive primary jurisdiction in this matter."

"The thing that comes within the jurisdiction of the CAB," responded Davis, "is its right to decide whether the acquisition of control of TWA by the financial institutions was in the public interest. If the board so decided, the additional defendants would then be cloaked with antitrust immunity, and Toolco's countersuit against them would be useless.

Judge Metzner seemed unconvinced. He replied: "Well, you are saying you came into court a year ago to sue the additional defendants and now you say, 'Well now, why are we suing the additional defendants here for a money judgment? Maybe you don't have jurisdiction, Mr. Southern District. We are going down to Washington to see if what we claim is really all right.' "

Davis: "Your Honor, the situation at the time we filed these counterclaims, and I believe a number of people believe, that the granting of exemption by the CAB [from the antitrust law] could only apply when the CAB acted. Now there has been no affirmative action taken by the CAB with respect to the acquisition of control by these additional defendants. It was not until *Panagra* came down that I was confronted with the fact that even though the CAB had not acted—as the court stated, as I read the Supreme Court majority opinion—it would be odd, I believe is the expression, that something which the CAB could find to be in the public interest and could grant exemption under the antitrust laws should run afoul of the antitrust laws and the two systems collide."

Asked Davis: "What kind of time, money, and effort am I spending here to establish factually a violation of the antitrust laws if then the next day, or while I am doing this, the CAB, not necessarily at my instance but at the instance of the additional defendants, should determine that the acquisition of control over this air carrier was in the public interest?"

Then Davis went on to say that he would make a more complete argument about what should be done with the counterclaims on February 18. But for the present he contended that all discovery should cease. In order to block the additional defendants from later claiming a right to examine Hughes, Davis launched into a complicated argument in which he asserted that their right to call for Hughes' testimony was dependent upon TWA's right because it was based upon the witness subpoena that he had accepted from TWA on behalf of Hughes. Because Hughes Tool had now chosen not to defend itself in the TWA suit, and thus was barring TWA from any further discovery proceedings, Davis claimed that the additional defendants also were barred from demanding the appearance of Howard Hughes on Monday.

The lawyers for the additional defendants were aware of Davis' aim to choke off the discovery proceedings. Bruce Bromley, who had just returned from California where he had been setting up arrangements for Hughes' deposition, took immediate exception to Davis' statement. "Your Honor, Mr. Davis has now told you," said Bromley, "that my rights to examine Toolco through Hughes is some way dependent upon TWA's right. You know, I think full well, that it was nearly a year ago, to wit, on February 13, 1962, that the additional defendants represented by me served an appropriate notice under the appropriate rule to examine Toolco through Hughes and we are entitled to have him there for that purpose. Unless Mr. Davis tells Your Honor that he is now prepared to consent to a dismissal of his counterclaim with prejudice, then we are entitled to go ahead on Monday.

"Of course, some of the other additional defendants served the same notice," Bromley continued. "So I don't understand his constant repetition of a statement that Mr. Davis must know is not true, that is to say that we have no independent right to examine Hughes. And he has not said whether Hughes is going to show up on Monday in response to that notice or not."

"Your Honor," declared Davis, "apparently Judge Bromley misunderstood me or——"

"I don't think I misunderstood you," declared Bromley.

Judge Metzner remarked that he had a distinct recollection that in one of his pretrial orders he had given specific orders that after TWA had completed its deposition of Mr. Hughes, the additional defendants would be entitled to proceed with their examination of him. After a discussion at the bench with Judge Metzner, who looked up his previous ruling that assured the additional defendants of their independent right to examine Hughes, Bromley declared that he was returning to California the next day. "I would like the special master to be there Monday morning so that I may note an appropriate default under my notice," Bromley stated. Like a Greek chorus, the other lawyers for the additional defendants echoed Bromley's request.

For a half hour or so, the argument had focused on the additional defendants. Now, seeking to call attention to TWA again, Sonnett rose to make what was perhaps the climactic speech of his legal career.

"In all of the procedural maneuvering that appears to be going on," he began, "I think it well to recall what Your Honor said many months back, which was that the plaintiff should not be lost sight of in the maze of pleadings or the complexity of the pleadings that have resulted. The TWA position is a very simple one. From the outset it was represented that Mr. Howard R. Hughes, as a witness, was subject to the jurisdiction of the court for his deposition to be taken for use in this proceeding on behalf of TWA. TWA's right to depose him, both on the complaint and answer, since the complaint still stands denied, and on the counterclaims, we think is perfectly clear. Indeed, it has been ordered repeatedly by this court."

Sonnett went on: "I am not aware that there was any counsel in this room representing Howard R. Hughes, and TWA has not taken the position and will reserve the question of whether the Hughes Tool Company can or cannot produce Mr. Howard R. Hughes, and we are not particularly concerned because that is why we used the witness subpoena in the first place, to be sure he would be there.

"For Mr. Davis to stand here and, with his tongue in cheek, to say to this court that the expenses of this litigation and of these depositions are so great—even, by the way, if they flew to California on TWA, they would get 78 per cent of the profit—that they won't participate in discovery proceedings is obviously absurd. I deny that Mr. Davis has any authority to state to Your Honor definitively or otherwise what Hughes will or will not do on Monday morning. I don't think he can commit that man to his behavior at all. He can say to you, if he is authorized to say it, that the Hughes Tool Company won't be there, but on behalf of TWA I say to Your Honor that is completely immaterial. I submit to Your Honor, TWA has a right under your orders, under the process of this court and those of the court in California to the sworn evidence of this man. Now, if there be any reason why he cannot appear, let him say so. But we have a right to that evidence. Who knows, if he is persuasive enough, he might persuade me that there is something in his derivative counterclaim. Up to date I haven't seen that to be true, but he might.

"So far as TWA is concerned," continued Sonnett, "the obligation on Monday is for Hughes to appear personally, and we will take whatever action is necessary to see that he does. This is, as TWA sees it, another stall or attempted stall. It is an attempt to bait us away from getting at the merits of the controversy by offering us some phony maneuver for a partial default judgment, unlimited damages. The damages I think we will collect in this case are $135 million [Sonnett by now had increased TWA's damage claims to match those in Toolco's countersuit]. That is the amount that they alleged we were hurt, tripled, and we will prove it. We will also establish our right to the divestiture that we seek in this complaint.

"These sorts of maneuvers do not reach that point at all. They will try to foreclose us from the sort of record that I want to present to Your Honor, whether it is on default or trial, so you will conclude, as I have, that the only proper remedy for the violations of law here, in addition to damages, is a divestiture of this stock. That is the only cure for this situation. This is an effort to lead us down a garden path to some very unsatisfactory results. I think we should go forward on Monday."

Sonnett's argument obviously made an impact on Judge Metzner, who put a question to Chester Davis.

"Mr. Davis," he asked, "have you or the Hughes Tool Company directed Mr. Howard Hughes not to appear on Monday?"

"No, Your Honor," replied Chester Davis. "I am not aware of any directions, certainly none that was emanating from me."

"Suppose Mr. Hughes shows up on Monday," said Judge Metzner.

"Well, I am perfectly willing to stipulate that the place of deposition be here rather than in California and to make this the place and we will note the default of his appearance," responded Davis. Then, addressing his opponent, Davis said: "I am perfectly willing to have a proceeding, if it will help your record, Mr. Sonnett, on Monday, if that is the date you want. We can do it in this court-room, you can do it in my office, you can do it in Mr. Rankin's office, and then you can note the fact the tool company is failing in refusing to produce Mr. Hughes, and then you can have your record and you can take your remedy on it."

Davis went on: "I do not understand what remedy it is that TWA is seeking when it has the opportunity to prove these damages that you can claim you can establish. My purpose, of course, is to obtain something which will enable me to get a review on the law as to whether or not you are entitled to be here in the first place. And then I am prepared, if I am wrong in that regard, to pay the consequences to the extent to which you are able to prove damages."

"May I briefly respond, Your Honor," asked Sonnett, "because I think—although again I have trouble understanding [how] Mr. Davis can talk so much and say so little—I don't know yet whether Mr. Hughes has seen fit to issue instructions to this board of directors of the tool company or whether he hasn't about this matter. There is no counsel here speaking for him, and I haven't any illusions personally that anything Mr. Davis says is going to produce Mr. Hughes anywhere at any time unless Mr. Hughes decides to comply with the process of the court, and he is under that process.

"This is only an attempt to create another procedural diversion. If there is going to be a default on Monday, let there be a default, that is within their power, it is within Mr. Hughes' power—but I know of no procedure for anticipatory defaults—otherwise let him withdraw his answer and let's have a judgment on the complaint for the relief we seek."

Judge Metzner responded: "Well, I understand one of the reasons we are having this conference is to discuss an anticipatory default so that people don't go to a great deal of trouble and effort running out to California and coming back on the same day."

Sonnett: "I have people out there who have been there for six or seven days, about six people in an office, ready to go."

Judge Metzner: "And there are a lot of people who are not out there, and I have been given to understand that this conference was called for the purpose of discussing this anticipatory default and to notice Judge Hall [Peirson M. Hall, the senior justice in the Southern District of California] that he should discontinue any arrangement efforts he is making for this deposition to take place. It was done on the basis of Mr. Hughes not going to appear. Let us not have everybody running out there. Now, Mr. Davis says that as far as the defendant Hughes Tool Company is concerned, they will admit today that Mr. Hughes will not appear on Monday and that as a result you may then take whatever steps you wish to pursuant to Rule 37. I would also like Mr. Davis to state for the record that if by any chance Mr. Hughes should appear at the courthouse on Monday, despite what has transpired here this afternoon, that that will be no defense to any proceeding taken by TWA."

"I will so state, Your Honor," said Davis, who was delighted at having fended off Sonnett's attempt to cut through Toolco's defense.

But Sonnett, who had always placed great value on holding the threat of personal involvement over Hughes, refused to give up. "We are going to have people there in any event, Your Honor, with respect to whatever you direct, and I mean that only in that sense, that I don't think Mr. Davis can call the turn on Mr. Hughes' movements any more than I can," he said. "There is a process outstanding from that court, the courthouse is arranged, the amplifiers are in, the place is swept. We had a report this afternoon there are people out there with files all ready to go.

"I think he either will show up or not show up," declared John Sonnett. "It is that simple."

Judge Metzner seemed bothered by Sonnett's insistence on taking Hughes' testimony. "Mr. Davis is telling you he is not going to show up," he insisted, "and Mr. Davis has been the conduit through whom the orders of the court have been transported to Mr. Hughes, and one of those orders was that if Mr. Hughes did not show up, the court would entertain a motion for a default judgment and an assessment of damages. If Mr. Davis now tells you that Mr. Hughes is not going to show up, and even if he is going to show up, he is not going to use it as a defense to any motion in this court pursuant to Rule 37, I would think that takes care of that phase of the case."

Then Judge Metzner added: "I am bothered about the counterclaims."

"So am I," responded Bruce Bromley. He demanded that Toolco should agree to dismiss its countersuit if it did not intend to produce Hughes on Monday.

"I think the plaintiff [TWA], in so far as his complaint is concerned, is amply protected by the record made here this afternoon, and you may then move for your default judgment," said Judge Metzner. "But the counterclaim problem bothers me, and I do not see, Mr. Davis, how you can do anything else but take the dismissal with prejudice on your counterclaims. Otherwise, the additional defendants are perfectly justified in going out to California and noting the default of Mr. Hughes and coming back and moving for a dismissal with prejudice." By "dismissal with prejudice," Judge Metzner meant that Toolco's countersuit would be quashed and never could be revived.

Understandably, Davis did not want to give up the countersuit. "I am perfectly prepared to state, if that will facilitate the procedural matters," he replied, "that the tool company, in so far as these counterclaims are concerned, does not intend to pursue litigating those counterclaims in this court until after there has been a determination by the CAB, and if that has been——"

Judge Metzner interrupted Davis. "You don't have any control of that," he told him. "Once you instituted your action—and you are in the position of a plaintiff in that regard—the defendants acquired priority of deposition. You cannot come in now and say 'I am not going to push this; I am going to sit back and wait a while, and you, Mr. Defendant, have to wait for me.' Once you initiated that proceeding by way of counterclaim and the defendants have their right to proceed, you cannot tell them to stop."

"Your Honor," declaimed Davis in a sweeping all-purpose statement, "I can only take a position that I do not consent to any order that the court may issue at the instance of these additional defendants for whatever reason they advance."

To that, Judge Metzner remarked that Special Master Rankin might fly out to California to record Hughes' failure to appear and thus lay the groundwork for the motion to declare Toolco in default. But Davis insisted that such a trip would be unnecessary. He offered to meet with the lawyers for the additional defendants on Monday, just as he would meet with Sonnett, to enable them to note Toolco's default.

Turning to the lawyers for the additional defendants, Judge Metzner said: "You have heard Mr. Davis' suggestion, and if I can reiterate it, there is no necessity of your going out to Los Angeles to note Mr. Hughes' default—or rather, to take Mr. Hughes' deposition—because he is not going to show up. If he does and you are not there, this is no defense by them to any motion by you for a dismissal with the prejudice of the counterclaims. Since essentially this is a Hughes Tool Company matter, a dismissal with prejudice of the counterclaims, I would think sufficiently protects the additional defendants."

After months of delays and elaborate legal maneuvers, the events now were rushing with confusing rapidity toward a showdown. Rather than wait until February 18, the date scheduled for hearing Davis' motion to suspend the countersuit until after the CAB's decision, Judge Metzner decided to deal with the issue at once. Said he: "We might as well then consider the motion at this time for a stay of the proceedings on the counterclaims and deny that stay and from then on we come to the question of what is the state of the record come Monday if Mr. Hughes does not appear; and as I understand it, even if he does appear, it will make no difference."

"That's correct, Your Honor," affirmed Chester Davis.

"Because if he appears, as far as the Hughes Tool Company is concerned, he has not appeared," continued Judge Metzner, "and they will not use his appearance as any defense to a motion made by the additional defendants for a judgment of dismissal with prejudice."

Then Judge Metzner asked, "Is there anything else left on that?"

By then, it was 6:25 on the evening of February 8.

"Only one more thing before I forget it," answered Judge Bromley. "Your Honor's stay of the tax documents having expired an hour and twenty-five minutes ago——"

Declared Judge Metzner: "That is a third ground [for a default judgment]."

"A third ground," affirmed Bromley, who also wanted to make a record. "I ask for their production to the special master, who is here in the courtroom," he said. "Where are the documents, Mr. Davis?"

When Davis failed to reply, Judge Metzner spoke: "You might as well make your record, Mr. Davis."

"I restate my position, Mr. Bromley," declared Davis.

"You are not producing the tax documents?" asked Judge Metzner.

"That is correct, Your Honor," responded Davis.

Sonnett spoke up again. It was obvious that he was extremely reluctant to lose his hold on Hughes as a witness. "I want to be doubly sure," said Sonnett (who seemed to be ignoring much of what had already transpired that day), "that there is no stay with respect to TWA's deposition of Mr. Hughes on Monday in California."

"No," replied Judge Metzner, "I am afraid, Mr. Sonnett, that we have agreed here—at least I think we have—that there is no point in your going out to California on Monday because Mr. Hughes is not going to appear and that Toolco says that since he is not going to appear, and if he does appear, in order to protect what he may feel are individual problems regarding failure to appear, you are still free to make application under Rule 37 for a dismissal or for a judgment on your complaint."

"I am sure that binds Toolco but it doesn't bind Mr. Hughes," asserted Sonnett.

"Suppose that is so," remarked Judge Metzner. "That is the only part you have in the lawsuit right now." In effect, Judge Metzner was accepting Davis' position that Toolco, as the defendant, was completely responsible for Hughes and would bear the penalty of his actions. To Sonnett's dismay, Hughes, the man, was slipping from his grasp.

But Sonnett, who did not want to accept that, renewed his argument that TWA, regardless of Toolco's position, had an independent right to compel Hughes to testify on Monday. Sonnett quickly rephrased the court's ruling in a way that he would have liked to understand it. "Therefore Your Honor's direction today is without prejudice to whatever rights TWA may have to enforce the subpoena in California directed to Mr. Hughes," summarized Sonnett, who wanted the court's approval to proceed with the examination on Monday.

"What do you mean by that?" asked Judge Metzner, surprised.

"Well, we may see fit to seek some way of attempting to induce Mr. Hughes to appear and testify," replied Sonnett. It was a threat to force Hughes to appear, perhaps by having him declared to be in contempt of court for failure to appear for his deposition.

"I see no reason for that at the present time," snapped Judge Metzner, who seemed startled by Sonnett's determination to hunt down Howard Hughes.

"At the present time I can't see anything very clearly except to be sure that I can't see Monday morning very clearly," Sonnett responded, easing away from his harsh insistence on Hughes' testimony.

"Well, if you feel that as far as you are concerned, TWA, I will continue the stay of the deposition for that purpose only," said Judge Metzner, who apparently hoped to block Sonnett from complicating the situation by trying to drag Hughes into the deposition proceedings on Monday. "If you want to have it lifted at some time in the future you may come in and apply to have it lifted.

"In other words," concluded Judge Metzner, "the understanding of the court is that you have now an anticipatory default for failure to appear which will ripen at ten o'clock Monday, February eleventh, on consent of Hughes Tool Company, the only defendant here with the responsibility, I assume, to answer in money damages to your claim. And then you are free to move for a dismissal—I mean for a judgment on your claim."

"If Mr. Davis accepts what Your Honor has just said, I have no problem about Monday," stated Sonnett. "I wish he would say yes or no to that."

"Do you understand what I just said, Mr. Davis?" asked Judge Metzner.

Davis: "I understood what you said, Your Honor, a long time ago, and I thought I made myself quite clear on the record, and I don't understand how Mr. Sonnett wants to take testimony——"

Judge Metzner: "Now, Mr. Davis, we have a simple question, yes or no?"

Davis: "I understand everything you said, Your Honor."

Judge Metzner: "And the answer is yes?"

Davis: "That's correct, Your Honor."

Sonnett: "Thank you."

Judge Metzner: "All right."

Despite Judge Metzner's ruling of an anticipatory default, lawyers for TWA and the additional defendants, who were in Los Angeles anyhow, assembled on February 11 in the hearing room in the Federal Courthouse that had been set aside for Hughes' appearance. The loudspeakers were in place. The earphone for Hughes rested on the back of a chair. Signs were attached to two rows of benches, reserving them for the press.

At ten o'clock, a clerk of the court called out, "Is Howard R. Hughes present?" He repeated the question three times.

There was no reply.

Part Three

16.   The Severest Sanction

"Haven't you put him over the barrel?"
                                      Judge Metzner to John Sonnett

When Howard Hughes failed to appear at the Federal Court Building in Los Angeles on that fateful day in February 1963, he and his lawyers could hardly have imagined the full ramifications of that action. Chester Davis explained the reason for Hughes' absence as a "business decision" taken by the Hughes Tool Company in the belief that even in the event that TWA could prove that Hughes had harmed the airline, the amount of those damages would be less than the expense of continuing the litigation. Hughes had been advised that despite the great magnitude of TWA's claims against him, the most he might lose by his failure to appear would be $5 million. Even so, until the very last moment, Toolco executives could not be 100 per cent certain that Hughes would stay away from the deposition, though the betting leaned very heavily in that direction. Some Toolco veterans, who still had contact with Hughes, could only be vastly relieved that he chose to forego his day in court. At this time, Hughes was very nervous, short tempered, and irritable. Some of the Hughes people feared that if he did get on the stand, he might, through a lapse of memory or flash of temper, either perjure himself or so offend the presiding judicial officer that he would risk a contempt of court citation.

Among Hughes' opponents, his failure to appear produced some pronounced emotional letdowns. Fred Furth felt the most let down of all. For nearly two years he had led the unsuccessful hunt to flush Hughes from hiding. Now his immediate reaction was that he had failed once more. But after he and some of the other lawyers found their way to a bar near the Federal Courthouse, the realization began to dawn on him that in a real sense he had gotten Hughes after all. By keeping the spotlight of the search on him, Furth had built up the pressure for Hughes' appearance in court. "I guess we got him," concluded Furth, who was feeling no pain. His companions nodded in agreement.

Meanwhile, back in New York, John Sonnett was already seeking to exact the greatest possible victory from Hughes' defiance of the court order that demanded his appearance. In a written motion to the court, Sonnett argued that Hughes had defaulted the case and thus should be subjected to the most severe possible penalty: in legal parlance, Toolco's defense should be struck, which meant that Toolco should be considered to be guilty of each and every one of the charges in TWA's complaint and should be punished to the full extent demanded by the airline. And that was some punishment! The penalties included the forced divestiture of Hughes' holdings in TWA, a permanent injunction barring Hughes and his aides ever again from interfering with TWA, and the dismissal of the $443 million countersuit "with prejudice." Finally, there was the question of the assessment of damages. Originally Sonnett had estimated that Hughes had damaged TWA to the amount of $35 million—a sum that under antitrust law would be tripled. But after Toolco put the damage figure at $45 million in its countersuit, Sonnett requested the court's permission to raise TWA's own claim to that amount.

The lawyers for the additional defendants also were seeking to use Hughes' default as a means to force Toolco to drop the huge claims against them. Under the general coordination of Bruce Bromley, the lawyers drew up an impressive set of briefs that documented Hughes' evasive tactics and his refusal to surrender the documents that the additional defendants claimed would conclusively prove that *he,* and not they, was to blame for the late delivery of TWA's jet fleet. In essence, the lawyers for the additional defendants argued that if Hughes would not cooperate in allowing them to prove their innocence, then Toolco's charges against them should be dismissed for good.

While his opponents were engaged in seeking to score conclusive victories in the huge intertwined litigation, Chester Davis was fighting a determined delaying action. He was behaving almost as if default either had not occurred or was inconsequential. He asked the court for reargument of the case. He also applied for a stay on the assessment of damages until after the CAB had ruled on Toolco's complaint against the additional defendants and had given its opinion on whether the board's approval of Toolco's control of TWA in 1950 had conferred antitrust immunity on Hughes and his corporate alter ego.

On February 21, 1963, ten days after Hughes' dramatic absence, the lawyers assembled once more before Judge Metzner. The issue was, "What would be the legal consequences of Hughes' failure to obey the court's order to give his testimony?"

As the session began, Judge Metzner disposed of preliminary matters by quickly striking down Chester Davis' application for a reargument of the case. "This court," he declared, "will not stay any further proceedings in this action." Then Judge Metzner turned to quiz Sonnett about the request to increase the amount of damages by $30 million. "Isn't it perfectly possible," he asked, "that a defendant may be willing to suffer a default for $105 million but will not suffer a default for $135 million? Haven't you put him over a barrel?"

Replied Sonnett: "We want three times $45 million simply because of what they say in the counterclaim." Despite his insistence on that figure, Sonnett realized that the court would be unwilling to make an assessment of the damages until after hearings in which the TWA side would demonstrate that by committing the offenses alleged in the complaint, Hughes had damaged TWA in the amount of so-and-so many dollars. In Sonnett's estimation, that was all that remained to be done. His position was that by refusing to show up for his deposition, Hughes had committed a default that denied him the right to contest the merits of the case. Hughes was guilty as charged of breaking the antitrust laws of the land and had forfeited his right to any defense. Now, after totaling up the bill, all that was left to do was to say: "Pay up, Howard Hughes."

"We think that [the amount of damages] is the only question that is open on the record and that Your Honor should have a hearing on the subject," explained Sonnett, who also insisted that the proceeding should take place before the court, not the special master. "Unless this has firm judicial control, the hearing will turn out to be ten months instead of ten days," he warned.

In rebuttal, Davis said that he welcomed the damage hearings, because they would finally force TWA to produce the facts that underlay the charges in the complaint. He said that Toolco expected TWA to establish that each alleged offense actually was committed and to prove the causal relationship between the offense and the damages. Sonnett and Davis thus took diametrically opposed positions. While Sonnett regarded the allegations in the complaint as admitted to be true by Hughes' default, Davis insisted that, in effect, nothing had been admitted and that TWA should be required to establish the truth of the complaint before the airline could collect a cent. "What is the course of conduct that tool company engaged in while it was a 78 per cent owner of TWA which harmed TWA? What is the course of conduct that Toolco engaged in which was outside the specific approval of CAB?" he asked. "Let them put any officer of TWA, or whoever else they want—the leading institutions who participated in these transactions—let them put them on and prove what we did or give some evidence of what we did . . . That is all I want to know— what did we do?"

Judge Metzner did not hand down a decision after the February 21 hearing, and because he was still presiding over that long criminal trial, he did not have another opportunity until May 2 to deal with the Hughes case. When he did convene a pretrial conference that evening, it was obvious that he had not been impressed by Davis' earlier argument or subsequent briefs. After a verbal exchange with Davis about the legal significance of Hughes' non-appearance, Judge Metzner delivered his own pronouncement on the consequence of the default. It was markedly similar to John Sonnett's. Declared Judge Metzner: "The facts of the complaint are admitted, not in the sense of an admission saying, 'Yes, I did it,' but they are true, and the only thing left is how much."

On May 3 Judge Metzner handed down the judgment in the case. Its severity shook the defenses of Hughes' forces. Even at this advanced stage in the proceedings, the court had still less drastic alternative courses of action. For example, as a punishment for Hughes' failure to obey the order to give testimony, the court could have imposed on Toolco a fine of X thousands of dollars a day until it managed either to produce Hughes or made a clear-cut surrender. But Judge Metzner's judgment ruling placed the maximum penalty on Toolco. "The default," he wrote, "was deliberate and willful . . . A judgment by default shall be entered in favor of TWA against Toolco and the counterclaim asserted by Toolco against TWA shall be dismissed with prejudice [i.e., cannot be revived]." Judge Metzner also approved Sonnett's motion to increase the damage claim to $45 million so that the total penalty now loomed as $135 million on the antitrust charges, plus another $10 million on a separate claim of post-1960 interference on TWA's business. A few days later Judge Metzner also dismissed Toolco's countersuit against the additional defendants, with prejudice.

Those rulings represented a powerful, if not wholly unexpected, defeat for Chester Davis. But his old sense of robust optimism must have returned as he read the last paragraph in the judge's order. Despite the severity of sanctions against Hughes, the judge in the closing sentences gave Davis exactly what he wanted—the opportunity for review. Wrote Judge Metzner: "I am of the opinion that this order involved a controlling question of law (see *Pan American Inc. v. United States*) as to which there is a substantial ground for difference of opinion. An immediate appeal from this order is justified, since it may materially advance the ultimate termination of this litigation."

Who could have imagined this turn of events? Though he had lost important and potentially damaging decisions, Davis now had Judge Metzner's endorsement to test his theory of the case at a higher level. Meanwhile, the Hughes side also was making encouraging progress with its complaint at the Civil Aeronautics Board. The importance of the CAB had been greatly magnified by Judge Metzner's decision. If the appellate court followed the *Panagra* precedent and held, as the Supreme Court did, that the board had prior jurisdiction in cases that involved the exercise of its expertise, Howard Hughes might still emerge as the victor over his foes in the eastern financial establishment. Certainly, he was gaining important allies within the CAB. In response to Toolco's complaint filed in February 1963, the CAB's Bureau of Enforcement in April had petitioned the board for permission to investigate the charge that certain financial institutions had unlawfully seized control of airlines. The Hughes forces followed up the Bureau of Enforcement's action by insisting that the board should open a full-scale investigation into possible conflicts of interest among TWA's financial backers.

In addition to his new CAB campaign, Howard Hughes also began to raise cash. Through a team of underwriters headed by Merrill Lynch, Pierce, Fenner & Smith, Hughes arranged to sell the $80.9 million in warrants and subordinated debentures that he had acquired as part of the Dillon, Read plan in December 1960. Why was Hughes collecting all that money? The answer, as it gradually emerged during the next few months, was that Howard Hughes was preparing for his master coup to regain control of TWA. Even so, the pace of events in the case had slowed measurably. After the hectic times of "the night court proceedings," the new tempo of developments seemed very slow.

One reason was that the lawyers were occupied in preparing thick stacks of briefs and reply briefs for the United States Court of Appeals, Second Circuit, which on June 6, 1963, had agreed to hear the appeal on both TWA's complaint and Toolco's countersuit. The Court of Appeals, however, limited the reviewable questions, in its words, to two: "(1) whether the U. S. District Court for the Southern District of New York had jurisdiction of action and (2) whether the exercise of its regulatory power by the Civil Aeronautics Board in the premises by the issuance of orders permitting defendants to act as defendants acted constitutes a good defense to the antitrust claim of TWA."

Those two questions focused directly on Davis' defense theory in *TWA v. Hughes.* However, they ignored his appeal for a reversal of Judge Metzner's dismissal of the counterclaims with prejudice. On that front, Davis argued that the District Court had erred in refusing to grant a stay of proceedings on the counterclaims until the CAB had acted on Toolco's complaint to the board and that even if it was not an error to deny a stay, the court should have permitted Toolco to make a voluntary dismissal of the countersuit so that Toolco could have raised the charges at a later date.

Predictably, TWA and the additional defendants, the victorious beneficiaries of the District Court's decisions, supported Judge Metzner's rulings with long and learned briefs.

Leo Tolstoi, who delighted in the dramatic coincidences of war and politics, would have been fascinated by the Hughes' legal battle. November 13, 1963, was one of those times that thrust the competing themes of the conflict into poignant, almost exaggerated focus. On that day, even as the Court of Appeals heard the argument on both the suit and countersuit, Merrill Lynch made the sale to the public of Hughes' TWA debentures and warrants. The proceeds from that sale—some $80 million—could help Hughes to overcome or nullify whatever the judges might decide. It was a race between judicial power and financial might.

In the court hearing, the judges wanted an answer to a basic question: What would Hughes do if they reserved the lower court's ruling and sent the cases back for trial? Would he be prepared this time to obey a court order to give testimony? Chester Davis could not give a clear answer. He explained that he had indeed accepted a subpoena on Hughes' behalf but that Hughes had never informed him whether he actually was or was not going to appear. Davis attempted to gain the court's sympathy for Hughes by explaining that he was an eccentric who was also not available even to his business associates and that his refusal to appear in public was not an act directed against the courts. He even contended that as an eccentric, Hughes deserved the protection, not the punishment, of the courts. Replied one of the judges: "If he is an eccentric, Mr. Davis, as an officer of this court, I am sure you agree that we cannot permit him, in effect, to carry on a judicial filibuster so that orders of the court are not complied with."

On that uncompromising note, the judges closed their questioning of Chester Davis. It was not a promising omen. But, in a sense, the money that Hughes raised that day through the sale of some of his TWA securities was more important at that moment than the opinion of the judges. While the Court of Appeals pondered its judgment, Hughes, helped by the extra millions, began to put into operation the final phase of his grand plan to regain control of TWA. That masterful strategy had begun two years earlier when he had saved Northeast from bankruptcy and in the process had forced the CAB to take back its earlier harsh condemnation of his stewardship at TWA. Now that the CAB had allowed him to take control of Northeast, it could hardly stop him from paying off TWA's debts and regaining control of the airline in which he still owned 78.23 per cent. And in the event Hughes did regain control of TWA, would he and his skillful lawyers find some way to settle the lawsuit? Most people assumed they could. Surely, once Hughes was back in control, TWA would not press a suit against him. If minority stockholders insisted on a financial settlement of the complaint, Hughes could oblige them. He could pay into TWA a substantial sum of several or, if necessary, many millions. After all, he would only have been transferring funds from one corporate pocket, Toolco, to another, TWA.

The Toolco lawyers took the position that the CAB had no authority to block Hughes from resuming his lawful control of TWA. Still, just to make doubly sure, Hughes on April 9, 1964 had formally requested the Civil Aeronautics Board to permit him to acquire the $92.8 million sinking fund notes from the Metropolitan and Equitable, on which rested their power to appoint two of the three voting trustees. In addition to the purchase of the notes, Hughes would have to pay a penalty to the note holders for earlier retirement of the loan; the sum had now declined to 18 per cent of the principal. The effect of Hughes' purchase would be to give him the right either to appoint all the voting trustees or to dissolve the voting trust entirely. In either event, Hughes once again would be TWA's undisputed master.

TWA's management had been greatly alarmed. In a series of public announcements, Tillinghast had sought to hold the CAB to its 1960 pledge—that "guarantee to the bankers"—that it would conduct a "searching inquiry into the public interest factors affecting this control" before Hughes would be permitted to reacquire the direction of the airline. The TWA executives warned that Toolco was attempting to use the public power of the CAB "as a private weapon to escape the responsibility of Hughes Tool's past misconduct." TWA vowed that "We will answer this latest maneuver in hearings before the CAB and, if necessary, in the courts."

Even as Toolco and TWA began to spar on the issue of Hughes' resumption of control, the Court of Appeals on June 2, 1964 handed down its decision on the two interrelated cases. The ruling, written by Chief Judge J. Edward Lumbard, totally undercut the legal fundaments of Howard Hughes' position. In the first case— that of *TWA v. Hughes*—the Circuit Court ruled that no, the CAB's 1950 approval of Toolco's control of TWA did not immunize Hughes or his tool company from the effect of the antitrust laws. The three judges also declared that the District Court, and not the CAB, possessed primary jurisdiction for dealing with the antitrust charges in TWA's complaint.

The Court of Appeals was equally unsympathetic to Davis' arguments on the countersuit. Its ruling clearly reflected how adversely Hughes' refusal to obey Judge Metzner's orders had affected the judges in the higher court. Said the decision: "Judge Metzner was fully justified in entering judgments dismissing the counterclaims against TWA and the additional defendants. The sanction of judgment by default for failure to comply with discovery orders is the most severe sanction which the court may apply and its use must be tempered by the careful exercise of judicial discretion to assure that its imposition is merited. Hughes' deposition was absolutely essential to the proper conduct of this litigation. Yet he and Toolco seized upon every opportunity to forestall this event . . . Indeed, Hughes and Toolco seemed to look upon the entire discovery proceedings as some sort of game, rather than as a means of securing the just and expeditious settlement of the important matters in dispute. . . . Hughes' conduct is particularly intolerable in a large and complex litigation such as this one."

The Court of Appeals concluded: "In light of all these circumstances, the District Court was not obliged to employ sanctions less severe than the dismissal of the counterclaim with prejudice."

Chester Davis made an immediate motion to the Court of Appeals for a rehearing of the case, but he was turned down. So how did matters now stand for Howard Hughes on the legal front? In a word, badly. His $443 million countersuit was irrevocably dismissed. In the TWA complaint, Hughes was presumed to be guilty as charged.

If ever there was a time for Howard Hughes to speed up his effort to regain control of TWA, it was now. With increasing frequency, Hughes' lawyers began to visit the Washington headquarters of the Civil Aeronautics Board for private meetings with the board members. The lawyers must have been very convincing. On July 10, 1964, a little more than five weeks after his setback in the Court of Appeals, the Civil Aeronautics Board gave Hughes what he wanted. Without holding the customary public hearings or conducting any sort of investigation, the board in Order No. E-21057 approved Hughes' motion to resume active control of TWA. The CAB reasoned that no special investigation procedure was required since Hughes was only reacquiring a control situation at TWA that had been approved in the past by full-scale CAB investigations. Only one condition was attached to the approval. Because it is contrary to public policy for one individual to control more than one airline, Hughes would have to rid himself of control of Northeast. "Toolco may," said the board, "exercise its option to acquire the TWA notes . . . at such time as it submits a plan satisfactory to the board which would effectively divest Toolco of the power to simultaneously control both TWA and Northeast."

True to its earlier threat, TWA petitioned the Court of Appeals in New York for a review of the CAB decision. In a brief to the same three judges who only a short time earlier had so decisively ruled against Hughes, John Sonnett argued that Toolco was seeking to escape from the consequences of the antitrust action by an end run in Washington that would enable Hughes to settle the suit on his own terms. The Court of Appeals put the case down for argument during the September 1964 term.

But even as TWA sought to contain Toolco's breakthrough in the CAB, Hughes' forces were preparing for yet another try in the nation's courts. After checking with the most prestigious fellow Texan in Washington in those days (it was 1964), Hughes engaged the law firm of Arnold, Fortas & Porter, whose senior partner, Abe Fortas, was appointed to the United States Supreme Court the next year. Aided by Chester Davis, who remained Hughes' chief counsel, the Fortas firm petitioned the Supreme Court for a writ of certiorari to review the decisions of the district and appellate courts. The imposition of the default judgment, the Fortas firm contended, was far too severe a penalty, because such a sanction should be applied only if the failure to proceed with discovery was tantamount to an admission of a lack of merit in the defaulting party's defense. Hughes, the Washington lawyers stressed, defaulted for sound legal and business considerations. They also argued that Toolco should have been granted a voluntary dismissal or indefinite stay on the countersuit, since the prosecution of the countercomplaint was suspended only to allow the CAB to exercise its prior jurisdiction in the case. In addition, the brief cited several points in the proceedings in the district and appellate courts in which Hughes had been the subject of what the Fortas lawyers characterized as overhasty or unsupported judicial actions.

Hundreds of cases are appealed each year to the Supreme Court, but only a handful are accepted. Hughes was one of the fortunate few. On November 16, 1964, the Supreme Court announced its

intention to review both the default judgment and the dismissal of
the countersuit. The cases were put down for a relatively early
hearing—March 1965. The prompt scheduling put a tremendous
work load on the lawyers who now had to produce the briefs, reply briefs, and memoranda that set out the opposing views. Each
side managed, though, to turn out a thick stack of briefs. Also, all
sides agreed to a selection of material from the case so far. This
material, which included excerpts of the court record, depositions,
and other evidence, was printed in six thick volumes, which were
submitted to the justices of the Supreme Court. Yet the very bulk
of the case posed severe problems. How could the justices, who
are so extremely busy, be expected to read some four thousand
pages of briefs and basic record? And even if they did dedicate
a week or so to briefing themselves on the Hughes' case, who
could be sure that from all that maze of paper and conflicting
arguments the justices could draw a clear picture of the essential
elements in the case?

Questions such as those weighed heavily on the minds of John
Sonnett and Chester Davis as they prepared their oral arguments
for the Supreme Court. Each man would have only one hour to
state his argument and answer questions posed by the justices before the red light in the chamber would flash on, indicating that
time was up. In those sixty minutes, he would have to condense
the incredible complexities of *TWA v. Hughes* into a brief and
intelligible statement, show the correctness of his own cause, and
try to persuade the high court that his interpretation of the law was
the right one. All that in one hour!

At precisely 1:35 P.M. on March 3, 1965, Chief Justice Earl
Warren, flanked on either side by the eight associate justices, leaned
slightly forward in his highbacked chair. "Mr. Davis," he said.

Chester Davis rose to his feet and began. "I have lived three
and a half years with this case now and I can't tell you how much
I appreciate the opportunity to address the Court with respect to
the issue which is involved," he exclaimed, in what surely must
be one of the most natural and unassuming introductions in the
annals of the highest court's oratory. Then Davis quickly re-

counted his view of the case—that Hughes and Toolco had gained CAB approval for control of TWA and that all transactions between Toolco and the airline had been approved by the CAB whose blessing had conferred immunity from antitrust laws on Hughes, that the bankers and insurance executives had conspired to take control of TWA away from Hughes, and that lender-controlled management had initiated the present lawsuit as a maneuver to prevent Hughes from ever regaining his rightful control of his property. Finally, Davis repeated to the justices his familiar point that the complaint failed to identify a violation of the antitrust laws. "I don't think it is possible to find a violation of the antitrust laws," he declared. "This is our subsidiary. We own 78 per cent of it. Why would we hurt it? What difference does it make [to] the antitrust laws whether the orders for aircraft are made by Mr. Tillinghast or Mr. Hughes?"

Toward the close of his argument, the justices interrupted Davis to question him along a quite different line. Associate Justices William Brennan and Byron White were concerned about the fact that the most severe possible sanction had been imposed on Hughes by the courts below.

"When and under what circumstances would you have a chance to have reviewed the propriety of the entry of a default judgment?" asked Justice White.

"Well, presumably if the matter went to a hearing and a final judgment," replied Davis, who then explained the circumstances that led him to break off the discovery proceedings. "There came a time," he stated, "when I found through discovery and through documents produced to me from these leading institutions that part of their technique was to insist upon taking the deposition of Mr. Hughes in California. It was going to be an extended, burdensome, and expensive one. After the court denied any motion to dismiss, refused to submit the matter for interlocutory appeal, refused to certify it," he continued, "I came to the conclusion—I did it, if I was wrong, I'm sorry, but I did it—that my client was better off resting on the merits of his position than to undertake the burden of expense of the kind of discovery they were contemplating."

In his relaxed and reflective moments, John Sonnett used to say that other lawyers might be better at this or that legal skill than he, but no one could beat him for thinking on his feet. He was in top form that day—and indeed he needed to be. Sonnett led off making a dramatic, if deflating, suggestion. "The writ of certiorari should be dismissed as improvidently granted," he told the justices. "The reason for that," he went on, "is that the questions upon which certiorari was granted need not be answered because the judgment below is clearly correct under the grounds." Sonnett then quickly presented the other main points of his argument—that the complaint did indeed adequately state causes of action under the antitrust laws, that the CAB "does not have exclusive primary jurisdiction of the matters alleged in the complaint," and that "the CAB did not exempt from the reach of the antitrust laws any of the conduct alleged in the complaint."

On the two final points, which directly contradicted Davis' defense theory, Sonnett received support from the Civil Aeronautics Board. In a memorandum, which the CAB filed with the Supreme Court as amicus curiae, the board stated that in its opinion the Federal Aviation Act had not superseded the workings of the antitrust laws in regard to the issues in TWA's complaint and that CAB approval of transactions between Toolco and TWA did not immunize those transactions from possible antitrust prosecution.

The CAB brief could hardly have been more helpful if Sonnett had written it himself. Nonetheless, the justices were curious about another aspect of the case. Most notably, they wondered how an assessment of damages could fairly be made, since the case had never actually gone to trial.

"What is left before the master?" asked Justice White, who was seeking to determine the status of the case in the event the Court confirmed the default judgment.

"The computation as to the amount of damages," replied Sonnett.

"How do you do that?" inquired Justice White, who wanted to know how the causal relationship would be established between the alleged offense and the damages. "I mean," he continued, "how much does the default judgment foreclose? Don't you have to show the damages which were caused by the conspiracy?"

As Sonnett began to explain that the complaint fully explains who caused the damages, Justice White broke in with another question:

"So, the assumption is that what the default judgment says was what was alleged to have happened?"

"That is correct," responded Sonnett, "subject only to our proof on what will be obviously expert evidence as to the amount of the damages."

But Justice White continued to question Sonnett about whether the default implied that the charges in the complaint were true. Finally, Sonnett declared: "By reason of the one, two, three deliberate defaults, Your Honors must take as admitted the allegations of the complaint, which are factual."

"What is there for Mr. Rankin to do except multiply by three?" interjected Justice Brennan, in a reference to the tripling of damage awards in the antitrust cases. But Justice White was still curious about whether Sonnett thought Toolco, in refusing to proceed with the discovery process, had really taken a gamble of such magnitude. "Do you really [believe that] they made that decision based on the assumption—if they were wrong on the CAB jurisdiction that it would cost them $35 or $45 million?"

"Oh, I don't think that is much money to the Hughes Tool Company," replied Sonnett.

"You are really saying that they made a $45 million business decision?"

"So they said and I take them at their word," said Sonnett.

The justices also were puzzled why Sonnett, despite a long search, had failed to locate Hughes. "On behalf of TWA, I tried to have a subpoena served on Howard Hughes for several years, spent a lot of money, and couldn't find him," Sonnett told them.

"If there had been a warrant out, you don't think they could have found him?" asked Justice White in what everyone understood as a hypothetical question of the FBI's efficiency.

"Maybe so," responded Sonnett, "but our fellows, who were ex-FBI agents, couldn't." While the justices laughed, he continued: "Suffice it to say, the tool company was under a valid obligation to produce Mr. Hughes. Mr. Hughes said, 'I am not going to be bothered,' and that was that." Concluding his argument to the Supreme Court, Sonnett declared: "This is not the case where a man cannot testify. It is a case of a man who would not testify. It is that simple."

The next day, Davis and Bruce Bromley argued the countersuit before the Supreme Court, but those proceedings were anticlimactic compared with the first day. The fate of the largest civil legal battle in history now rested with the nation's highest court. So what did it do? To almost everyone's surprise, it took John Sonnett's advice. In a rarely invoked procedure, the Court five days later issued a terse one-sentence unsigned order. The order stated merely that the Court's earlier decision to review the cases had been "improvidently granted." The justices gave no explanation whatsoever for their action, but apparently the two days of arguments had convinced them that either the cases required no review or were not yet in a state where the Supreme Court should pass a definitive judgment.

In any event, the practical effect of the Court's puzzling behavior was a severe defeat for Howard Hughes. By its failure to reverse the Court of Appeals in either action, the Supreme Court left the situation unchanged—the $443 million countersuit was irrevocably dismissed while the severest sanction, the default judgment against Hughes, was allowed to stand and with it, the presumption on the part of Hughes' opponents that his failure to obey the court's order rendered him guilty as charged in the complaint. Now *TWA v. Hughes* would go back to the District Court where the special master would preside over the damage hearings to determine the exact amount that Howard Hughes would be compelled to pay to TWA.

And as Justice Brennan had mused, "What is there for Mr. Rankin to do except to multiply by three?"

17. The Sweet Rewards of Defeat

Even as Howard Hughes was being defeated in the nation's highest court, he was also running into snags and delays in his bold attempt to outrun the course of justice by buying back control of TWA. Earlier, in the summer of 1964, the CAB had handed Hughes a great tactical advantage by approving his request to resume control of TWA, provided he divest himself of control of Northeast. But that proviso was proving to be extremely bothersome. How could he get rid of the ailing airline? Its weakness had served his purposes during the negotiations with the CAB. However, Northeast's continued weakness now worked against his plans. During the past two years, Hughes had committed $23 million to keeping Northeast alive. Even so, Northeast, which expected to lose at least $2 million in 1964, still remained an unattractive commercial proposition. The other airlines, notably Eastern and National, which might be interested in buying Northeast, only wanted to dismember it in order to reduce competition on the New York–Florida route. If Hughes sold Northeast for that purpose, the transaction would almost surely be blocked in the courts by New Englanders, who through a judicial stay already had managed to block an earlier CAB order that lifted Northeast's certificate to fly the East Cost route.

If he was to succeed in the maneuver to regain control of TWA, Hughes needed to divorce himself from Northeast in a quick and uncomplicated manner that would avoid legal complications. His lawyers, notably Raymond Cook, came up with a novel solution that, ironically enough, took a page from the Hughes' initial defeat at TWA. It was to give Hughes' entire 55 per cent stock interest in Northeast, plus a pledge of $3 million in operating funds, to a trustee. The trustee would be totally free to dispose of Northeast as he saw fit. In that way, Hughes, who would be released from the Northeast situation, would be free to resume control of TWA.

On October 7, 1964, the Toolco attorneys announced their plan in Boston. Howard Hughes, they said, had decided to turn his interests in the airline over to an independent trustee. He could have hardly chosen a more capable and prestigious person. Louis J. Hector, a Miami attorney, had been a member of the Civil Aeronautics Board in the late 1950s. When he resigned in protest over the CAB's confused administrative practices, he wrote a two-page letter to President Eisenhower that won wide admiration throughout the airline industry as a classic indictment of Washington's bureaucratic bungling. In announcing Hector's appointment as the trustee, Northeast's president, James Austin, explained at a press conference that Hector now was, in effect, the personal owner of the airline with full power to do with it as he saw fit.

But would this arrangement satisfy the requirements of the CAB? "We have high hopes," Raymond Cook told newsmen. "We see this arrangement doing what we have set out to do— divest Toolco of Northeast."

But even as Hector assumed his unique trusteeship of Northeast, Hughes' opponents at TWA began a new court action to prevent Toolco from regaining control of TWA. In a blocking maneuver, John Sonnett renewed TWA's petition to the Second Circuit of the Court of Appeals for a review of the CAB decision to allow Hughes to regain control of TWA without first holding a public hearing.

December 7, 1964, was a Pearl Harbor day for Howard Hughes. On that day the Court of Appeals ordered the CAB to suspend its earlier approval of Hughes' resumption of control of TWA until it first held a "full evidentiary hearing" to determine whether it was in the public interest for him to do so. The default judgment was haunting Howard Hughes. "The charges against Toolco stand undenied," the court wrote. "They present a picture which is entirely inconsistent with the requirements of the public interest."

The CAB vowed that it would appeal the decision to the Supreme Court. Nonetheless, it would be many months before the issue could reach the highest court, if indeed the court deigned to hear the case. Whatever the ultimate outcome on the appeal, the immediate effect of the Circuit Court's ruling was to badly throw off the timing of Hughes' comeback plans. Three months later the Supreme Court handed down its declaration, which left standing the lower-court decisions.

Those two sets of court developments combined to reverse completely the tide of battle in the legal struggle. The case was now headed in a direction Howard Hughes had sought at all costs to avoid. It was going back to the District Court for hearings before the special master, who would assess the damages that Hughes allegedly had inflicted on TWA. Unlike Sonnett, who had wanted to proceed at once to an assessment of damages immediately after Hughes' default, Howard Hughes and his lawyers had wanted for two good reasons to pursue the appeal. For one thing, they had felt their interpretation of the law was right and that the Supreme Court would rule in their favor. Equally important, they believed that the more restrained and dignified legal proceeding associated with a Court of Appeals or Supreme Court would provide a far better climate for reaching a possible negotiated settlement than the incriminating and acrimonious mood of damage hearings, which were bound to be filled with furious charges and countercharges.

Throughout the period from the default in February 1963 to the Supreme Court hearing in March 1965 there had been numerous attempts at reaching a compromise settlement. Howard Hughes had told his lawyers that he would be willing to pay $50 million to get the case settled. But he was unwilling to accept the one condition on which Tillinghast always insisted—that Hughes should sell his TWA stock and get out of the airline forever.

Now, under the worst possible conditions, the attorneys for

Howard Hughes soon would be entering the damage hearings. Because of Hughes' default, the TWA complaint was regarded by the courts to stand unchallenged and its charges to be true. This assumption posed a terrible dilemma for Chester Davis and the distinguished Wall Street firm of Donovan, Leisure, Newton & Irvine, whom Davis had engaged to handle the damage hearings. The judicial reasoning, in essence, had been: If you preclude your opponent from investigations that might prove the validity of his charges or his defense, then you cannot turn around and claim that those charges or defense positions are not true.

Yet Davis and James V. Hayes, the Donovan, Leisure partner who took on the courtroom and hearing duties, were fully convinced that essential elements of TWA's complaint were unsupported by fact. Hence, as the preparations for damage hearings got underway in late 1965, Davis and Hayes contended that the default should not be construed as an admission that TWA's charges were true. They argued that TWA should be compelled both to prove that Hughes broke the antitrust laws and to demonstrate that the offense resulted in damages to the airline. They also argued that Toolco, despite its default, had the right to defend itself and that accordingly, the special master and the court were obliged to take judicial notice of federal agency records, notably those of the Civil Aeronautics Board, and testimony from the depositions and other evidence that refuted the charges in TWA's complaint. Furthermore, they claimed that they had the right to introduce new material to discredit the claims of the plaintiff. In short, Davis and Hayes insisted on the right to test the charges in an adversary proceeding just as if no default had ever occurred.

Naturally, John Sonnett continued to hold exactly the opposite position. He maintained that the default foreclosed Toolco from any further defense and that the only remaining task was to fix the exact amount of damages. In order to speed up the assessment, Sonnett asked Special Master Rankin to draw up an interim tentative findings of fact, which would serve as the guideline for TWA's presentation of its testimony at the damage inquest. Rankin duly complied with the request. But Sonnett was very unhappy with the results because Rankin omitted from findings the "fact" that Toolco was a manufacturer of aircraft. Since that allegation was essential to the antitrust charge against Hughes, Sonnett appealed the finding to Judge Metzner. The court, however, refused to make any substantive alteration in the special master's report, but it did use the occasion to restate the effect that the default would have on the damage hearings. In an order issued on November 16, 1965, Judge Metzner wrote, "Liability is not an issue for the Special Master except in a very limited sense. The sufficiency of the complaint has already been established by the denial of the defendant's motion to dismiss. By virtue of the default, the defendant has admitted the truth of the well-pleaded allegations of the complaint."

The key words were "well-pleaded," a term that became highly controversial. Perhaps sensing the future debates about the meaning, Judge Metzner sought to define it by writing that "Allegations are not well pleaded if they are shown to be indefinitive or erroneous by other statements in the complaint; or where they are contrary to facts of which the Court will take judicial notice; or where they are not susceptible of proof by legitimate evidence; or where they are contrary to the uncontroverted material in the file of this case." Hence, Davis and Hayes would have at least a limited opportunity to refute TWA's charges. But the judge also added a remark that showed how heavily the default had weighted the scales of justice against Howard Hughes in the damage hearings. "If evidence merely tends to show that an allegation is not true, the allegation must be taken as true in this default . . . attempts by a defendant to escape the effect of default should be strictly circumscribed. It should not be afforded an opportunity to litigate what already had been deemed admitted in law."

With those admonishments ringing in their ears, Chester Davis and James Hayes prepared to enter what was certain to be a one-sided battle with John Sonnett over a very crucial question: How much does Howard Hughes owe to TWA?

Meanwhile, Hughes was suffering setbacks in his maneuvers at the CAB. After having been initially satisfied with the transfer of Hughes' interest in Northeast to the trusteeship of Louis Hector, the CAB now announced that it was unhappy with the arrangement, since Hector obviously had to be mindful of Hughes' aims and interests. But before the CAB could take action, a solution arrived from a very unexpected quarter. The Storer Broadcasting Corporation of Atlanta, a highly profitable chain of radio stations that was looking for expansion opportunities, began to dicker with Hector for the purchase of Northeast. During the summer of 1965, Storer bought Northeast by assuming some $40 million of its debts and paying about $6 million in cash to Hughes. Now freed of the Northeast albatross, he could have moved to regain control at TWA, except for one big problem. That was the judicial order, won by TWA in the Court of Appeals in December 1964, that commanded the CAB to hold a public hearing before Hughes could be allowed to get back into TWA's corporate cockpit. The CAB had appealed the appellate court's decision, but on October 11, 1965, the Supreme Court refused to review the decision, thus leaving in force the necessity for a public hearing, which almost certainly would have involved tremendous clamor for personal testimony from Howard R. Hughes. The consequence: After all those years of pressuring and persuading the board members and after an estimated expenditure of $20 million in unrecoverable funds at Northeast, Hughes abandoned his attempt at the CAB to confound his enemies and emerge victorious from the lawsuit by regaining control of TWA. For the second time in his great battle with the financial establishment, Howard Hughes, as 1965 ended, was completely on the defensive, his options and alternatives reduced to almost nothing.

At last, on May 2, 1966, the damage hearings formally commenced. As a result, TWA was finally compelled to state the "well-pleaded" charges upon which its case rested. For five years Chester Davis had been challenging John Sonnett to reveal the facts behind the complaint against Howard Hughes and his tool company. Now, as a result of the default, Sonnett did not have to prove that the violations actually took place—that was assumed to be true—but he did have to demonstrate what amount of damages were caused by which specific violations.

And what a clever and ingenious case Sonnett had devised! He ignored entirely the whole pre-1956 period covered in the complaint. Instead, Sonnett, who had a preference for simplicity, concentrated only on the period that dealt with the orders and acquisitions of the jets. In essence, his case said simply this: "You, Howard Hughes, promised to supply sixty-three jetliners on a timely basis to TWA, which would have met precisely the airline's needs. But you delivered too few planes too late. Therefore you owe TWA the money that the airline otherwise would have earned if it had had the entire fleet at the originally promised dates. You ask why you are guilty, Mr. Hughes? The reason is that you violated the nation's antitrust laws by dominating TWA and forcing it to accept aircraft only from you. If TWA had been free to act as it pleased, it would have ordered exactly the same numbers and types that you did, but it would have gotten the planes on time."

And who was the chief witness who would testify to the correctness of this line of reasoning? It was none other than Robert W. Rummel. Hughes' adversaries could hardly have created a more ironic situation. This was the man, then a lanky young flier like Hughes, who had conducted the crucial stress analysis of Howard's revolutionary record-setting H-1. This was the man who since 1943 had participated with Hughes in the development and selection of each and every new TWA plane. This was the man whose loyalty to Hughes earlier had been unquestioned. He had worked in secret with Hughes, sometimes withholding his knowledge of future plans even from his direct superiors at TWA. Over the years, Rummel had met Hughes in countless clandestine rendezvous at dozens of nondescript hotels, had waited in his own home or in hotel rooms "on the hook" for days and weeks for Hughes' telephone calls, and had carried on long-distance conversations with him that sometimes lasted nine or ten hours. "Once in a while we would take a ten-minute break," Rummel remembers.

When he had been questioned by Chester Davis during the 1962 depositions, Rummel had praised Hughes so highly for helping TWA find the most suitable aircraft that his testimony had contradicted a cardinal point in TWA's antitrust complaint. That point was that Hughes had excluded other planemakers from the TWA market. In his testimony, Rummel had cited a number of examples of how Hughes had encouraged the planemakers to compete with one another in order to get the best plane for TWA.

But Rummel, who had retained his position as a TWA vice president under the new management, had begun to see Hughes' activities at TWA in a quite different light. With the help of one of Sonnett's senior aides, Corey Dunham, Rummel produced a twenty-four-page affidavit, to which were attached six detailed annexes totaling thirty-six pages. This affidavit became Exhibit A in TWA's damage case against Hughes. In the document Rummel recited the well-known facts that Toolco in 1956 and 1957 had ordered sixty-three jet aircraft, but that TWA did not receive this sixty-three-plane fleet. Instead, six Boeing 331 Intercontinentals were diverted to Pan American and of the thirty promised Convairs only twenty were delivered. Wrote Rummel: "By the end of 1960, TWA's jet fleet totalled only twenty-eight aircraft, not sixty-three. That twenty-eight-plane fleet was greatly inadequate for TWA's needs. Moreover, even if all forty-seven jet aircraft ultimately received by TWA from Toolco had been received by the end of 1960, TWA's jet fleet would not have been adequate to meet TWA's needs at that time." Concluded Rummel: "In my opinion, the sixty-three-plane fleet, in the numbers and types ordered by Toolco—had it been ordered and delivered on a timely basis—would have been adequate to meet the needs of TWA for jet aircraft through 1960."

There was one other main assumption to TWA's case against Hughes—that if he had not dominated the airline, TWA on its own would have been capable of financing the sixty-three-plane jet fleet that it so urgently had needed. Sonnett had a team of investment bankers standing by to testify that if Hughes had not been in control of TWA, the airline would have been able to take care of itself.

These were hard and hurtful charges that TWA was making against Howard Hughes, who had been willing to ransom his fortune in order to provide aircraft for the airline. Yet from a strictly financial standpoint, TWA's attacks on Hughes unintentionally turned out to be of almost boundless benefit to him. The TWA lawsuit had the subtle effect of changing the public's opinion of him and thereby affording him a fantastic opportunity for a financial coup. Prior to the controversy with the bankers in the late 1950s, Hughes had been identified in the public mind as being synonymous with TWA. As such, it would have been impossible for him to have sold his huge chunk of TWA stock. At the very first hint of his impending exodus, the stock price would have collapsed. But now John Sonnett's cleverly conceived case—and the huge amounts of attendant publicity—had persuaded the public that Howard Hughes was an undesirable influence at TWA. The sooner he got out, the better off the airline would be.

It turned out to be a stroke of good fortune for Howard Hughes. He was finally in a position where he could sell out without pulling down the price of the shares. And it was a time to think about selling. Under Tillinghast's management, TWA had really taken off. From the dismal days in 1961 and 1962, when TWA lost millions and seemed headed toward bankruptcy or a shotgun marriage with Pan American, the airline had made an almost incredible recovery. Tillinghast, who had dropped the idea of a merger with Pan Am, had expanded and improved TWA's operations; the airline finally had gotten enough new jets, including the more powerful Boeing 707 fan jets and the sleek trijet 727s. The airline was also helped in the early 1960s through the purchase of the four Convair 880s that Hughes had originally diverted to Northeast.

Like a jet, TWA's net profit climbed from $19.7 million in 1963 to $37 million the next year and to $50.1 million in 1965. TWA's per-share price rose on the stock market even faster than the profits. From a low of $7.50 per share in 1962, TWA's stock increased during the next three years more than eleven-fold in value and was still climbing.

And who was the big winner? Howard Hughes, of course. It was one of the supreme ironies of the legal battle. His enemies had made him rich in a generally financially unrewarding industry that until now had done nothing but soak up his fortune. But they had also robbed him of the special joy he used to feel for TWA. Out of control for five years now, he no longer recognized the airline as something he had built. It was larger, jet-powered, unfamiliar, and impersonal. "I can no longer run my hands over TWA," he remarked. As early as autumn 1964 he had already begun to discuss selling at least a part of his TWA holdings, notably the 1.3 million shares he had gained through a conversion of a part of the debentures. (He had refused to deposit these new shares with the voting trust.) But the stock market turned downward in February 1965, and Hughes dropped that idea. Then in early April, Hughes telephoned one of his financial advisers. "How long will it take to make preparations to sell the whole batch?" he asked. "Thirty days" was the reply.

Actually, the preparations for the sale, which was the second largest secondary offering in history (smaller only than the Ford family's sale of the auto company's shares in 1956), was accomplished in only twenty-nine days. With the help of 387 American and twenty-three foreign underwriters, Merrill Lynch, Pierce, Fenner & Smith handled the complex details of offering. When the impending sale was actually announced in April 1965, TWA's stock was trading at about $80; then after a dip to $76.50 it rallied to an all-time high of $96.84 before beginning a slow slide to $86. At $86, Hughes decided to sell before the price fell any further. The next morning (it was May 3), Howard Hughes' 6,584,937 TWA shares, which then amounted to 75.18 per cent of the airline's stock, were snapped up by private and institutional investors at an unparalleled pace. In only thirty minutes after the stock went on sale, every share had been sold. Hughes' sense of timing was superb. Except for an immediate post-sale rise to $87.50, TWA's shares during the next seven years never again approached the eighties.

As the proceeds of the sale, the largest sum of money ever to pass at one time into the hands of a private individual reached those of Howard Hughes. After deductions of about $3.00 per share for underwriters' fees and other expenses, Howard Hughes received a check of $546,549,771. The check was handed over to Toolco officers and attorneys in Wilmington to avoid a New York City tax on stock transfers, which would have amounted to more than $260,000.

Hughes' opponents at TWA were delighted that he had sold out. But they also were puzzled. His voluntary exodus accomplished one of the main objectives of Tillinghast and Sonnett—to solve the "Hughes problem" by getting him out of the airline. But why had not Hughes capitalized on the sale by trying to link it to a settlement of the lawsuit. "Look, Howard," Greg Bautzer had told him, "we can get this thing cleared up." But Hughes refused to permit a linkage between suit and sale.

Howard Hughes was taking a gamble of gigantic proportions. As long as he retained his holdings in TWA, even if he had to pay a high amount of damages in the lawsuit, his loss would have been considerably cushioned by the fact that he was paying his money into an enterprise in which he already owned more than three quarters of the stock. Thus, the debit in Toolco's account would be at least partly offset by the gain in TWA's net worth. In fact, if the millions in damages made the airline a more attractive property on the stock market, the increase in value of Hughes' TWA stock conceivably could cover whatever penalty he might have to pay. But now that he had sold out, Hughes no longer could benefit from any funds that he might be forced to pay into TWA. He had abandoned his fail-safe device. Nonetheless, he insisted that he had been correct in refusing to link the sale of his TWA shares to a settlement of the lawsuit. Hughes had not wanted the sale to become bogged down and delayed in a legal morass, which almost certainly would have accompanied his efforts to reach an out-of-court settlement. Even more important, Hughes remained convinced that he had done TWA no wrong, that he would be vindicated in a court of law, that despite all the disappointing setbacks and the handicap of the default judgment, he still would emerge victorious. That was a very sanguine view of the events as they faced Howard Hughes in mid-1966. But then, Hughes, as his travel plans soon were to reveal, seemed to be in a gambling mood.

18.   The High Roller of Las Vegas

The City of Los Angeles, which in the mid-1960s was one of the
Union Pacific's few remaining long-distance passenger trains, had
run into an unexpected delay during a routine after-midnight stop
in Ogden, Utah. The delay meant that the old streamliner, which
on that trip was hauling two very special cars—a New Haven
sleeper and an executive carriage—would reach Las Vegas well
after sunup. That fact greatly disturbed the main occupant of the
private cars. Howard Hughes was making a major move. After
a temporary and troublesome sojourn in Boston, he was traveling
to the gambling capital of the United States, and he wanted to
slip into town quietly and unseen.

For the past several months Hughes had been unsettled and
uncertain about his own plans. In July 1966 he had left his rented
mansion in Bel Air and, surrounded by elaborate security and
secrecy precautions, had boarded a special car attached to the
Santa Fe's Super Chief for a long ride that ultimately had brought
him to the Ritz-Carlton in Boston, where he and his retinue had
occupied the hotel's entire fifth floor. The choice of transportation
was dictated by a nationwide air strike, but Hughes, who had developed a fear of flying, also preferred rail travel. He repeatedly
told aides: "I will never fly again unless I am at the controls."

The popular assumption was that Hughes had gone to Boston
for medical treatment, possibly an ear operation to improve his

near deafness. In reality, Hughes had chosen Boston simply as a way station where he could decide upon a new permanent base. In his mind there were two leading candidates, both places he had gotten to know during the late 1950s when he was testing aircraft for TWA—and for his own amusement. One was Montreal, where he had flown to test the Bristol Britannia. The other was the Bahamas, where he had spent many pleasant weeks shooting landings in the JetStream Constellation that Carter Burgess so urgently had wanted to get back into service for TWA.

As Hughes pondered these choices with his usual thoroughness of attention to detail and customary self-defeating indecision, he became increasingly disenchanted with his situation in Boston. He found the Boston newsmen to be an especially unbearable breed of journalists. They harassed him by turning on fire alarms for his floor of the Ritz-Carlton and then, in an attempt to gain a glimpse of him, would come storming in behind the firemen.

While he was still debating where to go, Hughes received a message from Edward P. Morgan, a Washington attorney who was doing some work for Toolco. In his memo, Morgan suggested Las Vegas as the site of Hughes' next sojourn. That recommendation was quickly buttressed by a pledge from Hank Greenspun, the energetic publisher of the Las Vegas *Sun*. Hughes knew Greenspun slightly from his visits to the city in the late 1940s and 1950s. In those days, Hughes used to fly over from Los Angeles for a few days of rest and diversion. Sometimes he would bring along a movie actress. He liked Las Vegas so much that he had bought a huge tract of land near the city, which is still shown on the real estate maps as "Husite." One night in the early 1950s, as he was piloting a Wall Street banker over Las Vegas for the sensational view of the city's lights on the otherwise black desert, Hughes turned toward him. "Someday, I am going to go there and clean that place up," he said.

Hank Greenspun now gave Hughes a pledge that greatly appealed to him. If Hughes came to Las Vegas, he would not be bothered by the press. For a man of Hughes' wealth, Las Vegas had other appeals too: the State of Nevada has no personal, corporate, or inheritance taxes. As a result, Hughes asked Robert Maheu to investigate the possibilities of his living and investing in Las Vegas. In early November 1966 Maheu registered at the Desert Inn under the assumed name of Robert Murphy, a precaution taken to avoid the speculation that the presence of a well-known Hughes operative would be bound to attract. After a short period of intensive investigations, he gave Hughes a positive report on the Las Vegas situation.

Maheu was in Las Vegas, preparing for his employer's arrival when a radio call came from the stalled City of Los Angeles in Ogden. The caller was Jack Hooper, a former Los Angeles police sergeant who was the director of Hughes' security force. Hooper said that he could rent a locomotive that could barrel ahead of the City of Los Angeles, towing the two Hughes cars. Maheu approved of the plan. At 4 A.M. on Thanksgiving Eve 1966, Howard Hughes stepped from his rail car at the Carey Avenue crossing of the Union Pacific tracks in North Las Vegas. He was placed on a stretcher in the back of a Ford station wagon and driven to the front door of the Desert Inn. While his guards shielded his arrival, he walked through a private entrance near the front door, turned left twice, and boarded a waiting elevator that whisked him to the penthouse on the ninth floor.

No gambler had ever arrived in that gaudy, incredibly superficial city with a bankroll that matched Hughes'. He brought along about $446 million in liquid assets, which represented the proceeds of the sale of his TWA shares (after paying federal capital-gains tax). The TWA sale pushed Hughes' fortune well into the billionaire bracket. He embarked upon a spending spree that astounded even the jaded residents of Las Vegas, who were accustomed to visiting high-rollers playing for very big stakes.

No outsider knows for sure whether Hughes started his buying spree according to a plan or from a fit of pique that he felt necessary to obscure by massive purchases. But there is no doubt that his original purchase was motivated by a high percentage of pique.

After Hughes had taken over the entire top floor of the Desert Inn, he began to bargain for the purchase of the hotel. The owners, a syndicate of old-time Las Vegas figures, including the noted gambler Morris (Moe) Dalitz, soon became disgusted with his dilatory tactics. They wanted him either to buy the hotel immediately or get out, because his suites were needed to house visiting high-rollers, who were customarily given free, plush accommodation in anticipation of the big money they most likely would drop on the Desert Inn's green felt gaming tables. True to his old tradition of cliff-hanging negotiations, Hughes had stalled right down to the last. Then, as the final deadline was within minutes of expiring, Hughes, acting through an attorney, began to raise a big fuss about a $30,000 item in the purchase price, which totaled $13 million. That tore it. The Desert Inn's owners, who were sitting downstairs in the grill room, were outraged. They told Bob Maheu that they were going to seize Hughes that very evening and put him out on the street. Maheu, who already was acting as Hughes' representative in Las Vegas, took them at their word. He was also exasperated beyond measure by Hughes, who earlier had agreed to the purchase on the present terms. "Give me one hour," Maheu begged the Desert Inn owners. Then, using his special elevator key, which sends the lift to the ninth floor (otherwise it stopped at the eighth), Maheu rushed up to the penthouse. He went into one of the rooms opposite Hughes' three-room suite and scrawled on a legal pad: "You finally have taxed my patience to the full limit. If you cannot keep your word, then there is nothing more I can do to help you. You don't owe me a penny." Maheu rapped on the middle door of Hughes' suite. Ray Crawford, one of the Mormon nurse-secretaries, who attended Hughes round the clock, opened the door.

"Give this to Mr. Hughes right away," commanded Maheu. Hughes reacted swiftly to Maheu's message. A few minutes later Hughes' attorney told the Desert Inn owners that the sale would be consummated as agreed to earlier. Then a call came for Maheu from Crawford. "The Man wants me to beg of you not to leave," Crawford said. "He will call you in the morning at eight."

True to his word, Hughes rang Maheu the next morning at eight. "Jesus Christ," cried Hughes, "don't you ever scare me like that again! Promise me you'll never leave." And that, so Robert Maheu claims, is the way their relationship was cemented in the early days in Las Vegas. Certainly, over the ensuing months the development of the relationship between the two men indicated a remarkably high degree of mutual trust, respect, and loyalty. Robert Maheu became in effect the visible alter ego for Howard Hughes, the corporeal, corporate manifestation of the unseen billionaire, whose influence streamed out from the penthouse, touching in some way every life in Las Vegas and beyond that, throughout the state. Maheu, a large and impressive man, played tennis with the state governor, took an active and constructive role in Las Vegas' community life, and encouraged other executives to do likewise. Hughes had built for him a mansion on the grounds of the Desert Inn. Maheu set a cultivated tone. The first time he entertained for lunch the casino managers, many of whose formative years had been spent in Las Vegas' mob-dominated period, Maheu tapped his water glass for attention. Then, to the astonishment of his Las Vegas colleagues, Robert Maheu said grace.

Because of the legal considerations in Nevada, Hughes would have had to invent a Bob Maheu if he had not already existed. Under the state's strict gambling laws, which were devised to chase organized crime out of Nevada's gaming industry, the supervisory agency required that a casino license could only be issued in the name of one individual. That was to put squarely onto one person the liability and responsibility for the casino's operation. Also at that time, an individual was not allowed to control more than one casino.

With Maheu as the front man, Hughes began to buy up Las Vegas at a rate that at first stunned and then delighted residents of the city. Within one year from the time of his clandestine arrival, he had purchased, in addition to the Desert Inn, The Sands, the Castaways, the Frontier, the North Las Vegas Air Terminal, television station KLAS, Alamo Airways, and the 518-acre Krupp Ranch, which had belonged to the late widow of a relative of Germany's munitions king. Hughes electrified Las Vegas with hopes and speculation about what else he might do. Breaking a silence of some fifteen years, Hughes mused in a press release that, with luck, Las Vegas might just become the southwestern terminus for the supersonic transports whose passengers could be shuttled by helicopters or smaller STOL (short take-off and landing) jets to downtown areas of Los Angeles, San Francisco, and other cities in the general area. To handle SSTs, however, Hughes insisted that Las Vegas would need a new airport further away from built-up areas than the present one, McCarran Field, which already was being crowded by the city's sprawl. When a federal aviation expert pooh-poohed Hughes' suggestion, saying that McCarran Field was situated on the best site in the valley, Hughes replied in another press release with a flash of his old combative wit. "It is a perfect site for an airport," he wrote. "It has only one trouble. Somebody built a city on the same site." Hughes also was aware of the public clamor for some clue about his plans. In still another press release, almost on the anniversary of his first year as Las Vegas' most famous recluse, Hughes made a promise. "I will go this far," he wrote in a classic display of hedged introspection. "I will promise some kind of small industrial effort in some part of Nevada with no agreed or committed time schedule. Now I know that this does not sound like much. I guess you just have to make your own estimates. I promise one thing: it won't be as favorable a schedule as you expect, or as favorable a schedule as you would like it to be, or as favorable a schedule as I would like it to be."

Actually, Hughes never did start even a small industrial venture in Nevada. But he continued to buy up real estate, hotels, and casinos at a dizzying pace. In 1968 he took a lease on McCarran Field. He removed a conspicuous example of overbuilding from the Las Vegas skyline by buying and completing the unfinished Landmark Hotel (the scene of the "James Bond" film *Diamonds Are Forever*). In a move reminiscent of his rescue of Northeast Airlines years earlier, Hughes purchased Air West, a regional carrier, for the considerable sum of about $90 million. To the delight and enrichment of many a poor prospector, Howard Hughes also began at a furious pace to buy up mining claims throughout the state. In all, he spent some $30 million for an estimated fifteen hundred claims.

Hughes became such a dominant economic force in the state

that politicians catered to his whims and desires. The law forbidding an individual to control more than one casino was amended to enable Hughes to buy a whole string of them. Members of local and state commissions, notably the gaming boards, often were convened in sudden meetings to go through the motions of approving yet another Hughes plan. Though unseen, he had become the most powerful single force in the state. In fact, during all these often frantic purchases and negotiations, Hughes never once left the penthouse. Even so, he was remarkably well informed. He watched television, read a thick stack of newspapers that were brought in from all over the state, and pored over long reports, which were prepared at his request by Maheu and other members of his staff. Hughes peppered his aides, most notably Maheu, with memos. Written on lined legal pads, they often spelled out the exact scenario for handling situations, including the proper psychological approach. At other times, the memos cajoled, inspired, and occasionally complimented the recipient. Down to the smallest details, Hughes was running the show. Samples from the memos:

On wanting more information from an aide: "I wait up. Please call me now and I will not have to wake you later. I cannot eat and cannot sleep. I am so absorbed."

A lesson on business procedures (to Maheu): "As usual in preliminary exploration, I must be able to talk frankly with you without even the slightest hint being accidentally dropped to anyone. Also, I must be able to talk to you freely and openly with no fear that you may go ahead and proceed to carry out some of the things we discuss. In other words, I am just thinking out loud but I do not want any of this, or subsequent messages, to be considered as greenlighting any plans already made until I tell you specifically that I have passed out of the talk stage and am ready to take some decisions. Okay? H."

On how to get a lower price from Moe Dalitz (to Maheu, who was negotiating for purchase of the Stardust Casino): "You may be surprised how many times a man like Moe will make concessions for a friend. I mean, for example, that I believe Moe would go further as a gesture of personal friendship to you than he ever would as the result of negotiating pressure brought by me. You see, if I try to bargain Moe into a deal his pride asserts itself and he says, 'Never!' Whereas as a favor and gesture of personal friendship to you when you are depressed by the treachery of a trusted employee who betrayed your trust, Moe might easily do for you what he would not do for me. Anyhow, please try. Howard."

On Hughes' preference for dealing with one issue at a time (to Maheu): "I just simply have a one-track mind. Please forgive me, H."

On trying to recruit Vice President Hubert H. Humphrey to the ban-the-nuclear-testing movement (to Maheu): "There is one man who can accomplish our objective other than [Lyndon] Johnson—and that man is H.H.H. Why don't we get word to him on a basis of secrecy that is *really really reliable* that we will give him imediately full unlimited support for his campaign to enter the White House if he will just take this one on for us. Let me know. H."

On the necessity to line up Hank Greenspun's support on the anti-testing issue (to Maheu): "I simply beg that you obtain, without one minute's delay, Hank Greenspun's all-out support. I am positive from his past editorials that this is 100% his kind of battle . . . I am sure that he will make a real crusade out of this if we encourage him and if he knows that he has us to back him up. Please let me know—I am positive that this is the most critical item, time-wise, that lies before us at this minute. H."

On how to handle a possible competitor (to Maheu, who was supposed to arrange for a Las Vegas *Sun* columnist to interview a rival casino owner and, in the process, goad him): ". . . to trigger Mr. X off so that the 'wild man' will start raving and ranting and baring his teeth and threatening dire destruction to all who get in his path. If X would put on one of his standard performances in front of Price [the columnist] we would have it made. H."

Intramural psychological warfare (to Maheu): "Welcome back! You may not be aware of this, but I have simply felt that you were not with me lately. It seemed that all we did was quarrel and bicker."

On dealing with the Nevada Gaming Control Board (to

Maheu): "Now re a statement to the commission, I feel you should tell them that outside of the Stardust we have no further plans in Southern Nevada. I urge we say nothing re Northern Nevada."

More advice on how to get better deals (to Maheu): "You must put it in this framework—that your job is in jeopardy."

On building the mansion (to Maheu): "Bob, please go ahead and buy the two lots in the name of H. T. Co., and please proceed to build likewise at the company's expense. I think we might get the building job done more economically if the architect and the builder think it is for you at your expense. Many thanks, Howard."

On tactics for trying to get President Lyndon Johnson to stop the underground nuclear tests (to Maheu): "There is only one bad thing. If Johnson sends a message back that he wishes he could, but due to the shortness of time, etc. etc.,— If that happens we really have had it but good. After that nobody would touch it."

On one test itself (to Maheu): "Who is to say it will not be discovered later that detonating bombs under the ground and poisoning and adulterating the earth for all the future of mankind is not equally as dangerous as an explosion in the air. One thing is sure—extra sure—if they shoot that bomb on Friday, nobody can go back and undo it. H."

Hughes was sometimes a deceptive tactician. He was developing an obsession about retaining his position as the biggest hotel and casino operator in Las Vegas, and he wanted to sidetrack potential competitors before they even got started. When he learned that a group of outside financiers was coming into Las Vegas to build a hotel, he devised a scheme to try and discourage them. It was questionable at that time whether the city had any need for additional hotel space. Hughes compounded the problem by announcing that he would spend $150 million to expand The Sands by 4,000 new rooms. That would make it economically unrewarding, to say the least, for anyone else to put up a hotel.

To give his scheme a special aura of authenticity, Hughes even composed the press release that detailed his grandiose plans. Under his guidance, The Sands would become "the most complete vacation and pleasure complex anywhere in the world—a complete city within itself—shops open twenty-four hours a day, one entire floor devoted to family recreation, the largest bowling alley and billiard and pool facility in the world, an ice-skating rink, rooms for chess and bridge, Skee-Ball, table tennis and a theater for first-run unreleased motion pictures." It would be, according to Hughes, "a resort so carefully planned and magnificently designed that any guest will have to make a supreme effort to be bored, whether he is a sophisticated VIP of the jet-set, or one of the children of a family spending their vacation with us."

There would also be indoor and nighttime golf, added Hughes. The indoor course would be "so carefully designed that shots will feel just like shots outdoors and the spin of the ball in a slice or hook is even measured electronically and indicated to the players."

Unfortunately for Hughes, his rivals were not frightened away by his press release. Months later, after people began to ask questions about why no ground had yet been broken at The Sands for the new project, Bob Maheu figured out a disarming and purely fictional reply. The explanation was that Toolco scientists and engineers had discovered that the existing Hughes hotels in Las Vegas already had suffered severe structural damage from earlier nuclear testing in Nevada. Since underground tests were going on again, it would be too dangerous to try to erect a large structure of the sort envisioned by Hughes.

Maheu bounced his story off Hughes, who was delighted. "Bob, the more I think about it the more I like it," he replied in a memo. "The idea of saying we postponed it because of the tests is terrific."

That, however, was the only benefit the resumption of underground testing did have for Howard Hughes. In 1968 he had become increasingly agitated about the resumption of tests at the Atomic Energy Commission site 75, north of Las Vegas. Originally, Hughes had been influenced in his choice of Las Vegas for its pure, unpolluted desert air. Now the government planned to explode a nuclear device in the one-megaton range as the test of warheads for antiballistic missiles. The test was code-named Boxcar and

Hughes was determined to derail it. His obsessive fear of contamination was raised to an almost hysterical pitch by his suspicion that underground blasts would render radioactive the state's underground water supplies. Anxious to avoid a showdown with Hughes, the AEC assembled a number of its top scientists to reassure Hughes' own scientific advisers about the safety of the tests. Hughes, however, refused to be mollified. He sent Maheu off on a secret mission that led to clandestine meetings with Vice President Hubert Humphrey, who agreed to the creation under White House auspices of a high-level committee of private citizens who were opponents of nuclear testing. Not surprisingly, the committee issued a report that stated that Boxcar's hazards to the environment outweighed its potential advantages to the national security. But President Johnson had the report suppressed. Frustrated on that front, Hughes secretly supplied funds to the St. Louis Committee for Environmental Protection, headed by the distinguished scientist Barry Commoner. Hughes paid for members of the group to travel to Las Vegas for a protest demonstration. Among other warnings, the St. Louis group cautioned that Boxcar's underground shock wave might crack the nearby Hoover Dam.

But neither pressure nor threats deterred the AEC. A few days before the test, Hughes scrawled a long memo to Maheu that provided a prophetic insight into the thought processes of a man who had chosen to imprison himself in a penthouse. Wrote Hughes: "I think that the AEC must be made to realize that I am dedicated to the minimum request made of them [to delay the explosion]. That if they do not grant it, I will ally myself completely with the all-out anti-bomb faction throughout the entire U.S. That this group had only been waiting for a strong leader and I am ready to dedicate the rest of my life and every cent I possess in a complete no quarter fight to outlaw all nuclear testing of every kind and everywhere. . . .

"If they ride roughshod over me and go ahead with the tests, I will have nothing to discuss with them, that they could not even get an appointment to get in the office, that all the horses and tractors in Nevada could not even get them through the door."

Despite Hughes' threats, Boxcar was detonated right on schedule. A few windows shook in Las Vegas, but otherwise there were no reverberations. For all practical purposes, he had lost his battle with the AEC. In 1968 Howard Hughes also lost his multimillion attempt to take over one of the nation's three coast-to-coast radio and television networks, the American Broadcasting Company. When the Federal Communications Commission declared that it would expect Hughes to appear personally in hearings before it approved his control of ABC, he managed to wiggle out of his bid.

Though Hughes was suffering setbacks, he also was continuing to make a greater impact on Las Vegas than any other individual had ever done in the city's gaudy history. As the hermit in the penthouse, he held a special fascination for the city that otherwise is accustomed to the most blatant exposure of flesh and of human emotions. When the governor of Nevada finally was granted an audience, albeit by telephone, the event was a sensation. The Las Vegas *Review-Journal,* one of the city's two major papers, printed a two-line banner headline—in blue ink, no less. For the first time in three decades, Nevada was obsessed by something besides gambling. There were rumors galore—that he would buy up one, or both, of the city's newspapers; that he would build a huge industrial complex near Las Vegas; that he was going to buy up more lots along the Strip; that he was out to bust the Mob; that he was personally responsible for cutting off Frank Sinatra's credit at The Sands. That development led to a fight between the enraged singer and a Hughes manager and cost Sinatra a couple of front teeth. Nightclub comedians along the Strip tried, almost always unsuccessfully, to make jokes about Hughes. "Our father who art in the Penthouse, Howard be thy name . . ." was an example of how poorly Hughes lent himself to humor.

But Hughes was providing a much more important service to Las Vegas—he was giving it an economic resurgence. When he arrived in 1966 the city was in the midst of a real estate depression:

rents were low, unoccupancy rates were high, and land prices were down. Thanks to Hughes' massive investments, real estate prices along the Strip and in other choice areas had quadrupled within three years and home rentals and the price of houses had risen at a rate of 15 to 35 per cent per year. Hughes' presence also attracted other large and respectable corporations to Las Vegas, which began to change its image from a mob-run fleshpot to that of a respectable entertainment center, which also could be a good place to locate a plant or regional office. "Hughes has revolutionized this town," enthused one Las Vegas entertainer. "We have left behind the era of 'the Green Felt Jungle' and are now entering into 'the Greenback Forest.'"

While Hughes was seeding Nevada with greenbacks, his opponents in Manhattan were seeking to establish their case for collecting from him their huge settlement. After a number of procedural delays, the damage hearings, as we have seen, had finally begun in May 1966. They lasted until April 9, 1968. During those twenty-three months, the testimony of the witnesses covered nearly 11,000 pages. In addition, more than 800 separate exhibits, comprising some 60,000 pages, were produced as evidence by both parties. A large part of the hearings turned into a battle of computers as each side produced ream upon ream of printouts that sought to prove the validity of its own case and to undermine the contentions of the other side.

The hearings were an extremely costly and drawn-out exercise in the construction of hypothetical models. Essentially, TWA sought to establish that if it had not been dominated by Hughes, it (a) would have been able to finance the full sixty-three-plane fleet it required and (b) would have received the planes on a timely basis, enabling it to retain its competitive position against the other major airlines. Then, through the testimony of experts—for which TWA paid total fees of $1,642,667.71—the airline tried to place a dollar amount on the damages that it allegedly had suffered from Hughes' acts.

By contrast, Toolco, which contested each of TWA's points,

sought to explode the airline's theories by showing that TWA was better off with less planes (since 1960–61 was a time of over-capacity and financial losses among the airlines because of the introduction of too many new jets) and that, in any event, TWA could never have financed the sixty-three-plane fleet on its own.

The airline's lead witness, of course, was Robert Rummel, who testified that if TWA had ordered its Boeing jets only a little later than Pan American and American, it would have received all thirty-three Boeings no later than July 1960. He also asserted that TWA could have taken delivery on all thirty Convair 880s by September of that year if it had been free of Hughes' domination. As it was, six Boeings and ten Convair 880s were not delivered at all, and the remaining planes were generally delivered far later than would have been the case if TWA had placed the orders and pursued the deliveries without the interference of Howard Hughes. To buttress Rummel's testimony, TWA produced a Boeing vice president, John B. Connelly, who testified that Rummel's assumptions about reallocation of 707 deliveries conformed with Boeing's practice to try to give major customers fairly equal treatment if they placed their orders at roughly the same time.

On the financial front, Edward J. Morehouse, the senior vice president of the investment banking firm of Drexel, Harriman & Ripley, presented a highly complex report on TWA's behalf. The report claimed that a "non-captive" TWA could have raised capital in the mid-1950s, when other major airlines were arranging long-term loans. At that time, the interest rate was much lower than the 6 per cent the airline was later forced to pay because of Hughes' delays. In an even more complex study, Edward L. Wemple, a partner in the aviation consulting firm of Coverdale & Colpitts, constructed a model of how TWA would have improved its flight schedules if it had received the sixty-three planes on time. Another TWA expert witness, R. Dixon Speas, the president of R. Dixon Speas Associates, which dealt in the sale of used aircraft, pointed out that TWA would have gotten higher prices for its piston-engine planes, if it had been able to put them on the market earlier. Finally, John C. Biegler, a partner in the public accounting firm of Price, Waterhouse & Company, synthesized all those reports into one comprehensive statement that compared the theoretical earnings of a non-captive "reconstructed" TWA with the dismal performance of "historical" TWA.

In totaling up the damage claim, TWA asserted that Hughes had caused the airline to lose $71.7 million in profits during the period of October 1, 1955, to December 31, 1963. To that figure were added other sums, including $12.3 million for the additional capital that would have been paid into TWA by shareholders under Morehouse's theoretical financing program; $20.3 million, representing the higher interest charges that TWA had to bear because of Hughes' lateness in arranging long financing for the jets; $527,000 for extra cost in refresher and standby pay for TWA crews who had to wait for the late planes; and $43,000 for refresher training for certain maintenance personnel. In all, TWA's damage bill against Hughes came to the grand total of $104.9 million, which as a penalty under antitrust practice would be tripled to $314.7. That was about the same amount that Hughes had spent in Las Vegas.

In rebuttal, Toolco attacked TWA's case as "ingenious extravaganza, spun from opinion testimony without substratum in fact, logic, or law." Toolco also contended that TWA failed utterly and irretrievably to meet the legal requirement to prove a causal relationship between Toolco's alleged antitrust violations and the resulting injuries to TWA. Declared Davis and Hayes: "Plaintiff first ran into trouble when it was faced with the necessity of translating the sound and fury of the complaint into colorable claims of antitrust damage. Translation proving impossible, transmogrification was substituted." The Toolco attorneys claimed that TWA's theory on damages "demonstrates a total lack of substance to plaintiff's case." Furthermore, they pointed out that when Special Master Rankin in late 1968 struck from the interim finding of fact the part of TWA's complaint alleging that Toolco was a manufacturer of aircraft, the basis for the antitrust action was destroyed.

In addition, Davis and Hayes produced their own experts, probably at a cost at least as high as that of TWA, to challenge the airline's hypothetical reconstructions. In reply to Rummel's contention that the smaller jet fleet was inadequate, Toolco contended that the very same firm of Coverdale & Colpitts, which now was criticizing Toolco's cutbacks, at the time of the cutbacks in 1959 had been asked for advice. It had endorsed the reductions in the number of aircraft, as did TWA's own management.

On the issue of raising funds through the sale of stock, Toolco attacked Morehouse's report as "20/20 hindsight"—"an academic mathematical exercise unhampered by inconvenient historical facts and tailored to reach a foregone conclusion." As its witness, Toolco put on the stand Gene M. Woodfin, a partner of Loeb, Rhoades & Company. In a rebuttal to Morehouse's suggestion that in 1955 a sale of TWA shares should have been made to raise money for the jets, Woodfin testified "that such an expensive, premature and unnecessary financing would have been a bad business decision."

In reply to the assertion that the "reconstructed" TWA's sixty-three-plane fleet would have been profitable, Toolco put on two expert witnesses. They were Nathan S. Simat and L. John Eichner, of the aviation consulting firm of Simat, Helliesen & Eichner. The two men, who attacked the optimistic projections of Coverdale & Colpitts as unrealistic, charged that the method of linking higher profits to added jet capacity was totally fallacious and completely contrary to the historical realities. They pointed out that in the 1960–63 period the airlines were suffering acutely from over-capacity, which either drastically reduced their earnings or caused losses. Through the use of computers and various methods of statistical analysis, they attacked the conclusions of Coverdale & Colpitts on a wide range of technical issues. On the subject of the alleged higher price for an earlier sale of the used piston aircrafts, Simat and Eichner testified that earlier replacement of the smaller piston aircraft by the larger jets actually increased operating expenses, thus canceling any possible benefit of a better price for the older planes. On Toolco's behalf, a dealer in used airliners declared that the market had been so flooded in the late 1950s that it was impossible to state with certainty what price TWA's used Constellations and Martin 404s would have commanded at any given time.

By the time the damage hearings ended on April 9, 1968, Toolco was confident that its evidence had knocked down each and every one of TWA's claims and that none of them could qualify under Judge Metzner's guideline as being "well-pleaded" allegations. Under his ruling, a claim could only stand if it had a basis in fact. Equally important, Toolco believed that it had established another fundamental point—that TWA had failed to prove that there was any causal relationship between the damage claim and alleged antitrust violations. Though the court considered those violations to be true because of Hughes' default, the Toolco attorneys felt that TWA had been unable to demonstrate the linkage between allegations and damages.

But the special master who had presided over the damage hearings did not agree. He was Herbert Brownell, the former Attorney General of the United States, who had replaced Lee Rankin in 1966. (Rankin had asked to be relieved of his duties so he could accept the appointment as corporation counsel for New York City.) On September 21, 1968, Brownell released a highly detailed 323-page report. It was a devastating setback for Toolco, whose position now was much weaker than before it began its big defense effort.

In fact, according to Brownell's interpretation of the strictures under which the defendants were operating in the damage hearings, Davis and Hayes might as well have saved their breath. To Toolco's dismay, the former Attorney General even reinstated the crucial allegation in TWA's complaint that Rankin had tentatively dropped—that Toolco was a manufacturer of aircraft. That assertion, said Toolco, was not provable. Whatever else Toolco might have done, it certainly had not built airliners, which had been in competition with Boeing, Douglas, and the other planemakers. And if Toolco was not engaged in producing aircraft, as the TWA complaint alleged, how could it have engaged in restraint of trade? This allegation, as Hayes described it, was the arch of TWA's case without which it would collapse. Now, in his report, Brownell put back into the case the fundamental antitrust charge in TWA's complaint. In so doing, he completely rejected Toolco's reliance upon "judicial notice." "Judicial notice" means that the court will take into consideration facts that are derived through the collection of evidence or exist in records of other agencies. It was a concept that was vital to Davis and Hayes since they hoped to persuade the court to take notice of facts in the depositions and in the records of the CAB that refuted TWA's allegations. "Toolco's reliance upon judicial notice of official documents and records is misplaced," declared Brownell. "Although judicial notice may indeed be taken of official reports, such as reports of administrative agencies, the notice extends only to the existence of the report and its contents, and not to the accuracy of facts recited in the report." Brownell explained that "in the absence of a default, the CAB materials might be quite persuasive. However, they do not permit judicial notice to be taken of the assertation that Toolco was never a manufacturer or supplier of aircraft." The effect of this ruling was to deny Toolco the opportunity to go outside the narrow and skillfully drawn confines of Sonnett's complaint and to introduce facts and evidence that would refute TWA's allegations.

Worse still for Toolco, Brownell rejected its contention that despite the default, TWA still had an obligation to prove that the damages were proximately caused by violations of antitrust law. He ruled that because of the default, the causal relationship of alleged offense to damages was presumed to be true. According to Brownell's reasoning, TWA's allegations plus Toolco's default established the validity of the airline's damage claims. "The sufficiency of the complaint has been upheld," he declared, in reference to earlier court rulings, "and the default admitted all well-pleaded allegations of the complaint. Therefore, liability was an issue only to the extent that the defendants could show . . . that allegations in the complaint were not well-pleaded." However, since Toolco could not introduce evidence to prove that the claims were not well-pleaded, it was, in effect, trapped in a situation where it could not use the facts available to refute TWA's charges.

Having disposed of Toolco's defense, Brownell then reckoned up the bill. In arriving at final figures, he scaled down TWA's damage claims and rejected altogether the one that dealt with a higher return on the sale of used piston aircraft. Still, the award was huge. TWA had asked for a total of $104.9 million in damages, or $314.7 million after trebling. After a series of complex calculations, including a $29 million credit for the savings on interest that TWA unintentionally reaped because of Hughes' delays in finalizing the airline's long-term financing, Brownell awarded TWA the largest assessment in the history of United States civil law: $45,870,478.65. Multiplying by the punitive antitrust factor of three raised the sum to $137,611,435.95.

Toolco, vigorously objecting to Brownell's conclusions, presented a number of memos and briefs that pointed out alleged errors and inconsistencies in TWA's claims and in the special master's interpretation of them. But it was all to no avail. On December 23, 1969, just one day before Howard Hughes' sixty-fourth birthday, Judge Metzner confirmed the special master's award down to the last cent. On the last business day of 1969, the ninth anniversary of Howard Hughes' surrender of control of TWA to the lenders, the airline made a motion to the court that a final judgment in the case should be entered against Toolco and Raymond Holliday. In addition to the damage award of $137,611,435.95, TWA asked that the court should also order Toolco to pay for the cost of the suit, including attorneys' fees. That alone could run to $10,000,000 or more.

Howard Hughes faced a staggering bill of nearly $150 million. To raise so much money in a short time would mean selling off assets and running hundreds of millions through the tax mills. The amount was, in fact, so large that it threatened to unravel his entire financial empire. This case was, as Hughes' people called it, "the Big One"—the one that Howard simply could not afford to lose. He knew that, too. The proceeds from the sale of his TWA stock now were invested in Las Vegas. Despite his huge holdings, he was short of what now mattered most—ready cash. In his penthouse atop the Desert Inn, The Man was becoming very worried. He was wondering what he should do.

19.   Struggle for the Empire

Bob, please understand one thing which I do not think you have understood heretofore: You have the ball on the TWA situation. You do not need further approval from me until such time as you are prepared to recommend to me a specific sum of money. About legal representation is up to you.

If I am to hold you responsible for the overall outcome of the litigation, I must give you the complete authority to decide which law firm you want to handle each phase of it.

I repeat, Bob, you have full authority.

Most seriously, and with deep thanks for your recent attention to my personal situation.

Howard

A security guard from the Penthouse brought this memo in a sealed envelope to Bob Maheu in mid-January of 1970. As was his custom, Maheu, after reading the memo, made a copy and then returned the original. The peroration in Hughes' memo was a reference to the breakup of his marriage to Jean Peters, whom he had left behind in Los Angeles when he departed for Boston in 1966. The rest of the memo reflected his deep concern and growing anxiety about the course of the lawsuit. Hughes was frightened at the prospect of losing $150 million or more at one whack. He also was growing increasingly disenchanted with Chester Davis, who until now had not managed to win one single important decision before the courts.

As he returned the original to the penthouse, Maheu knew that the memo was extremely significant. But he hardly sensed then that it would set off a titanic power struggle within the Hughes empire—a power struggle that incidentally caught the imagination of a minor American novelist on the Mediterranean island of Ibiza.

The memo meant a considerable enhancement of the already impressive stature of Bob Maheu within the Hughes empire. Until now, Maheu's role, though powerful and important, had been generally restricted to Hughes' ventures in Las Vegas and the Far West. His title reflected that fact—chief executive of Hughes Nevada Operations. For his services, he was paid $520,000 a year. While princely, the amount also covered the salaries and operating expenses of the firm of Robert Maheu & Associates, which employed at least seven people, including one of his sons, Peter.

Headquartered in ostentatious offices in the Frontier Hotel, directly across the Strip from the Desert Inn, the Maheu firm represented Hughes socially, legally, politically, and economically in Nevada. Hughes had, of course, also built for Maheu at Toolco's expense a $600,000 French colonial mansion. When Maheu protested in a telephone conversation that the price of the then-abuilding house was running too high and offered to pick up part of the bill, Hughes (according to Maheu) demurred. Instead, he stressed how important it was for Maheu to have a beautiful home in which to entertain. "You don't know how much I would like to do it myself," Hughes told him. "You are me to the outside world. The more of this you accomplish, the less pressure there is on me to do anything like that." Even by Las Vegas standards, the mansion was too pretentious. In a dig at Maheu's power, some people called it "Little Caesars Palace"—after the incredibly ornate Strip hotel.

Bob Maheu, balding, well built, and impressive, occupied a very special place within the Hughes hierarchy. Unlike other Hughes executives, Maheu did not work for Toolco. He worked directly for Hughes. It was a privileged role that was bound to evoke some suspicion and jealousy among old-time Toolco executives.

Maheu, who was aware of all that, had been worried ever since the start of the Nevada operation that his own position could be undercut by the old-timers who held several crucial tactical advantages over him. For one thing, they could control the flow of information to Hughes in the penthouse. The nurse-secretaries owed great loyalty to Bill Gay, Hughes' former administrative aide, who originally had recruited them. For another, they controlled much of the money. Toolco, which still administered the bulk of Hughes' fortune, acted as the clearing house through which Hughes made payment in most of his business deals. Toolco's approval of a deal was automatic if Hughes gave the word, but in the absence of his explicit approval, the Toolco people could cut off Maheu from access to large amounts of money.

Maheu's relationship with Hughes rested on a purely personal understanding. When Hughes first moved to Las Vegas, he told Maheu that he intended to live there the rest of his life. According to Maheu, Hughes had told him that the two men would be together—so Maheu remembers the words—"for the rest of their natural lives."

In March 1968, sixteen months after Hughes had arrived in Las Vegas, Maheu, by now acutely aware of the hostility of some of the Toolco old guard, asked for a guarantee to secure his position in the event something happened to his personal employer. Hughes replied with a memo that seemed to promise Maheu that he would be appointed to the supreme position within the empire —that of trustee of his Toolco stock. "Bob, I have your message," Hughes wrote. "I do not feel your apprehension in the least bit unjustified. If I give you my word to find a solution promptly, such as a voting trust for my Hughes Tool Company stock, and if I put the formalities into a state of effectiveness for your scrutiny without any unreasonable delay, will you consider it done as of now, so your mind will not be filled with these thoughts in the near future? I will assume an affirmative answer and proceed accordingly."

Hughes never fulfilled that promise. He did, however, fully support Maheu, and he kept the channel of communication between them continuously open through telephone calls that sometimes numbered as many as twenty or thirty a day. On some days Maheu spent as many as twenty hours on the telephone with Hughes. Despite the closeness of their relationship, Hughes refused to allow Maheu to see him in person. "Let's get together and work this out eyeball to eyeball," Maheu would insist when the two men would have disagreements on business deals, which was relatively frequent. But Hughes would beg off. "I just can't bring myself to do it," he would tell Maheu.

Thus, on that January day in 1970 when Maheu found himself in charge of the TWA litigation, he realized that the tensions between him and the Toolco group were likely to increase. In order to avoid unnecessary conflict, Maheu was eager to observe the niceties of protocol with the Toolco board of directors. Since Toolco and its chief operating officer, Raymond Holliday, were the defendants of record in the lawsuit, Maheu told Hughes that he thought that he should have a resolution of Toolco's board of directors empowering him to handle, and, he hoped, to settle, the TWA litigation. Hughes passed the word to the Toolco directors, who issued to Maheu the necessary authorization to handle all the phases and aspects of the TWA suit, including a settlement.

The authorization arrived none too soon. On April 14, 1970, Judge Metzner, who already had confirmed the damage findings of Special Master Herbert Brownell, handed down a final judgment in favor of TWA. The judgment awarded TWA the full damages plus $7,500,000 in attorneys' fees and $336,705.12 in costs. The total sum: $145,448,141.07, to which was added interest at the rate of 6 per cent per year from the day of judgment. Thus the bill was increasing monthly by more than $700,000—a not inconsiderable amount even for Howard Hughes.

Hughes would most certainly appeal the District Court's judgment. But what were the chances for success? Obviously they were meager. With the sole exception of the 1965 Supreme Court hearing, which had ended in something of a standoff, Hughes at each crucial stage in the litigation had suffered defeats of the most severe possible nature. It did not require any special legal insight to see that for Hughes the opportunities for changing that ruinous pattern were running out. Nor did it require any extraordinary knowledge to realize that now, as the case passed from the District Court to the Court of Appeals, was the time to make a maximum effort to seek a reversal.

In secret, Maheu began to study the situation. Without informing any of the Hughes-employed lawyers, he engaged the services of a law professor who was an expert on drafting appeals, to advise him on strategy for the TWA suit. Maheu also listened to Davis explain his approach to the appeals problem. Present at the session were lawyers from the Donovan, Leisure firm, which had represented Toolco in the damage hearings. Maheu found Davis' approach far too preoccupied with justifying his own conduct in the case. According to Maheu, the Donovan, Leisure lawyers agreed with him that a new and different approach was needed.

For further advice Maheu went to three other law firms. Two were in Washington—former Defense Secretary Clark Clifford's firm of Clifford, Warnke, Glass, McIlwain & Finney; and Welch & Morgan, the "Morgan" being Ed Morgan, a close friend of Maheu who frequently was engaged in matters concerning the Hughes interests. The third was the Beverly Hills firm of Wyman, Bautzer, Finell, Rothman & Kuchel, of which Gregson Bautzer, the lawyer-about-Hollywood, was a partner.

As Maheu recalls it, the advice from the three firms triangulated perfectly. In essence, they told him that a whole new strategy had to be devised for the appeal. That strategy should rest on the assertion that Howard Hughes had been insufficiently represented in the lower court; figuratively, he had not had "his day in court." It is an old and tested formula that appeals to the judicial sense of fair play, which dictates that every man is entitled adequately to defend himself before he is judged. But the problem was that such an approach would involve the repudiation of the conduct of case up until then. That meant that a scapegoat would have to be found. And who would that sacrificial billy be? It could only be Chester Davis. According to some of the advice, the name of Chester Davis should not even appear on Toolco's brief to the Court of Appeals, since the basis of Toolco's argument would be a statement that would go something like this: "Your Honors, this case has been mishandled and Howard Hughes, poor man, has not been properly represented in court; his case has not been adequately presented nor have the fundamental issues of law in the case been properly adjudicated. Therefore, Your Honors, a miscarriage of justice has been allowed to take place. But now we are starting with a clean slate because the lawyer who allowed all these errors to take place has been dismissed. Your Honors, here is the real case." Then would follow an attack on TWA's antitrust charges against Hughes.

Maheu broke the news to Chester Davis by telling him that he would, of course, continue as general counsel of Toolco, but that his name must be dropped from the appellate brief and that the new strategy would be to repudiate his handling of the case. "Tough about that, Chester, but you see how things are," was Maheu's approach. Chester Davis was not cooperative. The legal profession, he once joked, is the second oldest but it has one great advantage over the older one—a lawyer can kick his client out of bed. But Chester Davis did not like being kicked out himself. Not only did he refuse to accept the decision, but he also opened a counterattack against Maheu.

It was a highly ironic turn of events because both Maheu and Davis were outsiders in the Hughes empire. They were relative newcomers who could not claim familiarity with the origins of the Hughes fortune or relate the stories about how they knew-Howard-when—a prerequisite to membership in Toolco's inner circle. Of the two, however, Chester Davis was in a far stronger position to gain acceptance. He was, after all, a lawyer who was no rival for the ultimate executive authority in Toolco. By contrast, Maheu was establishing a power base in Las Vegas that someday could overshadow the Houston hierarchy. After Hughes enhanced Maheu's status by empowering him to handle the TWA litigation, anti-Maheu alliances began to form within the empire. Hence, Davis was able to find supporters in the highest echelon of Toolco executives, most notably in Frank W. (Bill) Gay, the Mormon elder who by remote control from Los Angeles was able to control the flow of information to The Man. At some point, alarming reports began to reach Howard Hughes, remote and isolated in the penthouse. No outsider, so far, is privy to the exact details, but in essence, the reports informed Hughes that Maheu had developed into a disloyal and avaricious employee, who was taking his trusting employer for everything he was worth. Allegedly, Maheu was pocketing part, or all, of the finder's fees, which ran into the tens of thousands of dollars and sometimes even more, for all the hotels, casinos, real estate, and mining claims that Hughes was buying in Las Vegas. He was also supposedly taking kickbacks from suppliers who were selling to Hughes' establishments. By nature and bitter experience, Howard Hughes was extremely suspicious and unforgiving. During talkative periods, he liked to tell his nurse-secretaries about his childhood and early manhood. One of the stories related how Hughes, then a teen-age radio buff, got gypped by a parts dealer. The experience convinced him, he used to say, that people were out to take him.

Hughes never gave Maheu an opportunity to answer those allegations, which still have never been proved. But there is no doubt that Hughes believed them. Nearly two years later, during a telephonic press conference, when he was asked about his reason for firing Maheu, his anger flared. He gave a highly libelous explanation, implying, in effect, that Maheu was a thief.

The charges against Maheu laid the groundwork for what was certainly one of the most bitter power struggles in American business history. The architects of the struggle were Chester Davis and Bill Gay. During the summer and early fall of 1970 they consulted together a number of times, and Gay in turn talked with members of the penthouse staff about the possible ways and means of firing Maheu.

Maheu, meanwhile, sensed growing tension toward him among

the penthouse staff. In retrospect, he now is convinced that fewer of his memos were being passed on to Hughes. He was also increasingly less able to get through by phone to Hughes. The aides would tell him "The Man is asleep" or "He doesn't want to be disturbed."

There was, however, one perfectly valid, and non-conspiratorial reason for strange behavior in the penthouse. Howard Hughes was becoming seriously ill. For nearly four years he had neither stirred from the penthouse, nor glimpsed the outside world. The windows of his three-room suite, which looked out over the Desert Inn swimming pool and lushly green golf course to the glorious panorama of the desert and mountains beyond, remained tightly covered by thick black drapes—a fitting color for a self-created coffin.

In just about every way 1970 was a very bad year for Hughes. The fiction of his marriage to Jean Peters finally fell asunder and he made the painful arrangements for her to divorce him. She had not visited him since he moved into the penthouse, and he had dealt with her only by telephone. He had suffered two catastrophic defeats in the TWA litigation. His hotels and casinos in Las Vegas were losing money. His health—both physical and mental—was deteriorating. His eating habits, historically atrocious, had weakened his system. The richest man in the world was suffering from nutritional anemia. He also suffered from chronic constipation. He sometimes sat for an entire day on the toilet. More and more often he was dropping off into a coma-like sleep that lasted for two and three days. At other times, he would sit for hours crumpled into a chair, his face held in his hands. At one point, his aides counted that he sat without moving or eating for fifty-two hours.

As early as 1969 one small room in the penthouse (it was located directly across the hall from the center room in Hughes' suite) had been set up as a clinic so that blood transfusions could be administered by a Toolco doctor to Hughes, who needed help in combating his anemia. For a short period following a transfusion, Hughes would regain a measure of his old vigor and combative self-confidence. But by September 1970 Hughes aides were so concerned about the condition of The Man that they resorted to an action that could only have been brought about by the gravest possible emergency. They called in an outside doctor. He was a Las Vegas heart specialist named Harold L. Feikes. Dr. Feikes attempted to give Hughes a blood transfusion, but he was in such poor shape that it was nearly impossible to find a vein. After Dr. Feikes went home, he was visited by sheriff deputies, who were curious about the events in the penthouse. Rumors abounded in Las Vegas that The Man was very sick. As a result, there was anxious concern in the city and throughout Nevada about Hughes, by now the largest private employer in the state on whose enterprises rested one-sixth of Nevada's economy. Feikes protested to the deputies that he could not divulge a patient's condition without the patient's consent. But, after they had assured him that the report would be kept strictly confidential in the sheriff's office, the doctor jotted down his diagnosis of Hughes' condition. It made saddening and chilling reading. His weight was about ninety-seven pounds. Since he was 6 foot 4 inches, Hughes must have resembled a living skeleton. Long hair drooped half way down his back. He was suffering from pneumonia. More important, the index of his red blood corpuscles was down to four, a reading which meant that Howard Hughes was "not working"—not enough oxygen was being carried to his brain to enable him to be a functioning, lucid human being.

As Hughes lapsed into illness, Maheu received a message from the penthouse. The Man was not feeling well and he wanted Maheu to carry on as best he could. Aside from all his other concerns, Maheu was most anxious to save Hughes from defeat in the TWA litigation. He was pressing ahead with his plan to remove Chester Davis' name from the appellate brief and to bring in new law firms to handle the case. But by now, Maheu's own position had been so weakened by the innuendo against him and by his lack of access to Hughes that his opponents sensed that the moment to strike had come.

On November 12 Chester Davis sent a tough-worded message to Maheu, telling him to stop interfering in the lawsuit. It was

Chester's responsibility and he would handle it. Maheu replied immediately in equally uncompromising terms. In a Telex he told Davis: "To date you have lost this case at every level with catastrophically adverse financial and other injury to the defendant . . . I deeply resent your presumptuous request that I 'cease interference with counsel in charge and responsible for the case.' There has been no interference on my part other than taking steps to accord other counsel an opportunity to salvage a case which you have tragically lost."

Though Maheu might be leading in the battle of words, Davis was outmaneuvering him in action. On the second morning after that exchange, a very important paper was pulled off the telecopier in the penthouse by one of Hughes' nurse-secretaries. It had been transmitted from the Manhattan law offices of Chester Davis. It was the text of proxy that, if signed by Hughes, would place the power of his wealth and influence behind Maheu's enemies. The proxy would empower three men to vote Hughes' stock in his Nevada holdings and to make any managerial decisions that they deemed essential for the operation's welfare. The three were Chester Davis, Bill Gay, and Calvin Collier, the Toolco secretary-treasurer. The proxy, which had apparently been drafted by Davis, after consultations with Gay, would mean that Hughes, who until now had jealously guarded his proprietorial right to vote his stock, would be transferring his authority to others.

Before the proxy could become effective, Hughes would have to sign it. His condition was so poor at the time that he may not even have known that such a document had been prepared. At about 10:30 on the morning of November 14, the proxy was taken into Hughes' room by Howard Eckersley, the chief nurse-secretary who also was a notary public. Another nurse-secretary, Levar B. Myler, accompanied him. Hughes, who disliked having unnecessary germ-carriers in his presence, asked Eckersley what Myler was doing there. Eckersley, who was to notarize the signature, explained that Myler would be a witness.

It was a poignant scene. Slumped into a chair, wan, sick, and irritable, was Howard Hughes. For more than four decades, his pride and fortune had rested on his unchallenged and untrammeled control of his enterprises. Now, a recluse and physical wreck, he was about to abdicate the right to run a large section of his empire. Eckersley handed him the proxy, but Hughes either could not or would not move to a desk or table where he would have a firm support on which to sign the paper. Instead, he tried to sign it on his lap, using a legal pad as support. But the pad was too flimsy to provide a stable writing base on Hughes' emaciated thighs. He asked Myler to gather up a whole stack of legal pads, which were scattered about the room. They were piled on Hughes' lap. Placing the proxy on the yellow pads, he scrawled across the paper his distinctive signature. Eckersley notarized the proxy.

So what happened next? For the moment, nothing. Hughes entrusted the proxy to Myler, who handled the important document in a most unusual way. He locked it in a safe-deposit box in the Nevada State Bank in Las Vegas—a box to which only he and his wife had access. In theory, at least, Mr. and Mrs. Myler held the keys to the Hughes kingdom.

The next act in the power struggle took place about two weeks later. On Thanksgiving Eve 1970, four years after he arrived clandestinely by private train in Las Vegas, Howard Hughes secretly left the penthouse. At about eight o'clock in the evening, he pulled a sweater over his shirt and put on a fedora. His undetected exodus was ridiculously simple. While access to the penthouse by way of the elevator was carefully guarded, Jack Hooper and his security experts had decided that there no longer was any need to keep a guard outside the door that led from Hughes' quarters to the fire-escape steps. Those steps ran down one end of the Desert Inn to an unobtrusive exit at a dark corner. Instead, Hooper simply had the exterior handle removed from the fire-escape door so that it could not be opened from the outside.

Thus, while the Hooper guards kept their vigilant watch by the elevator, eying the closed-circuit television monitors, Howard Hughes and a small group of his penthouse aides, walked down the fire escape and slipped into several waiting autos. As a decoy, a convoy of black sedans with California license plates that were registered to the Romaine Street communications center, sped away toward the Las Vegas airport, McCarran Field. But Hughes and his aides, who were traveling in station wagons, headed in another direction for Nellis Air Force Base outside Las Vegas. At about that same moment, a Lockheed JetStar, a four-engine corporate plane leased from the Lockheed Aircraft Corporation landed at Nellis and taxied to a position along the flight line. The officer of the day later reported that he saw a stretcher being wrestled, with great difficulty, through the narrow door of the JetStar. Actually, Hughes climbed the steps into the plane; the wrestle involved a filing cabinet. As the JetStar took off, the pilot informed the Nellis tower that Albuquerque was their next destination. The plane refueled there and then headed for Nassau in the Bahamas. Hughes' aides had arranged with the Bahamian officials for special treatment for The Man, who was not forced to subject himself to the gaze of an immigration official. Hughes was whisked the five miles or so in a panel truck to a back entrance of the handsome Britannia Beach Hotel on Paradise Island. A waiting elevator carried him to the ninth floor of the hotel where the northern part of the floor had been readied as the new hideaway.

For several days no outsider even knew that Hughes had left the Desert Inn. The security guards continued to stand watch, the shades in the penthouse still were drawn. Nothing seemed to have changed. Then Hank Greenspun, who once had owned a small fraction of the hotel and continued to remain in close contact with many members of the staff, received a tip from one of them that the Desert Inn's most famous guest had made a precipitate departure. Greenspun telephoned the news to Bob Maheu who was absolutely nonplussed. At once Maheu put through a call to the penthouse. A second-echelon aide curtly informed him that Mr. Hughes no longer was there. Meanwhile, Greenspun, who by now had made a specialty out of publishing exclusive stories about Hughes, was preparing to banner his biggest scoop yet. The next day, December 3, the Las Vegas *Sun* carried a huge headline: HOWARD HUGHES MISSING. On December 4 Hughes received a copy of the paper in the packet that was regularly delivered to him in the Bahamas. He was angered by the headline. According to Levar Myler, who was with Hughes on Paradise Island, Hughes said that Bob Maheu had to be behind this, because Greenspun would not have dared print any such thing without Maheu's encouraging him. Hughes then instructed Myler to release the proxy. By telephone, Myler told his wife in Las Vegas to take the document from their safe-deposit box and hand it over to the Toolco official who would call the next day. By pure accident, Hughes' action meshed well with plans that were already under way at Toolco. At three meetings in November, Toolco's board of directors had discussed the problem of firing Maheu. On December 3, the day of the *Sun*'s disclosures, Toolco's executive committee passed a resolution to sever Robert Maheu from all his connections with the company.

With the groundwork well laid, Chester Davis moved into action. He sent a message to Bob Maheu's friend and lawyer in Washington, Edward Morgan, asking him to come the next day at 2 P.M. to Suite 1901 in the Century Plaza Hotel in Beverly Hills. Also invited was Richard Danner, the managing director of the Frontier in Las Vegas, where Maheu's staff was headquartered.

On December 4, as Morgan and Danner entered Suite 1901, they found the atmosphere distinctly hostile. Their unsmiling hosts were four Toolco men: Bill Gay, Calvin Collier, Raymond Holliday, and Chester Davis. With his characteristic directness, Davis told Morgan that Maheu was fired. To which Morgan replied: "Well, I know the first question Bob Maheu will have is 'why?' So I think you should give me a bill of particulars to take back to him."

Davis said that Mr. Hughes had lost confidence in Maheu and was very disappointed with the business results of the Nevada operation. (In fact, the business was still going poorly; on a turnover of about $500 million, the Nevada operation was earning less than 5 per cent, and among the hotels and casinos, only The Sands was showing an impressive profit.) But Morgan countered by asking if the Maheu situation could not be worked out in an orderly manner.

Chester Davis, however, had used up his patience. "I've delayed the matter long enough," he declared. "I want this done today! We have ordered his salary cut as of now." In a flourish of rhetoric straight out of the Old West, Davis added: "Bob Maheu must either quit by sundown or be fired." As an added unpleasantry, Raymond Holliday buttonholed Danner: "They are going to fire 155 people," Holliday told him. "You are No. 5 on the list and I wish you were higher."

The words of the Century Plaza showdown still ringing in their ears, Morgan and Danner caught a flight to Las Vegas. By late afternoon, they reached the Frontier where they reported what had happened to Bob Maheu and Tom Bell, who was Hughes' personal lawyer in Nevada. But even as Maheu and his allies were pondering the significance of the Century Plaza ultimatums, the Davis-Gay-Collier triumvirate was already following up the warnings with a full-scale attack. The Toolco group telephoned The Sands with an urgent command: Clear all the guests out of the eighteenth floor—Davis and his allies were taking over that top floor. That same evening Davis, Gay, and Collier arrived in Las Vegas and set up a command post atop The Sands. Surrounded by security guards, they began to direct the most bizarre invasion of Las Vegas hotels and casinos in that city's checkered career. At their command was a small army of special agents from Intertel, a private security outfit. The Toolco attack was no spur-of-the-moment affair. It obviously had been planned for some time. The aim of the operation was in one swift swoop to seize control of Hughes properties. Speed and surprise were essential because of the nature of the business that the Toolco group was trying to take over. Literally millions of dollars would be floating around the casinos and some of it, in the course of a gambling evening, would not yet be logged in. In the event of confusion or delays in the Toolco take-over, a casino dealer or cage boss could easily pocket a small or not-so-small fortune—and no one would be the wiser. There was also the problem of the security force in the casinos. Maheu's closest ally was Jack Hooper, the chief of Hughes' security service, which also guarded the casinos. It would be impossible to seize the cash assets in the casinos unless the Hooper guards were first brushed aside.

At about eleven o'clock on the evening of December 4, Maheu, who was still huddled with his friends and supporters in the Frontier, began to receive reports about strange happenings in the casinos. Intertel guards were moving in, and with them came auditors from the firm of Haskins & Sells, who were demanding access to the cages, the enclosed areas in which the cash, vouchers, and chips are kept in casinos. In most instances, the casino managers were refusing to allow the auditors to enter the cages, and Hooper's guards were refusing to yield to the Intertel agents. At The Sands and the Castaways, however, the auditors did manage to get into the cages where they confiscated the chips, the cash, and the "markers" (the IOU's that patrons had signed for gambling credit). They were packing these liquid assets into paper bags for removal to more secure premises. Meanwhile, a real, though bloodless, miniwar war was underway in and around the Hughes properties. In the casinos, agents of the two opposing security forces were engaged in a nervous confrontation, but there were no fights or shootouts. Outside, operatives from one side were shadowing agents from the opposition in hopes for clues about the next move or countermove. Meanwhile, electronics experts on both sides were "sweeping" their respective headquarters for electronic "bugs" placed there by the enemy. Davis sought to use the suspected bugs to get across his message to Bob Maheu. Looking at a point in the ceiling of The Sands that was suspected to house a listening device, Davis cried: "If you are up there, you son of a bitch, you are going to go to jail."

Bob Maheu and his supporters were appalled at the clumsiness of the Davis group. Under Nevada law, it was strictly illegal for any person who did not hold a license from the Gaming Control Board to enter a casino cage. Tom Bell, whose brother Lloyd was the undersheriff of Clark County, in which Las Vegas is located, got in touch with Sheriff Ralph Lamb, who was also concerned about the illegal entry of unlicensed men into the sacrosanct areas of the casino cages. He said that he would have the auditors removed by force if necessary. But he also warned that he might lift the licenses on the Hughes' casinos for allowing such an irregular situation to come into being. That threat had a telling effect on Maheu, who had decided to ignore his discharge by the triumvirate. If he still exercised power for Hughes in Nevada, as he believed he did, The Man would never forgive him for tolerating a situation to develop that at the worst could cost the casinos their operating licenses and at the very least would annoy the Gaming Control Board. Thus, Maheu ordered the immediate expulsion of the auditors from the cages at The Sands and Castaways. He also decided that he would try to slow down the pace of the Toolco takeover in Las Vegas. "I think we owe it to Mr. Hughes to hold things up and not to handle as fast as they are trying to," Maheu told his supporters. In order to block the Davis-Gay-Collier *Blitzkrieg,* Maheu decided to go to court to seek a restraining order. When told by Bell that he would have to post a $10,000 bond for the restraining order, Maheu signed a marker for that amount and Danner fetched the money from the cage at the Frontier.

The next morning (it was Saturday, December 5) Maheu won a temporary restraining order in the Clark County court, which enjoined Davis, Gay, and Collier from seeking to exercise any control over Hughes' property in Nevada. But on Monday, December 7, the Toolco forces struck back by gaining a court order of their own that prohibited Maheu from exercising control over Hughes' properties. In addition, Toolco filed a suit against Maheu, Hooper, and Hooper's security outfit, Elgin Enterprises, charging them with interference in Toolco's right to administer Hughes' Nevada properties.

Another legal battle was in the making. It was especially bitter because of the personal vendetta between Davis and Maheu. As the two opposing sides appeared on December 7 before Clark County Judge Howard Babcock, Davis openly goaded Maheu. "Somebody is going to go to jail over this," Davis would say. During court breaks, he addressed Maheu directly: "Bob, are you going to take the stand? 'Cause if you do, I'll bury you." But as Davis baited Maheu, Hank Greenspun, who had sided 100 per cent with Maheu, took a seat directly behind Chester Davis' chair at the counsel's table. "Go, Chester, go!" Greenspun would stage whisper. Everyone, including Davis, knew exactly where Greenspun wanted the high-powered Manhattan lawyer to go.

While the court battle was beginning, Governor Paul Laxalt sought to use his good offices to mediate the conflict. It was, after all, bad publicity for Nevada. On the evening of December 7 the governor assembled both sides in the Morocco Motel on the Strip. Also present were members of the gaming board. Laxalt, whose law firm was employed by Toolco, sought to persuade Maheu to withdraw his claim to represent Hughes. The governor was prepared to turn over the casino licenses to the new Toolco triumvirate. But Maheu refused to cave in. Even so, at 1:30 A.M. the next morning, the governor's belief in the validity of Davis' cause was enhanced by a telephone call from Hughes himself. For about thirty minutes Hughes spoke with Laxalt and then with Clark County District Attorney George Franklin. He joked about his health, saying it was improved, and expressed his unconditional support for the Davis-Gay-Collier triumvirate. According to Franklin, he also said: "I'll be home shortly. I intended to go on a vacation for fourteen months and will return to Las Vegas and spend the rest of my life there."

Maheu and his supporters, however, remained unconvinced that his firing and the empowerment of the triumvirate represented the rational will of Howard Hughes. It was understandable that Maheu, for reasons of self-interest, would feel that way. In a counterattack to the Toolco suit, he launched a $50 million legal action charging that his verbal lifetime contract with Hughes had been improperly terminated. There were other factors, however, that raised doubts in Maheu's mind as well as in those of many other people about whether Howard Hughes was in any condition to give the orders. The unsettling reasons were:

His health. In the rush to spirit Hughes away from Las Vegas, his climate-control equipment, which had insulated his room in the Desert Inn from outside germs and humidity, had been left behind. His state of health only two months earlier indicated that a trip would be a terrible, perhaps killing, strain. That raised the suspicion that he had been led away unknowingly—or against his will. In fact, Maheu's side later produced a witness in the trial who swore that he had seen a thin man being partly led and partly carried away from the Desert Inn. That witness testified that the man had called out: "Won't someone please call Bob Maheu or Pat Hyland [the chief of Hughes Aircraft]!" But Judge Babcock disregarded that testimony as "not worthy of belief."

The selection of Gay and Davis as Hughes' trustees. There was overwhelming evidence, leaked out by the people who had gotten hold of Hughes' supersecret penthouse memos, that he bore a severe and lasting grudge against Bill Gay. That grudge rested on two counts. The first and less serious was a miscarried business venture. Several years earlier Gay had started a division, known as Hughes Dynamics, which was intended to make "software" (tapes, etc.) for computers. It lost an estimated $9 million before Hughes found out about its failure and shut it down. The second was much more serious; it was an emotional involvement. Hughes had entrusted Gay with the responsibility for preserving his marriage to Jean Peters. When the marriage failed, Hughes blamed Gay. He spelled out his feeling in a memo that was written in response to one by Maheu, in which Maheu had asked whether Hughes would join him in making a substantial wedding present to Bill Gay's daughter, Mary. Maheu had written that Gay's daughter would be upset if she failed to receive a wedding present from Hughes. In reply, Hughes wrote: "Re Bill, apparently you are not aware that the path of friendship in this case has not been a bilateral affair. I thot [sic] that when we came here and I told you not to invite Bill up here and not to allow him to be privy to our activities, you had realized that I no longer trusted him. . . . my bill of particulars against Bill's conduct goes back a long way and cuts very deep. Also, it includes a very substantial amount of money—enough to take care of any needs of his children several times over." After he had finished writing that memo, Hughes, who continued to brood about Gay, sent a second memo. "Bob, I have read your message about Bill again and the more I read it the more angry I get," wrote Hughes. "I certainly cannot get very sympathetic about Mary Gay getting very shook up when Bill's total indifference and laxity to my pleas for help in my domestic area, voiced urgently to him, week by week, throughout the past 7 or 8 years have resulted in a complete, I am afraid irrevocable, loss of my wife.

"I am sorry but I blame Bill completely for this unnecessary debacle. And this is only the beginning. If I compiled here a list of the actions or admissions in which I feel he had failed to perform his duty to me and the company, it would fill several pages. I don't usually discuss this subject, but the whole episode [Mary's wedding] you describe to me seems very insignificant indeed compared to the instances when I feel he has let me down—utterly, totally, completely.

"Regards, H."

Maheu and his supporters also doubted whether Hughes would ever again vest his trust in Davis. Maheu recalled that a few years earlier, when talking by telephone to Hughes about hiring a lawyer for some special work in Nevada, he had run through the names of candidates. According to Maheu, when he came to Chester Davis, Hughes nearly went through the telephone. He says that Hughes shouted: "God damn it, Bob, you must be losing your mind. If we allow this man to come to Las Vegas, in twenty-four hours the whole city will be devastated, and in forty-eight hours the entire state of Nevada will be in chaos."

The choice of the Bahamas. Hughes, who had enjoyed his sojourn in the Bahamas in the late 1950s, had in recent years considered buying the beautiful Britannia Beach Hotel on Paradise Island. He had ordered his aides to prepare a thorough investigative report on the economic and political outlook for the Bahamas. Their findings were put down in a report labeled "The Downhill Racer." The thesis was that the rise of black politicians, combined with the decline of the old British colonial influence in the islands, would lead to an explosive situation. On reading that report, Hughes, who had no love for blacks, was alarmed. He adamantly declared to Maheu and others, so they report, that he would never in a thousand years consider going to the Bahamas.

Fear of flying. Maheu says that Hughes had developed a phobia about flying and had repeatedly said that he, Hughes, would never travel by air again unless he himself were at the controls.

The use of Hughes' name. In the past, Hughes always had been determined that his name should not be used for publicity purposes. But now his name was being employed, in a promotional sense, both for his new airline (it became Hughes Air West) and for the ventures in Las Vegas. Even more important, a few of his closest aides, including Howard Eckersley, became involved in a fraudulent Canadian stock deal that had made use of their association with Hughes. Many people, who had known Hughes, felt that he would never tolerate such happenings for one second—if he were in a condition to do anything about it.

Had Howard Hughes been kidnapped? Was he the victim of a conspiracy within Toolco? Las Vegas was seized with wild speculation and rumors. Sheriff's deputies made two forays to the top floor of the Desert Inn, but having failed to penetrate beyond locked doors into Hughes' now vacant personal premises, they abandoned their efforts and announced that they had found no evidence of foul play.

Even so, a considerable number of people in Las Vegas remained convinced that Hughes had been spirited away against his will. There were also charges, voiced mainly by Tom Bell, Hughes' Nevada lawyer, and Hank Greenspun, that the trip might have endangered Hughes' life. Bob Maheu pledged: "I will not leave a stone unturned until I am thoroughly convinced Mr. Hughes is well and this [action] is his wish." Maheu meant that he would not contest his firing (even though he would still press for compensation) if he were convinced that it reflected the rational will of Howard Hughes.

True to his word, Maheu, with the help of his son Peter, decided to conduct a search for the vanished billionaire. Under the direction of Peter, who had apprenticed in the dark art of investigation as an employee of the Central Intelligence Agency, a nine-man task force, composed mainly of private investigators, was recruited for a sort of "Mission Impossible." According to Bob Maheu, their assignment was to determine the state of Hughes' health and to ascertain, if possible, whether he had gone to the Bahamas voluntarily. But there were rumors, vehemently denied by Maheu, that the task force's real mission was to free Hughes from his "protectors" and bring him back to the mainland.

While the other members of the Maheu task force went to the Bahamas, Peter stayed in Miami where he kept in touch with a network television team in the event his men turned up anything newsworthy. On December 8 the nine men arrived on Paradise Island and rented rooms on the eighth floor of the Britannia, directly beneath Hughes' quarters. The very next day, about noon, there was a firm rap on the door of the suite that the Maheu team was using as a command post. In walked a high-ranking Bahamian police official accompanied by eight armed constables. They placed the eight Maheu men present under arrest. The police were accompanied by James Golden, a former United States Secret Service agent who had been in charge of security for President Richard Nixon. Now Golden was employed by Intertel.

As Golden and the Bahamian police looked about the room, the ninth member of the task force unsuspectingly walked in and was arrested. A search of the rooms turned up, among other things, air and marine charts of the Bahamas and Florida's east coast, including the U. S. Coast Guard's boating guide with routes and destinations in Florida marked in ink; a number of cameras with telescopic lenses; binoculars; a two-way radio; and a dozen clandestine surveillance devices. The nine men were questioned, held for twenty-four hours, and then deported to Miami as "undesirables." Their electronic bugging devices were turned over by the Bahamian authorities to the Miami office of the Department of Justice. A federal grand jury was quickly convened in Miami to determine whether the Maheu investigators and their sponsors had violated United States laws against the exportation of electronic surveillance devices. According to some reports, the grand jury also was asked to consider indictments against several persons for conspiracy to commit a kidnapping.

After three years, no indictments have been handed down against either the Maheus or their agents. But the questioning of Peter Maheu before the grand jury did disclose that the mission had turned up at least one intriguing bit of intelligence, which fanned fresh rumors about Hughes' fate. Some of the agents had managed to slip into the ninth-floor hallway, which ran past Hughes' suites. There, leaning against the hall wall, was a large 6-foot 3-inch-long cardboard box. From it was oozing some sort of liquid.

"Could the box have contained a body on ice?" asked a federal prosecutor.

"It could have been anything," replied Peter Maheu.

20.   Project Octavio

I have noticed in this curious world that anything is possible, and that what seems highly improbable is merely beyond the current reach of one's imagination.

So wrote a little-known American novelist in the preface to his 1969 book *Fake!,* which dealt with the work and woes of Elmyr de Hory, a masterful art forger. The power struggle within the Hughes empire caused Clifford Irving's imagination to make a gigantic reach toward pulling off the literary hoax of the century. That hoax had profound effects on Howard Hughes. It forced him, after years of silence, finally to speak out on his own behalf. It compelled him to flee the pleasant seclusion of the Bahamas, escaping, as it turned out, only a short while before police would have seized him. Perhaps most important, it made him consider the impact that his odd life style was having on the way people felt about him. The Irving hoax, of course, did not affect the outcome of the legal battle one way or the other. But it certainly was the most novel by-product of that conflict.

From his home on the Mediterranean island of Ibiza, a haven for both hippies and artists, Irving followed in the world press the developments in Las Vegas, Hughes' mysterious flight to the Bahamas, and the ensuing court battle in Nevada. For a man who was fascinated by intrigue and forgery, as his interest in De Hory had clearly indicated, the Hughes episode was made to order. Irving was fascinated to read that for the first time some of the secrecy that surrounded the Hughes empire was being stripped away. Most of all, he was struck by the revelation of the handwriting of Howard Hughes, which until now had remained a closely guarded secret.

A sample of Hughes' slanting scrawl was made public in the Las Vegas legal conflict that pitted Bob Maheu against the Toolco triumvirate of Davis, Gay, and Collier. It was inevitable that each side would attempt to influence the court by submitting handwritten memos from the vanished Hughes that supported their totally opposed positions. And there was plenty to contest. On December 24, 1970, which was Hughes' sixty-fifth birthday, Judge Babcock had affirmed the right of Toolco to terminate Maheu's employment. Exactly one week later, Maheu struck back by filing a $50-million damage suit, charging that Toolco's action was a breach of an oral contract with Hughes, who had promised him employment for his entire lifetime.

Most of the Hughes memos that were introduced in the hastily convened court actions were treated as confidential and not placed in the public record. But in the confusion a few documents did find their way into the open evidence. Newsmen seized on them and for the first time ever reproductions of Hughes' handwriting appeared in many newspapers and magazines.

After he saw a small portion of Hughes' handwriting and signature in a *Newsweek* article entitled "The Case of the Invisible Billionaire," Clifford Irving decided to undertake an audacious scheme. He would write a fake autobiography of Howard Hughes, which he would pass off to his publishers as genuine. It was an ingenious plot, which for reasons of Irving's later difficulties was never fully told. After he was caught, he understandably downplayed his plans. Actually, he was quite clever and resourceful. As he devised the plot, the chance for success rested on four conditions:

1. That Irving would be able to copy Hughes' handwriting,

using the *Newsweek* sample as a guide, to lend a special air of authenticity to the project;

2. That Hughes had so stirred up the world's interest that a publisher (namely, McGraw-Hill, with whom Irving already had a $150,000 contract for four other books) would be so eager to print the "authorized" biography that he would not ask too many questions;

3. That Hughes was too sick to deny the legitimacy of the autobiography and that even if he did, his denial would not be credible because of his reputation for eccentricity;

4. That Irving, relying on the fact that Hughes had a compulsion for secrecy, could establish himself as the sole conduit through which the publisher could communicate with Hughes and that all investigators could be kept at bay by warning them that any snooping would cause Hughes to cancel the project.

As an added precaution, Irving would even demand to handle both the signing of the contract with Hughes and the delivery of the checks that would "pay" Hughes for his "autobiography." In a truly inspired touch, Irving decided that the checks should be made out to "H. R. Hughes," enabling Irving's wife, Edith, to cash them under the assumed name of "Helga R. Hughes." ("H. R. Hughes," by the way, was a form of signature that Howard Hughes had never used.) The transactions would be made through Swiss banks where the long-honored code of total confidentiality about customers' accounts would shield the Irvings from prying investigators. If any other publication bought serialization rights for portions of the Hughes autobiography, the contract would strictly forbid them from conducting independent investigations into the authenticity of the autobiography. Irving would also make it plain that any advance publicity or breach of total secrecy would mean only one thing: Howard Hughes would immediately repudiate the book on which the publisher could expect to make hundreds of thousands of dollars, perhaps even millions.

Having devised what seemed like a foolproof system, Irving wrote a letter—a "teaser," he put it later—to Beverly Loo, an old friend who was then McGraw-Hill's subsidiary rights manager.

He told her that he had sent a copy of *Fake!* along with a letter to Howard Hughes, whom Irving's father, a New York cartoonist, had known briefly in the 1940s. Hughes had written back, Irving related, in a cordial manner that indicated that he might not be adverse to Irving's doing a book on him. (Irving had, in fact, forged the "reply.") With a beguiling air of innocence, Irving told Loo, "Some wheels are beginning to turn in my brain." He ended his letter by asking: "Do you know if there is a biography of Hughes, or anything in the works for the near future? Let me know, but please don't mention it to anyone."

Since Irving seemed to be on to a literary scoop of sensational proportions, Beverly Loo naturally encouraged him to press on. Meanwhile, Irving began to prepare two additional letters from Hughes that ended with the billionaire's declaring that he was "not horrified" by Irving's suggestion that he collaborate with Hughes on an autobiography. On February 10, 1971, Irving, who had been formally advised by McGraw-Hill to stop work on a half-finished novel to pursue the Hughes book, arrived in New York from Ibiza for two days of interviews with top-ranking executives at the publishing house. He managed to impress them the first day with the forged letters, but that evening, when he bought a copy of *Life,* in which the full Hughes memo was reproduced, he nearly got sick. He had made the forgeries using only the final snippet and signature from that memo. When Irving studied the handwriting in the entire one-page document, he was appalled at how poor his forgery was. He worked most of that night to write new letters, based on the memo reproduced in *Life.* They were masterful fakes, and he substituted them for the earlier ones. The next day McGraw-Hill, which did not detect the difference between the two sets of letters, empowered Irving to make an offer to Hughes of $500,000 for the autobiography—$100,000 upon the signing of the contract, another $100,000 on the delivery and acceptance of the interviews, which would form the basis of the autobiography, and a final $300,000 on the acceptance of the manuscript plus a preface by Hughes himself. In September 1971, after Hughes supposedly had demanded more, McGraw-Hill increased the total advance to $750,000.

Originally, Irving had intended for the imaginary interviews with Hughes to take place at Paradise Island in the Bahamas. But a romantic triangle complicated Irving's plot. On his February trip to New York from Ibiza, he had stopped over in London to visit Nina van Pallandt, an attractive Danish baroness (by marriage) and folk singer who had been a neighbor on Ibiza. Finding Nina looking pale, Irving promised her a week in the sun. He had intended to take her with him to Paradise Island, but because of the crowds of winter-weary Americans flying to the sun in mid-February, he had been unable to make flight reservations to Nassau, the airport nearest Paradise Island. "I felt the beginning of panic," Irving later wrote. "How could Howard Hughes not be able to arrange air tickets to Nassau? And what would I say to Nina, who expected to spend five days in the sun?"

Irving's solution was to make air reservations to Oaxaca in Mexico, with a night's stop in Mexico City. Hughes, he told the unsuspecting Nina would contact him in their Mexico City hotel. That night Irving confided in Nina the details of the plan. She laughed and thought him quite mad, but acknowledged that the *world* was mad. They flew to Oaxaca where he had spent three months in 1955. Nina wondered if McGraw-Hill would believe his story. Irving said that he had no idea whether they would or wouldn't.

For a couple of good reasons, they believed it. For one, Irving had a reputation of reliability at McGraw-Hill; he had always produced his manuscripts on time, a rare attribute in authors that produces grateful responses from publishers. Also, of course, the McGraw-Hill executives understandably were excited to be participants in what was bound to become a literary coup. And Irving made it very easy for them to become converts to his cause. In addition to the "letters" from Hughes, he produced wonderfully detailed accounts of his interviews with him. He even had an artist friend draw sketches of his first meeting with Howard Hughes, whose thin face was a mask of lines and creases. According to Irving's conspiratorial account, Hughes had used the code name "Octavio." To the few executives privy to the secret of the autobiography, the undertaking became known as "Project Octavio."

After the supposed Mexican meetings on February 13, 1971, Irving pretended that he had talks on March 4 and 5 with Hughes in San Juan, Puerto Rico. On the second day, according to Irving, Hughes signed the letter of agreement, granting McGraw-Hill the right to publish the autobiography. During the next nine months, he said, there were many sessions with Hughes in Nassau, Beverly Hills, Palm Springs, and at three different sites in Florida. Irving assured his publishers that he was making good progress. That he was—but not as he described it. At the start of the project, Irving had engaged as his researcher an old acquaintance and journeyman writer named Richard Suskind. Suskind, who lived near Ibiza on the island of Majorca, traveled to the United States where he pursued the conventional sources of information on Hughes. He and Irving dug for Hughes lore in newspaper morgues in Howard's hometown of Houston; they visited the Northrop Institute of Technology in Inglewood, California, where much material on Hughes' aeronautical achievements is kept; they studied Hughes' career as a film director and producer at the Academy of Motion Picture Arts and Sciences. They talked with people who had known Hughes—or said they had known him.

While Suskind pursued the mundane chore of digging through files and clippings, Clifford Irving—through a combination of his own unprincipled cleverness and incredibly good luck—managed to gain access to the two greatest, and at that time highly secret, sources of information about Hughes in existence outside Toolco's own file. They were so good, in fact, that they gave the Irving manuscript a ring of unmistakable authenticity that not only impressed and delighted the editors but also temporarily persuaded even highly experienced and skeptical newsmen, some of them veterans of decades of Hughes watching, that the "autobiography" was genuine.

Source No. 1—The Dietrich-Phelan manuscript. While engaged

in research in California, Clifford Irving on June 13, 1972, happened to meet an old acquaintance who came to play a crucial, but still not completely explained, role in the creation of the "autobiography." He was Stanley Meyer, a onetime producer of the "Dragnet" television series, whom Irving had known when he was a fledgling writer in California in the early 1960s. Through a series of complicated, and perhaps not entirely accidental, "coincidences," Stanley Meyer was at that time engaged in a project involving another book about Hughes. The source of the Hughes lore for this book was Noah Dietrich, Hughes' former chief lieutenant and self-styled "hatchet man," who would be listed as the author. Dietrich's helper, and the actual writer, was James Phelan, a fine and thorough investigative reporter, who was an experienced observer of Hughes' machinations. Under Phelan's expert questioning, Dietrich filled some hundred recording tapes with the memories of his thirty-two years with Howard Hughes. Augmenting those recollections with his own reporting, Phelan produced a first draft of a book. After he had finished, Phelan himself realized that the text needed to be rewritten. "We lost Howard and there is too much Noah," he told Dietrich. Phelan volunteered to do the new version. But Meyer, who was relaying Phelan's manuscript chapter by chapter to a literary agent in New York, persuaded Dietrich that a new writer should be brought in. Meyer was engaged in a strange, seemingly contradictory game. At the same time, while he was apparently helping with the preparation of the Dietrich-Phelan book for publication, Meyer was also helping to block the project. As he received the Phelan-written chapters, Meyer would personally drop off a copy at the Wilshire Boulevard offices of Greg Bautzer. In turn, Bautzer would send the chapters to Hughes. Since Dietrich, as part of his severance settlement, had signed an undertaking not to write about Hughes, Meyer's action alerted the Hughes forces to be prepared to oppose the publication of the book.

It was, however, in his other role as assisting in the Dietrich project that Meyer drew Irving aside and asked him, as Irving later reported, "How would you like to write Noah Dietrich's autobiography?" Irving could hardly stifle his laughter. He explained that he was already busy writing a book on the world's four richest men, including Howard Hughes. This was the "cover" story that Irving, with McGraw-Hill help, had devised to justify doing research on Hughes without disclosing the true nature of his project. But, busy as he was, Irving agreed to take an overnight look at the manuscript. Irving later described the scene that evening as Suskind and he read the Dietrich-Phelan manuscript:

"Dick, sprawled face down across the bed reading the manuscript, cackled like a mad chicken.

" 'This makes it for us,' Dick said. 'Man, we're home free.' "

In addition to the Dietrich-Phelan manuscript, Irving had received from Meyer several transcripts of Noah's original taped recollections. He also was given a highly confidential Time Inc. memo that Phelan had earlier turned up through his own digging. The document was a ten-page single-spaced memo to James R. Shepley, then the *Time-Life* chief of U.S. and Canadian correspondents who subsequently became president of Time Inc., from Frank McCulloch, who from 1957 to 1960 was *Time*'s Los Angeles bureau chief. McCulloch, a highly persistent reporter, was the last newsman to see Hughes face to face. The memo was the transcript of a long and detailed telephone conversation with Hughes in the late 1950s. Hughes, who feared that a forthcoming *Fortune* piece would handicap his efforts to raise financing for TWA's jet fleet, was imploring McCulloch to intercede with his superiors at Time Inc. to delay the article's publication. The monologue was a masterpiece of Hughes at his best, with passages of superb wheedling, pleading, and begging interspersed with tempting offers of better stories yet to come and subtle threats against his detractors. Clifford immediately recognized the instructive value of that document. As he later wrote: " 'Study this,' I said to Dick, 'and get it stuck in your mind. When the time comes, one of us is not only going to have to know all about Howard Hughes and think like Howard Hughes, but talk like him as well. And this memo is going to be our guiding star.' " Before giving back the papers to Stanley Meyer the next day, Irving had the entire batch Xeroxed. Then, as he returned the documents to Meyer, Irving said that, sorry, he was not interested in doing the rewrite job. He was put off by Dietrich's unsympathetic attitude toward Hughes, he explained.

Source No. 2—Time Inc.'s confidential files. By the spring of 1971, McGraw-Hill had sold the magazine serialization rights of the Irving book to *Life* even before it was written. Irving, who was still looking for authentic material on Hughes, was delighted. The sale opened to him a rich source of Hughes lore. He managed to persuade the editors of *Life* to let him peruse the *Time-Life* file on Hughes by telling them that he was seeking to double-check the truth of some of the stories that Hughes had told to him. A number of these highly confidential files were not kept in the regular editorial reference facility, which was open to all Time Inc. editorial personnel. Irving was given a spare *Life* office, where the secret as well as non-confidential files had been placed.

Swapping information is a recognized practice in journalism, but a generally accepted part of the code is that the newsman given access to another organization's files uses that material only for background and cross-checking purposes. Irving had a different aim: he arrived at the *Life* offices with a large Spanish straw bag in which he had hidden a camera. In the solitude of his office Irving photographed between 350 and 400 pages of *Time-Life* files, which included additional reports by McCulloch of conversations with Hughes as well as extensive behind-the-scene reporting by *Time-Life* correspondents whose digging over the years had given Time Inc. publications an edge over their competitors in writing about the elusive billionaire.

Those two great finds—the Dietrich-Phelan manuscript and the Time Inc. files—provided Irving and Suskind with almost everything they needed. In adapting the Dietrich recollections to their own needs, they performed a brilliant transformation—they made the salty and outspoken Dietrich into the far less quotable and reticent Hughes. That gave their autobiography authenticity and a well-defined central character. Furthermore, the Time Inc. files provided depth and background.

During the summer of 1971 Irving and Suskind returned to Ibiza where they began to compose the transcripts of the Hughes interviews that would form the basis of the autobiography. To produce the tapes, they hit upon an ingenious solution—they simply interviewed each other, taking turns at playing Howard Hughes. When they asked "Hughes" questions that he could not answer, they fabricated the replies. They used their imaginations to make up a series of totally bogus experiences for Hughes, including his friendship with Ernest Hemingway, his discovery of true love with the wife of a diplomat in Central America, and his visit to the late Albert Schweitzer at his mission hospital in Africa. They even added the touch that Hughes became disenchanted with Schweitzer when he found that the great physician-theologian locked his doors at night to prevent the local Africans from pilfering his home. Prudently, they "gave" the tapes to Hughes before anyone else could hear them.

In early September Clifford Irving flew to Manhattan, lugging the Hughes transcript, which ran to more than a thousand pages. Like his art forger friend De Hory, who was better at making copies than in doing original works, Irving proved more skilled at producing fakes than he was at writing his own books. The next morning, as editors from McGraw-Hill and *Life* gathered in his suite at the Elysee Hotel, they were visibly impressed by the tone and detailed richness of the transcripts. To the editors, the quality of the book was the best proof of its authenticity. As *Life*'s managing editor, Ralph Graves, later said: "Even the boring parts were persuasive." As a result, Irving collected a $275,000 check for Hughes from McGraw-Hill, bringing the total advance on the book to $375,000.

At 6 P.M. on Tuesday, December 7, 1971, McGraw-Hill issued a 550-word press release that announced that it was publishing the authorized autobiography of Howard Hughes. The book would go on sale March 27, 1972, and *Life* would run three

10,000-word installments. The release also disclosed some intriguing details about how the book had been done. For the past year, the release said, Hughes and American writer Clifford Irving had spent almost a hundred sessions together in "various motel rooms and parked cars throughout the Western Hemisphere." During those sessions, Irving had interviewed Hughes, and tape-recorded the replies. The release also quoted at length from Hughes' preface to the book, which outlined his reasons for finally lifting the veil of secrecy from his life: "I believe that more lies have been printed and told about me than about any living man —therefore it was my purpose to write a book which would set the record straight and restore the balance. . . . The words in this book—other than some of the questions which provoked them —are my own spoken words. The thoughts, opinions, and recollections, the description of events and personalities, are my own. . . . I have lived a full and, perhaps, what may seem a strange life—even to myself. I refuse to apologize, although I am willing now to explain as best I can. Call this autobiography. Call it memoirs. Call it what you please. It is the story of my life in my own words." Hughes praised his collaborator, Clifford Irving, whom most readers had never heard of. He explained that he had selected Irving "because of his sympathy, discernment, discretion, and, as I learned, his integrity."

In retrospect, there was very little reference in the McGraw-Hill release to Clifford Irving, who had, after all, pulled off one of the greatest coups in literary history. Irving was identified only as the author of several books, including *The Losers* and *The Thirty-eighth Floor*. McGraw-Hill failed to mention Irving's most recent and most successful book, which had a prophetic name. It was *Fake!*

Thus was the hoax launched by an unsuspecting publisher on an unsuspecting public. So far, at least to the best of his knowledge, Irving's four chief conditions, upon which depended the success of his bogus venture, were being met. But Irving clearly had not anticipated the interest that the announcement of the Hughes book would cause. Immediately, it was front-page news across the United States. As a result, a large number of newsmen began to dig furiously for more news and facts than those in the McGraw-Hill release. Many journalists telephoned Hughes' two chief public relations men, who were members of the firm of Carl Byoir & Associates—Dick Hannah, a vice president in Los Angeles, who had handled the Hughes account for twenty years, and Arelo Sederberg in Las Vegas, a former Los Angeles *Times* business writer. Hannah and Sederberg over the years had established reputations for leveling with the press whenever they were able to. The first callers found Hannah and Sederberg very cautious. During the first half hour or so, as one long-distance telephone call after another flashed onto their switchboards, Hannah and Sederberg, who had both been caught by surprise, counseled skepticism about the book. But they were unable to make a categorical dismissal of McGraw-Hill's claims. Within one hour, after checking with Toolco executives, they became more assertive. "The Hughes Tool Company denies the existence of a Hughes autobiography," they told reporters.

That denial made no dent whatsoever on the publishers in New York, so carefully had Irving prepared both McGraw-Hill and *Life* to expect denials from the Hughes Tool Company. Irving had told them that Hughes had explicitly said none of his associates were to know about the book. In a rebuttal to Toolco's denial, McGraw-Hill issued a confident statement: "We have gone to considerable efforts to ascertain that this is indeed the Hughes autobiography. And we believe what we say is correct." Time Inc. expressed its confidence in the project.

They could hardly be blamed for their confidence, for there was a compelling reason for discounting Toolco's denial. That reason rested in the uneasy state of Hughes' relations with the new Democratic administration in Nevada, which had replaced the friendly Republican regime of Governor Paul Laxalt. The incoming governor, a tough young Irishman named Mike O'Callaghan, and the new chairman of the state Gaming Control Board, Bill Hannifin, had been demanding that Hughes should appear in person to explain what he intended to do with his gambling empire in Nevada before the board would consider his request to license Toolco executives to run the establishments during his absence from the state. The governor was impatient with Hughes' refusal to make a personal appearance. "I am told that he is in good health but that it would be traumatic for him to see anyone," said O'Callaghan, who added: "I am getting fed up with the intrigue that surrounds the whole matter. I am tired of shadowboxing."

In November 1971 the Gaming Control Board nonetheless had finally relaxed its demand for Hughes' personal testimony and had agreed to accept a handwritten letter from him that was to be authenticated by his fingerprints from both hands, which were to be impressed on the writing sheet. Thus, shortly after Hughes had managed to fend off demands for his personal appearance in Nevada, the entire situation was disrupted by the McGraw-Hill announcement that not only was he capable of meeting an outsider, but he also was able to travel "throughout the Western Hemisphere." Governor O'Callaghan immediately declared that Hughes had better meet with members of Nevada's Gaming Control Board—or else. Under those circumstances, it was imperative for Toolco to deny the existence of the autobiography—whether it was authentic or not. Furthermore, Hughes himself had still not been heard from. His silence enhanced the credibility of Irving's explanation that The Man had kept the project secret from his aides and Toolco executives.

Exactly one week after the McGraw-Hill announcement, on the evening of December 14, Frank McCulloch, by then the chief of *Time* magazine's large New York bureau, received a long-distance conference call from Dick Hannah and Perry Lieber, another of Hughes' PR men. Saying that Hughes was repudiating the Irving book, they added: "The old man wants to talk with you."

"I'd be delighted," replied McCulloch, who, knowing Hughes' penchant for procrastination, assumed that the conversation, if it took place at all, would certainly not be held for weeks or even months. To McCulloch's surprise, Hannah and Lieber said Hughes would call later that same day. Project Octavio had been kept so secret at Time Inc. that McCulloch only knew about the Irving book from what he had read in the papers. McCulloch tried to stall for time, but the Hughes men insisted that the call had to go through that day. McCulloch informed Jim Shepley and Ralph Graves that Hughes was going to call and deny the authenticity of the book. At that news, a group of McGraw-Hill executives, with Clifford Irving in tow, hurried to the thirty-fourth headquarters floor on the Time & Life Building. A large number of concerned men, including McCulloch, from both corporations gathered in the office of Don Wilson, Time Inc.'s vice-president for corporate and public affairs. As they chatted, Chester Davis' arrival was announced by the reception center on the ground floor. McGraw-Hill officers retired to other offices and Clifford Irving, who feigned to be bored by the whole affair, went to dinner. Davis was angered by the refusal of McGraw-Hill and Time Inc. to accept his explanation that the book was a hoax. He hoped the telephone call would persuade Time Inc. to reject Irving's claims. Holding the phone in a manner so that no one could see which digits he selected, Davis dialed a Miami number and charged the call to his credit card so that no one could get the number from the Time Inc. telephone bill. On his second try, the call went through; Davis handed the phone to McCulloch.

In the 1950s Frank McCulloch had spent hundreds of hours on the phone with Hughes. He immediately recognized the twangy voice as genuine. "How do you want to handle this, Howard?" asked McCulloch, who wanted to make a full transcript of the call.

"Like we always did," replied Hughes. "We'll talk it through, off the record."

"I'd like to tape it," said McCulloch.

"No, not this one," answered Hughes.

"I'll take notes, then," parried McCulloch.

"Okay," agreed Hughes, and the two men launched into a thirty-minute phone conversation in which Hughes categorically denied any involvement whatsoever in the autobiography. As the call was about to end, Davis began to gesticulate in the background. He then gave McCulloch a message that he was authorizing him to put the conversation on the record and instructed him to pass that word on to Hughes. Hughes was not pleased. He told McCulloch to put his lawyer on the phone. No one knows what Hughes said to Davis, but Davis, after putting down the telephone, began gulping whiskey from a water glass. Davis also quickly changed his instructions. The conversation was to remain off the record.

A few minutes later Clifford Irving telephoned McCulloch from a restaurant.

"What did Howard say, Frank?" asked Irving.

"He says that you are a phony and that he never heard of you or your father," replied McCulloch, who by now had become somewhat suspicious of Irving.

"And what do you think?"

"I think you are a phony, too."

Weeks later Irving confessed to McCulloch that when he heard that, he nearly fainted.

After several attempts by the Hughes forces to induce Time Inc. to cooperate in exposing the hoax, the two opposing sides went their separate ways—the Time Inc.–McGraw-Hill group, which remained convinced that the autobiography was genuine, sought more evidence in support of the book's authenticity while the Hughes side moved toward more extreme measures to expose the fraud.

Largely at McCulloch's urging, McGraw-Hill and Time Inc. began an extensive investigation of the "Hughes" handwriting and signature that Irving so skillfully had reproduced. On the holographic evidence rested much of their confidence in the genuineness of the manuscript. Time Inc. correspondents managed to turn up more samples of Hughes' signatures and handwriting, including even the latest letters he had sent to the Nevada Gaming Control Board. McGraw-Hill and *Life* decided to test the links in the holographic chain. On December 17 the highly respected handwriting firm of Osborn Associates was engaged to compare Irving's "Hughes" documents with the samples of signatures that were believed to be genuine. Meanwhile McCulloch, who had been given portions of the Hughes "autobiography" to read, was impressed with the ring of authority. Well he might have been, since some of the selections came from his own files. As an added test of Irving's credibility, McCulloch was given an opportunity to grill him. They met for two hours in a McGraw-Hill conference room. A copy of the manuscript was on the table, and by coincidence it was opened to a page that mentioned McCulloch. The passage dealt with a phone call between Hughes and him. Spotting his name, McCulloch, who was unaware of Irving's session with the *Time-Life* files, read the passage and, impressed with its accuracy, asked Irving how he had gotten it.

"Howard gave it to me," replied Irving. "He taped all your conversations and gave me copies."

McCulloch accepted that explanation. At that stage, McCulloch was dubious about Irving but still felt the book itself was genuine. Meanwhile, Chester Davis continued to bombard Time Inc. and McGraw-Hill with warnings that the book was fraudulent. Irving had a defiant counterproposal: Davis and he should take polygraph ("lie detector") tests to determine which of them was lying. Davis was unreceptive to the challenge, but to Irving's utter dismay, McGraw-Hill and Time Inc. liked the idea that Irving should take a test. The results, which they assumed would be negative, would help refute Davis' charges. It was now December 23. Irving, who was planning to spend Christmas on Ibiza with his wife, Edith, and their two children, warned that he had to catch a flight at 7 P.M. that evening for Madrid. Still, he had no choice but to submit to the test. It was a rushed job, and the results were inconclusive. But Irving emerged sweating and shaking from the session. "Ain't nobody ever going to get me in one of those things again," he cried, rushing off to catch the plane. On December 29 the handwriting experts of Osborn Associates presented the publishers and Irving with a most welcome post-Christmas present: the handwriting on the Irving documents and the specimens, they declared, were all the work of the same man—Howard Hughes.

As the New Year began, it seemed as if Irving might still succeed in pulling off the hoax. But the improbability of the undertaking continued to pique the curiosity of Frank McCulloch and *Life* correspondent William Lambert, a Pulitzer Prize-winning investigative reporter who also had become interested in the case. Drawing on his old reliable connections within the Hughes empire, McCulloch learned that The Man had not left the Britannia Beach Hotel since his arrival in the Bahamas in November 1970. Hence Irving was lying on the important point about where the interviews with Hughes had taken place. Meanwhile Lambert conferred with Intertel, which was investigating the hoax for Hughes, and also started to scout ways and means of prying information from the Swiss banks about the accounts into which, it had been learned, money had been deposited in the name of H. R. Hughes.

In rapid succession, the stitches of Irving's finely balanced plot began to unravel a bit. On January 7 Howard Hughes, who was outraged at the inability of his aides to quash the book, broke his silence of fourteen years. In a two and a half hour telephone interview with seven journalists in Los Angeles, he flatly denied any involvement with the autobiography. "I don't know him," Hughes said of Irving. "I have not heard of him until a matter of a few days ago." Hughes stated that he had not traveled to the places cited in Irving's fanciful itinerary. He also expressed his suspicion that the plot was far too complicated to have been the work of only one man. "To assume that it's all an accident certainly takes a lot of assuming," he said. Hughes took for granted that the man behind the plot was Bob Maheu, who in his words was directing a "devastating, horrifying program of harassment against me."

"Why did you fire Maheu?" asked one of the journalists.

Hughes replied with a libelous accusation that Maheu had been stealing from him.

Would Hughes ever return to the United States?

"If some of these people would get off my back, I could come closer to [returning]. I don't deny one thing," he continued. "I don't want to spend the rest of my life sitting in some courtroom being harassed and interrogated by some disgruntled discharged employee. That I will frankly admit."

Two days later, parts of the Hughes interview were run on nationwide television. They showed, of course, only the journalists who questioned him. In a countermove that same day, Harold McGraw, the president of McGraw-Hill Book Company, and Jim Shepley, the Time Inc. president, went on TV to reiterate their belief in the authenticity of the book. The next day the experts from Osborn Associates buttressed their earlier oral report with an unequivocal written verdict: "The evidence that all of the writing was done by one individual is, in our opinion, irresistible, unanswerable and overwhelming." Pleased by the publicity of Hughes' denial, which was certain to increase sales, McGraw-Hill and *Life* announced that they were advancing the publication dates of the book and magazine series from March to February. In reply to a suit by Davis, who sought to block the publication of the book, McGraw-Hill and Time Inc. executives, editors, and correspondents, on January 18, submitted affidavits that spelled out their belief in the authenticity and authorized nature of the autobiography. Just as Irving had hoped it would, Hughes' reputation for devious schemes had weakened the force of his denial. As McCulloch wrote: "Nor is my belief in the authenticity of the autobiography shaken by the denials, which I have heard from a man I believe to be Howard Hughes. Such actions are perfectly consistent with the Hughes I know."

But the very next day—by now it was January 19—just as the confidence of McGraw-Hill and Time Inc. was at its very apex, the Irving hoax began to come apart.

Break No. 1—"Howard" was "Helga": Thanks to the investigation of two *Time* correspondents, the Swiss Credit Bank revealed to Time Inc. and McGraw-Hill that the "H. R. Hughes" who had deposited and withdrawn $650,000 over the past eight months from their Zürich bank, was a brunette in her mid-thirties. Appalled by that information, McGraw-Hill and Time Inc. filed on January 19 secret complaints in Zürich that enabled the Swiss police to start work on a possible fraud and forgery case. Robert Peloquin, the chief of Intertel, also had learned that a woman was involved. In Zürich he showed pictures of Edith Irving to the teller who had cashed the "H. R. Hughes" checks. "It is very, very close" was the teller's response. That was good enough for the Swiss police to send a man to Ibiza. There, Clifford Irving remained totally unruffled, at least to the outside world. He even insisted that the Zürich affair was a dark plot to cast doubts on the honesty of him and his wife. Edith was even more disarming. She would open the door of their Ibiza home to visiting newsmen with the mischievous comment, "Hi, I'm Helga Hughes." At that time, no one really believed her.

Break No. 2—Discovery of the identity of the alleged contact man between Irving and Hughes: Irving repeatedly had stated that his go-between to Hughes was a man—about six feet tall in his late thirties or early forties—called George Gordon Holmes. McCulloch and a Los Angeles *Times* reporter, John Goldman, deduced that the description fitted one of Hughes' former aides, John Meier. At about 7:30 on the evening of January 27, McCulloch and Goldman decided to test their hunch by paying a visit to the Park Avenue residence of Martin S. Ackerman, a lawyer. By then, Irving had returned to New York City and had engaged Ackerman as his attorney. The two newsmen were shown to an upstairs sitting room by Mrs. Ackerman. After some small talk, she asked: "Well, group, what brings you here?"

"Tell Cliff," said McCulloch, bluffing, "that John and I know it's Meier."

" 'Meier' what?" she parried, apparently hoping to learn the first name.

"Just Meier," replied McCulloch. "Your husband and you and the rest of us are caught with a phony," McCulloch added ominously.

Mrs. Ackerman went downstairs where her husband and Irving had sought refuge in the kitchen when they had learned the identity of their visitors. When she passed on McCulloch's message to them, Irving nearly collapsed. He was confused by the phonetic sameness of Meier (the John whom he did not even know) and Meyer (the Stanley, who had let him read the Dietrich-Phelan manuscript). In a seizure of panic, Irving jumped to the incorrect conclusion that McCulloch and Goldman knew about Stanley Meyer and thus had broken open his plot. It was better to make a statement to the authorities before McCulloch and Goldman published their stories. Hence, Irving and Ackerman rushed to the Manhattan district attorney's office, where Irving made the first installment in what became an unfolding confession of his hoax.

Later that evening McCulloch and Goldman finally did meet an ashen Clifford Irving at the Ackermans'. "I've been to Hogan [Frank Hogan, the Manhattan DA] and told him," Irving said to the two reporters.

"Shut up!" advised his lawyer.

"You shut up!" replied the client. "I'm going to tell these guys. My wife is 'Helga,' but she was doing this at Hughes' direction."

Those revelations literally stopped the presses—*Life*'s, that is. The magazine had already begun to print its February 4 issue, whose cover carried a drawing of Hughes according to Irving's description. Inside was an article by Managing Editor Ralph Graves, who expressed continued, if somewhat hedged, support for the genuine nature of the autobiography. At McCulloch's suggestion that same evening, a new slash was placed across the cover picture. "Clifford Irving says Howard Hughes looks like this— but did he ever see him?" it said. Graves' article, which was amended to cast serious doubt on Irving's project, also broke the devastating news that "Helga Hughes" was Irving's wife.

Break No. 3—Irving's letters to Hughes: In an effort to convince his critics that he had a direct link to the furtive billionaire, Irving wrote two letters to a Florida address he claimed was a pick-up point for his correspondence with Hughes. During late January the letters were studied by United States postal inspectors. They reached a conclusion that until then had occurred to almost no one. The forger was none other than Irving himself.

Break No. 4—The Danish Pastry: By now legal authorities, as well as newsmen, were digging into Irving's story. With remarkable coincidence of timing, the postal inspectors and reporters reached a key source on the very same day: February 2. That source was Nina van Pallandt, the beautiful Danish folk singer who had traveled with Irving to Mexico for his alleged first meeting with Hughes. Postal inspectors traced Nina to an outlying island in the Bahamas called Treasure Cay. What she told their agent completely exploded Irving's story about his Mexican rendezvous with Hughes. The United States Postal Service kept its information secret. But McCulloch and Golden, who had picked up vague reports about Nina, were also trying to track her down. That morning McCulloch had been trying to pry some tips about her whereabouts from a federal agent in New York City. "Read Robert Louis Stevenson," he was advised. Robert Louis Stevenson? What could that mean? It became clear to McCulloch when, in searching through hotel directories, he spotted the listing for a hotel in the Bahamas called Treasure Cay. Nina happened to be walking through the lobby when McCulloch's call to her came through. He read her the Mexican portion of Irving's affidavit, which Irving had submitted to a New York state court in December in an effort to rebut Chester Davis' attacks on the book. When she heard about Irving's mythical meetings with Hughes in Mexico, Nina exclaimed: "I'm flabbergasted." So, too, was Clifford Irving when he learned that day that Nina's sweet lips no longer were sealed.

Break No. 5—The Phelan connection: Like many other experts in Hughesiana, James Phelan had tended to believe that because of the quality of Irving's material, the "autobiography" had to be genuine. Despite the denials of Howard Hughes and Toolco, Phelan felt that the parts he had read or heard about rang true and could only have come from Hughes or a source near to him. Then suddenly one day it struck him who that source was—it was Jim Phelan.

The realization came to Phelan as he was sitting in the pleasant living room of his bungalow in Long Beach, California. He was reading an article in the February 10 issue of the New York *Times* by its San Francisco correspondent, Wallace Turner, an accomplished "Hughes watcher." Turner had been writing a remarkable string of stories that revealed parts of the as-yet-unpublished "autobiography." Suddenly Phelan came to one of Irving's anecdotes in the "autobiography" that concerned an incident in the 1940s when Hughes caught Perry Lieber, then his public relations man at RKO, in a ruse. Hughes, who had reached Lieber by telephone at Hedda Hopper's home, had instructed Lieber to go to a pay booth and wait for a call, but Lieber, wanting to save himself the trouble, had given Hedda's unlisted number to Hughes, pretending it was a phone booth. Hughes, however, recognized the digits as Hedda's private line and scolded Lieber. Turner, who tried that anecdote out on Lieber, quoted him as saying: "You've shaken me. I don't want to lend more credence to that book, but that story was never published. I have never used it in a speech and I cannot remember ever telling it to anyone. How could Irving have learned of it?" In Phelan's manuscript, that's where. It had slipped Lieber's mind, but he had told the story ten years earlier to Phelan, who in turn had told it to Dietrich. Dietrich felt that the story was such a fine example of Hughes' passion for secrecy that he insisted on including it in his book.

On seven previous occasions Phelan had put in telephone calls from California to McGraw-Hill executives, volunteering to read the Hughes "autobiography" for accuracy. They had always refused his help. But now, after he told them of his discovery, they invited him to come to New York. Phelan also called his old friend Frank McCulloch, and as the two men exchanged information and ideas, the anatomy of the hoax plot began to take shape. After Phelan rang off, McCulloch telephoned Clifford Irving at the Hotel Chelsea, in lower Manhattan, where he was registered under his actual family name of Rafski.

"I talked to Stanley Meyer," McCulloch told him, embroidering a bit on his telephone conversation with Phelan. "He gave you a big hand up. And you know what else—Jim Phelan is on a plane to New York and we are going to McGraw-Hill and we are going to place page by page his manuscript alongside yours."

For a moment Clifford Irving did not speak. Slowly, he exhaled, "Wow . . . Wow . . . Wow." Then he said: "God damn, Frank, you got to admit it's a real pisser!"

The rest, so to speak, is history. Phelan's manuscript revealed that his version of the Dietrich memoirs was the chief source of Irving's material. Federal and state grand juries met. The Swiss issued a warrant for Edith Irving's arrest, and the whole plot was exposed for what it was—an elaborate hoax by an exceptionally gifted con man and masterful forger.

As the case was winding up, Frank McCulloch resigned from Time Inc. to start a new education magazine, called *Learning Today,* in Palo Alto, California. In his honor, a big farewell party was given in the Ponte Auditorium in the Time & Life Building. Instead of stumbling through the customary goodbye speech, McCulloch had prepared several doggerel verses, which dealt with his career at *Time.* For the final one, he asked the audience to hum along to the tune of "The Last Time I Saw Paris." Then he declaimed:

> *The last time I saw Howard*
> *My heart was light and gay,*
> *If you'd kept your*
> *Cotton pickin' hands off,*
> *I'd have made a million bucks that way.*

"That song is signed 'Clifford Irving,' " he said. A few minutes later, McCulloch was told that there was an urgent phone call for him in the lobby.

"I did not write that," said the caller. It was Clifford Irving.

"Touché," replied Frank McCulloch.

What undoubtedly had happened was that the private detective, whom Irving had hired to keep tabs on McCulloch, had called Irving and told him about the verse. In that way Irving had the last laugh, at least until a few months later. On June 16, 1972, he was sentenced to two and a half years in prison. Edith served two months in a United States jail, and then went to Switzerland where she began serving a two-year term for fraud and forgery.

Before he went to prison, Irving dashed off his account of the hoax, *What* Really *Happened.* But he was severely handicapped by the legal consideration that he was compelled to abide by the account in his confession. It only partially covered the entire episode. But if he made any changes or additions that conflicted with the confession, he could face new perjury charges. Also, he was permanently enjoined by Hughes Tool Company's suit from quoting any part of his famed Hughes autobiography. Thus it seemed that his best work would go forever unpublished, a cruel blow for any author.

21. The Court of Last Resort

Perhaps the most discomforting effect of the Irving hoax for Howard Hughes was that it ruined his stay in the Bahamas. He had been living quietly and unobtrusively on Paradise Island for more than one year, but the excitement in the U.S. and elsewhere over the autobiography in January and February 1972 awakened black-power politicians in the Bahamas to the fact that they had a very rich and famous white man in their midst. True to the earlier forecast by Hughes' investigators in their report entitled "The Downhill Racer," the militant blacks had been voted into office four years earlier, ousting from power the white business-oriented politicians. The islands were gripped by a sometimes surly and nearly always assertive attitude toward whites. The attitude now focused on Hughes.

Questions were asked in Bahamian parliament about whether Hughes and his aides were obeying the immigration regulations that require residency and work permits for long-term visitors. After a quick investigation showed that Hughes' aides did not possess valid work permits, Bahamian police suddenly appeared on the ninth floor of the Britannia Beach Hotel. They seized two of Hughes' aides and deported them from the islands. Hughes' intelligence operatives in Nassau picked up an alarming tip: the next day the Bahamians were coming back for The Man himself. Was the tip correct? The Hughes security people were unwilling to take the chance. In frantic haste, James Golden, who now was employed by Hughes, not Intertel, arranged for a Miami-based yacht, the converted Coast Guard cutter *Cygnus,* to pick up The Man and his party at a quay near the hotel. During the early morning of February 16, 1972, Hughes was spirited aboard the yacht and, without so much as a nod to the Bahamian authorities, sailed away to Miami. Before dawn the next morning, Hughes was carried by stretcher from the yacht and was driven in a panel truck to the airport. There a chartered Eastern Airlines 727 jetliner was waiting to whisk him to his next hideaway.

The new hideaway turned out to be Managua, Nicaragua, where he and his staff took over all seventeen rooms on the penthouse floor of the pyramid-shaped Intercontinental Hotel. Hughes came at the invitation of the country's President and perennial strong man, Anastasio Somoza Debayle. Hughes, some insiders insist, had always wanted to own a country. The next best solution was to have a friend who did. For decades, the Somoza family has been the dominant political and economic power in that country of 1.7 million. Somoza's reason for issuing the invitation to Hughes was that he wanted more private American investment for the country. Hughes' aides, who knew how to say the right thing, assured him The Man "has definite ideas about investment there." Actually, the only investment Hughes made was a small one in the national airline. In return for buying a one-quarter interest, Hughes induced the Nicaraguans to take off his hands three Convair 880s, which had remained in the Toolco possession after he lost control of TWA in 1960.

After slightly less than a month's stay in Managua, Hughes was ready to move on. But before he left, he made a revolutionary change in his behavior. On the morning of March 13, 1972, a Hughes aide asked the United States ambassador in Managua, Turner Shelton, if he would arrange a personal meeting between Hughes and Somoza. Then Hughes began to have severe second thoughts. During the afternoon, he complained that he had a stomach-ache and could not go through with the meeting. But he did. At about 10:45 that evening, after he already had boarded a chartered Grumman Gulfstream executive jet, General Somoza, accompanied by Ambassador Shelton, entered the plane. For the first time in at least fourteen years, Hughes conversed face to face with someone outside his immediate retinue. As it turned out, he enjoyed the conversation enormously and could hardly stop talking. Ambassador Shelton later reported to newsmen: "He is tall, of course, and thin. He has a short trimmed beard that covers his face, and there is a Vandyke on his chin. His hair is cut short in the old style and it has gray in the back. Sort of salt and pepper. His hand shake was strong. His speech was in normal tones, and his remarks were cordial, friendly, and affable."

The ambassador's description of Howard Hughes provoked only derision in some of Hughes' opponents who once had known him fairly well. "A strong handshake?" remarked one of his enemies in Las Vegas. "He never had a strong shake in his whole life." Others felt that the description of Hughes' physical condition was so favorable that Somoza and Shelton must have met with a Hughes double. Yet in all likelihood they did indeed meet Howard Hughes. His motivation for the meeting was highly personal. Ever since the Irving hoax he had been brooding over what his friends, whom he no longer saw or talked with, would think of him. He was worried about the image he was getting in the world and was distressed by the reports that his hair was half way down his back and that he was ill—though at one time both reports had been correct. Hence, Hughes wanted outside observers with good credentials to witness—and report—the fact that he was not the hippielike creature that press reports made him out to be. During his stay in the Bahamas, Hughes had regained his health and had recovered his ability to pull himself together. His weight, once down to only ninety-seven pounds, now was about 150.

After talking with Somoza and Shelton for about seventy-five minutes, Hughes flew off to a new hideaway—this time Vancouver, Canada. Once again, custom authorities accorded him special treatment. An officer came on board the plane to verify that a man was in the cabin, but he was allowed only to catch a glimpse of one leg of Hughes' pajamas. Then, in the usual secretive manner,

Hughes was spirited off to the Bayshore Inn, a tall tower that commands a sweeping view of Vancouver's magnificent shoreline. Hughes and his aides took over the entire top two floors, a total of twenty-four rooms in all.

Meanwhile, back in the courts of law, the great legal battle over TWA was heading toward its denouement. By now, the case had been going on for nearly eleven years. In slow stages, it was reaching the last act. After the extended damage hearings, Special Master Herbert Brownell took nearly one year to study the mountains of conflicting evidence and render his report, which largely granted TWA's claims. Then, Judge Metzner took nearly nineteen months before he handed down a final judgment on the damages. On April 14, 1970, he entirely accepted Brownell's figures and awarded TWA an amount that even for Howard Hughes was a bit staggering. It was $145,448,141.07.

Both TWA and Toolco appealed Judge Metzner's decision. TWA wanted a bigger damage award (an additional $76 million to $104 million before trebling) and a higher interest rate (up from 6 per cent to 7½ per cent). Since the damage assessment was so large, an increase of 1½ per cent in the interest rate would raise the carrying charge by some $2 million per year. That interest would accumulate either until Toolco exhausted all legal options and had to pay up or won a reversal of the judgment. By contrast, Toolco's pleas to the appellate court were more fundamental. It asked for a reversal of Judge Metzner's ruling on a number of grounds, most notably that the entry of a default judgment, which carried such drastic consequences, was a denial of due process of law for the defendants. Toolco also asserted that there were serious errors in the lower court's reckoning of the damage award, provided that damages could be proved at all, an issue that Hughes' lawyers still contested.

The case was argued before the appellate court on May 7, 1971. It was the third time in eight years that the dispute in one form or the other had found its way to the appellate level. On September 1 the three judges handed down a unanimous decision that once again was a great victory for TWA. The airline lost only on one issue: the judges refused to grant TWA an increase in the damages. But they did approve the airline's request to raise the interest rate to 7½ per cent. Similarly, the appellate ruling fully endorsed the airline's insistence on the personal testimony of Howard Hughes. It was a point that Judge Metzner also had supported. "Clearly the court was entirely correct in concluding that the litigation would continue its desultory course without the appearance on stage at the earliest possible moment of the prince of the drama," wrote Circuit Judge Irving R. Kaufman. Contrary to Toolco's arguments, the appellate judges found that TWA's complaint was sufficient to support the antitrust charges.

Furthermore, on the crucial issue of the significance of the default judgment, the circuit court completely supported the opinion of Judge Metzner that the refusal to proceed with discovery established the liability of the defendants and prevented them from making any further defense. "Toolco cannot elect to default and then defend on the merits," declared the three judges. "It cannot have its cake and eat it too." To allow Toolco to do that, continued the court, "would usher in a new era in the dynamics of litigation if a party would suffer default judgment to be entered against it and then go about its business as if the judgment did not exist and as though . . . the slate was wiped clean and a new day had dawned. To state the proposition is to expose the folly of it." The appellate judges added that even though the case had not come to trial, it seemed likely to them that TWA would have been able to prove its antitrust charges in court.

The appellate ruling could hardly have been more favorable to TWA. It was, as one of the lawyers put it, a judicial imprimatur on TWA's legal reasoning. That encouragement came at an important moment. By now, John Sonnett had died, a victim of brain cancer. The direction of TWA's case had passed to his former chief aide, Dudley Tenney. As Tenney himself was keenly aware, he was not the household word in the legal profession that Sonnett was. Nor was he the accomplished and pugnacious debater. But he was a thoughtful student of the law, a talented writer, a good organizer of the team efforts that are necessary for backing up and briefing

the lead lawyer in a big case. Tenney had directed TWA's efforts
at the appellate level, and the victory thus was an endorsement of
his leadership.

Tenney and the other lawyers for TWA naturally hoped that
the case would end with the appellate decision. TWA was eager
to collect the millions in damages that would help pay for the new
fleet of Lockheed 1011 Tristars. But predictably Toolco decided
to appeal the appellate decision to the United States Supreme
Court. In a defensive countermove, TWA submitted to the Supreme Court a conditional application for the certiorari, to be
granted only if Toolco's petition was successful. TWA hoped that
the Supreme Court would not agree to hear the case, but if it did,
the airline wanted to be able to argue for the higher damage award,
which the circuit court had refused.

As the two sides plotted their strategy for the next—and final
round—Toolco was seized by a sudden emergency. Over its corporate head hung a judgment for more than $145 million, which
was increasing daily at the rate of about $30,000 because of the
new higher interest rate. No matter what happened next in the
case, TWA demanded that Toolco give proof that it had the financial means to raise such a large amount. At the time of the final
damage assessment in 1970, Toolco had been required to post a
$75 million bond in the form of a letter of credit from the Bank
of America. In addition, Toolco had been obliged to maintain its
net worth at no less than three times the sum of the remaining
money due under the judgment. In response to TWA's demands,
Toolco asked that the same bonding arrangement be continued
until the nation's highest judicial council had ruled on the case.
But the Court of Appeals demurred. The appellate judges wanted
Toolco to post the entire amount of the judgment as a bond. At
this time (it was November of 1971), Hughes' Nevada operation
still was losing money, though the losses had been trimmed considerably. Hughes also had suffered heavy outlays for Air West, the
regional airline that he had purchased a short time earlier. Without mortgaging substantial parts of his Las Vegas or Houston
operations, he would have been hard pressed to raise another $75

million or so. Seeking a way out of the dilemma, Chester Davis appealed the circuit court's ruling to Supreme Court Associate Justice Thurgood Marshall. Justice Marshall ruled that Toolco's present bond was sufficient. The episode was a two-fold victory for Toolco: not only did it win the skirmish on the bond issue, but it also had had an opportunity to argue its case informally in advance to a justice of the Supreme Court. That may well have helped to engender interest in the case among the other justices.

Not that extra incitement was needed. Toolco's petition for a writ of certiorari was probably quite enough. It was a remarkable and forceful document, imparting a sense of urgency and indignation seldom seen in legal writings. The petition had a special tone for a very special reason. It was the result of a new legal cast at Toolco. For the effort in the Supreme Court, Chester Davis had decided to recruit a new team. In an attempt to underline the importance of the case, Davis chose two distinguished Washington law firms. They were Clifford, Warnke, Glass, McIlwain & Finney, whose senior partner, former Defense Secretary Clark Clifford, and Thomas Finney, an associate, became directly involved in the case; and the firm of Hogan & Hartson, where E. Barrett Prettyman, Jr. was assigned to assist Toolco's efforts. The Washington lawyers agreed that they needed a lead man, an outsider who had not been connected with the case. He should be someone of such high standing in the legal community that his presence would lift the case from the level of a corporate dispute to the higher plane of a battle of principles involving constitutional precepts.

With that description in mind, Barrett Prettyman placed a long-distance telephone call to Austin, Texas. He was calling Charles Alan Wright, then forty-five, a tall and square-shouldered professor of law at the University of Texas. His authoritative writings had marked him as the successor to his former teacher, Yale's James William Moore, as the nation's leading authority on federal procedure in civil cases. Prettyman told Wright that he represented a client against whom a large judgment was outstanding and asked if he could come down to Austin for a chat. To acquaint Wright with the case, Prettyman sent ahead a copy of the last decision by the Court of Appeals. When Prettyman arrived in Austin a few days later, Wright had already begun to form an opinion about the case. He felt that an injustice had been done to Hughes. It was a persuasion that made him an exceptionally forceful advocate. After a couple of meetings with Chester Davis, Maxwell Cox, and the Washington lawyers, Wright agreed to take the lead position. He began to draft the petition for certiorari.

John Sonnett had been a master at simplifying the complex issues in the case, and Charles Alan Wright displayed the same admirable talent. For the first time in the history of the case, Toolco's position was presented more clearly and concisely than TWA's. Wright's petition cut directly to the point. "What has happened in this case is an outrage," he wrote. "This case has been colored in the popular mind by the image of a man of great wealth so insistent on maintaining his privacy that he flouts the lawful processes of the United States courts. This image bears no resemblance to the reality of what in fact happened."

Wright continued: "The lower courts, mistakenly thinking that their authority had been flouted to protect the privacy of a wealthy man, have responded in a fashion that not only departs alarmingly from the usual course of judicial process but also represents a denial of due process." He explained that Toolco only made the decision not to allow Hughes to testify after it had been denied any other opportunity to test the legal merits of its case. "The decision of the Court of Appeals does tremendous violence to due process of the law, subjecting petitioners to the largest judgment ever awarded as a sanction for steps that, rightly or wrongly, they fully believed they were entitled to take in order to permit an orderly test of their legal position," he wrote.

Then Wright posed to the Supreme Court justices five questions concerning the case. The two most important ones dealt with the implication of default and the issue of antitrust immunity. Should a default be treated as a conclusive admission of liability for the damages alleged in the complaint? Does approval of control by the Civil Aeronautics Board confer immunity from the antitrust laws? If not, what worth is the CAB's protection? asked

Wright. "There is very little point in immunizing against antitrust attack only those acts that are not antitrust violations in the first place," he noted. The Texas law professor posed a sixth question that raised a new issue. He asked the Supreme Court to consider whether a subsidiary (TWA, in this instance) may sue its parent (Toolco) on antitrust charges simply because the parent determined the manner in which the offspring received capital equipment from manufacturers with whom the parent was not a competitor.

In reply, TWA tried to persuade the justices not to hear the case. "Nothing that has happened since this court's dismissal of the certiorari in 1965 . . . has made the case more worthy of consideration by this court," wrote the Cahill, Gordon lawyers. "The questions now advanced by the defendants as a basis for review . . . are merely artfully phrased efforts to extract from the controversy over the defaults and damages some legal issues of general significance. They simply are not there."

With that, Tenney and his team hoped to rebuff Wright's attempt to inject into the case those lofty constitutional issues that would attract the Supreme Court. But why should the justices want to hear the case anyway? It was not as if there had been any disagreement in the lower courts. In each instance they had unanimously ruled against Hughes. And what could the Supreme Court do if it did hear the case? It could, of course, send the case back for trial. But that would raise the same old question that Wright's petition so brilliantly cast in a quite different light. That question was, Would Howard Hughes appear as a witness? On the basis of everything that outsiders knew about Hughes, that answer remained a resounding "No." That would mean that the whole process of default and the determination of damages would begin again, burdening the courts for perhaps another decade.

Or the Supreme Court could scale down the judgment, deeming as excessive the award that now, because of interest, amounted to more than $160 million. But that would require careful research by the justices into the voluminous record of the case. Did the justices, among the busiest of men, want to tie themselves up

for weeks, or even months, on the details of only one case while
scores of other cases, many with more pressing social and legal
implications, waited for their attention? Not very likely. Another
possibility was that the Supreme Court might send the case back
to the Court of Appeals for further review. Still, since the opinions
of the lower courts were so settled, unless the Supreme Court
took time to issue specific new guidelines, it was highly unlikely
that the Court of Appeals would change its mind. There was yet
another option, but it was regarded by most experts as highly unlikely: the Supreme Court could simply toss out the case. Using
its famous phrase "reverse and dismiss," it could command the
Court of Appeals to quash the judgment against Toolco. But that
course of action seemed almost unthinkable. Even the Civil Aeronautics Board, to which Hughes had looked for protection, took
the position that its orders by no means conferred blanket immunity from the antitrust laws on those in control of airlines. Both
in 1965 and again in 1972, when the case was appealed to the
Supreme Court, the board declared that its orders did not immunize Hughes and Toolco from the antitrust violations alleged
in TWA's complaint. Hence the TWA side was hoping that the
Supreme Court would refuse to touch the case a second time.

On February 28, 1972, the Supreme Court dashed TWA's hopes
by announcing it would hear both Toolco's appeal and TWA's
cross appeal during the October term.

Once again, both sides were plunged into the preparations of
writing their briefs and compiling a record of the case for the
Supreme Court. In a joint effort, Toolco and TWA agreed upon
the selections of the record and evidence that should be submitted
to the Court. In all, that material filled fourteen printed volumes.
Then each side started to write its briefs. According to the schedule established by the Court, there would be an opportunity to
submit three rounds of briefs; first, the main brief, arguing the
case; second, a reply brief, answering the arguments of the other
side; and finally, a memorandum that would deal with whatever
loose ends remained before the oral arguments. In an exercise in
one-upmanship, Tenney engaged Professor James William Moore,

Wright's former teacher, as an adviser. The legal conflict thus assumed the additional dimension of a battle of the books, since Moore and Wright were the authors of the two rival treatises on federal practice and procedure.

As spring 1972 began, both sides were girding for the final showdown in a case that now had lasted eleven years. Wright wrote the main Toolco brief on which rode the chances of Howard Hughes finally to win, or irrevocably to lose, a judgment that was some thirty times greater than any award ever granted in an American court. (Some out-of-court settlements in the past had been sizable, but even they never exceeded $25 million or so.) In the brief, Wright stuck to the same dramatic approach as in his petition for certiorari. In a skillful restatement of the history of the case, he made Hughes and Toolco appear no longer as the transgressors who had defied the courts. Wright emphasized that by defaulting, Toolco had only sought a prompt test of the merits of its position.

Then Wright ticked off six main points, which he hoped would persuade the justices to reverse and dismiss the case. In essence, he argued that the District Court had erred in compelling Toolco and Hughes to proceed with the discovery proceedings before TWA had been forced to spell out the charges against them. He attacked the concept that the default established the truth of the legal conclusions in TWA's complaint. Wright stressed that while the default admitted the facts in the complaint, it did not concede the over-all conclusions of guilt; hence Toolco, he maintained, still was free to dispute whether the facts added up to antitrust violations. He argued that Toolco's actions were not violations of the antitrust laws, and even if they were, Toolco was shielded from antitrust prosecution by the blessings of the CAB. And if that were not enough, he contended that the damages were improperly assessed since they were not directly related to specific antitrust violations. He also disputed TWA's right to sue Toolco, since it had been a subsidiary when the alleged offenses took place. Finally he contended that the courts below had erred in allowing TWA to raise its damage claim after the default already had occurred.

"The case is really quite simple," concluded Wright. "The new management of TWA disagrees with some of the decisions Toolco made for TWA during the last six years of Toolco control. Its resort to federal court to litigate these differences of view has been rewarded beyond its fondest dreams—indeed, beyond the prayer for relief—by a huge judgment though it has never shown . . . how Toolco violated the antitrust laws . . . Toolco stands to lose a great deal if the decision below is affirmed, but the federal courts stand to lose even more . . ."

To which, in a 204-page brief, TWA replied, in a word, "Nonsense." In painstaking detail, TWA's brief sought to re-create the circumstances at the time of Toolco's default to show how the refusal to proceed with discovery proceedings was the product of personal whim, not a studied legal tactic. In an effort to counteract the presentation of Toolco's acts in their most favorable possible light by Professor Wright, Dudley Tenney attempted to demonstrate that Hughes and his tool company had been accorded every possible consideration by the courts, and that only after having refused to obey explicit court orders had Toolco been subjected to its due penalty. "Defendants address this Court as if they have been inexplicably punished by the lower courts and with the harshest possible penalties, for offenses purely imaginary, or technically only," Tenney wrote. "This is pure pretense. The default judgment against them . . . was as Judge Kaufman for the Court of Appeals points out 'inevitable' and 'inescapable.' It was not just proper but necessary. The reason for this was neither anger at Hughes nor a desire to punish contumacious conduct by Toolco. It was purely and simply remedial. . . . The courts below have taken only that action necessary to preserve TWA's right to justice, evenly administered. Since its foundation was the defendants' decision to deprive TWA of the opportunity to prove its case on the merits, it could only be interpreted—as it has been interpreted below—as relieving TWA of the necessity for producing such proof.

"The amount of TWA's recovery is that amount which TWA proved itself to have been damaged—in a lengthy evidentiary hearing in which defendants were permitted to produce whatever evidence on damages, including the proximate cause of those damages—they could find. TWA's case was held by the trier of those facts to be overwhelmingly proved, and his decision has been confirmed by the District Court and the Court of Appeals. Far from being an excessively minor offender, Toolco is instead the wealthy debtor that—having profited by more than $450 million on its TWA stock alone—is seeking by intransigence and legal strategems to avoid financial responsibility to others for its acts."

In the wake of the two main briefs followed a flutter of reply briefs and memoranda, but none of them substantially effected the main lines of battle that had been staked out in the two principal documents. However, time was so short and tensions so high that the lawyers were making last-minute changes in their submissions to the Supreme Court, often at incredible sums of money in printing charges. One brief, of which about five hundred were printed, ended up costing $500 per copy, because of the revisions of the already set pages.

Among the lawyers, the general expectation had been that the case would be heard during the last part of the Supreme Court's October term. Instead, the Court scheduled the argument for the first day. On October 10, Dudley Tenney faced Charles Alan Wright before the elevated bench of the justices of the Supreme Court. It was Tenney's first appearance in the Supreme Court; Wright was a veteran of nearly a dozen arguments. At precisely 2:05 in the afternoon, Chief Justice Warren E. Burger indicated that the court was ready to hear the argument in the fourth case of the new term.

Speaking first, Charles Wright began: "I want to go immediately to what seems to me to be the central overriding issue in this case: That I represent a corporation that has been ordered to pay the largest money judgment ever entered under the antitrust laws in a case that has nothing whatsoever to do with the antitrust laws." Added Wright: "Whatever else my client may have done, my client did not violate the antitrust laws, and even with all the benefits that my friends from TWA have by virtue of the default judgment, it is impossible to make a violation of the antitrust laws."

Wright then briefly recounted the history of the establishment of the voting trust and Hughes' loss of control at TWA. He explained that the motivation of the new trustee-appointed management in bringing an antitrust suit was to force Hughes to divest himself of his holdings in TWA.

"How does their motive bear on the issues here?" asked Associate Justice William Rehnquist.

"It bears in this way," replied Wright. "They got what they wanted ultimately: Toolco is out. And it seems to me, Justice Rehnquist, not unjust for us now to hold them strictly to their antitrust claim, not to feel sorry that, well, perhaps TWA simply picked a wrong theory. . . . I think that they followed their course with their eyes wide open, and that now they have to live or die with whether or not the theory they chose was a legally viable one."

Wright continued: "We still have not been told (a) in what respects did Toolco and the other defendants violate the antitrust laws, and (b) what is the immunity that you can get when the CAB approves acquisition under Section 408."

At the mention of the CAB immunity question, Chief Justice Burger broke in: "Of course, I'm sure, Mr. Wright, before we are through that someone is going to suggest that perhaps that should have been thrashed out at an earlier date before a default occurred."

Wright responded that Toolco had elected to default precisely because it wanted to get the CAB issue thrashed out at once. "We thought that we could get that legal issue before the court," said Wright. "We expected to prevail on it very quickly. We have not prevailed quickly. We hope to prevail now, nine years later."

Wright then elaborated on his contentions that TWA had no right to sue Toolco on antitrust. "For a parent to acquire goods for its subsidiary, even for a parent to decide what goods its subsidiary is going to have, or how many it is going to have—we have here no restraint on the competition of the sort to which the anti-trust laws are directed," he said.

Associate Justice Byron White took up Wright's line of reasoning. "And if the parent goes to the trouble of making the subsidiary promise not to get planes from any source except through the parent, you say that is just beside the point, that is just expressing what would happen anyway because it is in control," said Justice White. "Is that the way you look at it?"

Wright: "That is precisely my submission."

"So that a parent, in these circumstances," continued Justice White, "especially if approved by the CAB, can make the subsidiary promise not to buy planes any place else, with no problem under the antitrust laws?"

"Well, since the subsidiary cannot buy the planes in any instance without the consent of its parent, it hardly matters whether you coerce this terrible-sounding promise out of the subsidiary," replied Wright.

Countered Justice White: "You are just assuming that obviously, and maybe that is quite right, that the parent will have control of the board?"

"If I control 78 per cent of the corporation, I'd be surprised if the board of directors voted contrary to my wishes," retorted Wright.

"Well, yes," responded Justice White. "But the board of directors might say, well, we have obligations as directors, too."

Wright: "Yes."

Justice White: "To this corporate entity."

Wright: "Yes, and if we coerce our elected directors who control the board to do something that is wrong, something that is not in the best interest of the corporations, then I say that, of course, corporate mismanagement action will lodge, obviously."

Justice White: "But not an antitrust action?"

Wright: "Not an antitrust action, yes. That is the whole point of our case here."

Next, Wright turned to the issue of the significance of the default. The courts below, he complained, "took the view that by inviting default, as we certainly did, we had admitted the illegality of what we had done and we admitted that our illegal acts caused harm."

At that point Chief Justice Burger interjected: "Well, they treated it as though it was a negligence case, in which the defendants stipulated negligence and just went to trial on damages. Isn't that about right? A close analogy?"

Wright: "I think that that is what they did, and I think that that was giving it too much effect. We waived any right to dispute the facts. But we think that . . . even after a default a party still retains the right to challenge whether what he has done is a legal wrong. A defendant in a criminal case who pleads guilty may still appeal on the ground that the indictment did not state a crime, that the law was unconstitutional."

Justice White, who had been the keenest questioner from the bench in 1965 during the arguments by Sonnett and Davis, seized on the Chief Justice's point. "Well, of course, in the Chief Justice's example, it is stated that negligence was conceded."

"Yes," replied Wright.

"Your point," insisted Justice White, "is here you have never conceded the violation of the antitrust laws."

"That is right," said the lawyer from Texas.

"You have never conceded liability at any point," continued Justice White.

"We have never conceded liability," affirmed Wright.

At that moment, Associate Justice William J. Brennan, Jr., who had written the dissent in the landmark *Panagra* case, whose ruling was obviously in the minds of the justices, sought a further clarification. Brennan said: "You have conceded all the facts but you say they don't add up to antitrust liability."

Wright replied: "That is precisely what we are saying, Justice Brennan. That, as a matter of law, the facts that their complaint alleges and what the damage hearings established do not add up to an antitrust violation." Then Wright said he wanted to reserve his remaining few minutes of time for rebuttal.

Next came Dudley Tenney's turn. Few lawyers who have stood

in the Supreme Court have ever faced a greater challenge. He was the successor to John Sonnett, the brilliant and innovative attorney who had not lost even a single round in the lower courts. Tenney was also in a difficult tactical situation. The petitioner in the Supreme Court can try to wipe away the record in the courts below and emphasize the need for redress. But the respondent, in this instance Tenney, is burdened by his success. For better or worse, he is committed to the record and the lower court decisions in which he has prevailed. After a short introduction, Tenney launched into a recital against what John Sonnett would have called the blindness of those who refuse to see their own misdeeds. Tenney said: "As I hear them [Toolco] today, they are still denying matters alleged in the complaint. They are still arguing their factual view of these matters that were at issue. They are denying that they tried to establish themselves as the dominant factor in the supply of aircraft to the airlines, that they seized the TWA market, imposed boycotts, and prevented TWA from acquiring sufficient aircraft and arranging financing so that they could do this, so that the diversions of aircraft from TWA to its competitors had, as a very specific purpose, the establishment of defendants as a factor, a competitive factor, in the business of supplying aircraft to airlines."

That was the bare outline of TWA's case, and Tenney had put it well. But, in those opening moments, he hardly could have imagined what awaited him. Something about the case—its size, its scope, the involvement of the strange and intriguing Howard Hughes—had fired the interest of the Supreme Court justices. In the next twenty-five minutes, Dudley Tenney was subjected to one of the most severe grillings ever visited upon an attorney before the nation's highest Court. In that time he was questioned and interrupted by the Bench no less than fifty-six times—or roughly once every half minute.

No sooner had Tenney begun to discuss the contention by Wright that a subsidiary has no right under antitrust doctrine to sue its parent than Justice White broke in. "Mr. Tenney," he said, "if this Court should hold that a subsidiary does not have any post-acquisition antitrust claim available to it under the antitrust law against the parents, would you think that was something these petitioners could not raise because of the default?" Or, in layman's language, did a subsidiary, even after it had been taken over by the parent, still retain an independent right under antitrust to bring its corporate parents into court?

"Well," replied Tenney, "the defendants have presented this as a point. They have developed a new doctrine—it is new to me—under the antitrust laws. They have constructed a doctrine applicable to what they call a parent-subsidiary relationship that puts everything in that relationship outside of the scope of the antitrust laws. They say that as long as the parent controls the subsidiary . . ."

"The burden is not on them," broke in Justice White. "The burden is on you. You allege the antitrust violation."

"Right," added Justice Marshall.

"The burden is on me at a trial to establish the violations, Your Honor," replied Tenney. "There was no trial."

Ignoring that point, Justice White continued to engage Tenney. "And it stands where the plaintiff is the subsidiary against the parent. That is also your burden."

"As a legal proposition, it is my burden to establish that this is implicit in all of the antitrust decisions of this court," said Tenney. "However . . . I do not believe that there is such a thing as immunity for a parent's conduct with respect to a subsidiary, and I suggest that there should not be. . . ."

Now Justice Rehnquist took up the questioning. "Isn't it at least arguable that the parent-subsidiary immunity, as you refer to it, is not simply an arbitrary carving out of the petitioner, but is related in some way to the type of harm which Congress sought to protect potential competitors from. [That is,] how far it did intend to extend the protection of the antitrust laws insofar as a person seeking treble damages is concerned?"

"I do not think so, Your Honor," responded Tenney. "I have trouble believing that the public stockholders of a subsidiary that is not a wholly owned subsidiary . . . have been intended by Congress to be deprived of the rights that they otherwise would normally have."

Justice White then interjected another question. He wanted to determine how Tenney regarded the assertion by Wright, who had argued that the default did not admit Toolco's guilt under the antitrust laws. "But you don't contend, then, that the default admitted to any violation of the antitrust law?" asked White.

"The default?" asked a puzzled Tenney, wondering what was the import of the question.

"I mean as such," responded Justice White.

"As such here, Your Honor, it did not," conceded Tenney. "It admitted all of the conduct, it admitted the purposes, the antitrust . . ."

At that moment, Justice Brennan broke in to add: "Admits the historical facts."

"The historical facts and the anticompetitive purposes, the intent to monopolize . . ." continued Tenney.

"Those are historical facts. You are saying that those are facts from the past," interjected Justice Brennan.

"Those are facts," affirmed Tenney. "They are admitted. It also happens to be the case, of course, that there is a concession here, that the complaint states a cause of the action under the antitrust law."

"Yes," replied Justice White with an air of finality, "but the default does not concede a violation of the antitrust laws."

Tenney had not won on that exchange. Then he switched to a discussion of the related issue of liability. He argued that while Toolco did not admit to having damaged TWA, its default established the facts, which added up to the damages. "Liability has not been admitted by that," said Tenney, "but it stems from this."

"It flows," interjected Justice Brennan.

"It flows," confirmed Dudley Tenney.

Associate Justice Potter Stewart, however, remained troubled about whether too much effect had been given to that default, which the courts below had interpreted to mean that Toolco could not defend itself against the charges in TWA's complaint. Justice Stewart asked Tenney to consider what would be the proper disposition of the case if the justices decided to accept Toolco's argument that the default judgment had been a too drastic sanction and had been applied too severely by the courts below.

Tenney replied: "If this Court accepted the argument of the petitioners that they can refuse discovery of issues of this kind, refuse to proceed to a trial and still be entitled at a damage hearing to contest restraints of trade, contest anticompetitive conduct, contest all those things. If Your Honors accepted that, I think that you could remand this case. I think you might do some really ultimate damage to the entire system of procedure that civil practice has been based on for thirty years and perhaps even more."

Tenney's time was soon up. At the request of the Chief Justice, Tenney touched briefly on Toolco's claim that its acts enjoyed CAB-conferred immunity from antitrust prosecution. Tenney pointed out that the CAB as well the Justice Department disagreed completely with Toolco's position. He emphasized that in the present proceedings the Justice Department had submitted a brief for the Civil Aeronautics Board as amicus curiae in which the government lawyers pointed out the limited scope of the CAB's power to exclude persons and corporations from the force of the antitrust laws. As Tenney explained to the justices, the government brief specifically stated that the board's order authorizing Toolco's control of TWA and permitting certain intercompany transactions did not immunize the conduct alleged in the TWA complaint and admitted by the default. That, of course, was precisely the point that John Sonnett had made eleven years earlier when he first started the case. TWA, he used to say, was not suing Howard Hughes for what he had been permitted to do by the CAB. It was suing him for things that never had been submitted to the CAB for clearance, such as the diversion of aircraft, the intent to monopolize, and all the other things that no amount of CAB sanctification could shield from the antitrust laws of the land.

After Tenney had ended his argument, Charles Alan Wright, who had saved a few of his allotted thirty minutes for rebuttal, began to speak. As he had listened to Tenney's argument, Wright had quickly sensed that his opponent's concessions about the effect of the default provided him with an opening. For months Professor Wright had been reading TWA briefs in which first Sonnett and then Tenney had insisted that the default was tantamount to an admission of guilt and precluded Toolco from any further defense in the case. Now, under the questioning of the Supreme Court justices, Tenney had conceded that the default had established only the truth of the facts alleged in the complaint but that the defendants still retained the right to contest whether those facts added up to antitrust violations.

Said Wright to the Court: "It seems to me that, in an important respect, Mr. Tenney has, by what he has said today, confessed error. If I have heard him correctly, he has responded more than once . . . to questions from the Bench, that we are still free at this stage, after default, to challenge whether or not the acts pleaded in the complaint amounted, as a matter of law, to a violation of the antitrust laws."

The Texas professor then ticked off the devastating effects that the ruling of the Court of Appeals had had on Toolco's cause. As the appellate court saw it, the default established both Toolco's guilt and liability without TWA so much as having to demonstrate a causal relationship between the alleged violations and the alleged damages. "So that it seems to me," Wright continued, "the case was decided by both courts below on a theory that Mr. Tenney, I think quite properly, has now conceded to be unsound and contrary to the decisions of this court."

"Mr. Wright," asked Justice Stewart, "assuming we agree with that, should we do anything further than just to hold that and remand the case to the Court of Appeals?"

"It seems to me, Justice Stewart," responded the Toolco advocate, "that is a question of the judicial administration, and it would really be presumptuous of me to advise this Court." Wright did not want to tell the justices how to conduct their business.

But Justice White insisted: "Well, you do advise us through your brief, by arguing all those substantive issues."

Relenting, Wright replied: "Yes, and I would hope that I gave you such good advice that you might decide you would bring the case to end right now by simply saying, 'reverse and dismiss,' but . . ."

"Well, couldn't you?" insisted Justice Stewart.

"I would agree," Wright responded, "quite seriously, that ordinarily it is a tremendous advantage to this Court to have the considered opinion of the Court of Appeals on a difficult question, and that there would be valuable guidance, in this case, to have the Court of Appeals enlightened as to the proper standard, and then to review the thousands of pages in the record, the hundreds of pages in the complaint, and then say that these are violations or not."

"If we decide that there was not, and we send this back, what do we send it back to?" asked Justice Stewart.

As Wright paused for a moment, Justice White explained: "If we decide as my brother Stewart suggested, what is left to be decided below?"

"Well, then the question would be the substantive question," answered Wright. "What is the effect of immunity? Are these pleaded facts [by TWA] enough to make out liability?"

After a short further exchange with Justice White in which he and the justice agreed that the issue of CAB immunity was indeed ripe for decision, Wright ended his rebuttal.

At 3:06, exactly one minute over the allocated one hour, the Chief Justice signaled the end of the hearing. "The case is submitted," he said.

Dudley Tenney left the columned grandeur of the Supreme Court Building with the distinct premonition that something unfavorable was going to happen—perhaps that the Court would remand the case to the Court of Appeals for further investigation. But Charles Alan Wright departed a greatly encouraged man. In keeping with his custom after Supreme Court appearances, he headed toward the men's bar in the Madison hotel for a bit of succor. He had the heart-warming impression that seldom, if ever, in a Supreme Court confrontation had he seen his opponent subjected to so many hostile questions from the Bench while only relatively favorable or at least neutral ones had been directed to him. It was an occasion to raise a glass to.

Now both sides could only wait for the Supreme Court's decision. Wright's performance had given the Hughes side a reason for confidence. Still, the outcome remained unpredictable. In a law case of this magnitude, no one could be certain how much the argument in Court actually would influence the justices in their final decision, since they also would consider so many documents and additional facts that had hardly even been alluded to in the oral presentations. The hard facts were that the decisions taken by prestigious judges in the lower courts were so uniformly adverse to Hughes that it would have been an exercise in wishful thinking for Toolco to have reckoned on a reversal. Hence, Toolco had to plan for the worst possible eventuality. That would be that the Supreme Court would simply confirm the judgment below. In that event, Hughes would be required to pay to TWA a sum that with interest amounted now to nearly $170 million. For all his wealth, Howard Hughes did not have that much cash. One insider confided that Hughes was back in the same position in which he had been trapped in 1960 when he was forced to give up control of TWA—plenty of assets but too little cash.

Hence Hughes and his advisers decided that they had no real option except to collect the money for the judgment. But where to find it? Hughes turned to the bedrock of his fortune, the Hughes Tool Company. It remained the last great American industrial property still in the hands of only one man, and its wealth had been the basis of Hughes' power and independence. Now to save himself from financial ruin in the event of an adverse decision, Hughes pressed ahead with plans to sell Toolco to the public.

By now Hughes had returned to Managua. He had stayed in Vancouver a bare six months, leaving before Canadian authorities could raise a tax claim against him. In August 1972 he once more had taken up residence atop the Intercontinental Hotel in the Nicaraguan capital. At 5:40 on the morning of September 25, two representatives from the Wall Street brokerage house of Mer-

rill Lynch, Pierce, Fenner & Smith, were ushered into his presence
in the hotel. They were Julius H. (Dooley) Sedlmayr, a group
vice president, and J. Courtney Ivey, the firm's outside counsel.
In their presence Hughes signed the documents that authorized
Merrill Lynch to make the preparations for the sale.

It was a very odd transaction. Hughes was not parting with all
the various divisions and enterprises that collectively have become
known as the Hughes Tool Company. Instead, he was selling only
the oil-tool division and two foreign subsidiaries of Toolco. He
was retaining the rest—the Hughes Nevada Operations, the huge
real estate holdings, the aviation interests, including Air West, the
helicopter division. The mechanics of the sale, which featured a
couple of fast name changes, worked like this: the Hughes Tool
Company, which the world had come to know, if not always to
love, became a new entity called the Summa Corporation, possibly
from the Latin word meaning "highest." Then Summa spun off its
oil-tool division and the related foreign subsidiaries to a separate
new company. That creation—would you believe it?—got the name
Hughes Tool Company. Incorporated on September 14, 1972, in
Delaware, it was a new corporate being. To bring about the financial separation of the oil-tool division from the rest of the empire,
the new Hughes Tool Company handed over its stock, five million
shares in all, to Summa, which in turn, passed them along to Mer-
ril Lynch for sale to the public.

Why did Hughes sell the oil-tool division? And why, above all,
did he part with that famed name "the Hughes Tool Company"?
He had good reasons. The oil-tool division no longer was the dominant force in the drilling business. Competitors had edged into
what once was a Toolco preserve, and during the past decade the
oil-tool division had declined sharply in size and profitability. In
1971, the last full year reported for the stock prospectus, the oil-
tool division had had sales of only $82 million and profits of $4.3
million. More important, the patents on some of the oil division's
most commercially valuable drill bits soon were to expire. From
a purely economic standpoint, it was the right time to get out.

From a personal standpoint, Howard Hughes probably was

happy finally to break his association with the bit-making part of his empire. Though for years he relied on the oil-tool division's earnings, Hughes harbored a personal antipathy toward the enterprise. It was not his, not something he had built or created. It belonged to his father. Hughes had often seemed jealous of Toolco's great profitability in those years when it still was gushing forth $20 million to $30 million dollars annually in earnings. So now he would sever his last link to his family heritage and to Houston.

For Howard Hughes, the net proceeds from the sale were to be $130 million. Combined with his $75 million Bank of America letter of credit, he would have more than enough to meet the TWA judgment.

One week after the case was argued in the Supreme Court, Howard Hughes filed with the Securities and Exchange Commission the prospectus for the sale of the oil-tool division. When the stock actually went on sale a short time later, it was offered at a per-share price of $30. He might well have insisted on a great deal more. The public enthusiastically snapped up the shares. From its first day in the over-the-counter trading, the Hughes Tool Company became one of the most active issues, and its per-share price rose 70 per cent in three months.

On the evening of December 23, 1972, only hours before his sixty-seventh birthday, Howard Hughes was alone in his suite atop the Intercontinental. Suddenly the entire building began to heave and shake. Managua, which twice before had been leveled by earthquakes, was experiencing a third disaster. Though far more sturdy than most structures in the Nicaraguan capital, the hotel building cracked and the ninth floor—Hughes'—assumed a dizzying tilt. As Howard Eckersley, Hughes' chief personal aide, remembers: "I dressed and ran to find Mr. Hughes. He was so cool and insisted on staying until he was absolutely sure it was necessary to leave."

Even in an earthquake, Hughes remained quintessentially himself—reluctant to make any decision until the last possible moment. But even for Hughes, the master of patience and procrastination, the world was coming apart. The city's power failed, plunging Managua into darkness. The city was reduced to rubble and plagued by panic and fires. Accompanied by Eckersley and several other aides, Hughes made his way down the hotel's emergency stairs. He was put in a rented Mercedes sedan. Howard Hughes spent his sixty-seventh birthday parked in a field near the hotel, as Managua, leveled by the earthquake and a prey to looters, smoldered in ruins.

As soon as it seemed safe, Hughes was driven to the home of former President Somoza. To the Nicaraguan strong man, Hughes imparted his urgent desire to get out. "He was fairly disturbed," Somoza later said. "He is used to living in places where they do not have earthquakes." Somoza learned that the runways at the airport were not shattered by the earthquake. Without offering any financial aid for the quake victims, Hughes boarded one of his planes—a Learjet. Hughes' aircraft was seen waiting on the apron of the runway until other planes had successfully taken off. Ever cautious, Hughes was waiting, so the speculation went, to see if the others could safely take off before he allowed his own plane to roll. But roll it finally did. The next day his plane—he had transferred to a JetStar in Miami—landed at Gatwick, England, an airport near London that handles charter flights. Hughes has no valid passport, because he will not allow a photograph to be taken. Nonetheless, he was accorded special treatment in London. His plane taxied to a less busy part of the tarmac and immigration officials came out to the JetStar. They never saw Howard Hughes. Within a few minutes, he settled himself into a curtained Rolls-Royce, which drove him to his next hermitage, the Inn on the Park, a modern and elegant hotel just off Hyde Park. He and his aides took over a wing on the Inn's ninth floor. The windows of Hughes' room were masked over with black tape. The arrangements for his arrival were handled by the Rothschilds, an association that spurred rumors that Hughes had come to invest some of his fortune in Britain.

Then, on January 10, 1973, the Supreme Court of the United States handed down its opinion in *TWA v. Hughes*.

When the news arrived, Howard Hughes was in the Inn on the Park. "Howard did not stomp his foot and say, 'Hell, it's about time,'" said one of his personal aides. "But he was happy. He was absolutely ecstatic."

By a commanding margin of six to two, the Court decided that Hughes and his corporate alter ego, Toolco, were not guilty of antitrust violations as charged by TWA. Quite the contrary, the majority, in an opinion written by Associate Justice William O. Douglas, held that Hughes' acts at TWA all along had been immunized from the force of antitrust laws by the orders of the CAB, which had authorized him to assume control of the airline.

It was an astounding ruling. No one more clearly reflected the shock than Chief Justice Burger. In a dissent from the majority opinion, Burger, who was joined by Associate Justice Harry A. Blackmun, expressed a sense of amazement combined with consternation that the courts had allowed the case to continue so long when the basic issue could have been decided years ago. "To describe this litigation as the twentieth-century sequel to *Bleak House* is only a slight exaggeration," he wrote. "Dickens himself could scarcely have imagined that 56,000 hours of lawyering at a cost of $7,500,000 would represent the visible expenses of only one party to a modern intercorporate conflict, to say nothing of the time of corporate and management personnel diverted from their daily tasks. Indeed, today's ending is quite a surprise—as great a surprise for some of us as it must be for the parties. I suggest it will even surprise the victors, for in the oral argument to this court, only a few fleeting comments were devoted to the point that now becomes the dispositive issue in the case."

Bleak House, a discursive social commentary by Charles Dickens, contains the following passage, which the Chief Justice may have had in mind. "The one great principle of British law is to make business for itself," wrote Dickens. "There is no other principle distinctly, certainly, and consistently maintained through its narrow turnings. Viewed by this light, it becomes a coherent scheme, and not the monstrous maze that the laity are apt to think it. Let them but once clearly perceive that its grand principle is to

make business for itself at their expense, and surely they will cease
to grumble."

The Chief Justice clearly was displeased that the federal courts
were responsible for prolonging the conflict. "The history of this
case is so remarkable—indeed unique in the annals of modern federal jurisprudence—so far as I am aware—that I must preface my
dissent on the merits with a recital of the course of this litigation
over nearly a dozen years," he stated. "This protracted litigation,
conducted at enormous cost, now comes to an abrupt end on an
issue directly presented to this court nearly eight years ago but not
decided. As this strange history will demonstrate, resolution of the
issue when it was first before the court [in 1965] as now decided,
would have terminated this litigation without having parties invest
untold efforts and vast expenses in a now wholly irrelevant contest over the proper measure of damages."

The Chief Justice then recounted the twelve-year history of the
litigation. On the merits, he dissented chiefly for two reasons, notably, that the majority ruling too seriously reduced the scope of the
antitrust laws and that it extended the responsibilities of the CAB
into areas where that agency had neither the competence nor the
manpower to cope effectively. Still, the most poignant point in the
Chief Justice's dissent was the note of dismay at the lost effort,
the wasted money and needlessly expended energy that had been
consumed by the case, which, as the majority now held, should
have been tossed out of any federal lower court the very first day.

That was true, for the majority opinion had adopted the exact
same line of reasoning that Raymond Cook and Chester Davis
had argued from the day the TWA complaint was filed. An added
irony was that Justice Douglas, the author of the majority opinion,
also had written the majority opinion in the *Panagra* case in 1963.
That decision, the Hughes people had believed at the time, would
quickly rescue their case. Now, ten years later, Douglas and five
other like-minded justices were doing just that. They overlooked
all the other issues that were argued before them to seize on the
oldest question—that of immunity.

Justice Douglas declared that the *Panagra* ruling and the language on the Federal Aviation Act indicated that the courts below had erred in rejecting Toolco's defense that its acts were covered with antitrust immunity. The nature of the CAB's supervision of Toolco's relations with TWA, including the special monitoring of all aircraft transactions, showed that the agency's special powers to grant immunity extended to precisely the charges on which TWA had taken Hughes to court. "It is, therefore, difficult to understand how the Court of Appeals could conclude," wrote Douglas, "that the acts of Toolco in controlling, allegedly to the injury of TWA, the timing, the financing and the flow of new equipment to TWA was unrelated to any function of the Board under the Act. Clearly, such considerations were in the mainstream of the Board's paragraph 408 [granting of control] responsibilities to insure that only those acquisitions of control that are in the public interest are approved." The wording and the reasoning of the Douglas opinion suggested to some experts that he had gone back and read the Toolco briefs submitted to the Court in the 1965 hearing.

In any event, the compelling reason for the long self-imprisonment of Howard Hughes now dissolved. He no longer had to fear the consequences of TWA's lawsuit. He now was free, his fortune intact. He even faced the old problem that earlier had so bedeviled him: he had so much cash—some $105 million after taxes from the oil-tool division sale plus the deposit from the $75 million letter of credit—that he soon would have to invest it or face penalty taxes for excessive accumulation of profits. At sixty-seven he had the means and, hopefully, the health to undertake at least one more large venture that might give his life, toward its end, a new meaning.

During his January 1972 telephone press conference regarding the Irving hoax, Hughes hinted that if the TWA litigation ever were settled, he would come back out in the world once more. He talked enthusiastically about again piloting a plane or making a movie. His aides frequently said that he wanted to get back into life.

But could he? The years of self-imposed imprisonment had deeply affected him. Tragically, he had become alienated from the outside world. Despite his victory he was unable or unwilling to pull away even a little of the black masking tape from his window and look out on Hyde Park below.

Because of Europe's unseasonably warm weather during the winter of 1972–73, Hyde Park was almost as green in January as it would be in spring. Like a rich velvet carpet, it spread beyond his penthouse window. Along the wide bridle paths, young officers from the Queen's nearby Household Cavalry galloped their bays. Young women pushed baby carriages, and old people exercised their dogs. But Hughes saw none of the life around him. He had become conditioned to captivity. He could say, with Lord Byron's *Prisoner of Chillon:*

> *My very chains and I grew friends,*
> *So much a long communion tends*
> *To make us what we are:—even I*
> *Regained my freedom with a sigh.*

Index